AF352687

Spiraling into God

Spiraling into God

Bonaventure on Grace, Hierarchy, and Holiness

KATHERINE WRISLEY SHELBY

The Catholic University of America Press
Washington, DC

Cataloging-in-Publication Data is available
from the Library of Congress
ISBN: 978-0-8132-3671-1
eISBN: 978-0-8132-3672-8

For Tyson and Rebecca Shelby, of course;
and also for my mother, Kelly Jean Thompson Wrisley,
who embodied grace more than anyone else I know.

CONTENTS

Part I.
Theological Foundations for Bonaventure's Doctrine of Grace

Part II.
Bonaventure's Doctrine of Grace

Part III.
Theological Implications of Bonaventure's
Doctrine of Grace

ACKNOWLEDGMENTS

This book would never have appeared apart from a wide community of people who have continuously shown me the grace—both professionally and personally—necessary for completing it. It is revised from my dissertation, *The Vir hierarchicus: St. Bonaventure's Theology of Grace,* which I completed under the guidance of Stephen F. Brown, Boyd Taylor Coolman, and Timothy J. Johnson. First and foremost, I thank them for their mentorship, friendship, patient critiques, and incalculable time spent guiding my project from its inception to its completion. I am both a better scholar and a better person because I have been able to call myself a student of their individual and collective wisdom, and I could not have finished this book in its present form without each of them. Everything commendable here is thanks to their influence; any errors that remain (and I'm sure they abound) are entirely my own.

John Martino at The Catholic University of America Press likewise patiently guided me in revising my dissertation into a far more palatable book. I am deeply grateful for his assistance, as well as for the helpful comments of the two anonymous reviewers he employed in service of this aim, whose thoughtfulness most certainly improved the overall quality of the manuscript. Likewise, the Press's copyeditor, Elliot Polsky, provided invaluable help with respect to improving my writing while also raising comments and questions that pushed my work forward. Again, any errors that remain are a product of my own obstinacy and fault.

Thanks are owed as well to the Theology Department at Boston College, especially Rick Gaillardetz, for moral and financial support, both of which were necessary for this project's completion. Fellow graduate students at BC were cherished dialogue partners as I wrote the first drafts of these chapters: Jessica Coblentz, Justin Shaun Coyle, Daniel Horan, Ty Paul Monroe, Elyse Raby, Nicole Reibe, and Jordan Wood deserve especial thanks for their friendship as I completed those drafts. Holly Taylor Coolman and the Theology Department at Providence College similarly provided necessary support for completing many of the remaining edits, and I am grateful to have been afforded the opportunity to teach there during the difficult circumstances invited by the Covid-19 pandemic.

Many thanks are also owed—and then some—to David Couturier and Jill Smith at the Franciscan Institute at St. Bonaventure University for including me on several projects that contributed to this book's completion as well as for funding me on numerous occasions so that I could thus be included. Luke Togni, who currently works for the Institute, provided help during the final stages of copyediting when I no longer had my own institutional access to library materials. The Institute has nourished my growth as a young scholar in innumerable ways, and it provided (and continues to provide) an intellectual home in which the ideas put forth in this book could sprout and blossom. Portions of Chapters 2, 4, 5, and 9 have been revised from book chapters and articles invited by the Institute's hospitality as such, and I am grateful for their kind permission to reuse revised versions of those earlier pieces here. This book would not be what it is apart from the community of scholars that helped produce those projects, especially *Bonaventure Revisited: Companion to the Breviloquium* (2017), and *Bonaventure: Friar, Teacher, Minister, Bishop; A Celebration of the Eighth Centenary of his Birth* (2021).

Similarly, Marcella Mulder at Brill Publishing provided permissions to publish a revised version of my remarks from my chapter in *Ordo et sanctitas: The Franciscan Spiritual Journey in Theology and Hagiography. Essays in Honor of J. A. Wayne Hellmann, OFM Conv.*, edited by Michael F. Cusato, Timothy J. Johnson, and Steven J. McMichael (2017), which appears in Chapter 3. I am especially grateful to these editors for their helpful remarks on my research for that volume, which surely influenced my thinking for this book. McMichael's invitation to coedit Brill's *Medieval Approaches to the Virgin Mary: Mater sanctissima, misericordia, et dolorosa* (2019) inspired my work on Mary in Chapter 8.

Robert Porwoll approached me several years ago with a solicitation to contribute an essay on Thomas Gallus for a volume on the Victorines, which was recently published as "Thomas Gallus' *Explanatio* and Dionysian Thought," in *Victorine Restoration: Essays on Hugh of St. Victor, Richard of St. Victor, and Thomas Gallus*, edited by David Orsbon and Porwoll (Turnhout: Brepols, 2021); that invitation, along with their helpful comments on my essay, gifted me the space with which to spend time with Gallus on his own terms before applying his "angelic anthropology" to Bonaventure's doctrine of grace.

Kevin Hughes, Gregory LaNave, the Bonaventure Studium, and the organizers of the *Patristic, Medieval, and Renaissance Conference* held annually at Villanova University afforded me the opportunity to present conference papers related to my research on several occasions, in addition to providing friendship, encouragement, and treasured spaces for thoughtful dialogue. Beverly Kienzle has been a friend and pillar of support for my research for over a decade, and I am indebted to her for introducing me to the field of medieval sermon studies, an introduction that planted the seeds for my interest in Bonaventure's *Sermons on the Saints* in Chapter 8.

Finally, I'd know nothing of God's grace apart from my family. I could not have finished this book without their relentless faith in my abilities to accomplish what I would've otherwise thought impossible. My mother-in-law, Shauna Shelby, gave up several weeks of her time to watch my infant daughter so that I could focus on my work at various stages within the process of completing final edits. My sister, Lauren Wrisley, has been endlessly supportive precisely by permitting me space to not talk about theology. My interest in grace as a topic of study began through the influence of my father, Patrick Wrisley, with whom theological conversations on the back porch as a little girl certainly lit the spark for this project.

My mother, Kelly Jean Thompson Wrisley, passed away very shortly before this book was completed in its final form, and as I type these acknowledgments, I'm heading to scatter her ashes. Though this book is an academic study of sanctity and grace, I finish it with the conviction that I'd know nothing of these topics apart from her example. She breathed grace, and this book is for her.

My daughter, Rebecca, is currently too young to appreciate her role in helping me finish the text, but I wrote many of my final edits while she napped in my lap during the "fourth trimester." She has already taught me more about grace in her first few months of life than anything I read or wrote across several years of working on this project.

And last but certainly not least, my husband, Tyson Shelby, has been my rock throughout my writing process over those years. His unfailing love, countless sacrifices, and steadfast emotional support have carried me through my journey into Bonaventure's theology of grace. Beyond every other influence, the steady flow of grace he shows me in our everyday life is responsible for this book.

A Note on Translations and Editions of Bonaventure's Works

All translations are by the author unless otherwise indicated. All translations of Bonaventure's works are taken from *Doctoris Seraphici S. Bonaventurae opera omnia,* 10 vols. (Quaracchi: Ex Typographia Collegii s. Bonaventurae, 1882–1902), which are cited by parenthetical references indicating the volume and page number where the Latin can be found from the Quaracchi edition in the footnotes throughout the text. An exception to this rule applies for Bonaventure's *Sermones de sanctis,* whose critical editions are rather found in *Sancti Bonaventurae sermones de diversis*, vol. 2, ed. Jacques Guy Bougerol (Paris: Les Editions Franciscaines, 1993).

Abbreviations of Bonaventure's Works Used

I, II, III, and IV Sent. Commentarius in quatuor libros Sententiarum Petri Lombardi

Brev. Breviloquium

Comm. Jn. Commentarius in Evangelium Ioannis

Comm. Lc. Commentarius in Evangelium Lucae

De don. Spir. Collationes de septem donis Spiritus sancti

Itin. Itinerarium mentis in Deum

Hex. Collationes in Hexaëmeron

Leg. Maj. Legenda maior sancti Francisci

Leg. Min. Legenda minor sancti Francisci

Myst. Trin. Quaestio disputata de mysterio Trinitatis

Perf. evang. Quaestio disputata de perfectione evangelica

Red. Art. De reductione artium ad theologiam

Scien. Chr. Quaestio disputata de scientia Christi

Solil. Soliloquium de quatuor mentalibus exercitis

Trip. via De Triplici via

Abbreviations of Works by Pseudo-Dionysius

CD Corpus Dionysiacum, in *Patrologiae cursus completus, series graeca,* ed. J. P. Migne (3:119–1122)

CH The Celestial Hierarchy

DN The Divine Names

EH The Ecclesiastical Hierarchy

MT The Mystical Theology

Other Abbreviations

CC CM Corpus Christianorum, Continuatio Mediaevalis (Turnhout: Brepols, 1966–)

FAED 1 Francis of Assisi: Early Documents, vol. 1, The Saint, eds. Regis J. Armstrong, J. A. Wayne Hellmann, and William J. Short (New York: New City Press, 1999)

FAED 2 Francis of Assisi: Early Documents, vol. 2, The Founder, eds. Regis J. Armstrong, J. A. Wayne Hellmann, and William J. Short (New York: New City Press, 2000)

FAED 3 Francis of Assisi: Early Documents, vol. 3, The Prophet, eds. Regis J. Armstrong, J. A. Wayne Hellmann, and William J. Short (New York: New City Press, 2001)

PG Patrologiae cursus completus, series graeca, ed. J. P. Migne, 161 vols. (Paris: Garnier, 1800–1875)

PL Patrologiae cursus completus, series latina, ed. J. P. Migne, 221 vols. (Paris: Garnier, 1844–1864)

Spiraling into God

CHAPTER 1

General Introduction

Behold, I have described it for you in a threefold way, Prv 22:11. Since all forms of knowledge bear the mark of the Trinity, then all those things which are taught in scripture ought to represent in themselves a vestige of the Trinity. … And this threefold meaning of scripture corresponds to a threefold hierarchical activity, namely, *purgation, illumination*, and *perfection. Purgation* leads to peace, *illumination* to truth, and *perfection* to charity. When these are perfectly acquired, the soul is beatified [*beatificatur*], and to the extent that it is always turning around [*versantur*] these three activities, its reward will be increased.[1]

Thus begins one of the most famous of St. Bonaventure of Bagnoregio's spiritual treatises, *The Threefold Way.* Scholars of the Seraphic Doctor have long recognized the importance of the three "hierarchical activities" of purgation, illumination, and perfection for interpreting his theology and spirituality, which here provide the framework and foundation for his spiritual advice throughout the rest of this particular text. Several scholars have likewise noted a close connection between this "threefold way" and his doctrine of grace. Ephrem Longpré's seminal treatment of the subject, for example, considers how the soul is purified, illuminated, and perfected through grace,[2] even as Zachary Hayes's now classic book on the Seraphic Doctor's Christology assays

---

1. *Trip. via,* prol. (8, 3).

2. Ephrem Longpré, "Bonaventure," *Dictionnaire de spiritualité*, vol. 1, col. 1768–1843 (Paris: G. Beauchesne et ses fils, 1937).

the claim that "the structure of hierarchical thought may well shed light on the question of Bonaventure's theology of redemption." As Hayes there ascertains, "The broader structures of his thought lend themselves readily to the use of such a model, and the implications for soteriology were perceived with greater clarity with the passing of time" within Bonaventure's writings.[3]

The purpose of this book is to present a systematic account of St. Bonaventure's doctrine of grace through this model. I argue that an account of this sort can *only* be provided by attending to that doctrine through his theology of hierarchy, which, as Hayes once intuited, indeed sheds light on the question of the Seraphic Doctor's theology of redemption. I do so in order to answer a rather simple question—namely, what does *sanctitas* or holiness mean according to the Seraphic Doctor? This book offers an answer to this question by unpacking Bonaventure's definition of sanctifying grace as a "deiform" (or God-conforming) *influentia* that "hierarchizes" the soul, "purifying," "illuminating," and "perfecting" it from within so that the graced person may know and love God, neighbor, and creation in an ordered way. For the Seraphic Doctor, to be "holy" is to be thus "hierarchized" through sanctifying grace, which for him simply means that the human being has been made capable of relating to God, one's neighbor, and creation as God intended. The need for such a study is fourfold.

1. *A Systematic Account of Bonaventure's Doctrine of Grace.*   First, while the Seraphic Doctor's doctrine of grace appears frequently in scholarship treating various other aspects of his theology, there has yet to appear a definitive English monograph treating Bonaventure's theology of grace. Whereas the topic has been treated at length by Thomistic scholars,[4] a surprising dearth haunts the subject as it pertains to the Angelic Doctor's Franciscan counterpart.[5] The most extensive work

---

3. Zachary Hayes, *The Hidden Center: Spirituality and Speculative Christology in St. Bonaventure* (New York: Paulist Press, 1981), 158. I will return to his treatment of Bonaventure's soteriology in much greater detail in Chapter 7.

4. See, for one particularly useful study, Joseph Peter Wawrykow, *God's Grace and Human Action: 'Merit' in the Theology of Thomas Aquinas* (Notre Dame: University of Notre Dame Press, 1995).

5. Several scholars have nevertheless pointed to the usefulness of comparing their teachings on grace, making this dearth all the more surprising. See, for some examples, Christopher Cullen, "Bonaventure on Nature before Grace: A Historical Moment Reconsidered," *American Catholic Philosophical Quarterly* 85, no. 1 (2011): 161–76; and Kevin Hughes,

is that by Antonio Briva Mirabent, whose *La gloria y su relación con la gracia según las obras de San Buenaventura* argues that the state of grace is identical to the state of glory in Bonaventure's theology.[6] While Mirabent's work makes a fundamental contribution to Bonaventurean scholarship, it relies upon Bonaventure's more speculative texts, such as his *Commentary on the Sentences,* without necessarily extensively engaging his pastoral and hagiographical works in conversation with his philosophy. There are only sixteen references to Bonaventure's sermon literature throughout Mirabent's text,[7] while no reference at all is made to Bonaventure's theology of grace within either the *Legenda maior* or the *Legenda minor.* As I will explore with a more critical eye in Chapter 8, this hagiographical and sermon literature also deeply informs Bonaventure's theological project surrounding grace, and while other scholars have indeed provided important windows into that project,[8] there is yet no systematic presentation of grace across his speculative, hagiographical, and spiritual works. Most typically, moreover, scholars of the Seraphic Doctor tend to treat Bonaventure's theology of grace as a subtopic in relation to other themes—his Christology, Trinitarian theology, his "wisdom theology," his concept of *ordo,* or his teaching on prayer—rather than as a topic in its own right.[9] First and foremost, this

---

"Bonaventure *Contra mundum?* The Catholic Theological Tradition Revisited," *Theological Studies* 74, no. 2 (2013): 372–98.

6. Antonio Briva Mirabent, *La gloria y su relación con la gracia según las obras de San Buenaventura* (Barcelona: Editorial Casulleras, 1957).

7. See Mirabent, *La gloria,* for references to Bonaventure's sermons, at 128n1; 131n2; 196n4; 198n4; 199n1; 202n1; 277n4; 278nn3–4; 281n1; 282n3; 286n1; 289nn1–2, 5; and 290n2.

8. See again Longpré, "Bonaventure," col. 1768–1843, which remains one of the most insightful explications of Bonaventure's theology of grace to the present day. His discussion of grace is intended to lay the groundwork for his subsequent exposition of Bonaventure's contemplative theology, but in so doing, he provides a succinct and useful introduction to the Seraphic Doctor's teachings on grace, especially insofar as Longpré explores how the "perfection of the life of grace" consists in the Threefold Way.

9. Some of the most useful existing treatments of grace in the Seraphic Doctor's theology, upon which my own presentation of grace in Bonaventure's theology will build throughout the book (especially as it pertains to these topics), include, in alphabetical order: Christopher Carpenter, *Theology as the Road to Holiness in St. Bonaventure* (New York: Paulist Press, 1999); Cullen, "Bonaventure on Nature before Grace," cited above; Cullen, "Grace," in *Bonaventure* (New York: Oxford University Press, 2006), 153–64; Zachary Hayes, "Bonaventure's Trinitarian Theology," in *A Companion to Bonaventure,* ed. Jay M. Hammond, J.A Wayne Hellmann, and Jared Goff, Brill's Companions to the Christian Tradition 48 (Leiden: Brill, 2014), 189–245; Zachary Hayes, *Hidden Center,* cited above; J. A. Wayne Hellmann, *Divine and Created Order in Bonaventure's Theology,* trans. Jay Hammond (St. Bonaventure, NY: Franciscan Institute, 2001); Timothy J. Johnson, *The Soul in Ascent: Bonaventure on Poverty, Prayer, and Union with God,* 2nd ed. (St. Bonaventure, NY:

book aims to perform the latter task at length and thus fill this glaring lacuna in Bonaventurean scholarship.

2. *Holiness and Bonaventure's "Wisdom Theology."*   Within these existing treatments of the subject, the Seraphic Doctor's doctrine of grace has nonetheless been treated most frequently within the context of his "wisdom theology." In the prologue to his *Commentary on the Sentences,* Bonaventure defines theology as *sapientia* (wisdom), an "affective" habit with both speculative and practical aims. He ultimately claims, however, that a theological habit is developed within the soul primarily "so that we might become good."[10] Subsequent scholarship has wrestled with the nature of this claim, particularly in light of texts like the *Itinerarium mentis in Deum,* which would rather seem to suggest that the end of theology is *not* "primarily" practical, but contemplative. Most scholars affirm that by defining theology as "wisdom," Bonaventure understood it as a habit indebted to faith, and several monographs have therefore explored the relationship between grace, the development of a theological habit, and the path to holiness (*sanctitas*) in Bonaventure's theology.[11]

Within this context, the "Bonaventurean Question" refers to a scholarly debate that asks whether or not the Seraphic Doctor's "wisdom theology" can be conceived as a science in the Aristotelian sense of the term.[12] Grace plays into this question because Bonaventure requires a

---

Franciscan Institute, 2012); Gregory LaNave, *Through Holiness to Wisdom: The Nature of Theology according to St. Bonaventure* (Rome: Instituto Storico dei Cappuccini, 2005); Laure Solignac, *La voi de la ressemblance: Itinéraire dans la pensée de saint Bonaventure* (Paris: Hermann, 2014). Cullen's chapter on grace in his broader work on Bonaventure's theology remains one of the most usefully concise treatments of the subject, but again, Cullen treats the topic as one theme among many. I will attend more fully to Carpenter's and LaNave's treatments of the topic of holiness in Bonaventure's works below. Shawn M. Colberg's more recent study of reward and merit in the work of both Bonaventure and Aquinas will also be of interest to those seeking to understand Bonaventure's doctrine of grace more fully; see his *The Wayfarer's End: Bonaventure and Aquinas on Divine Rewards in Scripture and Sacred Doctrine* (Washington, DC: The Catholic University of America Press, 2020).

10. *I Sent.* prooem., q. 3 (1, 13): "Scientia theologica est habitus affectivus et medius inter speculativum et practicum, et pro fine habet tum contemplationem, tum ut boni fiamus, et quidem principalius, ut boni fiamus."

11. See especially Carpenter, *Theology as the Road to Holiness*; LaNave, *Through Holiness to Wisdom.*

12. Stephen F. Brown has made monumental contributions to the subject of the "science" of theology in this sense; see his numerous articles, some of which are listed in this book's bibliography, for these contributions. I borrow the phrase "wisdom theology" from Timothy J. Johnson, "Wisdom Has Built Her House; She Has Set Up Her Seven Pillars: Roger

theologian to be a person of faith,[13] and thus "holy" or graced, in order to be gifted with a theological "wisdom" above human science. This question in its modern form began with the Quaracchi Fathers, who edited Bonaventure's *Opera omnia* in the late nineteenth century,[14] but it took flight in the work of Etienne Gilson, whose *The Philosophy of St. Bonaventure* synthesized what he called Bonaventure's "metaphysics of mysticism." In comparison to Aquinas, who argued that the "latent presence [of the supernatural] acts only to conserve and move beings in their proper nature in such a way that it remains possible to make a separate description of their nature as science knows it,"[15] Gilson argued that Bonaventure rather asserted that "the supernatural perfects beings in their own nature so that it perpetually completes them and reveals them to themselves, and that it is impossible to describe them in themselves without recourse to it, and this is the method of St. Bonaventure."[16] Gilson's explication of Bonaventure's doctrine of nature and grace in comparison to that of Aquinas within this account of the Seraphic Doctor's philosophy remains one of the most important to this day, but has since received significant criticism and calls for revision.[17] As Kevin Hughes writes of Gilson's text, although Gilson importantly established a place for Bonaventure's teaching on grace and theology alongside that of Aquinas, "This interpretation has established a powerful hermeneutical trajectory that can affirm the accomplishments of both Bonaventure and Aquinas, but it does so by an all-too-modern system of separations: mysticism/theological science; piety/reason; and, by implication or application, private/public."[18] What is needed is a method of reading Bonaventure's "wisdom theology" that

---

Bacon, Franciscan Wisdom, and Conversion to the Sciences," in *The English Province of the Franciscans (1224–c. 1350)*, ed. Michael Robson (Leiden: Brill, 2017), 294–315.

13. See LaNave, *Through Holiness to Wisdom,* 14–19. See also Hughes, "Bonaventure *Contra mundum?*" 374, where Hughes simply defines this as the question of "whether Bonaventure possessed a 'Christian philosophy' distinct from his theology, a concern one can find expressed consistently in the *scholia* to the Quaracchi editions of Bonaventure's works."

14. LaNave, *Through Holiness to Wisdom,* 14.

15. Etienne Gilson, *The Philosophy of St. Bonaventure,* trans. Dom Illtyd Trethowan and F. J. Sheed (New York: Sheed and Ward, 1938), 493.

16. Gilson, *Philosophy of St. Bonaventure,* 493.

17. See Cullen, "Bonaventure on Nature before Grace," 161–76; Hughes, "Bonaventure *Contra mundum?*"; and Leon Veuthey, *La filosofia Christiana di San Bonaventura* (Rome: Miscellanea Francescana, 1996).

18. Hughes, "Bonaventure *Contra mundum?*" 374–75.

brings these binaries together and sees "mysticism/theological science" and "piety/reason" as two sides of the same coin.

After Gilson, therefore, Bonaventure's doctrine of grace has been referenced almost exclusively within the context of his definition of theology as a "wisdom."[19] Two recent treatments of Bonaventure's doctrine on grace demand our attention here. Christopher Carpenter's work, *Theology as the Road to Holiness in St. Bonaventure*, judges *sanctitas* to be necessary for the theological task in St. Bonaventure's purview. In thus focusing on the role of *sanctitas* in Bonaventure's definition of theology, Carpenter's work deals considerably with the topic of grace and describes the "fall of the mind and its remedy by hierarchization" through grace.[20] While his assertion to this effect certainly agrees with my overarching claim in this book, his account of grace is nonetheless limited in many ways. Carpenter reads Bonaventure's account of the mind's hierarchization exclusively in terms of the Fall, for example, without necessarily discussing how human nature even in its prelapsarian state requires grace in Bonaventure's thought, an idea to which I will attend in much greater detail in Chapter 6.[21] Moreover, as Gilson's exposition of Bonaventure's theology leans heavily on comparison to that of Aquinas, Carpenter depends upon a Lonerganian reading of Bonaventure rather than letting his doctrine of grace stand on its own two feet.[22] Additionally, Carpenter's concern for defending the Dionysian understanding of hierarchy for the modern reader overshadows his discussion of the meaning of that concept as Bonaventure himself would have conceived it.

Gregory LaNave provides a far more robust account of grace in the third chapter of his work, *Through Holiness to Wisdom: The Nature*

---

19. See, for some examples, George H. Tavard, "The Spirit's Assistance," in *Transiency and Permanence: The Nature of Theology according to St. Bonaventure* (St. Bonaventure, NY: Franciscan Institute, 1954), 212–28; Hughes, "Bonaventure *Contra mundum*?"; and Cullen, "Bonaventure on Nature before Grace," 161–76. Cullen's article importantly challenges John Milbank's accusation that Bonaventure's doctrine of grace also supports a doctrine of "pure nature." According to Cullen, Milbank "cites Bonaventure as one of those who … emerges as a pivotal figure in the rise of a secularized rationality, i.e., a view of human reason as no longer intrinsically ordered to the transcendent final end of union with God." I will address this debate in Chapter 6, but I raise attention to Cullen's article here because he examines the Seraphic Doctor's teaching on human nature and grace by comparing it to his treatment of the relationship between theology and philosophy.

20. Carpenter, *Theology as the Road to Holiness*, 39.

21. Carpenter, *Theology as the Road to Holiness*, 39–40.

22. Carpenter, *Theology as the Road to Holiness*, 52–56.

of Theology according to St. Bonaventure, which similarly treats the relationship between grace and theology in the Seraphic Doctor's thought.[23] Like Carpenter, LaNave emphasizes the role of holiness in Bonaventure's development of a theological wisdom but ultimately seems to imply that Bonaventure understands the purpose of theology as more speculative than practical.[24] He affirms the role of grace in shaping the intellect through knowledge and love and discusses grace with respect to the Seraphic Doctor's theology of hierarchy, but his account emphasizes the "speculative" goal of theology in a way that nevertheless leaves questions regarding Bonaventure's claim from the *Commentary on the Sentences* that theology ought to be practiced primarily "so that we might become good" (*ut boni fiamus*).[25]

Such accounts of Bonaventure's theology all underscore the importance of the Seraphic Doctor's doctrine of grace within his definition of theology as "wisdom." What remains debatable when one reads this secondary scholarship, however, is the precise relationship between "holiness" and "theology" in this definition: Does theology lead to holiness, or does holiness lead to theology? Are all theologians holy? Are all saints, likewise, theologians? Moreover, within these scholarly portraits of Bonaventure's "wisdom theology," which are often at odds, should scholars interpret him as saying that the purpose of theology is more practical than speculative, as his prologue to the *Commentary on the Sentences* suggests, or should they rather regard the contemplative ecstasy famously described in the *Itinerarium* as that which characterizes the goal of theology in Bonaventure's thought? How exactly do the speculative and practical goals of theology hang together in his wisdom theology as "two sides of the same coin"?

Secondly, then, the present study contributes to this branch of Bonaventurean scholarship and this particular set of questions precisely by *removing* these considerations from its focus until its conclusion in Chapter 9. In order to understand the role of grace and *sanctitas* in the Seraphic Doctor's "wisdom theology," I contend that scholars should first take the time to actually understand his doctrine of grace.

---

23. See LaNave's discussion in *Through Holiness to Wisdom*, 71–121.

24. LaNave, *Through Holiness to Wisdom*, 190–91.

25. See again *I Sent.* prooemium, q. 3 (1,13). See also LaNave, *Through Holiness to Wisdom*, 190–91, where LaNave notes the seeming disparity between this passage from the prologue to the *Sentences* commentary and the "speculative" vision that so famously characterizes Bonaventure's project in the *Itinerarium*.

As will be unfolded throughout the book, Bonaventure's association of *sanctitas* with hierarchy can actually provide a method of resolving the "binaries" within his wisdom theology, whereby "contemplation/ praxis," "reason/piety," and "mysticism/theological science" are not at *odds* in his definition of theology as a wisdom, but rather walk hand in hand. In this way, the book will also therefore contribute to the scholarly conversation surrounding the Bonaventurean Question. Perhaps strangely, but certainly necessarily, it contributes to this conversation by intentionally bunting the question of the role of grace in Bonaventure's definition of theology as a "wisdom" until the very end. If grace is indeed so central to that definition, as other scholars have well noted, then what is sorely needed is a systematic account of his doctrine of grace as it informs his notion of *sanctitas*. I offer that account in the pages that follow.

3. *An Intellectual History of Grace.*   Third, I intend here to expose the historical importance of Bonaventure's theology of grace by placing it in conversation with the broader history of Catholic teaching on the same. Rather than focusing on the "usual" suspects within this narrative of influence, which during the thirteenth century would most typically include Augustine, Aristotle, and Thomas Aquinas, I highlight lesser-known influences whose work I argue is the key to reading Bonaventure's doctrine of grace. Most obviously, this will include Dionysius the Areopagite and his original definition of hierarchy. Additionally, however, I highlight what I take to be the irrefutable influence both of the Victorine theologian, Thomas Gallus, and of Bonaventure's teacher, Alexander of Hales, over the Seraphic Doctor's notion of sanctity. These latter sources remain in themselves understudied figures in the history of Christian theology, yet their influence over Bonaventure's own thinking about what it means to be holy—as will emerge especially in *Part II* of this book—is indisputable. My presentation of the Seraphic Doctor's teachings on grace through these sources aims to resurrect them as important "players" within the story of grace in the Catholic intellectual tradition.

4. *Opening Up Bonaventure's Theology.*   Fourth and finally, the present study aims to make Bonaventure's theology of grace more accessible to a wider audience of theologians interested in the topic in a broader way. Bonaventure's treatises on grace from his *Commentary on the*

Sentences, as well as his theology of grace within his *Sermons on the Saints*, remain unapproachable for most English-speaking readers. Through this book, I hope to make the content of these sources more readily available for a wider audience, flawed though my own reading of those sources might be.

Why Hierarchy?

Enlightened twenty-first-century readers will immediately balk at my preferred hermeneutic. The word "hierarchy," after all, bears with it an oppressive host of negative connotations in the contemporary theological mindset. Given that the word "hierarchy" will—and indeed, *should*—be problematic for modern readers, why have I chosen to highlight it as the key to unlocking the Seraphic Doctor's theology of sanctification?

Before readers immediately dismiss this entire book, let me begin by simply affirming that such a reaction would be quite warranted. Hierarchies in the modern sense are often *not* good, helpful, or by any means "holy." Most today would rightly understand a hierarchy as an authoritarian power structure, a top-down system of power in which those who are "higher" within that structure unjustly suppress and trample those who are "lower" beneath them within that same system. A corporation with billions of dollars in assets, for example, run by a CEO who reaps the benefits of a multi-million-dollar bonus while his employees across the country struggle to pay for health insurance, would represent a perfect example of such a negative hierarchical power structure. Within an explicitly theological context, feminist theologians, liberation theologians, and ecclesiologists alike can recognize how patriarchal power structures and hierarchies within the Church might harmfully suppress the laity, a problem made even more acute by the contemporary abuse crisis. More often than not, with all these examples, the modern mind will understand a hierarchy as an "'artificial organization of multiple activities' involving '*inequalities* of aptitude and functions,'"[26] whereby the "powerful" within that system indubitably trump those with less power, whether that power be understood

---

26. See Sarah Coakley, *God, Sexuality, and the Self: An Essay on the Trinity* (Cambridge: Cambridge University Press, 2013), 320; Coakley here quotes Louis Dumont, *Homo hierarchicus: The Caste System and Its Implications* (London: Paladin, 1972), 54. In general,

monetarily, with respect to gender, education, or a host of other social, political, or economic factors that have not at all been caused by the persons "below" who thus find themselves unjustly trampled. It bears repeating at the outset of this study that I *affirm* that hierarchies in this modern sense of the word are in these ways not at all good, helpful, or by any means "holy." They therefore should often be challenged and dismantled—especially by theologians seeking to understand God's justice as described in scripture.

In her own work on the theology of Dionysius the Areopagite, who *invented* the word, however, Sarah Coakley has argued that the word "hierarchy," "like 'power,' is a word much in need of nuanced and analytical reflection," because, as she further contends, "it is not obvious that 'hierarchy' in *all* its meanings (Dionysian or otherwise) is, or should, be abhorrent."[27] Dionysius himself, Coakley reminds us, defines a "hierarchy" as "the greatest possible assimilation to and union with God.... Hierarchy is a holy order and knowledge and activity which ... participates in the Divine Likeness."[28] As this book will show, Bonaventure himself bases his own definition of hierarchy on this, the Areopagite's original definition of the word. For both Dionysius and Bonaventure, the goal of a hierarchy is to make created beings "as like as possible" to the divine, or, to use Bonaventure's language, to make creatures deiform by transforming them into a similitude of the Trinity. As I will examine at length in the following chapters, the Seraphic Doctor reappropriates the Areopagite's original definition of hierarchy throughout his *Opera omnia,* even as he revises it to satisfy his own Franciscan and Scholastic tastes. In this *ressourcement* of Dionysian hierarchy, however, Bonaventure nonetheless retains the Areopagite's original insight that, most fundamentally, a hierarchy *means* a certain sacred order and activity that likens us to God, all the while using his own vocabulary for expanding that meaning.

Even more importantly—as Hayes once so perceptively intuited— the same vocabulary that frequents Bonaventure's reimagining of Dionysian hierarchy also happens to inform his vocabulary for grace. This is exhibited in part by his well-known inclination toward the Dionysian

---

Coakley's bibliography provides a useful entrance into the modern critique of hierarchy, especially from a feminist perspective.

27. Coakley, *God, Sexuality, and the Self,* 319.

28. Coakley, *God, Sexuality, and the Self,* 319.

triad of "purification, illumination, and perfection" in his account of the spiritual life, but his use of Dionysian hierarchy within his doctrine of grace extends far beyond that triad in ways that have hitherto been unexplored by scholars of the Seraphic Doctor. In his *Commentary on the Second Book of Sentences* (hereafter, *II Sent.*), for example, Bonaventure defines sanctifying grace as a created gift, an *influentia* or "inflowing" of light that flows down from God through Christ into the soul.[29] "Just as light from the sun flows into (*influit*) corporeal material in the air, through which it is formally illuminating air," writes the Seraphic Doctor, "so also spiritual light flows into [*influit*] the soul from a spiritual sun, which is God, by which the soul is formally illuminated, reformed, graced, and vivified."[30] As we will encounter in Chapter 4, Bonaventure's definition of grace here borrows language from his theology of hierarchy, wherein he frequently uses the word "*influentia*" to describe Christ's presence throughout his interpretation of the cosmos. As he will further elaborate in his later works, this *influentia* of grace within a faith-filled soul then causes it to become "hierarchical," gifting it with the virtues that lead the soul to meritorious action, as well as with the spiritual gifts needed for the soul to achieve contemplative union with the Triune God.[31] The Seraphic Doctor's clearest definitions of and explanations for grace, in other words, walk hand in hand with his teachings on hierarchy, so much so that it would be quite impossible to successfully interpret his doctrine of grace apart from first appreciating what he means by "hierarchy," "*influentia*," and "the Threefold Way" within the context of the latter.

And indeed, evidence for this association between hierarchy and grace is found not only throughout his speculative or academic writings (such as *The Commentary on the Sentences* and the *Breviloquium*), but can also be encountered in Bonaventure's pastoral and hagiographical texts, as well. Quite strikingly, he begins both his *Legenda maior* and *Legenda minor* by claiming that "*the grace of God our Savior has appeared in these last days* in his servant Francis,"[32] and therein extols Francis for being "endowed with the gifts of divine grace," "enriched by the merit of unshakeable virtue," and "totally aflame with a Seraphic

---

29. *II Sent.* d. 26, a. 1, q. 2 (2, 633–36).

30. *II Sent.* d. 26, a. 1, q. 2 (2, 636). I will examine this definition in its entirety in Chapter 4.

31. I will discuss Bonaventure's notion of the hierarchical soul at length in Chapter 5.

32. See "The Major Legend of Saint Francis," in *FAED* 2, 525.

fire," thereby proclaiming Francis "a hierarchical man," or a *vir hierarchicus*.[33] Inasmuch as the Poverello is the paradigmatic example of sanctity in the Seraphic Doctor's doctrine of grace, painting a clear picture of what Bonaventure means by referring to Francis as a "hierarchical man" will illuminate his understanding of *sanctitas,* especially for those interested in how that notion relates to his "wisdom theology."

Simply put, it is my conviction that, in these ways, "the element of hierarchy" pervades the Seraphic Doctor's writings on grace, whether they be academic, mystical, pastoral, or hagiographical.[34] Though problematic in our own context, this book reads Bonaventure's doctrine of grace through his theology of hierarchy because it is the latter that provides the vocabulary, philosophy, and spirituality that makes sense of the former. In this respect, my preferred hermeneutic for reading Bonaventure's doctrine of grace in this book—that of hierarchy—provides a systematic account of that doctrine by relying on the Seraphic Doctor's own terminology for it. To be abundantly clear, my purpose here is *not* to offer a theological argument in favor of "hierarchy" as it is understood in the modern sense. Rather, I aim to articulate clearly how Bonaventure himself defined "hierarchy" so as to correctly interpret his doctrine of grace. In so doing, it is my hope that readers might also perceive how that doctrine might still be meaningful, even in our twenty-first-century context.

Such meaning might derive from the realization that the Seraphic Doctor uses "hierarchy" within his doctrine of grace as a way of describing how it is, exactly, that human beings most fundamentally relate to God and to one another. In its most basic iteration, as we will encounter in Chapter 3, Bonaventure understands a hierarchy to *mean* the Trinity. This in itself will be problematic for modern readers. For the Seraphic Doctor, however, this claim was paired with a very clear argument that a *perfect* hierarchy—or namely, the Trinity—is a hierarchy *without subordination,* or namely, an ordered relationship of three distinct but equal divine persons who relate to one another in perfect love. This insight is the foundation upon which Bonaventure will then construct his entire doctrine of grace: If for him the goal of grace is to

---

33. See "The Major Legend of Saint Francis," in *FAED* 2, 526; and "The Minor Legend of Saint Francis," in *FAED* 2, 684. Here, I have retained the translation provided by the editors of *FAED* 2.

34. Again, Hayes intuited this without necessarily expositing it at length; see *Hidden Center,* 158.

"hierarchize" the human being into a likeness of God, or into a similitude of the Trinity, this simply means making the human being capable
of perfectly ordered relationships, of *perfect love,* not only with respect
to God, but also with respect to *all of creation.* Bonaventure's doctrine
of grace does not teach that the human being is "hierarchized" for the
purpose of "ascending" to God in such a way that they will never again
need to relate to other people in the world around them; rather, for the
Seraphic Doctor, grace unites human beings to God in such a way that
they are then made capable of loving the world in a holy way, as well.
Or, phrased differently, we become most *like* God—we become holy—
when we relate to God and the world around us through perfect love.
While this is admittedly a gross oversimplification of Bonaventure's
Trinitarian theology and metaphysics, my focus on hierarchy within
his doctrine of grace aims to provide a systematic account of all these
ideas. To study hierarchy and grace in the Seraphic Doctor's writings
is to study the interrelationship of *all* created being through the love
of God.

Within his own expression of these ideas, Bonaventure will repeatedly use the symbol of Jacob's Ladder to help us envision these relationships along with him. Borrowing from his neoplatonic metaphysics,
his notion of the "hierarchical soul" describes three movements within
the soul that correspond with the neoplatonic triad of procession, return, and remaining: First, the graced soul "ascends" or "returns" to a
contemplative union with the Trinity, from which it, then, "descends"
or "processes" through meritorious actions. Sanctifying grace, for
Bonaventure, enables these two "movements" within the soul, thereby
helping it fulfill the double love commandment: "You shall love the
Lord your God with all your heart, and with all your soul, and with
all your strength, and with all your mind; and your neighbor as yourself."[35] Inasmuch as these "ascending" and "descending" movements
are activated in the soul by sanctifying grace in Bonaventure's theology,
he further teaches that the human being can, then, "remain" in God by
always circling between a contemplative union with God and meritorious actions with respect to her neighbor. Crucially, as will become
abundantly clear throughout this study, the symbol of Jacob's Ladder is
the Seraphic Doctor's favorite symbol for depicting these movements,

---

35. Lk 10:27. NRSV.

which, as I will further argue, are perhaps best understood as "spiraling." Like the angels that "remain" on Jacob's Ladder by ascending to God and descending back to the earth below in Jacob's dream at Bethel, Bonaventure holds that the "sanctified" soul can be called a "similitude" of the Trinity when it has been made capable of "remaining" in God through such ascensions and descensions. Francis can be called a "*vir hierarchicus*" only because, as Bonaventure insists in the *Legenda maior* and elsewhere, his soul had been shaped into a "Jacob's Ladder." I thus repeatedly return to this symbol in my *ressourcement* of the Seraphic Doctor's doctrine of grace with the hope that it will inform our own thinking about these movements.

I do not presume to work with one particular Bonaventurean text in order to expound these themes; rather, I seek to expose the interconnectedness of the Seraphic Doctor's doctrine of grace throughout his speculative, pastoral, and hagiographical works. With regard to his more speculative works, I will draw most frequently from Bonaventure's *Commentary on the Sentences*, the *Breviloquium*, the *Itinerarium*, the *Collations on the Seven Gifts of the Holy Spirit* (hereafter, *De don. Spir.*), and the *Hexaëmeron*. Reference to *On the Reduction of the Arts to Theology* (hereafter, *Red. Art.*), his *Disputed Questions on the Knowledge of Christ* (hereafter, *Scien. Chr.*), his *Disputed Questions on the Mystery of the Trinity*, his scriptural commentaries, and *The Triple Way* will be made when necessary, but I depend more upon the former than the latter, since these contain his most systematic and explicit treatments of grace. With regard to his more pastoral works and hagiographical literature, I rather rely upon the *Legenda maior*,[36] *Sunday Sermons*, and especially his *Sermons on the Saints*. With a host of other Bonaventurean scholars, I look for the "inner unity" of Bonaventure's thought across all these texts,[37] whose poetic style, as J. A. Wayne Hellmann has noted, often unfortunately "brings with it a freedom of expression and lack of precision."[38] Throughout the following pages, I try to remain attentive to the differences that might belie a claim to "inner unity" in his doctrine of

---

36. My justification for focusing on the *Legenda maior* rather than the *Legenda minor* will be addressed in Chapter 8.

37. Hellmann, *Divine and Created Order*, 2; see also Bonifaz Anton Luyckx, *Die Erkenntnislehre Bonaventuras* (Munich: Baeumker-Beiträge, 1923), 113; Gilson, *Philosophy of St. Bonaventure*, 36; Romano Guardini, *Systembildende Elemente in der Theologie Bonaventuras: Die Lehren vom lumen mentis, von der gradatio entium und der influentia sensus et motus*, ed. Werner Dettloff (Leiden: Brill, 1964), 155.

38. Hellmann, *Divine and Created Order*, 1.

grace, but as will hopefully be shown in the book as a whole, the larger narrative surrounding that doctrine across the course of his career overwhelmingly supports rather than subverts this claim to "inner unity."

Organization of the Book

Following the spirit of the Seraphic Doctor, I have organized the book into three Parts. *Part I* will treat the *Theological Foundations for Bonaventure's Doctrine of Grace*; *Part II*, *Bonaventure's Doctrine of Grace*; and *Part III*, *Theological Implications of Bonaventure's Doctrine of Grace*. Though the subsequent eight chapters are categorized according to the common titular theme of each broad section, I have nonetheless structured the text in a sequential way, whereby each chapter's argument lays the theological foundation necessary for fully understanding the next. Chapter 8, which treats the topic of sanctity, should thus be treated as the theological "climax" of the text, which is best approached by first reading Chapters 1–7.

Part I, Theological Foundations for Bonaventure's Doctrine of Grace, begins by introducing the theological contexts which I argue are necessary for approaching the topic of grace in Bonaventure's thought. In Chapter 2, *Historical Sources for Bonaventure's Doctrine of Grace*, three historical influences are introduced in service of this aim: Dionysius the Areopagite, Thomas Gallus, and Alexander of Hales. For each theologian, I highlight one aspect of their respective theologies that I argue will be indispensable for reading Bonaventure's own teachings on grace. I first discuss Dionysius's invention of the word hierarchy; second, I introduce the thirteenth-century Victorine theologian, Thomas Gallus, and his angelic anthropology, or notion of the "hierarchical soul"; and finally, I introduce Bonaventure's theological teacher at the University of Paris, Alexander of Hales, who defined sanctifying grace as a "created" gift as distinguished from the uncreated gift of grace, the Holy Spirit. Readers will immediately note that Chapter 2 occupies more space than any other chapter. I beg forgiveness for this length, but remain convinced that this is necessary both to give these sources their proper due and, at the same time, to lay the intellectual groundwork for approaching Bonaventure's use of them within his teachings on grace in later chapters.

After thus framing the book through these influences, I next consider another crucial foundation for those teachings in Chapter 3, *Bonaventure's Theology of Hierarchy*, wherein I explore his own understanding of what hierarchy means. This chapter will show how Bonaventure both borrowed from and revised Dionysius's definition of hierarchy, even as it will also introduce the Seraphic Doctor's hierarchical metaphysics, and especially his use therein of the neoplatonic triad of procession, return, and remaining. Inasmuch as Bonaventure employs his hierarchical metaphysics in his doctrine of grace, this chapter will lay the second half of the foundation upon which the remainder of the book's structure will be built.

From this foundation, *Part II* turns to an explicit analysis of his doctrine of grace. Building from Zachary Hayes's intuition that "The structure of hierarchical thought may well shed light on the question of Bonaventure's theology of redemption,"[39] *Part II* presents a chronological overview of some of Bonaventure's most significant expositions of grace to show how "the structure of hierarchical thought" was definitively a significant factor in those expositions throughout his theological career. In Chapter 4, *The Influentia of Sanctifying Grace in The Commentary on the Sentences and the Breviloquium*, I begin this overview by attending to Distinctions 26–27 of his *II Sent.* and Part 5 of the *Breviloquium*. Read together, these texts exhibit the Seraphic Doctor's most systematic explanations of grace; thematically, they walk together inasmuch as they both define sanctifying grace as a created *influentia*, or an "inflowing," a word I will have positioned within his hierarchical lexicon in Chapter 3. Though "the structure of hierarchical thought" will be less obvious in these texts than in his later works, Bonaventure builds his subsequent accounts of grace in the latter from this definition, so much so that it will be impossible to read the latter without first reading the former. Chapter 5, *The Hierarchical Soul in the Itinerarium and the Hexaëmeron*, next shows how the Seraphic Doctor indeed begins to make this association between hierarchy and grace more explicit after the *Breviloquium,* especially inasmuch as he began "borrowing" Thomas Gallus's notion of the hierarchical soul (which we will have previously encountered in Chapter 2) within his doctrine of grace in both these texts.

Read together, Chapters 4–5 thus narrate a "story" about how Bonaventure's theology of hierarchy informed his teachings on grace

---

39. Hayes, *Hidden Center*, 158.

throughout his theological career. Sanctifying grace in his writings is a created *influentia* that hierarchizes the soul so that it can become a similitude of the Trinity. By unfolding the story of his doctrine of grace in the four texts highlighted in Chapters 4–5, we will come to understand what this means. If Chapter 8 is the theological "climax" of this study, *Part II* is nevertheless its "heart."

While *Part II* therefore explores what grace is in Bonaventure's theology, *Part III, Theological Implications of Bonaventure's Doctrine of Grace*, considers why it matters. Chapter 6, *Grace in Bonaventure's Theological Anthropology*, shows how the Seraphic Doctor's very understanding of what it means to be human is rooted within his doctrine of grace. With recent critiques against this doctrine as it pertains to his understanding of human nature in mind, I argue that human nature is fundamentally ordered to beatitude by grace in his theology. Chapter 7, *Grace and Christ the Hierarch*, next shows how all these themes play out with respect to his Christology. I argue that his hierarchical metaphysics and teachings on grace are rooted within that Christology, especially his naming therein of Christ as the "Hierarch." For Bonaventure, grace is always gifted to humanity through Christ, the similitude of the Father to whom all human beings must be conformed if they are to become a similitude of the Trinity. In Chapter 8, *The Hierarchical Person: Bonaventure's Theology of Sanctity*, I finally examine Bonaventure's hagiographical literature and sermons to provide an account of what it means for the human being to be conformed to Christ and the Trinity through grace. This will indeed be the climax of the text inasmuch as this chapter will explicitly turn to the Seraphic Doctor's notion of sanctity. More specifically, I show how his systematic doctrine of grace figures into his hagiographical portraits of St. Francis and the Virgin Mary, the former of whom he names the *"vir hierarchicus,"* and the latter of whom he names the *"Purificatrix," "Illuminatrix,"* and *"Perfectrix."* Examining a selection of other saints from his *Sermones de sanctis* alongside these two, I show how the "shape" of holiness in his theology of sanctity can truly be called "hierarchical." Chapter 9 will then close with a *General Conclusion* that gestures at several further avenues of theological study in light of my overarching argument. Here, I will finally return to the question of the role of grace in Bonaventure's wisdom theology, the significance of which will only be fully appreciated once we have followed the narrative of grace in Chapters 2–8.

Part I

Theological Foundations for Bonaventure's
Doctrine of Grace

Introduction

My purpose within *Part I* is to introduce several key theological contexts that will be necessary for reading Bonaventure's doctrine of grace. These contexts are truly foundations for the remainder of this book inasmuch as I will construct my own arguments regarding that doctrine in *Parts II* and *III* atop them.

Chapter 2, *Historical Sources for Bonaventure's Doctrine of Grace*, first considers three such theological contexts, represented by three historical figures whose work would have influenced the Seraphic Doctor as a student of theology at the University of Paris: Dionysius the Areopagite, Thomas Gallus, and Alexander of Hales. The chapter highlights one particular aspect of each theologian's thought that will be indispensable for reading Bonaventure's own teachings on grace. My choice to include Dionysius here should already be obvious since it was the Areopagite who originally invented the word hierarchy; the Seraphic Doctor's own understanding of what hierarchy means within the context of his teachings on grace will be illuminated by attending to the Dionysian invention of the word. Thomas Gallus is a less obvious choice. This little-studied theologian from the early thirteenth century has come to be known as "the last of the great Victorines," and he is most famous for his "affective" reading of the Dionysian corpus and accompanying "angelic anthropology," or his suggestion that the soul itself can be made hierarchical for the purposes of being united to God in contemplative love.[1] His angelic anthropology will be readopted by

---

1. For the most significant book on Gallus, see Boyd Taylor Coolman, *Knowledge, Love, and Ecstasy in the Theology of Thomas Gallus* (Oxford: Oxford University Press, 2017).

Bonaventure within the context of his teachings on sanctifying grace, so spending time with Gallus's own angelic anthropology will help us make sense of the Seraphic Doctor's later teachings on the same. Finally, Alexander of Hales was Bonaventure's teacher and the first Franciscan chair of theology at the University of Paris. His definition of sanctifying grace as a created gift will offer a crucial context for approaching his student's later treatment of grace in *The Commentary on the Second Book of Sentences*, where Bonaventure will likewise define sanctifying grace as a "created" gift in distinction to the "uncreated" gift of grace, the Holy Spirit.

Chapter 3, *Bonaventure's Theology of Hierarchy*, will, then, move from these "external" theological influences upon his doctrine of grace to consider instead an "internal" theological context that will likewise be necessary for approaching that doctrine, namely, his own understanding of what hierarchy means. This chapter examines how the word was used by the Seraphic Doctor to describe how the created order of reality relates to the *ordo* within the Triune God; the chapter examines several key texts in which he actually defines hierarchy so as to explain his notion of hierarchical *ordo* as such. Most fundamentally, Bonaventure thinks that the word hierarchy *means* the trinity and unity of God. Creation, then, will be "hierarchical" to the extent that it is assimilated to or made like the divine *ordo,* which for him simply refers to the Trinity, the three equal but distinct divine persons who relate to one another through perfect love. In thus explaining Bonaventure's notion of hierarchy, the chapter will also examine his hierarchical metaphysics, and it especially considers his use of the neoplatonic triad of procession, return, and remaining: Inasmuch as he defines hierarchy as the trinity and unity of God, what does it mean for a rational creature to "return" to God through a hierarchy and then also "remain" in God? Attending to these concepts and questions will prepare us to see how hierarchy functions in his doctrine of grace in *Part II*.

CHAPTER 2

Historical Sources for Bonaventure's Doctrine of Grace

Of Bonaventure's scholastic context at the thirteenth-century University of Paris, Jacques Guy Bougerol has noted how, in order to study any aspect of the Seraphic Doctor's rich theology, we must first encounter "the openness of the intellectual life at the University of Paris" that nurtured him, inasmuch as the work of any scholastic theologian must always be read within the context of the scholarly community that shaped his thought in the University.[1] For our present purposes, this acknowledgment is the first foundation upon which our study of Bonaventure's doctrine of grace must begin. His teachings on grace were informed by a rich and diverse cast of characters, comprised of both his peers and teachers at the thirteenth-century University of Paris as well as his theological predecessors in the Christian tradition, whose writings he would have also encountered in this context.

This chapter highlights three such influences that will be indispensable for approaching the Seraphic Doctor's doctrine of grace in forthcoming chapters, represented here by three theologians whose work he would have read at the University of Paris: (1) Dionysius the Areopagite, (2) Thomas Gallus, and (3) Alexander of Hales. My choice to focus

---

1. See Jacques Guy Bougerol, *Introduction to the Works of Bonaventure*, trans. José de Vinck (Paterson, NJ: St. Anthony Guild Press, 1964), 18–19.

on these three theological influences in no wise intends to suggest that these are the only such influences upon Bonaventure's doctrine of grace. The formidable hand of the Bishop of Hippo weighed heavily upon all medieval accounts of grace, as Aage Rydstrøm-Poulsen has shown with respect to the development of these accounts in the twelfth century,[2] even as the introduction of the "New Aristotle" into the curriculum at the thirteenth-century University of Paris profoundly changed the tone and tenor of medieval treatments of grace in Bonaventure's day. The thirteenth-century University of Paris was a prime location for the meeting of a veritable army of such influences as the Seraphic Doctor would have encountered them through his studies. With respect to his teachings on grace, these would have included the anonymous author of the *Liber de causis*, his Victorine predecessors in the twelfth and early thirteenth centuries, and Bernard of Clairvaux, among a host of others. A consideration of all these sources would provide important historical, theological, and philosophical contexts for Bonaventure's own teachings on grace. A separate book could easily be written in several volumes on that subject alone.

I have chosen to focus on Dionysius, Thomas Gallus, and Alexander of Hales not because they are the only historical sources who informed the Seraphic Doctor's teachings on grace, but rather because they provide important—and in Gallus's case, previously unopened[3]—chapters within the "story" of those teachings as I will narrate them throughout the remainder of this book. Methodologically, the chapter will proceed in three parts that separately attend to each of these three theologians, highlighting particular aspects of their respective theologies that will be especially helpful for approaching that "story" in subsequent chapters.

I begin by providing a basic introduction to Dionysius the Areopagite, who first invented the word "hierarchy" in the early sixth century and whose influence upon Bonaventure is therefore key to this book's central argument regarding the relationship between hierarchy

---

2. For his massive work, which spans nearly 500 pages and provides a truly all-inclusive look at the use of Augustine in twelfth-century theologies of grace, see Aage Rydstrøm-Poulsen, *The Gracious God: Gratia in Augustine and the Twelfth Century* (Copenhagen: Akademisk Forlag, 2002).

3. The exception to this would be the book by Robert Glenn Davis, which discusses Gallus as a source for Bonaventure's notion of synderesis; see his, *The Weight of Love: Affect, Ecstasy, and Union in the Theology of Bonaventure* (New York: Fordham University Press, 2017).

and grace in the Seraphic Doctor's thought. In the second part of the chapter, I then turn to introduce a much less famous character within our story, namely, an understudied theologian from the early thirteenth century who is widely regarded as "the last of the great Victorines," Thomas Gallus. His "affective" reappropriation of Dionysian hierarchy includes, as we shall see below, the introduction of an angelic anthropology whereby he claims that souls are hierarchical, an idea that the Seraphic Doctor will subsequently readapt and revise within his later teachings on sanctifying grace. Finally, I introduce the most proximate source for the Seraphic Doctor's doctrine of grace, the first Franciscan chair of theology at the University of Paris and his teacher, Alexander of Hales. Introducing the Halensian doctrine of grace will provide an important lens into the *status quaestionis* surrounding grace as the Seraphic Doctor would have encountered it in his own thirteenth-century context. Foreshadowing Bonaventure's own treatment of grace, moreover, this section of the chapter will show how the Halensian teaching on grace uses Dionysian themes to describe the effects of sanctifying grace within the soul. All these "characters" and their respective theologies—Dionysius's initial definition of hierarchy; Gallus's notion of the hierarchical soul; and the Halensian understanding of sanctifying grace as a created gift that "purifies, illuminates, and perfects" the soul—provide indispensable contexts for approaching Bonaventure's later association of sanctity with hierarchy.

Each of these three sections will be divided into three parts, wherein I will first very briefly introduce the "character" in question in a general way; will secondly explain each character's "role in the story" with respect to his specific connection with the Seraphic Doctor, thus justifying my choice to shine a limelight on each character; and will thirdly expound upon particular aspects of each character's theology that will set the stage for my argument throughout the remainder of this book.

Dionysius the Areopagite: Hierarchy Defined

Dionysius the Areopagite: A Brief Introduction to the Theologian

Our survey begins in the early sixth century, with the anonymous writer known to us now as Dionysius the Areopagite. An introduction to his person and work can appropriately begin by simply dwelling on the significance of his name, which will help us approach his context. As Charles Stang has shown, this anonymous writer's entire theological project can be framed in accordance with his chosen pseudonym insofar as he purports throughout his writings to be none other than the "Dionysius" from the New Testament, Paul's convert from Greek paganism to Christianity as reported in Acts 17:34. This claim was irrefutably disproven by Hugo Koch and Josef Stiglmayr in the late nineteenth century, who separately published findings that all of the Areopagite's works—collectively known as the *Corpus Dionysiacum,* or the *CD*—borrowed extensively from the fifth-century neoplatonist philosopher, Proclus, and thus must have belonged to an early sixth-century pseudographer.[4] Nonetheless, Stang has recently underscored the importance of this pseudographer's chosen name in thus interpreting his works. The Biblical Dionysius converted to the Christian faith after he heard Paul preaching his well-known sermon to the Athenians as reported in Acts 17:22–23: "I see how extremely religious you are in every way. For as I went through the city and looked carefully at the objects of your worship, I found among them an altar with the inscription, 'To an Unknown God.' What therefore you worship as unknown, this I proclaim to you."[5] Stang argues that the sixth-century Dionysius adopts this name in his writings "in order to suggest that, following Paul, he will effect a new rapprochement between the wisdom of pagan Athens and the revelation of God in Christ," as well as to center his writings on Paul's suggestion that the soul can somehow enjoy a union with the "Unknown God" of Acts 17:23.[6]

We can draw from these remarks two important observations to help us understand who this pseudographer was and why his writings mattered within the history of Christianity (and thus also why he will matter for our present examination of Bonaventure's doctrine of grace): (1) that his project as a whole is concerned with wedding "the wisdom of pagan Athens" of his day, namely, neoplatonic philosophy, with the Christian tradition; and (2) that his project belongs to the category of "apophatic" or negative mystical theology inasmuch as it is concerned

---

4. See Charles M. Stang, "Dionysius, Paul, and the Significance of the Pseudonym," *Modern Theology* 24, no. 4 (2008): 541.

5. Stang, "Dionysius, Paul, and the Significance of the Pseudonym," 542.

6. Stang, "Dionysius, Paul, and the Significance of the Pseudonym," 542.

with the soul's union with the "Unknown God." The *CD* unfolds this project in five short but densely philosophical extant texts: his *Letters*, *The Ecclesiastical Hierarchy* (hereafter *EH*), *The Celestial Hierarchy* (hereafter *CH*), *The Divine Names* (hereafter *DN*), and *The Mystical Theology* (hereafter *MT*).[7]

With respect to the second of these two observations, scholarly interest in these works of Dionysius has recently surged due to his role in the "apophatic turn," or phrased differently, due to his role in the tradition of Christian mysticism that highlights negative theology as a path to God over and above the "positive" or kataphatic way. This tradition—rather than emphasizing a union between God and the soul whereby the soul can *know* God fully in an Augustinian sense—understood a mystical union between God and the soul as being characterized by "unknowing," or by an intellectual darkness in which the soul ceases to know anything as it is wrapped up in an ecstatic union with the Divine.[8] The Areopagite is nowadays especially lauded for the rich

7. See *Corpus Dionysiacum* (PG 3:119–1122). I rely on the translation of the *CD* in *Pseudo-Dionysius: The Complete Works*, trans. Colm Luibheid, ed. Paul Rorem (New York: Paulist Press, 1987).

8. This is due in large part to the enigmatic character of the *CD* itself. The question regarding *how* Dionysius's works should be interpreted is the subject of hot debate among scholars of the Areopagite, a debate that revolves around the question of whether or not his works should be interpreted as belonging more to the Christian mystical tradition or to the tradition of neoplatonic philosophy. It lies beyond the scope of this study for me to make a judgment regarding this argument; my goal is to simply introduce Dionysius's concept of hierarchy as it pertains to "telling the story" of the Seraphic Doctor's doctrine of grace. For a select bibliography on the thought of Dionysius, see Sarah Coakley, "Re-thinking Dionysius the Areopagite," *Modern Theology* 24, no. 4 (2008): 531–40, and the entire volume of accompanying essays treating the "apophatic turn" that thus appear with it; Hans Urs Von Balthasar, "Denys," in *The Glory of the Lord: A Theological Aesthetics*, vol. 2, *Studies in Theological Style: Clerical Styles* (San Francisco: St. Ignatius Press, 1985), 144–210; Alexander Golitzin, *Mystagogy: A Monastic Reading of Dionysius Areopagita* (Collegeville: Cistercian Publications, 2013); Alexander Golitzin, "Dionysius Areopagita: A Christian Mysticism?" *Pro Ecclesia* 12, no. 2 (2003): 161–212; Filip Ivanovic, ed., *Dionysius the Areopagite between Orthodoxy and Heresy* (Newcastle, UK: Cambridge Scholars, 2011); Andrew Louth, *Denys the Areopagite* (Wilton, CT: Morehouse, Barlow, 1989); Bernard McGinn, "Anagogy and Apophaticism: The Mysticism of Dionysius," in *The Foundations of Mysticism: Origins to the Fifth Century*, The Presence of God: A History of Western Christian Mysticism 1 (New York: Crossroad, 1991), 157–82; Eric D. Perl, *Theophany: The Neoplatonic Philosophy of Dionysius the Areopagite* (Albany, NY: State University of New York Press, 2007); John Rist, "Love, Knowing, and Incarnation in Pseudo-Dionysius," in *Traditions of Platonism: Essays in Honour of John Dillon*, ed. John J. Cleary (Brookfield, VT: Ashgate, 1999) , 375–88; Paul Rorem, *Pseudo-Dionysius: A Commentary on the Texts and an Introduction to Their Influence* (New York: Oxford University Press, 1993); and Stang, "Dionysius, Paul, and the Significance of the Pseudonym," 541–55.

apophatic emphases in his texts wherein the soul is instructed "to leave behind ... everything perceived and understood, everything perceptible and understandable, all that is not and all that is, and, with your understanding laid astride, to strive upward as much as you can toward union with him who is beyond all being and knowledge" through "an undivided and absolute abandonment of yourself and everything."[9] This intellectual darkness, which Dionysius here describes in *MT*, will pave the way forward for a long trajectory of mystical-theological reflection in the Christian tradition that thus also focuses on the *via negativa* as the proper posture of the soul-in-union-with-God. This trajectory will include, for example, such esteemed texts within the Christian tradition as *The Cloud of Unknowing* and the seventh chapter of what is perhaps Bonaventure's most famous treatise, the *Itinerarium*. Scholars in the twentieth and twenty-first centuries who have taken an interest in the *via negativa* find in Dionysius a rich source for considering the development of this tradition as it flowed forth from the Areopagite's pen in the *CD* and influenced countless theologians after him.

The Areopagite's role in this "apophatic turn" in the Christian mystical-theological tradition, however, is made even more interesting by the *first* of the above two observations—namely, that in his short but dense extant corpus there is an overwhelming synthesis between neoplatonic philosophy and the Christian tradition. Bernard McGinn has aptly summarized Dionysius's entire theological project by noting how "the theological center of Dionysius's concern is the exploration of how the utterly unknowable God manifests himself in creation in order that all things may attain union with the unmanifest Source."[10] Crucially, Dionysius borrows extensively from neoplatonic sources throughout the *CD*—especially Proclus, Plotinus, and Iamblichus, representatives of "the wisdom of pagan Athens" in his own day—to provide an account of how God manifests Godself in creation in order to lead rational creatures to this mystical union at the center of his project.[11] The extent to which he borrows from these neoplatonic philosophers is so great, in fact, that a lively debate continues to take place between scholars who wish to appropriate the Areopagite's thought either entirely to

---

9. *MT* 1.1, trans. Luibheid, 135.

10. McGinn, "Anagogy and Apophaticism," 161.

11. For an extremely thorough account of the neoplatonic influences upon Dionysius's thought, see especially Perl, *Theophany*.

the realm of philosophy or to that of theology depending on their own interests and specific field of study. It is not my task to place a stake in these debates,[12] but I highlight them here in order to shine light on the complexity of Dionysius's theology as a whole: Walking the *via negativa* with him throughout the *CD* is not an easy task, and my comments here can only but provide a very condensed introduction to his theology in order to set the stage for my later comments on Bonaventure's doctrine of grace.

Dionysius and Bonaventure

What, though, of the relationship between Dionysius and Bonaventure? First, we should note that while Koch and Stiglmayr disproved the Areopagite's claim to be the first-century convert of Paul in the nineteenth century, medieval theologians had no reason to dispute this claim and thus regarded the *CD* as authentic. Since medieval theologians—including Bonaventure—thought the *CD* was penned by one who held apostolic authority, they thereby assigned to the text a theological authority that was second only to scripture.[13] The Areopagite was, as it were, an especially beloved source for the Seraphic Doctor. Laure Solignac has shown how Bonaventure's entire theological project is "Dionysian" as much as it is "Augustinian,"[14] even while Jacques Guy Bougerol begins his seminal work on the historical sources for Bonaventure's thought by attending to the role of "Pseudo-Denys l'Aréopagite" in his works.[15] In other words, Bonaventurean scholar-

12. See Boyd Taylor Coolman's helpfully succinct summation of this debate in *Knowledge, Love, and Ecstasy*, 12: "Arguably, the most compelling feature of the Dionysian universe is its profound synthesis of Christian theology, scriptural exegesis, and ecclesial liturgy on the one hand, and the late antique Neoplatonism of Plotinus and especially Proclus, on the other. Much modern debate has revolved around the question of which is more fundamental: The Christianity or the Neoplatonism. For present purposes it suffices to refuse the dilemma, as Bernard Blankenhorn has recently done, and to acknowledge simply that the Areopagite is 'at once deeply Christian and Neoplatonic.'"

13. For an introduction to the *CD's* influence over medieval theologians in particular, see especially Rorem, *Pseudo-Dionysius*.

14. Solignac underscores the finer nuances of this synthesis throughout *La voie de la ressemblance*.

15. Jacques Guy Bougerol, "Saint Bonaventure et le Pseudo-Denys l'Aréopagite," in *Études Franciscaines* 18 (Supplément Annuel 1968): 33–123. This article was then reprinted as a book chapter with the same title, as well as the same pagination, in Jacques Guy Bougerol, *Saint Bonaventure: Études sur les sources de sa pensée* (Northampton: Variorum Reprints, 1989), 33–123.

ship already widely attests to the indubitable influence which the Areopagite's work held over the Seraphic Doctor's theology. Bonaventure would have read the Areopagite as a student at the University of Paris, and scholars generally agree that he favored Dionysius increasingly as a source until his death in 1274.[16]

Most importantly, however, in addition to this general acknowledgment of his influence over the Seraphic Doctor's theology, a brief encounter with the works of Dionysius the Areopagite is here necessary for a much more specific reason: Significantly, the Areopagite is actually credited as the *inventor* of the word "hierarchy."[17] Inasmuch as this book aims to explore the relationship between Bonaventure's theology of hierarchy and his doctrine of grace, my choice to shine a limelight on this particular character within my "story" of that doctrine should be quite obvious. Simply put, we cannot hope to comprehend what the Seraphic Doctor himself meant by the word "hierarchy" without first attending to the word's meaning in the *CD*, where it was *invented*. Bonaventure would have encountered the *CD* in Latin translations of the text provided by John Scotus Eriugena, John Saracen, Robert Grossetesste, and Thomas Gallus, the latter of whom we shall turn to momentarily,[18] and he will use excerpts from the Latin translation of the passage from *CH* 3 when he defines the word in his own way in *II Sent.*[19] As such, in order to pave the way forward for approaching Bonaventure's definition of the word, my comments below expound

16. See Bougerol, "Saint Bonaventure et le Pseudo-Denys l'Aréopagite," 105–12; and Hayes's summation of other scholarship attesting to this observation in his comments regarding the role of hierarchy in Bonaventure's soteriology in *Hidden Center*, 157–61.

17. Rorem, *Pseudo-Dionysius*, 21.

18. Bougerol, "Saint Bonaventure et le Pseudo-Denys l'Areopagite," 39. Bougerol identifies a total of 248 citations of the *CD* across Bonaventure's works (36), and shows the Seraphic Doctor most frequently used Eriugena's translation. Despite the fine scholarship of Bougerol, much work remains by way of studying Bonaventure's use of these sources and his reception of Dionysius, work that far exceeds the limitations of this study. For example, as careful and important as Bougerol's article cited above is for understanding Bonaventure's use of the Areopagite's thought, shifting trends in digital research necessitate that this number of citations perhaps be amended. The Brepols Cross Database Search Tool names 254 citations of Dionysius across Bonaventure's works, for example. A comparison of these citations with Bougerol's article might yield new insights into Bonaventure's use of the Areopagite's corpus as well as his use of the Areopagite's Latin commentators. While Bougerol does not lend too much significance to the influence of Thomas Gallus's reading of the Areopagite over Bonaventure's thought, moreover, this study will hopefully show that Bonaventure utilized the Abbot of Vercelli's Dionysian interpretations in crucial ways, especially with regard to his doctrine of grace.

19. For a discussion of this definition according to Bonaventure, see Chapter 3.

upon the Areopagite's original definition of hierarchy from *CH* 3. Though some seven hundred years removed from the Seraphic Doctor, this "invention" provides the theoretical foundation upon which the remainder of this book will be built.

Dionysius's Invention of Hierarchy

Before turning to this invention, however, a caveat bears repeating: Contemporary theological critiques of hierarchy warrant our acknowledgment, attention, and respect. The word nowadays is associated with patriarchal and oppressive power structures within the Church, even as liberation theologies have rightly highlighted the word's role in exacerbating the plight of marginalized poor peoples across the globe in the political sphere.[20] These critiques and others like them deserve

20. For a useful and short summation of this problem with respect to regarding the Trinity as a hierarchy, see Miraslov Volf, "'The Trinity is our Social Program': The Doctrine of the Trinity and the Shape of Social Engagement," *Modern Theology* 14, no. 3 (1998): 403–23. Volf's essay builds from a broader conversation in liberation theology that criticizes the notion of hierarchy—especially as it pertains to historical formulations for the Trinity—from a political perspective; see, for some examples, Leonardo Boff, *Trinity and Society*, trans. Paul Burns (Maryknoll, NY: Orbis Books, 1988), and Jürgen Moltmann, *The Trinity and the Kingdom: The Doctrine of God* (San Francisco: Harper and Row, 1981), 192–202. Elizabeth Johnson has likewise underscored the harmful ways in which hierarchy has been employed historically in theological discourse by the patriarchy; see *She Who Is: The Mystery of God in Feminist Theological Discourse*, 196–97 (New York: Crossroad Publishing, 2014).

Beyond these, the critique of hierarchy is so widespread in contemporary systematic theology that it is often simply presumed; I am grateful to private conversations with Dr. Elyse Raby for illuminating this for me. The field of ecclesiology is especially critical of what has come to be known as "hierarchology," a phrase coined by Yves Congar to describe the pyramidal organization of power that came to dominate the church in the thirteenth century during Bonaventure's lifetime. As Richard R. Gaillardetz has said of this critique, "the qualifier 'hierarchical' can serve an important purpose if we purge it of those pyramidal conceptions it gained in the thirteenth century, when medieval ecclesiology employed the neo-platonic cosmology of the late fifth- or early sixth-century figure, Pseudo-Dionysius the Areopagite, as a structuring principle for the Church. 'Hierarchia,' a term first coined by Pseudo-Dionysius, became in the thirteenth century an ontological schema for viewing the Church as a descending ladder of states of being and truth, with the fullness of power (*plenitudo potestatis*) given to the pope and shared in diminishing degrees with the lower levels of church life. This 'hierarchology' has remained in the Church, in varying degrees, up to the present"; see his "The Ecclesiological Foundations of Ministry within an Ordered Communion," in *Ordering of the Baptismal Priesthood*, ed. Susan Wood (Collegeville: Liturgical Press, 2003), 26–51, at 34. In the same article, Gaillardetz affirms that "a contemporary ecclesiology of communion must reject the ascending hierarchy of orders presupposed in the Middle Ages" in order for the Catholic Church to move forward post-Vatican II (43). See also Thomas F. O'Meara, "Beyond 'Hierarchology': Johann Adam Möhler and Yves Congar," in *The Legacy of the Tübingen School: The Relevance of Nineteenth-Century Theology for the Twenty-First Century*, ed. Donald J. Dietrich and Michael J. Himes (New York: Crossroad,

careful consideration among theologians who turn either to Dionysius or to his medieval interpreters as a locus for *ressourcement* in contemporary theological reflection. Historically, hierarchies within both the Church and the world at large have *unquestionably* served to oppress peoples rather than elevate human persons to God, a fact that must be acknowledged at the outset of any discussion of the word. As Sarah Coakley has recently suggested, however, when Dionysius invented the word, he meant something different. My ensuing remarks on this invention are intended in no wise to discredit contemporary critiques of hierarchy, but rather only to illuminate the meaning of the word as Dionysius himself intended it in its original context, so as to illuminate as well its meaning for Bonaventure.

The Areopagite's clearest definition, as it were, of hierarchy appears in the third chapter of *CH*. Within the broader context of the *CD*, *The Celestial Hierarchy* provides an account of that for which it is named: There, the Areopagite introduces nine orders of angels (taken from scripture) and describes their ministries and relations with God, one another, and humanity. These nine angelic orders are arranged by Dionysius throughout the text from "highest to lowest," an order he devises based on how he perceives their proximity to God. These consist of the seraphim, cherubim, thrones (what Dionysius calls the "First Hierarchy");[21] the dominions, powers, and authorities (what Dionysius calls the "Second Hierarchy");[22] as well as the principalities, archangels, and angels (what Dionysius calls the "Third Hierarchy").[23]

Before introducing these "three hierarchies" of heaven and describing their ordering to God and one another, however, Dionysius helpfully offers a definition of what he means by hierarchy in the beginning of Chapter 3. I here quote it in full, along with his subsequent explanation:

In my opinion a hierarchy is a sacred order, a state of understanding, and an activity approximating as closely as possible to the divine. And it is uplifted to the imitation of God in proportion to the enlightenments divinely given to it. The beauty of God—so simple, so good, so much the source of perfection— is completely uncontaminated by dissimilarity. It reaches out to grant every

---

1997), 173–91; Elyse Raby, *Toward an Intercorporeal Body of Christ: A Study in Ecclesial Body Images* (PhD diss., Boston College, 2021), 121.

    21. *CH* 7, trans. Luibheid, 161–66.

    22. *CH* 8, trans. Luibheid, 166–69.

    23. *CH* 9, trans. Luibheid, 169–73.

being, according to merit, a share of light and then through a divine sacrament, in harmony and peace, it bestows on each of those being perfected its own form. The goal of a hierarchy, then, is to enable beings to be as like as possible to God and to be at one with him. A hierarchy has God as its leader of all understanding and action. It is forever looking directly at the comeliness of God. A hierarchy bears in itself the mark of God. Hierarchy causes its members to be images of God in all aspects, to be clear and spotless mirrors reflecting the glow of primordial light and indeed of God himself. It ensures that when its members have received this full and divine splendor they can then pass on this light generously and in accordance with God's will to beings further down the scale.... If one talks of a hierarchy, what is meant is a certain perfect arrangement, an image of the beauty of God which sacredly works out the mysteries of its own enlightenment in the orders and levels of understanding of the hierarchy, and which is likened toward its own source as much as is permitted. Indeed for every member of the hierarchy, perfection consists in this, that it is uplifted to imitate God as far as possible and, more wonderful still, that it becomes what scripture calls a "fellow workman for God" and a reflection of the workings of God.[24]

This, then, is where the Areopagite "invents" hierarchy, thus setting the stage for all theological reflections regarding the word for centuries to come. To pave the way for understanding Bonaventure's theology of hierarchy in its relation to his doctrine of grace, three observations are warranted with respect to the passage above, which contains the first use of the word in Christian history.

First and most obviously, it is worth dwelling upon what a hierarchy actually is in the above passage. Most notably, the word does not mean here what it means today. In our modern context, a hierarchy is primarily understood as a social construct, a "repressive top-down system" of power that fundamentally involves "*inequalities* of aptitude and functions" among its various members that are founded upon an "artificial organization of multiple activities."[25] Here, however, when he *invents* the word, Dionysius rather defines a "hierarchy" as "*a sacred order, a state of understanding, and an activity approximating as closely as possible to the Divine*" (my emphasis).[26] This "sacred order," "state of understanding," and "activity," as he continues, serves the purpose

---

24. *CH* 3.1–2, trans. Luibheid, 153–54.

25. Coakley quoting Louis Dumont, in *God, Sexuality, and the Self,* 320n20; see also Louis Dumont, *Homo hierarchicus,* 54.

26. *CH* 3.1, trans. Luibheid, 153.

of perfecting rational creatures by making them like God or, in other words, by bestowing upon them a divine likeness. Crucially, this "triple aspect of order, activity, and science"[27] is not offered within his definition of hierarchy to posit a model for how society should be structured, but—as other scholars of Dionysius's thought have already well documented—to describe, using a complex synthesis of neoplatonic philosophy and Christian theology, how rational creatures relate to the One, Good God who created them.[28]

For example, the word "order" in this context, as René Roques has noted, indicates "an intelligible and sensible disposition that comes from God, the principle of all order," an order that harmonizes all creatures back to the unity of the One, Good God.[29] It does not imply an artificial division among creatures of different social strata, but rather for Dionysius simply refers to the fact that *all* rational creatures are ordered from and back to God as their Creator.[30] For Dionysius, rational creatures that thus participate in the activity of the hierarchies are granted access to a "share" of divine light through this Divine order, so that "through a divine sacrament, in harmony and in peace, [the divine light] bestows on each of those being perfected its own form,"[31] and they thus become "like" God; phrased differently, they become God-conformed or *deiform*. First and foremost, Dionysian "hierarchy" *means* that "order," "understanding," and "activity" through which rational beings thus become deified by being granted this divine likeness or deiformity. The word is, essentially, the Areopagite's shorthand way of describing how a rational creature relates to God by being like God.

Second, and closely related to this first point, we should here also note Dionysius's remarks concerning the goal of a hierarchy as such. If a "hierarchy" is a means of relating to God, then the goal of a hierarchy is for the rational creature to relate to God as perfectly as possible through it. And according to Dionysius, the rational creature relates to God most perfectly when it is made like God and is united to God, as

---

27. René Roques, *L'universe Dionysien: Structure hiérarchique du monde selon le Pseudo-Denys* (Aubier: Éditions Montaigne, 1954), 333: "Toute hiérarchie se caractérise par son triple aspect d'ordre, d'activité et de science."

28. For Dionysius's neoplatonism, see especially Perl, *Theophany*.

29. Roques, *L'universe Dionysien*, 333: "L'ordre hiérarchique est une disposition, intelligible et sensible, qui vient de Dieu, principe de tout ordre...."

30. This same concept of "order" is also an important theological theme for Bonaventure; see Hellmann, *Divine and Created Order*.

31. *CH* 3.1, trans. Luibheid, 154.

he writes in *CH* 3: "The goal of a hierarchy, then, is to enable beings to be as like as possible to God and to be at one with him."[32]

Significantly, in order to understand better how hierarchies lead rational creatures to this union with and conformity to God, readers of Dionysius look especially to his appropriation of the late-neoplatonic notion of remaining (*residuus*), procession (*exitus*), and return (*redditus*), as first systematized by Iamblichus and popularized by Proclus's statement that "every effect remains in its cause, proceeds from it, and reverts upon it."[33] In neoplatonism, these three movements are grounded in God, whereby the One eternally "remains" in itself but is nonetheless also the Source from which everything in existence flows forth as well as the End to which all rational creatures must strive. These movements of procession and return in neoplatonism comprise an intelligible circle of reality: All intelligible being "processes" from the One in the act of creation but then must "return" to the One to complete the circle of reality. The Areopagite, as it were, rehashes this idea throughout the *CD* with respect to his theology of hierarchy. In his introduction to *CH,* for example, he quotes Jas 1:17, "Every good endowment and every perfect gift is from above, coming down from the Father of Lights," so as to describe this procession and return of all creaturely beings from and to their divine source by using the imagery of Light: "each procession of the Light spreads itself generously toward us, and, in its power to unify, it stirs us by lifting us up. It returns us back to the oneness and deifying simplicity of the Father who gathers us in."[34] For Dionysius, rational beings who proceed forth from the Light of God in the act of creation can "return" to God through their participation in a hierarchy, since the Light of God "makes [itself] known to us" through the "representative symbols" of scriptures, the sacraments, and the liturgy.[35] A hierarchy has as its goal the rational creature's union with and conformity to God insofar as a creature's participation in hierarchical activities enables its own return, or *redditus*, to God.

---

32. *CH* 3.2, trans. Luibheid, 154.

33. Paul Rorem, *Biblical and Liturgical Symbols within the Pseudo-Dionysian Synthesis,* Studies and Texts 71 (Toronto: Pontifical Institute of Mediaeval Studies, 1984), 59. For Rorem's central thesis, see 63.

34. *CH* 1.1, trans. Luibheid, 145.

35. See *CH* 1.3–4, trans. Luibheid, 146–47. As Rorem's thesis suggests in *Biblical and Liturgical Symbols,* 63: "in the Pseudo-Dionysian corpus, the scriptures and liturgy are viewed as the divine procession into the world of the senses; their spiritual interpretation, correspondingly, is part of the divine return which uplifts the faithful."

Third, and building further from this, it is also necessary to say something more about how this return happens or, in other words, about how Dionysius thinks this goal is achieved. In the above selection I quoted from *CH* 3, he claims that a rational creature who participates in a hierarchy will be "likened toward its own source as much as is permitted"—that is, it will "return" to God—when "it is uplifted to imitate God as far as possible and, more wonderful still, [when] it becomes what scripture calls a 'fellow workman for God' and a reflection of the workings of God."[36] The "goal" of a hierarchy is achieved, in other words, because the rational creature who participates in a hierarchy is likened unto God with respect to a certain kind of activity, or better yet, *activities*. According to Dionysius, there are three:

Therefore when the hierarchic order lays it on some to be purified and on others to do the purifying, on some to receive illumination and others to cause illumination, on some to be perfected and on others to bring about perfection, each will actually imitate God in the way suitable to whatever role it has. What we humans call the beatitude of God is something uncontaminated by dissimilarity. It is full of a continuous light and is perfect, indeed it lacks no perfection whatsoever. It is purifying, illuminating, and perfecting; or rather, it is itself purification, illumination, and perfection. It is beyond purification; it is beyond light, it is the very source of perfection which is more than perfect.[37]

To become "as like as possible" to God and become "one" with God, a rational creature must participate in these three hierarchical activities, namely, purification, illumination, and perfection. If God—the source of all intelligible reality—remains in Godself through precisely these three activities as the highest and most transcendent sort of purification, illumination, and perfection, then, for Dionysius, rational creatures return to God inasmuch as they participate in these same three activities. A creature's proximity to God will therefore also depend on the extent to which he or she has thus been purified, illuminated, and perfected. In *EH*, for example, Dionysius will even appropriate these three activities to the different hierarchical orders within the Church, which are purified, illuminated, and perfected for the purposes of carrying out their own liturgical ministries: The hierarchs (or bishops) are charged with the work of "perfecting"; the priests are charged with the

---

36. *CH* 3.2, trans. Luibheid, 154.
37. *CH* 3.2, trans. Luibheid, 154–55.

work of "illuminating"; and the deacons are charged with the work of "purifying."[38] All people within the Church can thereby return to their Source in God through the hierarchical activity of the Church and, most especially, through the sacraments, which he claims, "bring about purification, illumination, and perfection."[39] Whether with respect to the angelic hierarchy or the Church, the Areopagite holds that these three hierarchical activities in particular are what cause rational creatures to become "fellow-workmen for God."

Dionysius is quite clear, moreover, that rational creatures within both the celestial and the ecclesiastical hierarchies can only truly become "fellow-workmen for God" when they then pass on their perfection, illumination, or purification to those below them in the hierarchies who have not yet been perfected, illuminated, or purified. As he writes in *CH*:

It is also right that those who purify should give of their superabundant purity to others. It is right too that those who give illumination—those minds clearer than others, joyfully full of the sacred radiance, and obviously able both to receive the light and to pass on what they acquire—that these should spread their overflowing light everywhere among those worthy of it. Finally, it is only proper that those charged with the task of creating perfection, as those who understand the perfecting impartation, should cause the perfect to be what they are by introducing them to an understanding of the sacred things so reverently beheld. And so it comes about that every order in the hierarchical rank is uplifted as best as it can toward cooperation with God. By grace and a God-given power, it does things which belong supernaturally to God, things performed by him transcendently and revealed in the hierarchy for the permitted imitation of God-loving minds.[40]

In other words, if rational creatures "return" to God and become "like" God and "one" with God through these three hierarchical activities, then it is not enough to participate in these activities in only a passive sense. For Dionysius, intelligible beings who have been purified, illuminated, or perfected by receiving the Light of God through their participation in the hierarchies can only be further uplifted into God

---

38. *EH* 6.5, trans. Luibheid, 248. It is important to note that Dionysius is nonetheless clear, especially in the case of the Bishops or Hierarchs, that these are always also "purifying" and "illuminating" in addition to doing the work of perfection; see *EH* 5.7, trans. Luibheid, 238.

39. *EH* 6.5, trans. Luibheid, 248.

40. *CH* 3.3, trans. Luibheid, 155.

inasmuch as they actively assist in purifying, illuminating, and perfecting those within the hierarchies below them who have not reached the same level of proximity to God. Dionysius's hierarchical "ranking" from the highest to lowest—of the seraphim down to the angels within the celestial hierarchy, and of the bishops down to the layperson within the Church—is based on this level of nearness to God by way of activity. Those who are *nearest* to God, namely, the "perfect," are only perfect because they cooperate as "fellow workmen for God" through hierarchical activity more than those in the hierarchies below them. They will cease being perfected if they cease actively assisting in the perfection of those below: To be perfec*ted*, they must also be actively perfec*ting*. Those who are illuminat*ed* remain as such only insofar as they are also participating in the hierarchical activity of illuminat*ing* those below. And finally, those who are purifi*ed* will only remain pure inasmuch as they are likewise participating in the hierarchical activity of purif*ying* those who remain "contaminated by dissimilarity." Dionysius's definition of hierarchy thus entails that all rational beings must become "fellow workmen" for God, assisting "lower" beings within the hierarchy and helping them become purified, illuminated, and perfected so that they, too, would become deified.

The "return," in other words, walks hand in hand with continuous "processions," and—to again recall that the Areopagite borrows a neoplatonic *triad* of movement—these two movements together are what constitute the rational creature's *remaining* in God through the hierarchies in Dionysian thought. As Boyd Taylor Coolman has noted:

Essentially, a Dionysian hierarchy is a dynamic structure or order (*taxis*), involving both knowledge (*gnosis*) and activity (*energia*), which reflects and imitates God and also conducts and unites to God. The purpose of any hierarchy "is assimilation and union, as far as attainable, with God." The dynamism of a Dionysian hierarchy ... is "animated" by the Neoplatonic metaphysics of procession (*exitus/proodos*), return (*reditus/epistrophe*), and remaining (*residuus/mane*). Every hierarchy thus has an ascending, descending, and remaining dimension or "valence" (as in a "vector" or "scalarity"), which simultaneously (not sequentially) constitutes it in a kind of dynamic equilibrium or *stasis*; or perhaps better: The dynamic simultaneity of procession and return establish an equipoise described as remaining.[41]

---

41. Coolman, *Knowledge, Love, and Ecstasy*, 23.

Dionysius's hierarchical system depends on the constant interconnectivity of all intelligible being: All intelligible beings within the hierarchies must continuously be related to one another and to God through these "ascents" and "descents." For the Areopagite, deification—understood as union with and conformity to God—does not occur apart from this hierarchical community, the "order" of rational creatures in the celestial and ecclesiastical hierarchies through which higher creatures assist the lower so that *all* may remain in the God-beyond-all-thought.

This idea accentuates the *relational* and *dynamic* character of hierarchy as the Areopagite originally conceived it. For him, participation in a hierarchy opens up the possibility for the creature's relationship with both God and other rational beings in the celestial and ecclesiastical hierarchies. Intelligible beings cannot achieve the goal of divine union apart from becoming a "fellow-workman for God" through hierarchical activity, defined by the Areopagite as the work of purification, illumination, and perfection whereby all beings within the hierarchies are dependent upon one another—the lower upon the higher, but also the higher upon the lower—in their common goal of returning to and then remaining in God. Eric Perl elegantly summarizes this idea, arguing that for Dionysius:

Each thing's participation in God, its being, lies in its fulfilling its proper place within the hierarchical structure of reality. But this means that its participation in God consists in its rightly relating to other beings above, below, and coordinate with it in the universal hierarchy. A being exercises its proper activities, its being, not in isolation but in relation to other beings. Hence, as Dionysius says, the love of all things for God, which is their reversion, their participation in him, and hence their very being, consists in their love for each other, according to the proper rank of each.... The higher being's love for or participation in God, its being, then, is its providence to the lower, and the lower being's love for or participation in God is its reversion, or receptivity, to the higher. Providing to the lower and reverting to the higher is the very meaning of occupying a given position in the hierarchical structure of the whole. Dionysian hierarchy, therefore, has nothing to do with domination and subservience, but only with love, the love of all things for one another which is the love of God in them all.[42]

The idea that a hierarchy can be characterized by a relationship of love, "the love of all things for one another which is the love of God in

42. Perl, *Theophany,* 77.

them all," will seem foreign to anyone who conceives of a hierarchy in the modern sense, as a social power structure in which higher beings necessarily suppress the lower. For Dionysius, who coined the word, however, "hierarchy" means a sacred order, a state of understanding, and activity through which rational creatures "remain" in union and conformity with God by way of relationships with one another.

In the same way that hierarchy meant something quite different for Dionysius than it does in our context, so too, it will mean something quite different for the Seraphic Doctor, both on its own and as he employs it within his teachings on grace. Through Dionysius's theology of hierarchy, we are indeed introduced for the first time to key themes and concepts that will characterize Bonaventure's teachings on grace, particularly to his metaphysics of light, the notions of image and likeness or similitude, and the concept of deiformity or God-conformity.[43] The intelligible circle that characterizes the neoplatonic vision of reality through the three movements of remaining, procession, and return is likewise a favorite image within Bonaventure's metaphysics. Similarly, the three hierarchical activities of purification, illumination, and perfection become a central feature of the Seraphic Doctor's thought, both with respect to his theology of hierarchy, but also in his description of the effects of sanctifying grace within the soul. Appreciating these continuities here serves the purpose of underscoring how—even as Bonaventure clearly adapts Dionysius's theology in his use of these themes in the thirteenth century—he nonetheless also revises and reshapes them for his own purposes. Introducing these themes as they were originally put forward by Dionysius exposes us to both continuities and discontinuities between himself and the Seraphic Doctor.

Before turning to these, however, it is necessary first to introduce another "character" in our story: Thomas Gallus. While my choice to shine a limelight on Dionysius as a source for the Seraphic Doctor's theology might be somewhat obvious, this character is much more obscure; his influence upon Bonaventure's theology of hierarchy and teachings on grace, however, are no less important, and we therefore jump ahead from the sixth century to the twelfth and thirteenth, where we find ourselves face-to-face with the Victorines.

---

43. For a discussion of these themes in Bonaventure's definition of grace, see especially Chapters 4–5.

Thomas Gallus: Hierarchy Ensouled

Thomas Gallus:
A Brief Introduction to the Theologian

Whereas Dionysius's popularity among theologians has surged in recent decades, Thomas Gallus is only now beginning to emerge as a formidable theological force from behind the shadows of his more famous twelfth-century predecessors at the Victorine school of theology in Paris, Hugh and Richard.[44] Whereas very little can be said with respect to the biography of the Areopagite,[45] a concise word is here necessary regarding the life of this little-studied Victorine. Gallus, known to his medieval successors alternatively as "Thomas of Paris" (*Thomas Parisiensis*), Thomas of St. Victor, or—as Bonaventure will refer to him in the *Hexaëmeron*—the "Abbot of Vercelli," was probably born in France in the late twelfth century. He became a Master of Theology at the University of Paris sometime between 1210 and 1218, during which time he also lectured to the students at the Abbey of St. Victor, and so is now

44. Relatively little scholarship has been produced on Gallus in comparison to Hugh and Richard of St. Victor; for a select bibliography on Gallus, see especially Coolman, *Knowledge, Love, and Ecstasy*; Boyd Taylor Coolman, "The Medieval Affective Dionysian Tradition," *Modern Theology* 24, no. 4 (2008): 615–32; and Boyd Taylor Coolman, "Thomas Gallus," in *The Spiritual Senses: Perceiving God in Western Christianity*, ed. Sarah Coakley and Paul L. Gavrilyuk (Cambridge: Cambridge University Press, 2012), 140–58. See also Declan Anthony Lawell, introduction to *Thomae Galli: Explanatio in libros Dionysii*, ed. Declan Anthony Lawell, *CC CM* 223 (Turnhout: Brepols, 2011), vii–ix, xxiii–xxxii; Declan Anthony Lawell, "*Ne de ineffabili penitus taceamus*: Aspects of the Specialized Vocabulary of the Writings of Thomas Gallus," *Viator* 40, no. 1 (2009): 151–84; Declan Anthony Lawell, "*Spectacula contemplationis* (1244–46): A Treatise by Thomas Gallus," *Recherches de théologie et philosophie médiévales* 76, no. 2 (2009): 249–85; Bernard McGinn, "The Victorine Ordering of Mysticism," in *The Growth of Mysticism*, 363–418 (New York: Crossroad, 1994); Bernard McGinn, "Thomas Gallus and Dionysian Mysticism," *Studies in Spirituality* 8 (1998): 81–96; Francis Ruello, introduction to *Un commentaire vercellien du* Cantique des cantiques: '*Deiformis anime gemitus*,' ed. Jeanne Barbet and trans. Francis Ruello (Turnhout: Brepols, 2005), 7–93; Kurt Ruh, "Thomas Gallus Vercellensis," in *Geschichte der abendländischen Mystik*, Die Mystik des deutschen Predigerordens und ihre Grundlegung durch die Hochscholastik 3, 59–81 (Munich: Verlag, 1996); Gabriel Théry, "Thomas Gallus et Egide d'Assise: le traité *De septem gradibus contemplationis*," *Revue néoscolastique de philosophie* 36 (1934): 180–90; James A. Walsh, *The Pursuit of Wisdom and Other Works by the Author of the Cloud of Unknowing* (New York: Paulist Press, 1988); James A. Walsh, "Thomas Gallus et l'effort contemplatif," *Revue d'histoire de la spiritualité* 51 (1975): 17–42; and Katherine Wrisley Shelby, "Thomas Gallus' *Explanatio* and Dionysian Thought," in *Victorine Restoration: Essays on Hugh of St. Victor, Richard of St. Victor, and Thomas Gallus*, ed. David Orsbon and Robert J. Porwoll (Turnhout: Brepols, 2021), 297–327.

45. Due to his anonymity, notes on the Areopagite's biography are, unfortunately, left largely to the field of speculation.

often dubbed "the last of the great Victorines."[46] Then, as Boyd Taylor Coolman's recent monograph on the Victorine recounts: "Around 1218–1219, at the request of the papal legate to England and France, Cardinal Guala Bicchieri, he (with two other canons) went to Vercelli to found an abbey and hospital dedicated to Saint Andrew. Apparently chosen for his typically Victorine combination of scholarly rigor and spiritual ardor, he became prior of the abbey in 1224, and abbot before 1226."[47] Gallus spent the next two decades as Abbot of Vercelli, "interrupted only by a year in England in 1238 and a brief period of exile in 1243," where he "died and was buried in the Basilica of Sant'Andrea at Vercelli in 1246."[48]

Gallus is an important figure within the history of the Christian theological tradition because of his work as a commentator on the entire *CD*. Following Hugh of St. Victor, who wrote his own commentary on *CH*,[49] Gallus took an especial interest in the works of Dionysius. Like Bonaventure, he would have had no reason to doubt Dionysius's claim to apostolic authority, but much more than Bonaventure, and to a far greater extent than Hugh, Gallus "readapted" the *CD* and made it his own.[50] His extant corpus consists of a few texts that loosely fall into three thematic categories, but which all bespeak his theology's indebtedness to and favoring of the theology of the Areopagite.[51] First, Gallus produced scriptural commentaries, including at least two commentaries on *The Song of Songs* which have been edited in full by Jeanne Barbet,[52] as well as a commentary on Isaiah (1218), a fragment of which appears in an edition by G. Théry.[53] As we will see below with respect to

---

46. For more on the biography of Gallus, see Coolman, *Knowledge, Love, and Ecstasy*, 5–6.

47. Coolman, *Knowledge, Love, and Ecstasy*, 6.

48. Coolman, *Knowledge, Love, and Ecstasy*, 6–7. Coolman's introduction to Gallus in this text also includes a lovely reflection on Gallus's tomb at Sant'Andrea, which can still be visited today.

49. Hugh of St. Victor, *In hierarchiam caelestem S. Dionysii* (PL 175:923A–1154C).

50. See Shelby, "Thomas Gallus' *Explanatio* and Dionysian Thought," 299–304.

51. Lawell provides a useful summary of these texts and their editions in his introduction to the critical edition of the *Explanatio*, viii–ix, nn. 3–7, and xxiii–xxxii. See also Shelby, "Thomas Gallus' *Explanatio* and Dionysian Thought," 304–5.

52. Gallus's composition of these is dated sometime before 1224, although there is still some question as to the precise date of composition. See Ruello, "Introduction," 29–31; Ruh, "Thomas Gallus Vercellensis," 63. For a critical edition of both of these commentaries on *The Song of Songs*, see *Commentaires du Cantique des cantiques*, ed. J. Barbet, Textes philosophiques du Moyen Âge 14 (Paris: Béatrice-Nauwelaerts, 1967), hereafter *In Cant*. My comments will refer to the first such commentary as edited by Barbet.

53. The only edition of Gallus's commentary on *Isaiah* we have is Gabriel Théry, ed.,

Gallus's notion of the hierarchical soul, these scriptural commentaries are a rich and fruitful source for his reappropriation of Dionysian theology.[54] Second, Lawell identifies two *opuscula* by Gallus, a sermon and short treatise on contemplation,[55] and finally, Gallus wrote several explicit commentaries on the works of Dionysius: his *Glose super Angelica ierarchia* (1224);[56] the *Extractio* (1238);[57] and his *Explanatio*, his commentary on the entire *CD* (1241–1244).[58] Whereas Hugh of St. Victor and Bonaventure looked to Dionysius as a useful source among others, interest in the Areopagite essentially dominated the Abbot of Vercelli's theological career. Through both his scriptural commentaries and his several commentaries on the Areopagite's corpus, Gallus's theological universe was thoroughly Dionysian from beginning to end.[59]

As a prominent commentator of the Areopagite in the medieval world, however, Gallus also stands out for another reason. Whereas Dionysius can be credited with inaugurating a trajectory of theological reflection in the Christian mystical tradition that was focused on the *via negativa,* Gallus can similarly be credited with rewriting that tradition in an "affective" key.[60] Broadly conceived, this "affective" interpretive tradition of the Dionysian corpus—which is generally thought to include Bonaventure, Hugh of Balma, and the unknown author of *The Cloud of Unknowing*, among others—was significant because it innovated the medieval interpretation of the *CD* by championing love *over* knowledge in its description of the soul's union with God that takes place in the *MT.* In that text, Dionysius describes Moses's ascent of Mt. Sinai as a mystical ascent into "the cloud of unknowing," where

---

"Commentaire sur Isaïe de Thomas de Saint-Victor," *La vie spirituelle* 47 (1936): 146–62, hereafter *In Is.*

54. See especially Coolman's use of these two commentaries in both *Knowledge, Love, and Ecstasy* and "Medieval Affective Dionysian Tradition."

55. Lawell, "Introduction," viii–xi, esp. n. 7: "two *opuscula* by Gallus have also come down to us: a sermon entitled *Qualiter vita prelatorum conformari debet vite angelice;* and a short treatise called *Spectacula contemplationis* (1244–1246)." Lawell acknowledges two further *opuscula* that could possibly also be attributed to Gallus, one of which he finds especially dubious, however. See also Shelby, "Thomas Gallus' *Explanatio* and Dionysian Thought," 304.

56. Lawell, "Introduction," viii; Thomas Gallus, *Glose super angelica ierarchia: Accedunt indices ad Thomae Galli opera*, ed. Lawell, *CC CM* 223A (Turnhout: Brepols, 2011).

57. See Lawell, "Introduction," viii, n. 4, for a list of editions of these works.

58. Edited for the first time by Lawell in *Explanatio in libros Dionysii, CC CM* 223 (Turnhout: Brepols, 2011). See also Shelby, "Thomas Gallus' *Explanatio* and Dionysian Thought."

59. See my discussion of this, along with accompanying bibliography, in "Thomas Gallus' *Explanatio* and Dionysian Thought," 299–304.

60. Coolman, "Medieval Affective Dionysian Tradition."

Moses is then united to God in an apophatic union that transcends all intellectual activities. As Coolman has well noted, the medieval "affective" interpretation of the *MT* suggests that Moses is united to the unknown God *through love* at the apex of this ascent, even though the *MT* itself "contains no references to charity, love, delight or to the affections generally."[61] Notably, this "affective" trajectory of Dionysian interpretation is rooted within Hugh of St. Victor's commentary on *CH*, where Hugh associates the cherubic and seraphic orders within Dionysius's account of the heavens respectively with knowledge and love. Hugh was the first to associate the seraphic order specifically with love, and to further suggest that love thus surpasses knowledge in the soul's mystical ascent to God.[62] Gallus would then extend this Hugonian insight and make it the centerpiece of his reading of the *CD*, essentially rewriting the entire Dionysian corpus in light of this claim. Indeed, it is Gallus—and not Hugh—who comments on and rewrites *MT* so as to suggest that Moses is united to God in "the cloud of unknowing" through love.[63] As Coolman observes, "the Abbot of Vercelli has extended Hugh of St. Victor's basic intuition—that Dionysius himself had taught the superiority of love over knowledge in the divine-human encounter—by doing what Hugh (nor, apparently, anyone else) had never done: interpolating that superior love into the very text of *The Mystical Theology*,"[64] an intuition which then inaugurates the "affective" trajectory of Dionysian interpretation in the High Middle Ages. In other words, though Gallus is only now emerging as an important and noteworthy figure in the history of the Christian theological tradition, his life's work represents one of the most significant moments in the history of Christian mysticism since it was he who definitively interpreted the *CD* in this "affective" tone.

Despite his importance within this tradition, there remains an incredible lacuna of scholarship surrounding this, the "last of the great Victorines." Critical editions of most of his works have only begun to appear on library shelves within the past decade.[65] Gallus's extant cor-

---

61. Coolman, "Medieval Affective Dionysian Tradition," 615–16.

62. See Hugh of St. Victor, *In hierarchiam caelestem S. Dionysii*, at *PL* 1023B–1026B, esp. 1023B–1023C.

63. See Shelby, "Thomas Gallus' *Explanatio* and Dionysian Thought," 299–304.

64. Coolman, "Medieval Affective Dionysian Tradition," 621.

65. This is in large part due to the monumental efforts of Declan Lawell and his production of the critical edition of the *Explanatio*.

pus is a wellspring waiting to be tapped by theologians interested in both the history of the Christian mystical tradition in general, as well as the Victorine theological tradition more specifically. As the present study aims to additionally emphasize, Gallus's theology is likewise an abundant and fruitful resource for those interested in the Franciscan theological tradition; the reasons why this is so will be treated in greater detail, below.

Thomas Gallus and Bonaventure

Much like his indebtedness to the theology of the Areopagite, Bonaventure's own dependence on and even favoritism of the Victorine theological tradition—especially as he inherited it from Hugh of St. Victor and Richard of St. Victor—has already been widely acknowledged by scholars. In his *Red. Art.,* for example, the Seraphic Doctor argues that all of sacred scripture teaches three truths: "the eternal generation and incarnation of Christ," which deals with faith; "the pattern of human life," which concerns morals; and "the union of the soul with God," which is "the ultimate goal of both." Theological doctors, he continues, are concerned with the first; preachers, with the second; and contemplatives, with the third. He then asserts: "The first is taught chiefly by Augustine; the second, by Gregory; the third, by Dionysius. Anselm follows Augustine; Bernard follows Gregory; Richard follows Dionysius. For Anselm excels in reasoning; Bernard, in preaching; Richard, in contemplation. But Hugh excels in all three."[66] Hugh and Richard, in short, were both directly named by Bonaventure as important sources for his theology, with Hugh receiving the highest praise from the pen of the Seraphic Doctor. What, though, of our Abbot from Vercelli?

Recognizing Bonaventure's indebtedness to Gallus in addition to Hugh and Richard requires, first of all, stepping back to appreciate three possible historical connections between Gallus and the thirteenth-century Franciscan school of theology.[67] First, several sources confirm that the Abbott of Vercelli enjoyed personal friendships with several of the early Franciscans. Purportedly, he was a close friend of none other

---

66. I have here used the translation provided by Zachary Hayes in *On the Reduction of Arts to Theology*, by Bonaventure, trans. and intro. Zachary Hayes, Works of St. Bonaventure 1 (St. Bonaventure, NY: Franciscan Institute, 1996), 45.

67. For my initial speculations on these connections, see Shelby, "Thomas Gallus' *Explanatio* and Dionysian Thought," 323–27.

than St. Anthony of Padua,[68] even as Théry has suggested the possibility that Gallus personally knew Brother Giles, postulating that Gallus even borrowed from Giles's *Dicta* "On Contemplation" when writing his own treatise on the seven steps of contemplation in 1224.[69] Such conjectures are substantiated, secondly, when we consider also that the Franciscans in Italy moved their *studium generale* from Padua to Vercelli in 1228. Gallus had been sent to Vercelli, we recall, as early as 1218, even as he had been appointed Abbot there in 1226, the year of Francis's death. The Franciscans studying at Vercelli would have been left under the direction and care of Gallus up until the time of his death in 1246, with the exception, of course, of his brief exile from there in 1243 and the year he spent in England in 1238. Third and finally, these historical records of direct associations between the "last of the great Victorines" and the Franciscans are made more intriguing by a postulation that as of now must be left in the realm of mere conjecture, but which is nonetheless worth considering.[70] Notably, Gallus was the last Victorine to hold a chair of theology at the University of Paris, which he would have given up around 1218–1219 in order to follow his vocation to Vercelli. Alexander of Hales, who we will meet below as Bonaventure's teacher at the University of Paris, became a Master of Theology in 1220–1221. Famously, his decision to join the Franciscans in 1236–1237 meant that he was the first Franciscan to hold a chair of theology at the University of Paris. It is not beyond the realm of possibility that Alexander stepped into Gallus's vacant chair in 1220 after the Victorine left for Vercelli, which would perhaps suggest that the Franciscan School of Theology at the University of Paris—which would include, of course, Bonaventure after Alexander—enjoyed an even closer relationship with the Victorines than is already acknowledged. All these connections suggest that Gallus's relationship with and intellectual influence over the early Franciscans is an area of study that needs much further examination and scrutiny; that the Abbot of Vercelli communicated

68. See Pierre Brunette and Paul Lachance, ed., *The Earliest Franciscans: The Legacy of Giles of Assisi, Roger of Provence, and James of Milan* (New York: Paulist Press, 2015), 7; McGinn, "Thomas Gallus and Dionysian Mysticism," 83; and Théry, "Thomas Gallus et Egide d'Assise," 189.

69. See Théry, "Thomas Gallus et Egide d'Assise," 187–89; Brunette and Lachance, *The Earliest Franciscans*, 7, 91n37.

70. I am grateful for private conversations with Stephen F. Brown, Boyd Taylor Coolman, and Jay Hammond, who have floated this as a possibility that needs further research and scrutiny.

with, enjoyed friendships with, and taught the early Franciscans is a high probability that cannot and should not be overlooked.

That Bonaventure was himself at least theologically influenced by "the last of the great Victorines" is, as such, a tributary argument within this book. Rather than proving that the Seraphic Doctor had any personal communication with the Abbot, however, I argue that Gallus served as a source for Bonaventure's doctrine of grace with respect to a very specific aspect of his Dionysian project—namely, with respect to Gallus's notion of the hierarchical soul.[71] Significantly, as we will encounter in *Part II*, the Seraphic Doctor will revise and readapt this notion in his descriptions of the effects of sanctifying grace within the soul. To be sanctified, for Bonaventure, is to be made "hierarchical," as shown in his famous reference to St. Francis in the *Legenda maior* as a *vir hierarchicus*. In much the same way that we cannot attend to his general definition of "hierarchy" without first attending to his source for this definition in Dionysius's *CH* 3, we likewise will not be able to approach the Seraphic Doctor's own claim that the Poverello was a "hierarchical man" without first regarding his source for this idea in the writings of Thomas Gallus.

Thomas Gallus's Angelic Anthropology

Indeed, in addition to highlighting the fact that Gallus stands behind the "affective" Dionysian tradition as its "architect," Boyd Taylor Coolman has also convincingly argued recently that the Abbot of Vercelli's notion of the "hierarchical soul" must be perceived as one of his most important contributions to this tradition. The notion appears most clearly not in Gallus's extensive commentaries on the *CD*, but rather, in the prologues to his scriptural commentaries on *Isaiah* and *The Song of Songs*.[72] There, the Abbot does something quite new with the nine orders of angels named by Dionysius in *CH*, actually claiming that the *soul itself* is "hierarchical," possessing nine orders within it that correspond directly with the celestial hierarchy. This "angelic anthropology" is necessary within the broader context of his "affective" Dionysian

---

71. A thesis that I begin to float in "Thomas Gallus' *Explanatio*," 325–26, which will be worked out in much greater detail in the pages that follow.

72. Coolman has recently underscored how his commentary on *The Song of Songs* especially ought to be lauded as an important source within the Gallusian corpus; see especially his "Medieval Affective Dionysian Tradition."

project inasmuch as Gallus will use it to explain how the soul achieves an affective union with the God-beyond-all-thought.[73]

My comments below by way of introduction to Gallus's angelic anthropology will be divided into two subsections. First, I simply offer a summary of this notion as Gallus presents it in the prologue to his commentary on *The Song of Songs*. This summary will help us see how Bonaventure explicitly reappropriates the notion within his doctrine of grace, since the Seraphic Doctor repeats Gallus's description of the function of these orders within the soul almost verbatim in his explanation of the effects of grace in Chapter 4 of the *Itinerarium* and even names Gallus as a source for this idea later in his *Hexaëmeron*.[74] We will not be able to perceive these parallelisms, as it were, without first attending to the specific nuances of Gallus's angelic anthropology as he originally iterated them.

Second, I comment on how we ought to understand this angelic anthropology in light of recent scholarship on the subject produced by Coolman. Beholding the finer points of the Abbot of Vercelli's angelic anthropology along with Coolman will help us more fruitfully encounter it within the Seraphic Doctor's doctrine of grace so as also to see how the latter theologian will expand it to fit within his own particularly "Franciscan" view of sanctity after the Victorine.

The Hierarchical Soul: What It Is   What, then, is the "hierarchical soul"?[75] In the prologue to his commentary on *The Song of Songs*, Gallus answers this question by first repeating Dionysius's assertion from *CH* that "each and every heavenly and human mind (*celestis et humana mens*) holds special first, middle, and highest orders (*ordinationes*) and virtues (*virtutes*), which are added according to each and every illumination of the hierarchies."[76] His subsequent explanation of this Dionysian assertion, however, adds new insights relevant to this claim that appear nowhere in the *CD*. According to Gallus, each of these three orders are disposed within the mind in a way that corresponds with the lowest, middle, and highest orders within the celestial hierarchy:

---

73. I treat this briefly in "Thomas Gallus' *Explanatio*," 306–9.

74. See my comments to this effect in Chapter 5, and my preliminary remarks to that effect in "Thomas Gallus' *Explanatio*," 325–26.

75. See also my treatment of this angelic anthropology in "Thomas Gallus' *Explanatio*," 306–9.

76. Gallus, quoting Dionysius's *CH*, in *In Cant.*, 66.

… namely, in the lowest: the angels, archangels, and principalities; in the middle: the powers, virtues, and dominions; and in the highest: the thrones, cherubim, and seraphim…. The lowest hierarchy of the mind consists in its very nature [*natura*]; the middle, in its industry [*industria*], which incomparably exceeds nature; and the highest, in an ecstasy of the mind [*excessu mentis*]. In the first, nature is operating by itself; in the highest, it is operating by grace alone [*sola gratia*]; and in the middle, grace and industry are working together [*operantur simul*].[77]

Gallus next proceeds with his explanation of this "angelized mind" by describing how each of these nine orders within the soul has very specific functions or operations. I provide a brief summary of these operations, below; admittedly, these will seem quite strange to anyone reading them for the first time. Though odd, this summary will nonetheless serve two crucial purposes: First, it will pave the way for our analysis below of the meaning of Gallus's angelic anthropology in light of Coolman's recent scholarship on the subject; second, it will help us compare Gallus's notion of the hierarchical soul to Bonaventure's own angelic anthropology in later chapters.

First, at the level of "nature" (*natura*), Gallus holds that the lowest order within the soul corresponds, of course, with Dionysius's order of the "angels." According to the Victorine, this consists in the "natural apprehensions" (*apprehensiones naturales*) of both the affect and the intellect, which announce these apprehensions to the soul in a simple way (*anime simpliciter annuntiant*).[78] From this, Gallus understands the order of the "archangels" to represent the dictations (*dictationes*) of both the intellect and the affect, through which the soul "dictates" or judges the natural apprehensions received at the level of the angels to be either true or false, suitable or unsuitable.[79] This leads to the order of the "principalities," which contains the soul's appetites. Here, the soul can either accept or flee from either good or evil,[80] and it thereby passes from operating only according to its natural capacities to the "middle" hierarchy, or namely, the hierarchy of what he calls "industry" (*industria*).

The "middle" three orders that then comprise the level of "industry" primarily concern a consideration of free will, wherein Gallus holds

77. *In Cant.*, 66.
78. *In Cant.*, 66.
79. *In Cant.*, 66.
80. *In Cant.*, 66.

that the soul is aided by grace to choose the good. At the lowest order within this middle hierarchy, the order of the "powers," for example, he describes how the intellect and affect voluntarily move away from that which is evil and toward that which is good.[81] The order of the "virtues" next contains "the forces of a mind with strength" (*valida mentis robore*) through which he thinks the soul is guided so that it can receive what he calls "divine lights" (*luminum divinorum suscepciones*).[82] Next, at the order of the "dominions," the affect and intellect are suspended in all their powers for the purposes of receiving these divine lights coming down from above as much as is possible for free will aided by grace.[83]

Third and finally, the Victorine recounts how the highest hierarchy within the soul is characterized by grace. Here, as he contends, the intellect and affect are first made capable for the reception of God at the order of the thrones, where the soul experiences an ecstasy of the mind (*mentis excessum*).[84] Next, Gallus asserts that every cognition of the intellect is drawn into the divine at the cherubic order,[85] which represents the fullness of knowledge (*plenitudine sciencie*) and the consummation of cognition (*cognitionis*).[86] He insists that the affect and intellect walk hand in hand until this point (*coambulant affectus et intellectus*),[87] where the cherubic intellect reaches the heights of knowledge. When the intellect cannot proceed any further, however, the affect then stretches forth into God at the level of the seraph.[88] The seraphic order, then, is portrayed by Gallus as the locus of the soul's affective union with God:

The ninth level chiefly contains sighs into God, the superintellectual extensions and infusions, boiling radiances and radiant boilings, to which the sublime ecstasies and exceeding sublimities of every intelligence cannot be drawn, but where only the affection can be united to God. In this order *most chaste prayers* are offered, by which we are drawn near to God, as it says in *DN* 3. This

81. *In Cant.*, 66.

82. *In Cant.*, 67. The reference to "divine lights" appears in this case in his prologue to his commentary on *Isaiah*, from which I here borrow; see *In Is.*, 155.

83. *In Cant.*, 67.

84. *In Cant.*, 67. For more on the order of the thrones in Gallus's angelic anthropology, see Coolman, *Knowledge, Love, and Ecstasy*, 126–37.

85. *In Cant.*, 67: "Octavus ordo continet omnimodam cognitionem intellectus attracti divina dignatione." As Coolman notes in *Knowledge, Love, and Ecstasy*, 24, the term "*cognitionem*" as Gallus employs it here is difficult to translate into English.

86. *In Is.*, 156; *In Cant.*, 67.

87. *In Cant.*, 67.

88. See again Shelby, "Thomas Gallus' *Explanatio*," 308–9.

order is embracing God, and having been embraced, it is made a friend of the Spouse, and it does not know a mirror.... In this order, the bride and Bridegroom lay down together on the bridal bed. From this flood of divine lights [*inundatio divini luminis*], it flows into [*fluit*] the inferior orders of the soul.[89]

As odd as Gallus's description of these nine orders might appear today, it is important to here pause to notice why the Abbott introduces this rather strange schema of the angelized soul. If, for Gallus, the apophatic union described by Dionysius in *MT* is best interpreted as a supra-intellectual union of love that takes place above the human person's intellectual capacity for knowledge, then the affective language of the *Song* here becomes in his hands the scriptural tool through which he can defend and unfold the affective Dionysianism at the center of his theological project.[90] And, moreover, by interpolating these nine orders of the celestial hierarchy into the soul itself in this text, he also quite significantly introduces an "anthropological twist" to Dionysius's conception of hierarchy. As Coolman assays, "No explicit theological anthropology comes down from Dionysius. By pursuing the matter at all, Gallus fills a lacuna in the Dionysian system. At the same time, Gallus' anthropology is distinctly Dionysian—it is in some sense a conception of the human which Dionysius *should have* held."[91] Dionysius's definition of hierarchy as a "sacred order, state of understanding, and activity approximating as closely as possible to God" is no longer merely a description of something that happens *outside* of the soul in the cosmos, but actually serves now to describe how the soul itself is hierarchically structured to relate to God through the affective union that crowns Gallus's own vision of the Dionysian mystical-theological enterprise. While he borrows the naming of these nine orders from the Areopagite, and likewise borrows the association of the cherubim with knowledge and of the seraphim with love from Hugh, his assertion that these orders can all be appropriated to the soul itself and accompanying description of their functions within the soul is something quite new.

The Hierarchical Soul: How to Interpret It   What, though, are we to make of this admittedly rather strange angelic anthropology? Recent

89. *In Cant.*, 67. For more on the importance of the term, 'extensiones', in Gallus's mystical theology, see Walsh, "Thomas Gallus et l'effort contemplatif," 28 and 32; see also Shelby, "Thomas Gallus' *Explanatio*," 308n56.

90. Shelby, "Thomas Gallus' *Explanatio*," 305–9.

91. Coolman, *Knowledge, Love, and Ecstasy*, 74.

scholarship by Coolman has underscored a crucial way in which this notion has often been misinterpreted with respect to one of its central points. As he has convincingly shown, Gallus's angelic anthropology indeed plays a key role in his affective Dionysianism inasmuch as he describes through it how the soul itself is hierarchical so that it may enjoy an affective union with the God-beyond-all-thought. Problematically, however, scholars have often tended to over-emphasize this affective union, interpreting the seraphic order in Gallus's angelic anthropology as a sort of "stopping point" in a bottom-up mystical ascent, or namely, in a merely linear way that is also anti-intellectual inasmuch as the Seraphic, affective union is thought to merely "leave behind" cherubic knowledge. Against this reading, Coolman emphasizes the fact that for Gallus, the intellect and affect notably work together throughout every level of the hierarchical soul up until the order of the seraph. Even there, moreover, the affective union described by Gallus ought not be conceived as a "stopping point" in a bottom-up, linear account of the soul's mystical ascent. Rather, as Gallus suggests in the passage quoted above, the "flood of divine lights" received by the soul at the level of the seraph, then, flow back down to the "inferior" or lower orders of the soul, as well.

Relatedly, therefore, and as Coolman has shown with painstaking detail,[92] the Victorine borrows Dionysius's use of the neoplatonic triad of procession, return, and remaining in order to describe the hierarchical soul in a dynamic rather than static and linear way:

… for Gallus, human existence is constituted by the same three dimensions of Dionysian metaphysics … namely, procession, return, and remaining. Seen from the perspective of the rational creature, "from below" or from within the rational creature (rather than "from above" or outside, so to speak), these dimensions acquire a distinct expression. Here, metaphysical procession (*exitus*) takes the form of a descending movement within the soul and a radical receptivity for receiving the divine "inflowing" from above. For Gallus, the creature is constituted as a creature just in so far as it receives "from above" and it is radically "upwardly postured" as it were, opened to receive all that it has, all that it is, *ex Deo*. Metaphysical return (*redditus*) for its part finds its anthropological expression in an ascending movement, an upward thrusting, ultimately self-transcending or ecstatic movement of the soul *ad Deum* and *in Deum*, that is, toward, to, and into God. Metaphysical remaining (*residuus*),

___

92. See especially Coolman, *Knowledge, Love, and Ecstasy.*

finally, corresponds to the fact that precisely through these simultaneously receptive and ecstatic modes of being, or by these states of receptivity and ecstasy, the rational creature achieves a state of ontological order, stability and simplicity, which enables it … to be related ideally and as it were maximally to God, by becoming a place of divine indwelling, a temple for the presence of God.[93]

In other words, as it "returns" to God by "ascending" to the order of the seraph, the hierarchical soul does not simply stop at the affective union with the seraph. For Gallus, once the soul has thus "ascended" within his angelic anthropology, the divine illuminations received by the soul through this affective union then likewise "descend" into the lower eight orders of the soul so as to fecundate each order within the "middle" and "lower" hierarchies with divine light as well. Precisely by way of this "descending" valence, in other words, the soul itself is hierarchical inasmuch as it is always receiving what Gallus refers to as "inflowings" of divine *theoriae* from the affection of the seraph.[94] The intellectual knowledge of the cherub, then, is made *fuller* through the seraph. This knowledge, then, filters down into the thrones, who receive the knowledge of the cherub and then likewise pass it down to the lower six orders within the soul. This "descending" movement of the hierarchy within the soul will then lead back up to the "ascent" to the seraph and vice versa, so that this dynamic interplay of ascensions and descensions is what finally characterizes the soul's "remaining" in God in Gallus's angelic anthropology.

The Abbot of Vercelli's affective union in this sense should not be regarded as a "stopping point" for the soul in some sort of linear, bottom-up ascent into God, but rather must be interpreted as the mode through which the entire soul can be called hierarchical: a dynamic, circulating system of interrelated orders enlivened by ecstatic love. As such, Coolman names three specific "movements" or "valences" within Gallus's angelic anthropology: (1) the "ascending" valence, through which the soul ascends to the charity of the seraph; (2) the "descending" valence, whereby the illuminations received by the soul at the level of the seraph then filter down to fecundate the lower eight orders within the soul; and finally, but perhaps most importantly, (3) the "spiraling" or "circling" valence, whereby the soul thus "remains" in God into perpetuity through

93. Coolman, *Knowledge, Love, and Ecstasy*, 74–75.
94. For more on these *theoriae*, see Coolman, *Knowledge, Love, and Ecstasy*, 174.

these constant ascensions and descensions, which are all made possible by the affective union at the level of the seraph.

As Coolman has further noted, this image of the soul is notably "not a simple circle, not a mere returning to the original point of departure, in order to merely set out on the same course again"; rather, for Gallus, "this dynamic movement *in Deum* is better characterized as a spiral," whereby "'new things' are continually flowing down into the hierarchized soul from her super-abundant Spouse.... There is here an epecstatic dimension to hierarchic human nature, a sense of continual and eternal progress. There is no *static* resting in God, no absolute cessation of the soul's movements.... Never fulfilled, in the sense of filled full, it is always spiraling."[95] For Gallus, this hierarchical dynamism is constitutive of human nature; or, as Coolman summarizes, "the soul always exists hierarchically or as a hierarchy ... a hierarchy is simply what one *is*."[96] The Victorine's angelic anthropology does not describe a bottom-up "ladder" of ascent as some sort of superimposed structure that the soul must follow to find union with God: What constitutes human nature is that it must always be ascending to the affective union of the seraph so that divine illuminations can "descend" from this mystical union to move it ever closer and closer unto God. In this sense, "grace does not 'overlay' a hierarchic structure upon a naturally unhierarchized soul. Rather, the soul itself is created as a hierarchy."[97] Inasmuch as the soul simply is hierarchical, it is always thus continuously "ascending," "descending," and "circling or spiraling." Gallus's angelic anthropology is a dynamic portrait of how the soul's interior orders are "always-having-to-be-filled"[98] by the ecstatic love between the Spouse and the soul at the level of the seraph in ever newer and deeper ways. Human nature, for the Abbot of Vercelli, is characterized by this dynamism, this continuous need to be thus fecundated and enlivened by the seraphic affective union with God so that it may perpetually "spiral."

Understanding how these three valences—ascending, descending, and circling or spiraling—thus function in Gallus's angelic anthropology is an important step for approaching Bonaventure's doctrine

---

95. Coolman, *Knowledge, Love, and Ecstasy,* 256.

96. Coolman, *Knowledge, Love, and Ecstasy,* 25.

97. Coolman, *Knowledge, Love, and Ecstasy,* 237–38.

98. I borrow this phrase—which will also fittingly describe the Seraphic Doctor's own view of human nature with respect to his notion of ontological poverty—from Coolman, *Knowledge, Love, and Ecstasy,* 98. For more on this notion in Bonaventure, see Chapter 6.

of grace. In the same way that the Seraphic Doctor both recycles and revises Dionysius's definition of hierarchy, he also recycles and revises these themes, both with respect to the hierarchies that comprise his understanding of the macrocosm and with respect to his teachings on the role of grace in his theological anthropology. In the fourth chapter of the *Itinerarium,* for example, he presents an abridged version of Gallus's notion of the hierarchical soul in order to describe how the soul is reformed into a similitude of God through grace, even as he explicitly names Gallus as a source within a lengthier explanation of his own angelic anthropology in *Hex.* 22. In both texts, the three valences of "descending," "ascending," and "circling or spiraling" that map onto the Dionysian triad of "procession," "return," and "remaining" in Gallus's angelic anthropology can similarly characterize the Franciscan's discussions of how grace causes the soul to become "as like as possible to God" in a hierarchical way. Like his Victorine predecessor, as we shall see, the Franciscan similarly holds that the "ascent" to the seraphic order is not simply a "stopping point" in the soul's journey to God, but is rather an affective union that fecundates the soul for ever more fruitful relationships with God.

The Seraphic Doctor nonetheless makes two important addendums to his predecessor's angelic anthropology. First, as Coolman has noted, whereas Gallus's angelic anthropology simply describes what the soul itself is, Bonaventure instead relegates the hierarchical soul entirely to the realm of grace.[99] Where for Gallus the soul simply is a hierarchy, for Bonaventure, sanctifying grace hierarchizes the soul. Secondly, we should also note that Gallus's account of the hierarchical soul is confined by the Victorine entirely to the realm of contemplation. His account of the soul's ascending, descending, and circling or spiraling movements describe the interior orders of the soul, and these do not necessarily need to extend so as to include a consideration of that which takes places in the created world outside of the soul, or namely, to include a consideration of the "active" Christian life. Bonaventure's revision of the Victorine's angelic anthropology, on the other hand, includes a Franciscan addendum with respect to the three valences of ascending, descending, and circling or spiraling, necessitated by the fact that Francis's own Seraphic union with God atop Mt. Alverna

---

99. See Coolman, *Knowledge, Love, and Ecstasy,* 237.

included his flesh as well as his soul, a "radiant boiling" that then led to his further ministry to the lepers in Assisi.[100] In his own discussions of the hierarchical soul, the Seraphic Doctor argues that the "flood of divine light" experienced by the soul through the affective union at the order of the seraph "descends" beyond its interior orders through works of mercy toward neighbors in the world, and indeed, to the rest of creation, as well.[101] Rather than being merely relegated to the realm of contemplation, in other words, Bonaventure's angelic anthropology necessarily extends beyond the soul to include the body, and so also includes the rest of the world. Bonaventure thereby "Franciscanizes" Gallus's angelic anthropology.[102]

Before we can approach such comparisons between our Victorine and Franciscan theologians, however, it is first necessary to introduce a final "character" within our story of the historical sources that thus inform the Seraphic Doctor's doctrine of grace. Within this doctrine, he borrows from and revises the Areopagite's definition of hierarchy; from Gallus, he borrows and revises an angelic anthropology; but through the influence of Alexander of Hales, Bonaventure develops an understanding of what, exactly, sanctifying grace actually is. This allows him to tie the foregoing themes together.

Alexander of Hales: Grace Defined

Alexander of Hales:
A Brief Introduction to the Theologian

Unlike Gallus, Alexander of Hales is already affirmed as a figure of great significance within the thirteenth-century theological climate, but even still, scholars are only now beginning in a sustained fashion to turn their eye upon those works associated with his name. Born sometime around 1185 in England, Alexander became a regent Master of theology at the University of Paris in 1220, roughly a year after Gallus left his

---

100. The importance of the "flesh" in Franciscan theology is highlighted by Emmanuel Falque and Laure Solignac in "Penser en franciscain," *Études franciscaines* 7, no. 2 (2014): 297–325. For more on Francis's sanctity as it relates to this notion, see Chapter 8.

101. See Chapters 4, 5, and 8.

102. Again, see Solignac and Falque, "Penser en franciscain," 297–325. This notion of embodiment is likewise important to Davis's reading of Bonaventure in *The Weight of Love*, esp. 107–26, as well as to Rachel Davies in *Bonaventure, The Body, and the Aesthetics of Salvation* (Cambridge: Cambridge University Press, 2020).

own chair at the University of Paris to take up his post in Vercelli, and he died in 1245, exactly one year before Gallus's death. In what caused a rather powerful stir among the theology faculty in Paris of his day, he pledged himself to the Franciscans in 1236 or 1237 and thus also in that year held the first distinctively Franciscan chair of theology at the University. Surrounding him there was a burgeoning group of eager young scholars who were also devoted to following the "spirit" of the Poverello through their theological studies, including among them Odo Rigaud, John of La Rochelle, and of course, Bonaventure himself.[103] As Kenan Osborne has commented regarding Alexander's theology, in light of his conversion to the Franciscan way of life, he nonetheless "felt no need to change his theology"; rather, "the spirituality of the Franciscan students had attracted him in a profound way, and it was he who in his classes began to harmonize the Franciscan vision and academic theology."[104] St. Francis had given permission to St. Anthony of Padua to teach theology, provided that he did not extinguish the spirit of prayer and

103. A concise introduction to Alexander of Hales and his relationship to his Franciscan students can be found in Hubert Philipp Weber, "Alexander of Hales's Theology in His Authentic Texts (Commentary on the *Sentences* of Peter Lombard, Various Disputed Questions)," in *The English Province of the Franciscans (1224–c.1350)*, ed. Michael J. P. Robson (Leiden: Brill 2017), 273–93. As Weber notes, "As there were many friars among Alexander's students, it was possibly through them that he came into contact with the order, which he entered when he was about 60 years of age" (274).

104. See Kenan B. Osborne, OFM, *The Franciscan Intellectual Tradition: Tracing its Origins and Identifying its Central Components*, The Franciscan Heritage Series 1 (St. Bonaventure, NY: Franciscan Institute, 2003), 42. As with Gallus, much remains for scholarship with respect to exploring "Halensian" theology. For a select bibliography, see Philotheus Boehner, *The History of the Franciscan School*, vol. 1, *Alexander of Hales* (St. Bonaventure, NY: Franciscan Institute, 1943); Boyd Taylor Coolman, "Hugh of St. Victor's Influence on the Halensian Definition of Theology," *Franciscan Studies* 70 (2012): 367–84; H. Daniel Monsour, *The Relation between Uncreated and Created Grace in the Halesian* Summa: *A Lonerganian Reading* (PhD diss., Toronto School of Theology, 2000); Walter H. Principe, *Alexander of Hales' Theology of the Hypostatic Union*, vol. 2, *The Theology of the Hypostatic Union in the Early Thirteenth Century*, Studies and Texts 12 (Toronto: Pontifical Institute of Mediaeval Studies, 1967); Lydia Schumacher, ed., *The Summa Halensis: Sources and Context*; *The Summa Halensis: Doctrines and Debates*; and *The Summa Halensis: The Legacy of Early Franciscan Thought*; vols. 65–67 of Veröffentlichungen des Grabmann-Institutes zur Erforschung der mittelalterlichen Theologie und Philosophie (Berlin: De Gruyter, 2020); Hubert Philipp Weber, *Sünde und Gnade bei Alexander von Hales* (Innsbruck: Tyrolia, 2003), as well as his "Alexander of Hales's Theology in His Authentic Texts," cited above. The general prologue to the *Summa minorum* put together by the editors of the Quaracchi edition of the text remains one of the most important resources on Alexander of Hales to this day; see "Prologue generalis," in *Summa theologica Doctoris Irrefragabilis Alexandri de Hales Ordinis Minorum* (Quaracchi) Tome 1, Book 1 (Quaracchi: Ex Typographia Collegii S. Bonaventurae, 1924), hereafter *Summa minorum*. My justification for referring to this work as the *Summa minorum* is detailed in n. 107, below.

devotion during his studies;[105] to the lament of some of his Franciscan brothers in his own day, Alexander's commitment to the Franciscans in the mid-thirteenth century ensured that this scholarly vocation within the Order would continue well beyond the preaching program of St. Anthony. And indeed, after St. Francis's death in 1226, Alexander's role in the Franciscan tradition cemented a permanent bridge between the spiritual charism of the Poverello's growing Order on the one hand and the intellectual life of the Order on the other.

Though the indebtedness of the Franciscan intellectual tradition to Alexander of Hales is thus widely acknowledged, it is important here to note that his influence at the University of Paris—and thus, within the larger history of the Christian theological tradition—nonetheless extended well beyond his own Franciscan brothers. Inasmuch as the thirteenth century saw the introduction of the "New Aristotle" into the theological curriculum at the University, and inasmuch as Alexander was one of the first theologians to encounter this "New Aristotle" in the early half of the thirteenth century, Alexander himself was one of the primary figures responsible for the introduction of the "New Aristotle" into the curriculum that thus revolutionized the academic discipline of theology during that time.[106] In addition to his familiarity with Aristotle, moreover, Alexander was also the first theologian to comment in a formal way on the *Sentences* of Peter Lombard, a practice which of course began to dominate the methodology of theological education in the thirteenth and fourteenth centuries, so that students after Alexander would have to provide a commentary on the entirety of the Lombard's *Sentences* to earn the title of "Master of Theology." In these respects, Alexander's theological influence spread well beyond the Franciscan order, including also the Dominican tradition and Thomas Aquinas. The entire landscape of the academic study of theology in the High Middle Ages well into the fourteenth century unfolded largely from his teachings.

His extant writings can roughly be divided into two categories. First, there is a collection of *reportationes* of his teachings collected from his students, such as his *Quaestiones disputatae antequam esset frater,* his *Glossa* on the *Sentences* of Peter Lombard, as well as some commentaries on scripture which are considered "authentically"

---

105. "A Letter to Brother Anthony of Padua," in *FAED 1*, 107.
106. See, for example, Osborne, *The Franciscan Intellectual Tradition,* 42.

Alexandrian. In addition to these, however, we have also the quite lengthy and magnanimous work known as the *Summa theologica fratris Alexandris,* otherwise known as the *Summa Halensis* or the *Summa minorum.*[107] Once thought to be an authentic work of Alexander, this work is now recognized as a compilation between Alexander and his students, with many authors lending their hands and heads to assisting in its production. Organized into four books,[108] the work foreshadows and predates the later, lengthier, and far more famous *Summa theologica* of Thomas Aquinas, although it is structured quite differently. Notably, like Thomas's *Summa,* it is not simply a commentary on the *Sentences* of Peter Lombard, but rather a monumental work of systematic theology that bears within it the very foundations of the Franciscan intellectual tradition.[109]

Crucially, despite the fact that Alexander himself probably did not write most of the *Summa* that bears his name, scholars widely agree that we can still regard it as at least "Halensian."[110] For example, based

107. A recent discussion of the *Summa's* relationship to Alexander's authentic theology can be found in Weber, "Alexander of Hales's Theology in His Authentic Texts," 289–93. Weber notes how the *Summa* itself was not actually completed until 1255, "when pope Alexander IV gave William of Melitona the task of completing the work," who then "added a few parts to the first three books ... and the fourth book, which also includes texts by Bonaventure" (291). Since all four books contain contributions by Alexander's students, Weber argues that "Alexander can be called the author as it seems that he started the work and probably gave it its structure. But only a part of the text came from his hand and even this part was maybe revised by his scholars" (291). Weber suggests that "the first three books of the *Summa* as a whole are not representative of [Alexander's] authentic theology" (291).

I have here chosen to refer to the *Summa* as the *Summa minorum* in acknowledgment of the fact that it was, as Weber contends, a compilation of writings from the earliest Franciscan theologians at the thirteenth-century University of Paris. Weber himself chooses to refer to it as the *Summa universae theologiae;* I have chosen *Summa minorum* instead because this title seems more appropriate for capturing the uniquely "Franciscan" character of the text. I also refer to the theology of the *Summa minorum* as "Halensian" in recognition of the fact that the text was at least produced by Alexander's students, if not by his own hand and if not always under his immediate direction. As will be seen in my argument below, the *Summa minorum's* teachings on grace are certainly derivative from Alexander's authentic texts, especially with respect to Alexander's suggestion that sanctifying grace is a created gift. Since the Quaracchi edition of the text remains the most definitive edition of the work, all further references to the *Summa minorum* here will cite both the volume number of the *Summa minorum,* followed by the volume number as it appears in the Quaracchi edition of the text in parentheses.

108. It is crucial to note that the Quaracchi editors never actually finished their edition of the fourth book of the *Summa,* which contains the *Summa's* treatment of the sacraments, penance, and prayer; Weber, "Alexander of Hales's Theology in His Authentic Texts," 290–92.

109. Osborne, *The Franciscan Intellectual Tradition,* 42, 53–68.

110. See again n. 107, above.

on what we can find in Alexander's teachings on grace in both his *Gloss* and his disputed questions before he was a brother, Alister McGrath has noted that: "it is possible to argue that the main features of the early Franciscan school's teaching on justification are essentially identical with the early teaching of Alexander of Hales. In other words, Alexander does not appear to have modified his theology significantly upon joining the Friars Minor, and subsequent Franciscan masters perpetuated his teachings as the authentic teaching of the Order."[111] Since McGrath's observations, the emergence of recent editions of Alexander's own authentic teachings—including an edition of his disputed questions on grace from before he was a brother[112]—make it easier for scholars to compare his "authentic" works to the teachings of the *Summa minorum*.

Much work remains with respect to unpacking the theology of all this "Halensian" literature. Scholars of the Franciscan intellectual tradition are only now beginning to probe the depths of the theological riches handed down to us in those works penned by Alexander or associated with his name, such as the *Summa minorum*. Franciscan scholars, and indeed, any scholar interested in the scholastic theology of the thirteenth and fourteenth centuries, have much about which to be excited as this Halensian literature becomes more widely available and thus more widely studied in upcoming years. My comments on the "Halensian" teaching on grace will only scratch the surface of the topic for the purposes of contextualizing Bonaventure's later teaching on the same.

Alexander of Hales and Bonaventure

More than any other character in our "story" of the historical sources that stand behind the Seraphic Doctor's doctrine of grace, my choice

---

111. Alister E. McGrath, *Iustitia Dei: A History of the Christian Doctrine of Justification*, 2nd ed. (Cambridge: Cambridge University Press, 1998), 161.

112. For the purposes of my present study, see especially *Quaestiones disputatae de gratia: editio critica*, ed. Jacek Mateusz Wierzbicki, Studia Antoniana 50 (Rome: Antonianum, 2008). Editions of Alexander's scriptural commentaries are also starting to emerge; see, for example, his *Postilla* to the Four Gospels, "I prologhi delle 'Postillae' ai vangeli synottici di Alessandro di Hales," ed. Alexander Horowski, *Collecteana Franciscana* 77 (2007): 27–62; and *Tractatus Magistri Alexandri de significationibus et expositione sacrarum Scripturarum*, ed. Alexander Horowski, in "Tractatus Magistri Alexandri de significationibus et expositione sacram Scripturam: Introduzione ed Edizione Critica," *Collecteana Franciscana* 79 (2009): 5–44.

to include Alexander of Hales in this narrative should be obvious. Any discussion of any aspect of the Franciscan intellectual tradition ought to begin by first attending to its development in the Halensian theology in which the entire theological tradition is rooted. Alexander of Hales was Bonaventure's teacher at the University of Paris, and Bonaventure himself was one of the theologians among Alexander's students who might have lent his hand to the composition of the *Summa minorum*. Salimbene reports that Alexander once said of his famed student that "I do not see in him that Adam sinned,"[113] underscoring the likelihood that their professional relationship was also one of friendship and mutual respect. Given this, attending to the Halensian teaching on grace will help us arrive at a clearer understanding of the immediate theological contexts that informed the Seraphic Doctor's teaching on the same subject.

The Halensian Understanding of Sanctifying Grace

As such, in what follows, I highlight two characteristics of the Halensian treatment of grace that will be necessary for understanding the Seraphic Doctor's doctrine of grace. Summarized in a succinct way, my discussion of these characteristics will consider, respectively, the Halensian understanding of what grace is and what grace does.[114] These two discussions can bring our "story" of the historical sources behind Bonaventure's doctrine of grace to a fitting conclusion, inasmuch as they will help us make the cognitive leap from discussions of Dionysian and Gallusian theologies of hierarchy to a more focused definition of grace as a topic in its own right. The Halensian understanding of grace is an especially fitting precipice from which to make this jump, inasmuch—as will be argued below—it plants the seed from which the

---

113. See Timothy J. Johnson, "Part III: On the Corruption of Sin," in *Bonaventure Revisited: A Companion to the Breviloquium*, ed. Dominic V. Monti and Katherine Wrisley Shelby (St. Bonaventure, NY: Franciscan Institute, 2017), 169n1, which attributes this claim—often attributed only to Salimbene—to Bernard of Bessa.

114. My thanks to Fr. David Couturier and the Franciscan Institute for funding my presentation of a condensed version of this material for a conference hosted by the Fondazione Collegio San Bonaventura, Frati Editori di Quaracchi at the Collegio Sant'Isidoro degli Frati Irlandese in Rome, entitled "International Symposium on Alexander of Hales and the Early Franciscan Masters," on 9–10 June 2018. That presentation was subsequently published as "Sanctifying Grace and the Threefold Way in the *Summa Halensis*," *Franciscan Connections: The Cord—A Spiritual Review* 68, no. 3 (Fall 2018): 10–16. This material has been reused in a revised form with permission from the Institute in this portion of the chapter.

Seraphic Doctor's own understanding of what grace is and what grace does will sprout up and flower, especially with respect to the role of hierarchy within that account.

First, I explore the Halensian definition of sanctifying grace as a created gift within the soul, which was a development from Peter Lombard's claim in his *Second Book of Sentences* that sanctifying grace simply is the Holy Spirit, the uncreated gift of charity that forgives sins. It is commonly affirmed that Alexander of Hales and those students who helped him compose the *Summa minorum* were the first theologians in the thirteenth century to distinguish between "created" and "uncreated" grace against Lombard in this way. Exploring this distinction, as well as the historical developments that led to it through the twelfth and early thirteenth centuries, will help us appreciate the theological *status quaestionis* surrounding grace as Bonaventure would have inherited it. I next examine a rather intriguing set of passages from Book 3 of the *Summa minorum* wherein the author (or authors) utilizes the Dionysian triad of purification, illumination, and perfection in order to describe the effects of this created gift within the soul. If, as this book argues, Bonaventure's definition of grace walks hand in hand with his theology of hierarchy, it is important to recognize that he finds precedent for this association in the *Summa minorum*. Both these discussions will help us understand the immediate theological context that thus informed the Seraphic Doctor's doctrine of grace as we will encounter it in *Part II*.

Two caveats must be addressed before thus proceeding, however. First, I have chosen here to refer to the "Halensian" definition of grace insofar as the following analysis will rely heavily upon the *Summa minorum's* treatment of grace in Book 3, and not only upon those writings considered to be "authentic" works of Alexander. As mentioned above, this is because the *Summa minorum*—though not entirely written by Alexander himself—is nonetheless widely affirmed to be "Halensian" in spirit insofar as the text was produced by his students.[115] The *Summa's* discussion of the effects of sanctifying grace through the Dionysian triad of purification, illumination, and perfection lays down an important stone in the foundation of Bonaventure's own treatment of grace, and its presence in this analysis will be crucial for moving forward to

---

115. See especially n. 107.

approach the latter theologian's work. References will be made when necessary to any significant divergences between the *Summa minorum* and Alexander's "authentic" teachings in footnotes.

Second, since my examination of the Seraphic Doctor's doctrine of grace will largely be confined to a consideration of his definition of sanctifying grace and his descriptions of its effects within the soul, my comments here will likewise be limited to a discussion of the Halensian treatment of sanctifying grace and will not necessarily extend to consider the Halensian approach toward helping grace, nor the distinctions between cooperative and operative grace, nor those between prevenient and subsequent grace. As scholars continue to unearth the theological riches of Halensian thought, these subjects should also be expounded at length with the attention and space they deserve.

The Halensian Distinction between Uncreated and Created Grace: What Grace Is   Approaching the Halensian definition of sanctifying grace requires first stepping back even farther to appreciate the historical context at the University of Paris that produced it. As indicated above, Alexander was positioned at a pivotal moment within the history of the Christian theological tradition as one of the veritable fathers of scholastic theology in the thirteenth century, as demonstrated especially by the fact that he was the first theologian to comment on the *Sentences* of Peter Lombard. Despite his novelty as a theologian, however, it would be a mistake to treat his work as if it existed in a vacuum. The academic life at the thirteenth-century University of Paris—along with all its scholastic methodological developments—irrevocably grew out of the academic life at the University of Paris in the twelfth century. Indeed, it was during the twelfth century that the University prospered and began to grow in significant ways under the direction of certain charismatic theological masters, such as Hugh of St. Victor and Peter Abelard. Throngs of interested young scholars would align themselves with the theology of one such charismatic figure or another, and the University of Paris budded into a thriving community of inquisitive academic minds urged on by their representative teachers, a tradition that certainly carried forward into the thirteenth century in the group of young Franciscan scholars who gathered around their own master, Alexander. Though his academic career belonged entirely to the thirteenth century, Alexander himself in a way stands between the twelfth- and thirteenth-century University of Paris, straddling both worlds as he inherited from the former to change the shape of theological study in the latter. To understand the novelty of his doctrine of grace, we must first acknowledge the former world.

For that, Aage Rydstrøm-Poulsen has already explored the particular nuances of theological debates surrounding grace in the twelfth century in his monumental book, *The Gracious God: Gratia in Augustine and the Twelfth Century*.[116] There, he narrates a sweeping tale of the story of grace in the twelfth century, beginning with a succinct summary of Augustine's teachings on grace, where he shows how, for the Bishop of Hippo, grace meant the forgiveness of sins and was seen as "the presence of divine love in the human heart."[117] From this, his book surveys Augustine's doctrine of grace as it developed in the twelfth century in the hands of Peter Abelard, the Victorine school of theology, William of St. Thierry, Bernard of Clairvaux, Peter Lombard, and subsequent theologians reacting to the Lombard's teachings at the University of Paris, among a host of others. For the most part, Rydstrøm-Poulsen argues, twelfth-century theologies of grace were deeply Augustinian.[118] In his *Sentences*, for example, Peter Lombard would define sanctifying grace as the love by which we love God and neighbor, claiming also that it is the gift of the Holy Spirit within the human soul that forgives sins.[119] In this way, the Lombard was thus "firmly rooted in the Augustinian tradition."[120] Following the Bishop of Hippo, the Lombard affirmed that sanctifying grace simply is the uncreated gift of charity that forgives sins, or, put differently, it simply is the Holy Spirit, who justifies the human being by dwelling within her to help her "love God above all things and her neighbor as herself."

A significant break in this tradition occurs in the twelfth-century University of Paris with Peter Lombard's peers, who began to suspect that the Lombard's explanation of grace in the *Sentences* did not

116. Copenhagen: Akademisk Forlag, 2002.

117. See Rydstrøm-Poulsen, *Gracious God*, 77, where he gives a very useful ten-point summary of the main "takeaways" from Augustine's doctrine of grace.

118. For his entire summation of Augustine's doctrine of grace, see Rydstrøm-Poulsen, *Gracious God*, 23–77.

119. This is famously rooted in B. 1, d. 17 of his *Sentences*; see *Petri Lombardi: Sententiarum libri IV*, ed. Joannes Aleaume, Francisco Garcia, Jacques-Paul Migne, et al. (Paris: Migne, 1841), 1.17.2.

120. See Rydstrøm-Poulsen, *Gracious God*, 483, and his preceding discussion of the Lombard's view of grace in 355–91.

sufficiently distinguish between different modes of causality or, more specifically, between the efficient cause (*causa efficiens*) and the formal cause (*causa formalis*) of grace. This break was introduced by Simon of Tournai (b. 1130, d. 1201), who argued that "man is righteous by the virtue of righteousness as the formal cause ... but he is made righteous by God as the efficient cause," so that "when a believer loves, his concrete love as formal cause is different from the source of this love, namely, the efficient cause."[121] In this way, Rydstrøm-Poulsen highlights Simon of Tournai's especial significance within the history of the development of the doctrine of grace since it was he who insisted that, "Human righteousness is one thing, the *causa formalis*, whereas the source of righteousness is another, *causa efficiens*. Likewise, human *caritas* is one thing, and its source, the Holy Spirit, is another."[122] In turn, this demand for "more precise distinctions and a clear language of causality in order to explain the interaction between divine and human nature"[123] in the late twelfth century is the point of departure from which we can approach the Halensian definition of grace in the early thirteenth.

Indeed, where Simon of Tournai is the first to demand a distinction between the *causa formalis* and *causa efficiens* of human righteousness, Alexander of Hales and the Halensian school of theology will nonetheless be the first to actually distinguish between a "created" gift of sanctifying grace and the "uncreated" gift of grace, understood to be the Holy Spirit. This distinction can be attributed specifically to Alexander, who uses it in both his *Disputed Questions* from before he was a brother and in his *Glossa* on the *Sentences* of Peter Lombard.[124] In his *Disputed Questions*, for example, he first defines grace as a "created similitude of

121. Rydstrøm-Poulsen, *Gracious God*, 435.
122. Rydstrøm-Poulsen, *Gracious God*, 484–85.
123. Rydstrøm-Poulsen, *Gracious God*, 485.
124. See especially Monsour's dissertation on this subject, "The Relation between Uncreated and Created Grace in the Halesian *Summa*," at 86: "According to Gérard Philips, there is no evidence that the term *gratia creata*, was part of written theological discourse before the first half of the thirteenth century. It occurs for the first time, it seems, in the body of writing the manuscript tradition attributes to Alexander of Hales (ca. 1186–1245). Thus, grace is spoken of as created, and also uncreated, in the *reportatio, Quaestiones Disputatae 'Antequam Esset Frater,'* dated by its modern editors between 1220 and 1236. Again, the two terms, *gratia creata* and *gratia increata*, occur in the *reportatio, Glossa in Quatuor Libros Sententiarum Petri Lombardi,* identified as Halesian in 1946, and dated by its modern editors between 1222 and 1229. In each of these works, however, the distinction receives little more than passing mention." More recently, the questions pertaining to the subject of grace from the *Quaestiones disputatae 'antequam esset frater'* have been edited in a new edition; see again *Quaestiones disputatae de gratia: editio critica,* ed. Wierzbicki; hereafter, *De gratia.*

the highest good" (*gracia est similitudo prima summe bonitatis creata*), which is the cause (*racio*) of the soul's union with God.[125] "Uncreated grace" is the Holy Spirit; "created grace," in contrast, is infused (*infusa*) by God into the soul and is accidental rather than substantial. This created similitude perfects the soul, elevating it from its "first being" (*primum esse*) to its "second being" or well-being (*secundum esse*) by assimilating it to God.[126] Comparable to light from the sun, which acts in matter below it by its own mediating light, so also does God act in the soul by moving the free will to meritorious works through the mediating light of created grace.[127]

Following this Alexandrian distinction, then, the *Summa minorum* similarly defines sanctifying grace (*gratia gratum faciens*)—the type of grace that "forgives sins" and justifies human beings—by first clearly defining the *uncreated* gift:

It ought to be said that when we consider grace, there is both a created grace [*gratia creata*] and an uncreated grace. Uncreated grace [*gratia increata*] is the Holy Spirit; and grace is called the Holy Spirit because it is called a gift [*donum*], and it is called a gift because it is also called love [*amor*]; for the Holy Spirit himself is love according to the Spirit's property [*proprietatem*], who as love proceeds from both the Father and the Son. And so, because it is a gift, so also it is love, because nothing is a gift unless by reason of love [*ratione amoris*] … because a gift properly speaking is given from love and liberality [*liberalitate*] and without coercion. Whence, in every gift, love should be given first, and so the Holy Spirit is called grace, because the Spirit is a gift, and it is called a gift from love. And this is that glorious gift which is spoken about in Jn 14:16: "I will ask my Father, and he will give you the Paraclete." For the Holy Spirit causes us to become graced by causing us to become deiform [*deiformes*]; but the Spirit does this, because the Spirit is love.… Because the Holy Spirit is thus love, and by all means it is the first power of loving [*virtus prima amoris*], whence, when it is given to us, it transforms us into a divine species [*divinam speciem*] so that the soul would be assimilated to God [*assimilata Deo*].[128]

125. *De gratia*, "1 Questio: De Gracia in Genere," 1 disp., mem. 1, ad ob. 2, 117.

126. *De gratia*, "1 Questio: De Gracia in Genere," 1 disp., mem. 2, a. 1, resp., 121. See also ad ob. 1, 122: "…etsi gracia copulet animam cum Deo, tamen hec copulacio non est per naturam nec quoad esse primum, set per assimilacionem et quoad esse secundum, quod est accidentale, non substanciale.…"

127. *De gratia*, "1 Questio: De Gracia in Genere," 1 disp., mem. 2, a. 1, ad ob. 3, 123.

128. *Summa minorum* 3 (4.2), p. 3, inq. 1, t. 1, q. 2, c. 1, a. 2, 959.

This definition of the *uncreated* gift of grace then yields in the *Summa minorum* to a definition of the created gift, sanctifying grace:

In another way, we ought to understand created grace [*gratiam creatam*] as a similitude and disposition belonging to the rational soul [*similitudinem et dispositionem ex parte animae rationalis*], from which it is held by God as one who has been received [*accepta*] and assimilated [*assimilata*], because there is both a transforming form [*forma transformans*], and this is uncreated grace [*gratia increata*]; but there is also a transformed form [*forma transformata*] which is left behind in the thing that has been transformed from the transformation, namely, in the soul [*anima*], and this is created grace.[129]

The *Summa* then explains that this created gift is necessary to prepare the one who receives it—or namely, the soul—for the uncreated gift: Without the created gift, the soul would not be properly disposed for the uncreated gift of the Spirit.[130] Simon of Tournai's call to distinguish between a *causa formalis* and a *causa efficiens* of human righteousness is fulfilled in the Halensian school insofar as Alexander and his students delineate between grace as both an uncreated and created gift. The former is the Holy Spirit; the latter is the "similitude" and "disposition" that transforms the soul into a suitable "recipient" for the former.

As McGrath has summarized this development, the introduction of a *created* gift in contradistinction from the uncreated gift of the Spirit leads to "the opinion that an *ontological* change is thereby effected within man…. The earlier medieval theologians expressed the change effected in justification in terms of a particular presence of God in his creature, which did not necessarily effect an ontological change."[131] Building upon but diverging from the earlier Lombardian view, the *Summa minorum* "conceives a special presence of God in the justified, such that an ontological change occurs in the soul. The presence of God in the justified sinner necessarily results in *created* grace—a created grace which can be conceived as a conformity of the soul to God,"[132] so that, as McGrath continues, "In this, the *Summa* makes an important advance on Peter Lombard's discussion of the divine presence in all creatures."[133] This "advance" takes hold within the

129. *Summa minorum* 3 (4.2), p. 3, inq. 1, t. 1, q. 2, c. 1, a. 2, 959.
130. See *Summa minorum* 3 (4.2), p. 3, inq. 1, t. 1, q. 2, c. 1, a. 2, 959.
131. McGrath, *Iustitia Dei*, 48.
132. McGrath, *Iustitia Dei*, 49.
133. McGrath, *Iustitia Dei*, 49.

thirteenth-century scholastic climate of the High Middle Ages because Alexander of Hales was the first theologian to actually begin the practice of commenting on Lombard's *Sentences*. Insofar as a student of theology beginning in the mid-thirteenth century would have had to write his own commentary on the *Sentences* to earn the title "Master of Theology," he would also have had to contend with these developments surrounding the Catholic doctrine of grace. Though he diverges from Lombard, Bonaventure follows his teacher in distinguishing between an "uncreated" and "created" gift of grace. Like the authors of the *Summa minorum,* he understands "created gift" as something that causes an *ontological* change within the soul, so that the lapsed human soul can become a "recipient" of the "uncreated gift" as a temple of the Holy Spirit. It is to the description of this ontological change within the *Summa minorum* that we now turn to better regard these themes in the Seraphic Doctor's own definition of sanctifying grace as a "created" gift.

The Effects of Sanctifying Grace in the *Summa minorum*: What Grace Does   As McGrath has already noted, this ontological change within the soul caused by the created gift of sanctifying grace is "conceived as a conformity of the soul to God" in both Alexander's authentic works and in the *Summa minorum,* or as a "similitude" or certain "disposition."[134] This language of God-conformity or deiformity, along with the notions of "assimilation" and the "similitude," echoes Dionysius's definition of hierarchy from *CH* 3 that I discussed above. It will be my task in *Part II* to show how Bonaventure reincorporates these same themes within his teachings on grace to claim that the effect of sanctifying grace is a hierarchical soul. In the same way that the Halensian teachings on grace must be contextualized with respect to the scholarly community at the University of Paris that produced it, however, Bonaventure's association of grace with Dionysian hierarchy was not entirely novel to him, even if he expands and revises the notion.

This is especially evident in Book 3 of the *Summa minorum,* in a Question that deals with "the effects of grace" in three chapters.[135] The

---

134. McGrath, *Iustitia Dei,* 49.

135. *Summa minorum* 3 (4.2), p. 3, inq. 1, tract. 1, q. 6: "De effectibus gratiae." To my knowledge, there is not a similar discussion of the "effects of grace" in Alexander's "authentic" works that so strikingly foreshadows Bonaventure's own later claim that sanctifying grace hierarchizes the soul by purifying, illuminating, and perfecting it. In his *De gratia,* for example, Alexander does not explicitly discuss the "effects" of grace in the soul. He

text first describes the "ontological" change that takes place in the soul through grace:

We should say that the effects [*effectus*] that are proper and essential to grace are to purify [*purgare*], illuminate [*illuminare*], and perfect [*perficere*]. For, since grace is nothing other than a similitude of the soul to God [*similitudo animae ad Deum*], as Augustine says, grace stretches [*intendit*] the soul to assimilate to God [*assimilare Deo*]; but these three actions—namely, to purify, to illuminate, and to perfect—must necessarily coincide [*concurrunt*] in order for this assimilation to happen, because the assimilation is nothing other than a movement from dissimilarity to similarity [*motus a dissimili ad simile*]. Whence, a soul will then be assimilated to God when it is moved from unlikeness to likeness, or from a likeness to a greater similitude, so that it would be even more like God. But Dionysius speaks of purification with respect to this dissimilarity, because purification removes that dissimilarity from the soul; and so, purgation is the removal of the dissimilarity from the soul, but the similitude [*similitudinem*] is introduced when the soul is illuminated and perfected.[136]

The authors of the *Summa minorum* here explicitly associate the "similitude" of the "created" gift of grace with the actions of purification, illumination, and perfection. Rather than relegating the three hierarchical

---

does, however, provide a question in consideration of the "consequences" of grace, where he discusses the differences between the virtues, gifts, fruits, and beatitudes (see *De gratia*, "2 Questio: Quatuor consequencia graciam: virtutes, dona, fructus, et beatitudines," 135–60). Alexander Horowski has examined this disputed question at length in comparison to Alexander of Hales's treatment of the gifts of the Holy Spirit in his *Glossa*; see "Doni dello Spirito Santo nella teologia di Alessandro di Hales," *Naturaleza y Gracia* 55, no. 2 (2008): 477–517. Horowski details at length how the spiritual gifts in Alexander's teachings on grace prepare the soul for the virtues, and ultimately, for the perfection of the spiritual life. Even more notably, Horowski's discussion notes how Alexander sees the spiritual gifts as *hierarchically* ordered to one another (see esp. 492) in the soul. Bonaventure will borrow from Alexander's claim that the consequences of grace are the virtues, spiritual gifts, spiritual fruits, and beatitudes in Part 5 of the *Breviloquium*, and, as Horowski notes, will also further develop and build upon Alexander's teachings on the gifts of the Holy Spirit in his own *Commentary on the Sentences* and in his *De don. Spir.* I have nonetheless chosen here to focus on the *Summa minorum*'s discussion of the "effects of sanctifying grace" in the soul because, as will be shown below and throughout my discussion of Bonaventure's own notion of the hierarchical soul in *Part II*, the *Summa minorum* explicitly associates the "effects" of sanctifying grace with the Dionysian triad of purification, illumination, and perfection. This favoring of Dionysius as a source is, we should further note, not at odds with Alexander's authentic works; his *Tractatus Magistri Alexandri de significationibus et expositione sacram Scripturam*, for example, notably begins with a consideration of how sacred scripture is given to us through the Father of Lights and by citing Dionysius; in that text, moreover, grace illuminates the meaning of scripture. See *Tractatus Magistri Alexandri de significationibus et expositione sacram Scripturam*, 21.

136. *Summa minorum* 3 (4.2), p. 3, inq. 1, tract. 1, q. 6, c. 1, 997.

activities to specific orders within the celestial and ecclesiastical hierarchies, however, the authors of the *Summa minorum* refer to them in an anthropological way: Here, a soul can only pass from "dissimilarity to similarity" when all three activities are at work within it. The ontological change caused by the created gift—namely, the conformity or "similitude" of the soul to God—is caused precisely insofar as that created gift causes these three activities. Or, phrased differently, the created gift of sanctifying grace causes an ontological change in the soul by purifying, illuminating, and perfecting it.

This, however, is only the first of three chapters within this Question in consideration of the effects of grace in the *Summa minorum*. Chapter 2 will next consider how, properly speaking, the effects of grace are to "vivify, assimilate, and gratify,"[137] and Chapter 3 similarly considers how, properly speaking, the effects of grace are "to justify, arouse, and elicit the movement of merit."[138] Following the authors' arguments in these two chapters will bring my "story" of the historical sources behind Bonaventure's doctrine of grace to a fitting conclusion.

First, the author of Chapter 2 indeed introduces the second triad of vivification, assimilation, and gratification by suggesting that grace is a similitude of both the first Truth and of the highest Goodness. He attributes this suggestion to Jn 1:4–5, which, as he says, tells us that "the Word *was life* and the *light of humanity,* shining *in the shadows,* and so also grace, which is a similitude of the Word, is compared to the soul as light and as life." As a similitude of the first Truth, the author explains, grace can be compared to the soul as light (*lux*).[139] In air, light causes three things: It first *purifies* air from dispositions which are contrary to it; it secondly *illuminates* air by "disposing the air with a disposition that is similar to itself" (*disponit aërem dispositione consimili sibi*); and thirdly, light *perfects* the air inasmuch as it "informs" (*informat*) the air. So, "just as light in the air performs these three aforesaid acts," as the authors of the *Summa minorum* write: "this can be similarly said

---

137. *Summa minorum* 3 (4.2), p. 3, inq. 1, tract. 1, q. 6, c. 2, 999: "Utrum proprii effectus gratiae sint vivificare, assimilare, gratificare."

138. *Summa minorum* 3 (4.2), p. 3, inq. 1, tract. 1, q. 6, c. 3, 1000: "Utrum proprii effectus gratiae sint iustificare, excitare, motus meritorios elicere."

139. *Summa minorum* 3 (4.2), p. 3, inq. 1, tract. 1, q. 6, c. 2, 1000. Notably, the comparison of grace to light is a point of obvious comparison between the *Summa minorum* and Alexander's own teachings on grace; see again *De gratia,* "1 Questio: De Gracia in Genere," 1 disp., mem. 2, a. 1, ad ob. 3, 123.

of grace inasmuch as it is compared to the soul as light (*lux*), because it first removes the dissimilarity of eternal light (*dissimilitudinem lucis aeternae*) from the soul, and with respect to this effect, it is understood as purifying; second, it disposes the soul to a disposition that is similar to it, so that the soul can be similar to grace in act (*similis in actu*), and then this is understood as illuminating; and finally, grace informs (*informat*) the soul, and then it is said 'to perfect' the soul."[140] The three activities of purification, illumination, and perfection are named by the authors of the *Summa minorum* as the "effects" of grace within the soul with respect to the fact that grace can be compared to light as a "similitude of the first Truth" (*similitudo primae Veritatis*).

Chapter 2 next continues, however, by then considering how grace is also "a similitude of the highest Goodness" (*similitudo Bonitatis summae*), and grace "should also be compared to the soul as life" (*vita*). In this way, the authors insist, grace can also be compared to the soul as love (*amor*), "and this love which impresses life is that by which the soul lives with God … and so in this way the act of grace is to vivify [*vivificare*]."[141] Once the soul has thus been vivified through love, "the transformation or assimilation [*transformatio sive assimilatio*] of the soul to God follows," because "this is the power of love [*vis amoris*] that transforms the lover into the Beloved … and with respect to this, the effect of grace [*effectus gratiae*] is understood as that which assimilates and conforms the soul to God."[142] When the soul has been assimilated to God, it finally gratifies God. "And so," the authors suggest, "because love is imprinted [*imprimitur*] on the soul, grace is said to vivify [*vivificare*]; because it is impressed [*impressus*] on the soul, it is said to assimilate [*assimilata*]; and because it is assimilated to the soul through love [*amorem*], it is understood in a general way to gratify [*gratificare*]."[143] The *Summa minorum's* introduction of this "second" triad of the effects of grace—namely, vivification, assimilation, and gratification—alongside the "first" triad of purification, illumination, and perfection, does not diminish the effects of the first three activities, but merely proposes another "mode" of grace as the "similitude." Where "purification, illumination, and perfection" conform the soul to God according to Truth,

140. *Summa minorum* 3 (4.2), p. 3, inq. 1, tract. 1, q. 6, c. 2, 1000.
141. *Summa minorum* 3 (4.2), p. 3, inq. 1, tract. 1, q. 6, c. 2, 1000.
142. *Summa minorum* 3 (4.2), p. 3, inq. 1, tract. 1, q. 6, c. 2, 1000.
143. *Summa minorum* 3 (4.2), p. 3, inq. 1, tract. 1, q. 6, c. 2, 1000.

"vivification, assimilation, and gratification" rather conform the soul to God according to Goodness.

This pattern continues in Chapter 3, where the *Summa minorum* next asserts that grace must also be considered as a "similitude of the highest power or strength" (*similitudo potestatis sive virtutis*). As such, it is comparable to a "cause of motion" (*motor*) and has another three-fold effect within the soul, whereby it causes merit by justifying, arousing, and eliciting (*iustificare, excitare, elicere*) the soul's rational faculties and free will so that the soul can know, desire, and find rest in the Good.[144] Here, then, a third "triad" of activities is introduced alongside the previous two, namely, "justification," "arousal," and "elicitation."

The author of this particular passage of the *Summa minorum* opens his discussion of this third triad by offering a helpful comment on how readers are to understand all three sets of grace's effects, writing:

We ought to understand that grace is compared [*comparatur*] to the soul as life [*vita*], as a cause of motion [*motor*], and as light [*lux*], because grace is a similitude of the highest Truth [*similitudo summae Veritatis*], and so it is compared to light; and it is also a similitude of the highest Goodness [*similitudo summae Bonitatis*], and so it is compared to life; and it is also a similitude of power and strength [*similitudo potestatis et virtutis*], and so it is compared to the soul as that which moves the will [*sic comparatur ut motor arbitrii ad animam*]. But Power [*potentia*] is attributed [*attribuitur*] to the Father, Truth [*veritas*] to the Son, and Goodness [*bonitas*] to the Holy Spirit, and for that reason, grace is a similitude [*similitudo*] of the whole Trinity and it assimilates us to the whole Trinity. Because it is comparable to light inasmuch as it is a similitude of the first Truth, we assume that there are three effects of grace; because it is also compared to life inasmuch as it is a similitude of the highest Goodness, we assume that there are three different effects of grace; and because it is compared to a motive cause, namely, inasmuch as it is a similitude of the highest power or virtue, there are also three effects of grace, namely, to justify [*iustificare*], to arouse [*excitare*], and to elicit the movement of merit [*motus meritorios elicere*].[145]

The doctrine of grace in the *Summa minorum* is here firmly rooted within the Halensian doctrine of the Trinity, where "Power" is a Trinitarian appropriation for the Father; "Truth," a Trinitarian appropriation for the Son; and "Goodness," a Trinitarian appropriation for the

---

144. *Summa minorum* 3 (4.2), p. 3, inq. 1, tract. 1, q. 6, c. 3, 1001–1002.
145. *Summa minorum* 3 (4.2), p. 3, inq. 1, tract. 1, q. 6, c. 3, 1001–1002.

Holy Spirit.[146] If the created gift of grace is defined by the authors of the *Summa minorum* as a "similitude," a "disposition" in the soul that causes it to be "assimilated" to God, the authors have, here in this discussion of the effects of grace, provided a more precise account of what that similitude looks like. To become a "likeness" or "similitude" of God, the soul must become a similitude of the entire Trinity: of the Son's Truth, the Spirit's Goodness, and the Father's Power. The effects of grace, as it were, must prepare the soul to become all three. Grace "purifies, illuminates, and perfects" the soul as "light" to conform it to the Son in Truth (the first triad of activity); it "vivifies, assimilates, and gratifies" the soul as "life" to conform it to the Spirit in Goodness (the second triad of activity); and it "justifies, arouses, and elicits" the soul as the cause of merit to conform it to the Father in Power (the third triad of activity).[147] Much like the three hierarchical orders of the soul within Thomas Gallus's angelic anthropology, moreover, these three sets of threefold activity ought not be understood in a merely linear way. The soul does not cease being "purified, illuminated, and perfected" through grace when it is "vivified, assimilated, and gratified" and then also "justified, aroused, and elicited to merit"; rather, all three triadic effects must happen within the soul simultaneously (*concurrunt*) if it is to be conformed to the Son, Spirit, and Father, respectively.

If we were thus to offer a shorthand response for the questions concerning what grace is and what grace does here in the *Summa minorum*, we might simply say that sanctifying grace is a created gift that causes the soul to become a "similitude" of the entire Trinity. Within this account of grace, quite notably, the authors of the *Summa minorum* explicitly incorporate the Dionysian triad of purification, illumination, and perfection as an appropriate description for the effects of sanctifying grace in the soul.

Inasmuch as Bonaventure reuses Thomas Gallus's angelic anthropology within his own account of the effects of sanctifying grace

---

146. On Trinitarian appropriations in the *Summa minorum*, see Justin Shaun Coyle, "An Essay on Theological Aesthetics in the *Summa halensis*" (PhD diss., Boston College, 2018).

147. That grace would make the soul into a likeness of the entire Trinity, we should further note, harkens back to Alexander's understanding of sin. In his *Disputed Questions on the Final Judgment*, for example, Alexander asserts that all three persons of the Trinity will serve as judges in the Final Judgment, because when one sins, one sins against the entire Trinity; see q. 1, Membrum 2, "De Ipso Iudice," in *Quaestiones disputatae secundum Alexandrum de Iudicio*, ed. Alexander Horowski, *Collecteana Franciscana* 75 (2005): 27–101, at 56.

within the soul, all these characteristics of the Halensian understanding of grace reappear there as well, albeit once again with significant Bonaventurean revisions and modifications. Rather than assigning the three Dionysian activities of purgation, illumination, and perfection entirely to the activity of the Son as Truth, for example, the Seraphic Doctor expands this insight surrounding the effects of grace to apply to each person of the Trinity, so that purgation pertains to the Father, illumination to the Son, and perfection to the Holy Spirit. Nonetheless, the *Summa minorum's* understanding of grace places the final stone within the foundation of our story of the historical sources that inform Bonaventure's doctrine of grace. In agreement with his teacher and Franciscan brothers at the University of Paris, he affirms that sanctifying grace is a created gift through which the soul is "purified, illuminated, and perfected" so as to become a similitude of the entire Trinity. Though much more could and should be said regarding the continuities and discontinuities between the Halensian and Bonaventurean iterations of what grace is and what grace does, these observations must suffice to pass from this part of the foundation for that doctrine onto the next.

Conclusion

In that same vein of thought, however, much more could also be said regarding the larger cast of characters that certainly also informed Bonaventure's doctrine of grace. My introduction to these three characters in particular—Dionysius the Areopagite, Thomas Gallus, and Alexander of Hales—has nonetheless introduced us to key definitions and themes that will be especially pertinent for approaching that doctrine throughout the remainder of this book.

First, Dionysius's invention of the word "hierarchy" in the early sixth century offers us the cornerstone from which the rest of this book will be constructed. In his *CH* 3, Dionysius defines a hierarchy as "*a sacred order, a state of understanding, and an activity approximating as closely as possible to the divine.*" A hierarchy has as its goal the rational creature's conformity to and union with God. The rational creature achieves this goal—and so "returns" to God—when it participates in the three hierarchical activities of purification, illumination, and perfection. Bonaventure's own definition of hierarchy in *II Sent.* borrows directly from Dionysius's "invention" of hierarchy from *CH* 3 in these respects, as we will see in the next chapter. Inasmuch as Bonaventure also incorporates his understanding of hierarchy within his teachings on the effects of sanctifying grace in the soul, and also especially insofar as he depends on the Dionysian triad of purification, illumination, and perfection within those teachings, encountering this definition was here necessary before moving forward to more fully appreciate these associations in the Seraphic Doctor's theology. In much the same way that the word hierarchy means something quite different for Dionysius than it does in our present context, moreover, the word also means something quite different for Bonaventure.

The Seraphic Doctor's own understanding of the word was informed in large part by his reading of the *CD* as translated by its medieval Latin interpreters, including the Dionysian commentaries produced by "the last of the great Victorines," Thomas Gallus. The Abbot of Vercelli contributed to the history of Christian mysticism by rewriting the Dionysian corpus in an affective key. In so doing, Gallus also put forward an angelic anthropology, claiming that souls themselves are hierarchical after Dionysius's description of the nine angelic orders. Within his broader theological project, this notion of the hierarchical soul explained how the soul could enjoy the affective union with God that crowned his Dionysian theological enterprise. As Boyd Taylor Coolman has recently argued at length, this angelic anthropology should be understood dynamically in Gallus's theology, and includes three valences—ascending, descending, and circling/spiraling—through which the soul strives to ever and ever greater levels of proximity and "likeness" to God. The Seraphic Doctor's encounter with the *CD* includes an encounter with Gallus's angelic anthropology as well; inasmuch as the Franciscan claims that grace hierarchizes the soul, he also reincorporates these three valences as appropriate descriptors for what it is, exactly, that grace does within the soul.

This chapter concluded by examining the most proximate source for the Seraphic Doctor's theology of grace, namely, his teacher at the University of Paris, Alexander of Hales, whose influence on Bonaventure is more widely recognized than that of Gallus. Against Peter Lombard, and following the demand for a distinction between the *causa formalis* and *causa efficiens* of grace originally introduced by the twelfth-century theologian, Simon of Tournai, Alexander and the students who assisted him in the composition of the *Summa minorum* were the first to define sanctifying grace as a "created" gift in distinction from the "uncreated gift" of the Holy Spirit. Before describing what grace does in the soul with respect to Gallus's angelic anthropology, Bonaventure first borrows this Halensian definition of what grace is from the community of Franciscan scholars at the University of Paris in the mid-thirteenth century. Insofar as this community also claimed that grace causes the soul to become a similitude of the Trinity by "purifying, illuminating, and perfecting" it, he perhaps also draws from them a path between Gallus's notion of the hierarchical soul and his own teachings on the effects of sanctifying grace in the soul.

These three characters set the stage for the narrative of Bonaventure's doctrine of grace as it will unfold throughout the remainder of this study. From Dionysius, the Seraphic Doctor borrows an understanding of what hierarchy means; from Gallus, he borrows an angelic anthropology; and under Alexander of Hales's influence, he formulates an understanding of what, exactly, grace is and what it does within the human soul so as to "return" it to the Trinity and help it "remain" there. By meeting these three characters, we are better prepared to meet Bonaventure, whose own theology of hierarchy we will encounter in the next chapter as the final foundation for approaching his doctrine of grace.

CHAPTER 3

Bonaventure's Theology of Hierarchy

In Chapter 2, I examined Dionysius's *CH* in order to underscore the idea that a "hierarchy," as it was originally conceived by the Areopagite, was "a sacred order, a state of understanding, and an activity" through which rational creatures could relate to God and other rational creatures within both the celestial and ecclesiastical hierarchies.[1] Far from indicating an oppressive top-down structure of power in which "higher" beings suppress "lower" beings within some sort of divine power-grab, the Areopagite invented the word to explain how rational creatures can become deified so as to enjoy a mystical union with God.[2] For Dionysius, this process of deification was the means through which rational creatures within the hierarchies could relate to other rational creatures in a holy way, as well, specifically through the three hierarchical activities of purification, illumination, and perfection. My goal throughout the remainder of this book will be to demonstrate the inseparability of Bonaventure's doctrine of grace from his own definition of hierarchy, which, as I will show below, the Seraphic Doctor both adapts and revises from the Areopagite.

Within this larger context, the present chapter simply aims to explicate what Bonaventure himself means by the word "hierarchy" within

---

1. See *CH* 3.1, trans. Luibheid, 153. For the Greek edition of Dionysius's works, see again *CD* (*PG* 3:119–1122).

2. Coakley, *God, Sexuality, and the Self,* 319–22.

his theology: How does the Seraphic Doctor define a "hierarchy," and in what ways does his definition both borrow and diverge from Dionysius's own definition in *CH* 3? Answering these questions is an additional step necessary for approaching Bonaventure's doctrine of grace, since—as I will be arguing in ensuing chapters—he quite seamlessly incorporates his theology of hierarchy into that doctrine.

Crucially, I do not intend the present chapter to replace previous scholarly examinations of Dionysian thought within Bonaventure's theology; rather, this chapter explains certain aspects of the Seraphic Doctor's view of hierarchy in order to affirm its presence, purpose, and significance within his doctrine of grace. Jacques Guy Bougerol and Romano Guardini remain unparalleled in their treatments of Dionysian thought within Bonaventure's writings, even as J. A. Wayne Hellmann's work on the concept of *ordo* within the Seraphic Doctor's theology contributes much to the conversation surrounding Bonaventure's understanding of hierarchy.[3] Building upon these previous accounts of the subject, most especially that provided by Hellmann, this chapter simply claims that "hierarchy" is one word used by Bonaventure to describe how the created order of reality relates to the *ordo* within the Triune God. Relatedly, for the Seraphic Doctor, it is also the means through which rational creatures can likewise relate in an ordered way to the rest of creation.[4]

What this chapter must therefore also accomplish is a precise explanation of Bonaventure's own concept of hierarchical *ordo*. It is well-attested that the Seraphic Doctor favors the image of the "intelligible circle" to symbolically depict his metaphysics.[5] As in Dionysius before him, the neoplatonic model of procession (*exitus*), return (*redditus*), and remaining is central to Bonaventure's conception of the relationship between the divine *ordo* and the created *ordo* insofar as he

___

3. See especially Bougerol, *Saint Bonaventure*, 33–167; and Guardini, "Die Hierarchien," in *Systembildende Elemente in der Theologie Bonaventuras*, 146–83. See also Hellmann, *Divine and Created Order*; Paul Kuntz, "The Hierarchical Vision of St. Bonaventure," in *Atti del Congresso Internazionale per il VII Centenario di San Bonaventura da Bagnoregio: San Bonaventura, Maestro di vita Francescana e di sapienza Christiana; Roma, 19–26 settembre 1974*, ed. A. Pompei, 233–48 (Rome: Pontificia Facoltà Teologica San Bonaventura, 1976); and Paul Rorem, "Dionysian Uplifting (Anagogy) in Bonaventure's *Reductio*," *Franciscan Studies* 70 (2012): 183–88.

4. Coakley, *God, Sexuality, and the Self*, 319.

5. See Hayes, *Hidden Center*, 15, esp. n. 9; *I Sent.* d. 37, p. 1, a. 1, q. 1, ad 3 (1, 639); *Red. Art.* 7 (5, 322); *Brev.* 5.1 (5, 253); *Hex.* 1.18–20 (5, 332–33).

holds that all created things emanate from the Trinity and thus must return to the Trinity in order to achieve their final rest (or, as Bonaventure likes to call it, their *status* or *fructus*) in God.[6] It is also well-attested that the Seraphic Doctor frequently employs the Dionysian triad of purification, illumination, and perfection in order to describe how rational creatures can themselves participate in the "return"—the *redditus*—back to God.[7] Hayes has noted how Bonaventure's use of the *exitus-redditus* model of reality is nonetheless complicated by his inclusion of Dionysian hierarchy within that model: How does hierarchical *ordo*—with its variegated grades of being and complex "levels" of proximity to God—fit alongside the simple image of a "circle" in Bonaventure's understanding of reality?[8] By probing what Bonaventure means by "hierarchy," this chapter aims also to articulate how the three moments of procession, return, and remaining function within Bonaventure's cyclical metaphysics. The chapter will introduce another symbol in addition to the "intelligible circle" in its explanation of hierarchical *ordo*—namely, that of Jacob's Ladder.

Jay Hammond has rightly emphasized the indispensability of symbols within the Seraphic Doctor's larger theological project, suggesting that Bonaventure uses them not to "prove anything," but "to express his theological vision," whereby "Symbols often 'enflesh' Bonaventure's discursive speculations, giving them greater rhetorical power as well as a more profound understanding of reality."[9] This chapter will argue that the symbol of Jacob's Ladder indeed "enfleshes" the Seraphic Doctor's "discursive speculations" surrounding the concept of hierarchy, and in so doing, will also offer a symbol that helps us conceive the neoplatonic triad of procession, return, and remaining in his metaphysics. Like Gallus before him,[10] the "return" or "ascending" movement to God in Bonaventure's theology of hierarchy does not end at a static "stopping

---

6. The very structure of Bonaventure's compendium to the study of theology, the *Breviloquium*, attests to this idea. See Joshua Benson, "The Christology of the *Breviloquium*," in *A Companion to Bonaventure*, 247–87; and Dominic Monti, "Introduction," in *Bonaventure Revisited*, 7–16.

7. Though Bonaventure employs this triad extensively throughout his writings, as we will especially see in Chapter 4, the most obvious example of this is in Bonaventure's spiritual text, *The Threefold Way*, which is about this triad.

8. *Hidden Center*, 15.

9. Jay Hammond, "Appendix: Order in the *Itinerarium mentis in Deum*," in *Divine and Created Order*, 198.

10. See my discussion of Gallus in Chapter 2.

point" whereby the creature achieves a neoplatonic escape from created reality in its pursuit of divine union: Rather, his moment of *status* is also a moment of *fructus,* wherein the "return" for Bonaventure indicates that the creature has been made "as like as possible to God"[11] by being ordered to ever more fruitful relationships with God and the rest of the created order of reality. Once the rational creature "returns" to God through her participation in a hierarchy, then she must "remain" in God by remaining in *all* these relationships. The symbol of Jacob's Ladder "enfleshes" Bonaventure's "discursive speculations" surrounding hierarchical *ordo* because, as will be shown below, it helps us arrive at "a more intuitive grasp" of these themes. In addition to simply defining the concept of "hierarchy" in Bonaventure's theology, my examination of this symbol here will also help construct a "foundation" for encountering this symbol within his doctrine of grace throughout the rest of this study: As readers will encounter in *Parts II* and *III,* the symbol haunts that doctrine frequently enough to warrant our raising its specter already here.

Structurally, the chapter will provide an *explicatio* of some of the most important texts that showcase Bonaventure's theology of hierarchy. I begin with an exposition of his initial definition of hierarchy from his *II Sent.,* followed by an examination of his definition of hierarchy from one of his final works, namely, the *Collationes in Hexaëmeron* (hereafter, *Hex.*). I conclude the chapter by turning to the Seraphic Doctor's explanation of hierarchy from one of his many sermons, namely, *Sermo 54 "De sanctis angelis"* from his *Sermones de sanctis* collection, where I will examine the image of Jacob's Ladder as a useful symbol through which to encounter his theology of hierarchy as I presented it in the previous two sections of the chapter.

I have chosen these three texts in particular to represent and explain Bonaventure's theology of hierarchy for three reasons. First, both Guardini and Bougerol have already highlighted the first two texts as useful windows into the Seraphic Doctor's hierarchical thought,[12] so

---

11. See again Dionysius's definition of hierarchy in *CH* 3, trans. Luibheid, 154: "The goal of a hierarchy, then, is to enable beings to be as like as possible to God and to be at one with him."

12. See Guardini, *Systembildende Elemente,* 148–49, where Guardini dismisses the "magisterial" definition of hierarchy mentioned by Bonaventure in *II Sent.* against both these treatments of the subject, which Guardini holds are more accurate representations of the Seraphic Doctor's thought. See also Bougerol, *Saint Bonaventure,* 131–37, where he

my focus on them here simply carries forward a previously established trend in Bonaventurean scholarship. Second, in agreement with what Hellmann and Luyckx have observed concerning the "inner unity" of Bonaventure's theology,[13] I contend that the Seraphic Doctor's understanding of hierarchy does not change in any major way between his earlier and later treatments of the subject. Focusing on his definitions of hierarchy in *II Sent.* and the *Hexaëmeron* alongside one another will provide clear evidence for this "inner unity" of his thought with respect to hierarchy across the course of his theological career. Finally, and perhaps most importantly, an *explicatio* of each of these three texts will serve the purpose of introducing key vocabulary and themes that will resurface in Bonaventure's doctrine of grace. His definition of hierarchy from *II Sent.* will, for example, provide the clearest articulation of what hierarchy *means* in any of his works, and will also introduce us to his hierarchical metaphysics and his use of the neoplatonic triad of procession, return, and remaining therein. His definition of hierarchy from the *Hexaëmeron* will rather acquaint us with the word "*influentia*" in his lexicon, the same term he will also use to define sanctifying grace. Finally, his explanation of the hierarchical *ordo* of the macrocosm in his *Sermo 54* will introduce the symbol of Jacob's Ladder in order to help us conceptualize his theology of hierarchy. All three of these topics as presented in all three texts—Bonaventure's most basic understanding of what "hierarchy" means; the word "*influentia*"; and the symbol of Jacob's Ladder—will be indispensable theological foundations for approaching his doctrine of grace in *Parts II–III*.

Bonaventure's Definition of Hierarchy in *The Commentary on the Sentences*

What, then, does hierarchy mean for the Seraphic Doctor? The foundation for his theology of hierarchy takes shape in the prologue to the ninth distinction of his *II Sent.*, where we encounter his first attempt at defining hierarchy in any of his works. Here, he gives *three* definitions, which when read together provide a resource for understanding what

---

presents these two definitions of hierarchy as the Seraphic Doctor's "general" notions of hierarchy.

13. See Hellmann, *Divine and Created Order*, 2n4; quoting Luyckx, *Der Erkenntnislehre Bonaventuras*, 113.

he means by hierarchy in all his subsequent works, including his use of the concept in his doctrine of grace.

Approaching this initial definition, however, requires first stepping back to the Lombard's text. In Bk. 2, d. 9 of his *Sentences,* the Lombard unsurprisingly employs Dionysius in order to introduce his readers to the nine angelic orders.[14] Despite pointing to the Areopagite in this introduction, however, the Lombard goes on to depend largely upon the works of St. Gregory the Great, and he never explicitly mentions the concept of hierarchy in his exposition. In contrast, Bonaventure's commentary on d. 9 opens with a prologue that introduces hierarchy so as to essentially re-flavor the Lombard's original text with a Dionysian spice. To explain the nine angelic orders as presented by his theological predecessor, Bonaventure writes that it is necessary to first ask three questions: "What is a hierarchy?" "What is an angel?" and "What is angelic order?"[15] Treating each of these topics sequentially, he begins the prologue by attending to the first:

Dionysius posits three definitions for this hierarchy in the book, *On the Celestial Hierarchy,* the first of which is this: "A hierarchy is divine beauty, as well as simple, the highest, and consummative." The second is this: "A hierarchy is a sacred order [*ordo divinus*], knowledge [*scientia*], and activity [*actio*] assimilating as much as possible to deiformity, and ascending proportionally into a likeness of God toward the lights that have flowed into it from above." The third is this: "A hierarchy is a likeness [*similitudo*] and unity [*unitas*] to God as far as is possible, holding itself to sacred understanding [*scientiae sanctae*] and action [*actionis*] as its guide, and fixing itself unchangeably to its own most divine beauty [*decorem*]; and as far as possible, reforming its worshippers."[16]

Bonaventure's "three definitions" here all derive from Dionysius's original definition of hierarchy as put forward in *CH* 3, which he would have encountered through Latin translations of the Areopagite's

14. Peter Lombard, *The Sentences: Book 2,* d. 9, ch. 1, trans. Guilio Silano, Mediaeval Sources in Translation 43 (Toronto: Pontifical Institute of Medieval Studies, 2008), 38.

15. *II Sent.* d. 9, prologue (2, 237): "Oportet igitur primo videre quid sit hierarchia; secundo vero, quid angelus, tertio, quid sit ordo angelicus."

16. *II Sent.* d. 9, prologue (2, 237–38). Bonaventure here employs the translation of *CH* 3 by John Scotus Eriugena. For all three definitions, see "De caelesti hierarchia," in *Dionysius Areopagita secundum translationem quam fecit Iohannes Scotus seu Eriugena,* Iohannes Scottus seu Eriugena, LLA 696 (Turnhout: Brepols, 2015). Compare to *CH,* trans. Lubheid, 151–52. There are obvious differences between all these translations, which may not be completely faithful to the Areopagite's original Greek text.

works by Jean Scotus Eriugena, John Saracen, Robert Grossetesste, and Thomas Gallus.[17] It bears repeating that the Seraphic Doctor interpreted *CH* 3 as coming from the pen of one who held an authority second only to scripture.[18] Although Hugo Koch and Josef Stiglmayr disproved the Areopagite's claim to be Dionysius, Paul's first convert to Christianity in Athens as presented by the author of Acts 17:22–34, in 1895,[19] medieval theologians including St. Bonaventure had no reason to doubt the Areopagite's claim. The Seraphic Doctor does not offer his citation of the text in the prologue to *II Sent.*, d. 9 in any sort of haphazard way, but rather intends it to illuminate the Lombard's text through the words of one whom he believed held apostolic authority.

As even a cursory glance comparing *CH* 3 with Bonaventure's commentary indicates, however, the Seraphic Doctor nonetheless significantly modifies the text. Contrary to Bonaventure's presentation of the Areopagite's thought in the above passage, Dionysius's text does *not* imply that these "three" definitions are meant to be understood separately or in any sort of ordered way, even as the "second" definition of hierarchy provided by Bonaventure is actually the first "definition" given by the Areopagite in *CH* 3.[20] Since Bonaventure continues the prologue with an explanation of each of these "three definitions," an analysis of that explanation will yield important insights into his own unique perspective on hierarchy in distinction to the Areopagite, which the Seraphic Doctor will more or less maintain throughout his theological career. Even more specifically, and quite strikingly, he here actually defines hierarchy according to the three movements of remaining, procession, and return, so that *Definition 1* describes God's "remaining"; *Definition 2*, the "procession" of all rational creatures from God; and *Definition 3*, the "return" of all rational creatures back to God.

17. See Bougerol, "Saint Bonaventure et le Pseudo-Denys l'Areopagite," 39.

18. See my comments on Dionysius and Bonaventure in Chapter 2.

19. Acts 17:22–34; see also Stang, "Dionysius, Paul, and the Significance of the Pseudonym," 541–55, for a fine analysis of the significance of this scriptural text for the Areopagite.

20. See again my discussion of this definition in Chapter 2. Luibheid's translation of both of these two definitions reads (where I have added the numeric order in brackets): "[1] In my opinion a hierarchy is a sacred order, a state of understanding and an activity approximating as closely as possible to the divine. And it is uplifted to the imitation of God in proportion to the enlightenments given to it. [2] The beauty of God—so simple, so good, so much the source of perfection—is completely uncontaminated by dissimilarity" (in *CH* 3, 154). Readers will note that Bonaventure's second definition is actually the first provided by the Areopagite, and vice versa. The third definition appears later in Section 2 of Chapter 3 (trans. Luibheid, 154).

Attending to all three definitions separately will thereby also introduce how these three movements function in Bonaventure's metaphysics.

Definition 1: The Remaining of the Divine *Ordo*

"A hierarchy is divine beauty, as well as simple, the highest [good], and consummative."

Bonaventure's choice to present this definition prior to Dionysius's own "first" definition of hierarchy might seem rather strange. Readers of medieval theology will note, however, that such seeming misplacements are rarely haphazard and almost always serve a crucial purpose with regard to the meaning of the text. Bonaventure's choice to examine this definition "first" presents no exception. According to him, this refers to the "uncreated hierarchy"[21] of God:

But the first definition, which is the uncreated hierarchy [*hierarchiae increatae*], expresses it with regard to trinity and unity [*trinitatem et unitatem*], so that trinity does not come before [*praejudicat*] unity, nor does unity come before trinity; but unity pertains to [*spectat*] the perfection [*perfectionem*] of the trinity, and the trinity pertains to the perfection of unity. So, when Dionysius says, "Hierarchy is divine beauty [*divina pulchritudo*]," there is shown to be [in the uncreated hierarchy] unity in trinity [*unitas in trinitate*]. For beauty consists in plurality and equality, as Augustine says in *On True Religion*. But so that it will be shown that plurality does not come before [*praejudicat*] unity, Dionysius says, "and simple," because plurality is indicated there, and nevertheless, the simplicity of unity is not carried away [*non tollatur*]. But, so that it will be shown that unity does not come before trinity, or plurality, he adds: "And the highest," because unity is thereby in God, and nevertheless God is the highest goodness [*summa bonitas*], through whom there is perfect communication [*perfecta communicatio*], and so a plurality of persons. Afterwards, so that he will show that unity pertains to the perfection of plurality, and vice versa, Dionysius adds, "and consummative" [*consummativa*]; which signifies that the highest perfection [*summa perfectio*] as well as each and every kind of perfection consists in trinity and unity [*trinitate et unitate*].[22]

In commenting on one phrase from *CH* 3, the Seraphic Doctor here manages to briefly summarize his Trinitarian theology with only a few

---

21. *II Sent.* d. 9, prologue (2, 238): "Prima autem diffinitio quae est hierarchiae increatae...."

22. *II Sent.* d. 9, prologue (2, 238). "*Praejudicat*" in this context is a difficult word to translate. I have chosen "come before," which does not quite capture the sense of "judging beforehand" that the word entails, but which nonetheless captures what the Seraphic Doctor conveys in the Latin with respect to the inseparability of God's unity and trinity.

sentences while also wedding it with hierarchy. While Dionysius discusses the unity and trinity of God in other texts, it is absent from this section of *CH* upon which the Seraphic Doctor's analysis rests, so that Bonaventure's commentary here is entirely his own. He intentionally moves this definition to the *forefront* of his discussion so as to order his ensuing introduction of the created hierarchies to his doctrine of God, the "uncreated hierarchy" who is both one and three. First and foremost, for the Seraphic Doctor, a hierarchy *means* the unity and trinity of God, whose beauty and simplicity provide the perfective source for every other created hierarchy.[23]

The elephant once again overwhelms the room. Readers hailing from a twenty-first-century theological perspective will most certainly—and rightly should—balk at Bonaventure's suggestion here that God is an "uncreated hierarchy." And indeed, if God is a hierarchy, does that not also imply that the three persons of the Trinity—Father, Son, and Holy Spirit—are *unequal* in some sense? By claiming that God *is* a hierarchy, moreover, is not Bonaventure thereby contributing to the historical construction of oppressive hierarchical power structures, both in the Church and society?[24]

J. A. Wayne Hellmann has already treated this question intermittently throughout his monumental study, *Divine and Created Order in Bonaventure's Theology*. There, he proposes the concept of *ordo*, or "order," as an organizing principle for the Seraphic Doctor's thought and argues that Bonaventure's view of the Trinity grounds his view of all creaturely order. There is an *ordo* in every creature which reveals the *ordo* of the uncreated God, from whom all creatures flow forth in the act of creation and to which all creatures are ordered through Christ, the *medium* between the divine and created orders. As Hellmann's chapter on the Trinity argues, creatures can be ordered to God in this

---

23. Bougerol has noted that this represents a divergence from the theology of Dionysius, who never used the term "hierarchy" with respect to God *in se*, but rather used the word, "thearchy," or alternatively, "divinity." See Bougerol, *Saint Bonaventure*, 132.

24. See again Miraslov Volf, "The Trinity is our Social Program," 403–23, in which Volf discusses the "hierarchical" vs. "egalitarian" view of the Trinity. Volf rightly dismisses the "hierarchical" view of the Trinity as being damaging to oppressed members of society. Volf's response underscores why a more nuanced understanding of what it meant for Bonaventure to call God a "hierarchy" might be an important step forward in overcoming oppressive hierarchies. Volf's essay belongs to a much wider conversation in liberation theology and depends especially on the work of Leonardo Boff in *Trinity and Society*. See also my Chapter 2, n. 20.

way through Christ because God as God is an *ordo* of divine persons. Bonaventure speaks of an *ordo* between the three persons of the Trinity, whereby the Father, Son, and Holy Spirit are distinguished from one another by their relations to each other in the order of origin: The Father gives himself totally to the Son, and together, the Father and Son spirate the Holy Spirit between them. This order of origin should not be conceived temporally but rather describes the eternal relations that distinguish the three persons of the Trinity, who nonetheless enjoy perfect unity.[25]

Bonaventure's claim that the Trinity is an uncreated hierarchy pertains to this notion of *ordo*.[26] The Seraphic Doctor's use of hierarchy with respect to the Trinity, as Hellmann rightly points out, refers to the *ordo* that both distinguishes the three persons within the Trinity while also affirming their unity. As the highest order, the persons of the Trinity must be *both* personally distinct *and* perfectly united: To claim that the Trinity is an "uncreated hierarchy" is, for Bonaventure, to affirm this perfect *ordo* within the Triune God. As Hellmann concludes, "Any group of persons will in some way be hierarchical if there is any unity among them, but hierarchy is only fully realized in the three divine persons where there is perfect equality."[27] His insights concerning Bonaventurean hierarchy and his notion of *ordo* are clearly reflected in Bonaventure's own analysis of the "first definition" of hierarchy in the prologue to *II Sent.*, d. 9 highlighted here. Through proposing the possibility of an uncreated hierarchy, the Seraphic Doctor intends to describe this perfect *ordo* within God, who is both trinity and unity, perfect equality, and the highest beauty. Crucially, Bonaventure's assertion of an uncreated hierarchy within God in no wise posits that the Father, Son, and Holy Spirit are unequal in any sense; rather, for Bonaventure, to say that God is an uncreated hierarchy underscores the *ordo* of relations that distinguishes the three persons of the Trinity while simultaneously affirming their divine unity and equality.

While the concept of a hierarchy within God should obviously be rejected according to the modern understanding of a hierarchy as an

---

25. See especially Bonaventure, "Whether a trinity of persons can exist together with unity of nature," in *The Disputed Questions on the Mystery of the Trinity*, q. 2, trans. Zachary Hayes, Works of St. Bonaventure 3, 138–58 (St. Bonaventure, NY: Franciscan Institute, 2000).

26. Hellmann, *Divine and Created Order*, 53.

27. Hellmann, *Divine and Created Order*, 53.

unequal social power structure, Bonaventure's assertion to this effect rather intends to explain *how* the three divine persons are at once three and one, or how the three persons within God relate to one another in an ordered way to form a perfect community of divine love. For the Seraphic Doctor, a hierarchy means, first and foremost, this divine *ordo* within God, the impeccable equality and unity of the Divine who is nonetheless a Trinity of persons. As he argues, "the highest perfection as well as each and every kind of perfection consists in trinity and unity."[28] In other words, a perfect hierarchy cannot be a power structure in which one member of the hierarchy "rules" over another in a way that would suppress or limit the other members of the hierarchy; rather, for Bonaventure, a perfect hierarchy preserves the distinction of the persons within it while yet insisting upon the equality of those persons, as well. The only perfect hierarchy—the uncreated hierarchy of the Trinity—is a hierarchy *without subordination*. Most fundamentally, therefore, a hierarchy means the communion of love that comprises the perfect, ordered relations between the three persons of the Godhead: It means God's "remaining" in God as God through this perfect *ordo*. This Bonaventurean revision of the Areopagite's original definition lays the intellectual foundation upon which the Seraphic Doctor then expands his notion of hierarchy to the created order of reality, as well.

Definition 2: The Procession of the Created *Ordo*

"A hierarchy is a sacred order, knowledge, and activity assimilating as much as possible to deiformity, and ascending proportionally into a likeness of God toward the lights that have flowed into it from above."

While Bonaventure claims that the "first" definition of hierarchy refers explicitly to the "uncreated hierarchy" within God, he then continues his exposition of the Areopagite's text by claiming that the second two definitions rather refer to "created" hierarchy.[29] "But they differ," he writes, "because the first primarily attends fully to the procession [*egressum*] from God; but the final definition fully attends to the return [*regressum*] to God, though each definition touches upon both."[30]

---

28. *II Sent.* d. 9, prologue (2, 462): "... in quo signatur quod in trinitate et unitate consistit omnimoda et summa perfectio."

29. *II Sent.* d. 9, prologue (2, 238): "Quia prima diffinitio est hierarchiae increatae; duae vero sequentes creatae."

30. *II Sent.* d. 9, prologue (2, 238).

Here, we encounter the "intelligible circle" of reality in Bonaventure's metaphysics. His suggestion that his second and third definitions for hierarchy refer to the movements of procession (*egressum*) and return (*regressum*), respectively, paired with his assertion that the first definition of hierarchy refers to God, serves to reinforce the threefold pattern of remaining, procession, and return that is so central to the Dionysian theological enterprise. For Bonaventure in *II Sent*, a hierarchy "means" all three movements: It means an "uncreated hierarchy" and so refers to God's remaining (*Definition 1*), and also means the procession and return of creatures to God with respect to the created hierarchies (*Definitions 2–3*).

Before turning to his discussion of the procession or *egressum* within *Definition 2* in particular, it is worthwhile to pause and note the simultaneity of the processive and regressive moments in his introduction to this "second definition." Where he claims that *Definition 1* refers exclusively to the uncreated hierarchy, *Definition 2* primarily (*principaliter*) attends to the procession (*egressum*) of the created order from God, and *Definition 3* fully (*penes*) attends to the moment of return (*regressum*), his accompanying observation that "*each definition treats both [utrobique tangatur utrumque]*" should not simply be glossed over. The moments of procession and return, though distinct, nonetheless bleed together in *Definition 2* and *Definition 3*, implying that where hierarchy is concerned for the Seraphic Doctor, both "moments" are always happening. This is useful to keep in mind as we consider each "moment" along with him, and it will be especially useful when we consider what he says about the "return," both here in his definition of hierarchy from the *II Sent.* and later when we specifically consider his doctrine of grace.

Bonaventure next expounds *Definition 2* by particularly dwelling on the egressive moment, explaining how the angelic or celestial hierarchy processes from God, which he insists takes place "by way of an image and similitude [*secundum rationem imaginis et similitudo*]."[31] He writes:

[Dionysius] first describes that hierarchy processing from God through the mode of image [*modum imaginis*], when he says: "A hierarchy is a divine order [*ordo*], understanding [*scientia*], and activity [*actio*]:" as an order, that

---

31. *II Sent.* d. 9, prologue (2, 238).

is as an ordered power [*ordinata potestas*], it corresponds to the Father; as understanding, to the Son; and as activity, to the Holy Spirit, according to memory [*memoriam*], understanding [*intelligentiam*], and the will [*voluntatem*]. But second, he describes it with regard to the cause of similitude [*ad rationem similitudinis*], when he adds: "assimilated as much as possible through deiformity, and ascending," etc.; and Dionysius is treating that assimilation [*assimilatio*] with regard to habit [*habitum*], when it says: "assimilated as much as possible to God," etc.; and with regard to act [*actum*], when it is further added: "And illuminations coming down from God have been given to it," etc. For the act of a similitude, or of assimilating grace [*gratiae assimilantis*], is to lead above [*sursum ducere*], just as its origin descends from above [*desursum descendere*].[32]

In my examination of the passage from *CH* 3 that Bonaventure here quotes, I underscored certain themes that would resurface within both his definition of hierarchy and his doctrine of grace, namely, the themes of light, image and likeness, and the soul's conformity to God. Here, in the Seraphic Doctor's own explication of this same passage, his words intimate the inseparability of that notion from his doctrine of human nature and grace, particularly insofar as he reframes Dionysius's definition of hierarchy as the procession of rational creatures from God through their "image" and "likeness" to God. These will be crucial terms when we consider the Seraphic Doctor's teachings on grace, human nature, and theological anthropology in Chapter 6, but what do they mean here with respect to his definition of hierarchy?

Bonaventure understands the soul to be an "image" of God because it has the three faculties described by St. Augustine in *On the Trinity*, whereby "it is *through* the faculties of memory, intelligence, and will ... that we discover the most suitable analogy in the natural order to the three Persons in the one God."[33] As the Seraphic Doctor describes at length in *Itin.* 3, a consideration of this divine image will lead the human mind to acknowledge its indebtedness to the Creator God.[34] Bonaventure's claim in *II Sent.*, d. 9 connects this Augustinian insight regarding the human mind as an image of the Triune God with Dionysius's definition of hierarchy: "Order" refers to the Father, and thus to memory; "understanding" refers to the Son, and thus to intelligence;

---

32. *II Sent.* d. 9, prologue (2, 238).

33. Stephen F. Brown, introduction to *The Journey of the Mind to God*, trans. Philotheus Boehner (Indianapolis: Hackett, 1993), xvii.

34. *Itin.* 3 (5, 303–6).

and "activity" refers to the Spirit, and thus to the will. Dionysius's hierarchical "procession" thus here transforms into a statement about the relationship between the mind and God in Bonaventure's hand, a seemingly impossible reconciliation of the Augustinian psychological analogy for the Trinity with the Dionysian insight that rational creatures relate to God through hierarchy.

Again, Hellmann's discussion of *ordo* as a guiding principle for Bonaventure's theology clarifies the meaning of this rather odd marriage between the thought of Augustine and the Areopagite. For the Seraphic Doctor, all of creation reflects the *ordo* of the Triune God at three different levels of being—namely, at the level of (1) the *vestige*, (2) that of the *image*, and (3) that of the *similitude*. (1) First, since every element of creation is ordered to God as its efficient and final cause, every created thing can be called a *vestige* of the Trinity. As Hellmann notes, "every creature has a relationship to God as a *principium creativium*, and so every creature is a *vestigium*," where a vestige is understood as "that first degree of cooperation [between the creature and God] which is rooted in the fact that all created things find their cause in God."[35] (2) While every created thing is thus a vestige of God by being related to God as its cause, only rational creatures are called an *image* of God, since, as Hellmann further reflects: "the image is ordered to God not only insofar as God is the cause, but also insofar as God is the object. The image of God is one who knows God."[36] To be properly named an "image" of God, a creature must possess the faculties of memory, intelligence, and will, "those distinctive powers of the image which give the image an essentially new relationship to the Triune God which the vestige does not enjoy,"[37] so as to know the Triune God in the mind. Wed to his notion of hierarchy, Bonaventure's claim that rational creatures process by way of an "image" serves the purpose of emphasizing this "new relationship" between the Triune God and the mind, a relationship which is nonetheless inherent within every creature that possesses memory, intelligence, and will: Creatures who process from God as an "image" of God are ordered to God in their very nature as rational beings. Like Gallus before him, the Seraphic Doctor here begins to combine Dionysian hierarchy with his

---

35. Hellmann, *Divine and Created Order*, 107.
36. Hellmann, *Divine and Created Order*, 107.
37. Hellmann, *Divine and Created Order*, 115.

theological anthropology.[38] A hierarchy is no longer simply a macrocosmic description of how rational creatures within the created order of reality relate to the God beyond all thought, but also appropriately describes the microcosm of the mind, which is itself a hierarchy of powers that reflect the trinity and unity within the uncreated hierarchy.

In addition to the vestige and image, however, the Seraphic Doctor also posits a third way in which creatures can be ordered to the Triune God, namely, (3) by way of a similitude, when the soul of the creature is completely conformed to God—or made "deiform"—through sanctifying grace. Following the Halensian understanding of grace, Bonaventure regards the creature's likeness to God as a gift of grace whereby, as Brown helpfully surmises, "God's presence in the soul by grace restores it from its bent-over form to its supernatural likeness or similitude to God."[39] As we shall see in *Part II,* it is impossible to divorce Bonaventure's notion of the similitude from his doctrine of grace, but for now, it suffices to underscore the fact that Bonaventure's notion of "similitude" also belongs to his definition of hierarchy. If a rational creature relates to the Triune God through the innate faculties of memory, intelligence, and will within her mind, she enjoys *unity* with the Triune God through the similitude gifted by grace. Read together, Bonaventure's exposition of hierarchical procession through the modes of image and likeness serves the purpose of describing how rational creatures are ordered to the uncreated hierarchy, the Trinity: As an image of God, the rational creature is ordered to the Trinity in her nature through memory, intelligence, and will; as a similitude of God, the creature becomes as like as possible to God so as to be at one with the Trinity.

Definition 3: The Return of the Created *Ordo*

"A hierarchy is a likeness and unity to God as far as is possible, holding itself to sacred understanding and action as its guide, and fixing itself unchangeably to its own most divine beauty; and as far as possible, reforming its worshippers."

Finally, the Seraphic Doctor concludes his presentation of these definitions by next explaining his reasoning for considering the "third definition" as a description of the rational creature's "return" to God:

---

38. For my discussion of Gallus's theological anthropology, see Chapter 2.
39. Brown, "Introduction," xvii.

But we thus understand the third definition in the following way; for there, as I said before, Dionysius is mainly describing the angelic hierarchy through a return [*regressum*] to God. Therefore, a hierarchy through returning [*regrediens*], or through its return [*regressus eius*], is noted in the aforesaid definition: first with regard to ability [*habilitatem*], when Dionysius says: "A hierarchy is a likeness and unity with God as far as is possible"; second, with regard to actuality [*actualitatem*], when Dionysius says: "holding itself to sacred understanding [*scientiae sanctae*] and action [*actionis*] as its guide"; third, with regard to immutability, when he adds: "And fixing itself unchangeably to its most divine beauty [*decorem*]"; fourth, with regard to the fruitfulness of plenitude [*plenitudinis ubertatem*], when he further adds: "and as far as possible, reforming its worshippers," namely, in this, that it would not only suffice for themselves [*quod non solum sibi sufficit*], but also, because of the plenitude of charity and grace, that it would enable them to assist others [*alios adiuvare*].[40]

Here, the rational creature "returns" to the Trinity through its participation in a hierarchy insofar as: (1) The hierarchy gifts the creature with the *ability* to be united to God through the gift of the similitude; (2) the rational creature is *actually* united to God through the sacred knowledge and activity of the hierarchy; (3) the rational creature is *immutably* united to God by beholding God's beauty through the hierarchy; and (4) the rational creature is made *fruitful* by being enabled to "assist others" in the hierarchy.

Any instance in which the Saint from Bagnoregio adds a "fourth" to his discussions of hierarchy should immediately warrant some pause on the part of his readers. Because his view of hierarchy is so intimately related to the Trinity, triadic patterns usually command his discussions of hierarchy, so that the inclusion of a "fourth" consideration more often than not indicates an important moment in his text. Indeed, this "fourth" consideration provides one key to understanding what Bonaventure means by the word "hierarchy" within his theology insofar as it underscores important data about how the moment of "return" (*regressum* or *redditus*) ought to be understood, both with respect to his teaching on hierarchy in a more general way, but also with respect to how he will employ these themes within his doctrine of grace.

Explaining why this is so requires returning to the previous definitions of "hierarchy" put forward by the Seraphic Doctor in Distinction 9.

40. *II Sent.* d. 9, prologue (2, 238).

First and foremost, a "hierarchy" for Bonaventure *means* the trinity and unity of God, referring most fundamentally to the perfect ordering of the three persons within the Godhead. Bonaventure's "second definition" of hierarchy, on the other hand, primarily describes the "procession" of all creatures from God, whereby rational creatures are ordered to the Trinity according to their very natures as rational creatures and can then be united to the Trinity through the gift of the similitude. Following these, *Definition 3* serves the purpose of indicating *how* the rational creature becomes "as like as possible to God" through this similitude by way of its participation in a hierarchy: The rational creature who participates in a hierarchy is "able" to be united to God, is "actually" united to God, is "immutably" united to God, and is reformed by what Bonaventure calls the "fruitfulness of plenitude" (*plenitudinis ubertatem*).[41] This "fruitfulness," as he further insists, is due to "the plenitude of charity and grace" which "enables" the rational creature within the hierarchy to "assist others" (*plenitudinem charitatis et gratiae, potens est alios adiuvare*). We should here note that the word "plenitude"—which the Seraphic Doctor repeats twice in this "fourth" consideration—is one of the Seraphic Doctor's favorite descriptions for God. For him, the Trinity is an overflowing-fountain of goodness, a "fullness" or plenitude that freely and lovingly pours itself outward in the act of creation. The opening sentences of the *Breviloquium* refer to this "plenitude of God," for example, from which the Seraphic Doctor then unfolds his entire compendium to the study of theology.[42]

41. I have chosen here and throughout the book to translate *"ubertas"* as "fruitfulness." The word *ubera* in Latin, of course, most commonly means "breasts"; curiously, the word also appears in Gallus's description of how the seraphic order overflows to fecundate the lower orders of the soul in his angelic anthropology; see Coolman, *Knowledge, Love, and Ecstasy*, 218. Coolman translates the word *ubertas* as "richness"; I have chosen "fruitfulness" because this coincides with Bonaventure's other descriptions of how the "return" should be characterized, and because this also connotes a certain vivacity. I cannot translate it as "breastfulness," in other words, but the word "fruitfulness" is nonetheless more redolent of the idea of life pouring forth from a mother's breasts to her child through her milk than "richness."

42. Bonaventure opens the *Breviloquium* by quoting Eph 3:14–19: "For this reason I bow my knees before the Father, from whom every family in heaven and on earth takes its name. I pray that, according to the riches of his glory, he may grant that you may be strengthened in your inner being with power through his Spirit, and that Christ may dwell in your hearts through faith, as you are being rooted and grounded in love. I pray that you may have the power to comprehend, with all the saints, what is the breadth and length and height and depth, and to know the love of Christ that surpasses knowledge, so that you may be filled with all the fullness of God [*plenitudinem Dei*]." See *Brev.* prolog. (5, 201). The phrase "fontal plenitude" is especially one of Bonaventure's favorite descriptors for the

His use of the word here in his summation of how a rational creature "returns" to God through its participation in a hierarchy highlights a central characteristic of his understanding of the *redditus* moment. To truly become as "like as possible to God," the rational creature must similarly become a *fruitful* creature whose goal is not merely a mystical union with the Trinity at the expense of other creatures, but a union with the Trinity that inundates the rational creature with a divine fullness through which she can be ordered to other creatures as well. Through hierarchy, in other words, rational creatures are ordered to God by also being ordered to one another. To reflect the *ordo* within God, rational creatures must "assist others" through the plenitude of grace and charity gifted to them by the divine similitude.

While this notion of assistance to "lower beings" within the hierarchies is certainly present in a nascent form in Dionysius's *CH* 3, it functions there in a somewhat mechanistic way. Rational creatures who receive divine illuminations from above assist others by shining light on those below them within the hierarchies, an "assistance" which behaves much like a pipe pumping water from a higher to a lower floor. So long as the creature participates in a hierarchy, it receives light and then passes it on, a movement that arguably takes place on a purely intellectual level in Dionysius's text. In what might be a revision to the Areopagite's account of this hierarchical assistance, Bonaventure's word choices for claiming that rational creatures are made capable of "assisting others" (*alios adiuvare*) hold some interesting connotations. For example, he uses "*adiuvare*" or a related form of the word exactly six times within the *Legenda maior*. Strikingly, each of these six instances is used with respect to miracles performed by the Poverello, all of which were acts of charity or works of mercy shown to suffering human persons.[43] Rather than being confined to the intellectual sphere

---

Father, who is the source of emanation for the other two persons within the immanent Trinity. His image of the Trinity as a plenitudinous, overflowing fountain, in other words, is derivative of his understanding of the Father's role within the intra-divine life of the Trinity.

43. In the first two instances of Bonaventure's use of the word, it is used in a negative sense to show how certain afflicted persons could not be helped by anyone or anything, until St. Francis comes along to heal the afflicted party. See *Leg. Maj.* 12.10 (8, 541): "Bononiae puer quidam unum ocolorum macula adeo habens obtectum ut nihil prorsus videre posset nec aliquo adiuvari remedio post signum crucis a capite usque ad pedes per servum domini sibi factum visum recuperavit tam limpidum ut postmodum ordinem fratrum minorum ingressus se longe clarius videre assereret de oculo prius infirmo quam de oculo semper sano"; and *Leg. Maj.*, miracula, §2.7 (8, 553): "Festinavit continuo pater ad filium et desperans obrutum non adiuvit sed eum sub onere sicut corruit sic reliquit." In *Leg. Maj.*,

or referring to a mechanistic motion of divine light from higher to lower beings, Bonaventure's own argument concerning the assistance of "higher" to "lower" beings within the hierarchies connotes intentional acts of charity that take place in the sensible rather than the intelligible realm. To "become as like as possible" to the Triune God through participation in the hierarchies means to assist other rational creatures through works of love and mercy, an interesting and noteworthy addendum to Dionysius's original text.

Simply put, the moment of "return" in Bonaventure's definition of hierarchy is not merely an "end point" within the "intelligible circle" of reality at which a rational creature arrives and simply stops moving. That the Seraphic Doctor would refer to the rational creature's "return" to God in other texts as both a *status* and *fructus* is indicative of this same idea: For him, to return to the Trinity through hierarchy is to be filled with a "fruitfulness of plenitude" (*plenitudinis ubertatem*) that in turn invites the rational creature to assist its neighbor through works of charity. It leads simultaneously to a *status* and a *fructus*, an end that is also fruitful, and thus also a "beginning" of sorts, the entrée into the creature's "remaining" in God. We likewise see here why the Seraphic Doctor had previously claimed that both *Definition 2* and *Definition 3* each refer to *egressus* and *regressus* simultaneously; within his definition of hierarchy, as soon as the procession begins, the return is initiated, and vice versa. These are not simply "points" on a circle but serve to describe the shape of hierarchy itself—all rational creatures who participate in a hierarchy are constantly always both processing and returning, and they never cease doing both.

---

miracula, §5.2 (8, 557), Bonaventure reports the story of a poor man who is oppressed and thrown in jail by a haughty knight, who assures the poor man that he will lock him away such that no one—not even St. Francis—will be able to help (*adiuvare*). St. Francis appears and breaks free the poor man from his shackles: "Nam cervicose respondens: tali te ait loco recludam et tali retrudam carcere quod nec Franciscus nec aliquis te poterit adiuvare." The remaining instances of Bonaventure's use of the word in the *Legenda maior* are all used by sufferers in the imperative, who cry out to St. Francis to help them in their affliction. See *Leg. maj.*, miracula, §3.3 (8, 554): "Absorbente autem profunda fovea corpus spiritus mentis sursum recurrebat ad beati Francisci suffragium clamans in ipso lapsu fideliter et fidenter: sancte Francisce adiuva me!"; *Leg. maj.*, miracula, §3.9 (8, 555): "Clamaverat autem Nicolaus praedictus cum primos ictus exciperet alta voce: sancte Francisce succurre mihi! Sancte Francisce adiuve me!"; and *Leg. maj.*, miracula, §10.6 (8, 564): "Positus itaque in angustia vehementi et auxilio desperatus humano coepit nocte quadam ac si praesentem cerneret beatum Franciscum talem coram eo assumere materiam querelandi: adiuva me sancte Francisce recolens meum servitium et devotionem tibi impensam."

The "three definitions" of hierarchy put forward by the Seraphic Doctor in the prologue to *II Sent.,* d. 9 collectively serve to describe how the created order of reality is related to the order within God. Most fundamentally, as he makes quite clear in *Definition 1,* a hierarchy means the unity and trinity of God and refers to the uncreated hierarchy, from which he says all rational creatures "process" and to which he says all rational creatures "return." *Definitions 2* and *3* pertain to this *egressum* and the *regressum,* respectively, though Bonaventure is careful to emphasize that neither of these movements should be regarded apart from the other. Rational creatures are related to God through "hierarchy" insofar as their participation in these movements leads them to become "as like as possible to God," or to become "deiform," when they will be filled with the "fruitfulness of plenitude" (*plenitudinis ubertatem*) that causes them to overflow with charity for others.

Bonaventure's Definition of Hierarchy in the *Hexaëmeron*

Frustratingly, Bonaventure's "three definitions" from the prologue to *Sent. II,* d. 9 fall within the context of his discussion of the Lombard's angelology. As such, these definitions technically apply only to the angelic or celestial hierarchy and not necessarily to the ecclesiastical hierarchy, a point he himself states at the conclusion of his discussion there.[44] A close examination of his definition of hierarchy put forward in one of his final works, the *Hexaëmeron,* however, will helpfully highlight the continuities between his earlier and later theology of hierarchy. Though my analysis of this definition will here jump two decades between the texts, this "jump" will substantiate my claim that there was indeed an inner harmony to his hierarchical thought across the course of his career as a theologian; I here highlight this definition in order to expose that inner harmony while also introducing another word within Bonaventure's lexicon for hierarchy and grace—namely, *"influentia."*

Instead of providing three separate definitions for hierarchy, as he did in his *II Sent.,* he limits his discussion of hierarchy in *Hex.* 21 to a single definition. "Hence, according to Dionysius, a hierarchy is defined as follows," he writes: "'A hierarchy is a sacred order, knowledge,

44. *II Sent.* d. 9, prologue (2, 238).

and activity assimilating as much as possible to deiformity, and ascending proportionally into a likeness of God toward the lights that have flowed into it from above.'"[45] Bonaventure's reduction of hierarchy to this definition might appear at first to drastically alter his previous discussion of the word from *II Sent.,* but his commentary on the Areopagite's definition begs for comparison between the two texts rather than contrast:

The order of power [*ordo potestatis*] corresponds to the Father, knowledge [*scientia*] to the Son, and activity [*operatio*] to the Holy Spirit. Whence, a hierarchy is called a power [*potentiam*], knowledge [*scientiam*], and activity [*actionem*]. For power without knowledge is sluggish, and knowledge without activity is fruitless [*infructuosa*]. And because it draws ever nearer to the eternal sun, it is necessary that it be a sacred order [*sacra ordinatio*]; and from this, it follows that it should be deiform [*deiformis*], because it forms it, or the creature, partly through nature [*partim per naturam*], partly through grace [*partim per gratiam*], partly through glory [*partim per gloriam*]: through an image [*imaginem*], through a similitude [*similitudinem*], through deiformity [*deiformitatem*]. And so it ascends to the lights placed inside it, ascending [*ascendens*] through an *influentiam*. But this *influentia* is not simply something uncreated [*quid increatum*]; nor does it follow that this *influentia* is of an *influentia* [*influentiae sit influentia*], because this *influentia* leads back into God [*reducit in Deum*]; for it means a continuous act [*continuationem*] with the First Principle and a reduction [*reductionem*] into it, not as some distant thing. Whence a true *influentia* is that which processes [*egreditur*] and returns [*regreditur*], just like the Son goes forth from the Father [*exivit a Patre*] and returns [*revertitur*] to him.[46]

Bonaventure's words here enjoy a striking continuity with the three definitions of hierarchy he put forward in his first major theological work. His affirmation that the "order," "state of understanding," and "activity" of a hierarchy refer to the three persons of the Trinity once again grounds his discussion of hierarchy within his argument that the Trinity itself is an uncreated hierarchy. The themes of image and likeness, procession and return, and grace also again feature prominently within his explanation of Dionysius's definition. Essentially, the definition of hierarchy Bonaventure provides in the *Hexaëmeron* represents an abridged summary of the same themes discussed at length in his first major work.

<hr>

45. *Hex.* 21.17 (5, 434).
46. *Hex.* 21.17–18 (5, 434).

Of especial significance in this respect is the Seraphic Doctor's repeated insistence here that a rational creature's participation in a hierarchy cannot be "fruitless" (*infructuosa*). Following his third definition of hierarchy from *II Sent.*, this insinuates that the "return"—the rational creature's reduction into the First Principle—once again cannot be conceived as some sort of static end, a point at which the rational creature arrives in God so as to simply stop moving. Bonaventure's association of the rational creature's reduction into the First Principle with the Son's procession and return from the Father is similarly noteworthy inasmuch as the Seraphic Doctor here underscores the eternal relationship between the Son and the Father within the intra-divine life. Within the immanent Trinity, the Son never stops processing from and returning to the Father; once again, the implication here is that these two activities do not cease.

Two notable additions in comparison to *II Sent.* still present themselves to the reader. First, when asserting that a hierarchy conforms a soul to God through nature and grace, which corresponds with his previous discussion of the image and similitude from the prologue to *II Sent.*, d. 9, the Seraphic Doctor adds that a hierarchy conforms a soul to God through glory, as well. As Antonio Mirabent has argued, "grace" and "glory" differ for Bonaventure only as a method of describing the difference between the state of the wayfarer *in via* and his enjoyment of heavenly glory. Otherwise, "grace" and "glory" do not differ at all in Bonaventure's theology.[47] He offers his definitions of hierarchy in *II Sent.* as an explanation of the Lombard's angelology, whereby the angelic experience of "glory" is already presumed. His addition of "glory" to nature and grace in the *Hexaëmeron* simply expands his definition of hierarchy to apply to wayfarers within the Church as well.

Second, and more importantly for my ensuing discussion of grace, the Seraphic Doctor adds the word "*influentia*," or "inflowing" to describe how a rational creature processes and returns to its source in God through the hierarchies in the *Hexaëmeron*. In his own discussion of Bonaventurean hierarchy, Hellmann underscores the importance of this word, arguing that it "is Bonaventure's term for indicating the far-reaching and all embracing presence of Christ," or "the share of God's inner life offered everyone in the person of Christ" which "has its origin

---

47. See Mirabent, *La gloria*; and Hellmann, *Divine and Created Order*, 124.

in the Trinity" and "descends first upon the celestial hierarchy ... and then finally upon the terrestrial hierarchy."[48] Jacques Guy Bougerol's extensive study of the word similarly argues that it has a Christological connotation in the theology of Bonaventure, who uses it to describe the mode of the Son's procession from the Father in *II Sent.* The Father's power inflows into the Son as an *influentia,* and then the two together spirate the person of the Holy Spirit. According to Bougerol, *influentia* is thus one of Bonaventure's words for describing how the Father and Son relate to one another in the uncreated hierarchy.[49] As evidenced in the *Hexaëmeron,* the word retains this Christological connotation in Bonaventure's definition of hierarchy: Just as the Son processes from the Father and returns to the Father through an *influentia,* so too do rational creatures process and return from the Triune God through Christ's *influentia* in the celestial and ecclesiastical hierarchies. The word "*influentia*" is part and parcel to Bonaventure's hierarchical vocabulary. By it, he describes how the uncreated hierarchy of the Trinity relates to the angelic and ecclesiastical hierarchies through the person of Christ, who is the *medium* between God and creation and through whom the power of God saturates the created hierarchies to unite them to the Trinity.

In addition to its Christological connotation, moreover, both Bougerol and Hellmann have also established an association between Bonaventure's notion of *influentia* and his metaphysics of light. As Bougerol details, the Seraphic Doctor's immediate Franciscan predecessors and peers at the University of Paris employed the term within their respective doctrines of grace. Alexander of Hales, for example, compared grace to the light of the sun: God, as the "sun of justice," is the source of grace.[50] John of La Rochelle, another of Bonaventure's predecessors in the Franciscan school, then adopted Alexander's analogy and carried it one step further, going so far as to claim that not only can grace be compared to light, but that grace can be called light. John of la Rochelle utilized the word, "*influentia,*" to express this idea, a term that was then also adapted by both Philip the Chancellor and Eudes Rigaud, among others.[51]

---

48. Hellmann, *Divine and Created Order,* 126.

49. See Bougerol, "Le rôle de l'*influentia* dans la théologie de la grâce chez Bonaventure," *Revue Théologique de Louvain* 5 (1974): 284, n. 45.

50. For this comparison, see especially my discussion of the effects of grace as "purification, illumination, and perfection" in the *Summa minorum* from Chapter 2.

51. Bougerol, "Le rôle de l'*influentia,*" 276–78.

Bonaventure would have been familiar with this vocabulary and will likewise employ it within his doctrine of grace. His use of it within his definition of hierarchy honors this interpretive tradition while also recalling the opening sentences of Dionysius's *CH*. The Areopagite there recalls Jas 1:17, "Every good and perfect gift is from above, coming down from the Father of Lights," in order to use the image of light as a metaphor for understanding how the hierarchies relate to "the Father of Lights." Bonaventure's use of the concept of *influentia* in *Hex.* 21 shows how the metaphysics of light in the Franciscan School of Theology was thereby wedded with medieval teachings on hierarchy. In the same way that the Areopagite understood the relationship of the hierarchies to God through light, the Seraphic Doctor regards the concept of *influentia* as descriptive of the Trinity's relationship to every hierarchy. This *influentia* is the ray of light that "processes" and "returns" from the Son so as to unite every hierarchy with God and one another. As Hellmann has already observed, "Bonaventure explains [the] interaction and communion between the hierarchies with concepts such as influence of light," so that "verbs such as *influere, illuminare,* and *hierarchizare* are used to indicate the communion that exists between the divine order of persons and that order found in the created celestial and terrestrial hierarchies."[52] Just as the sun's light illuminates everything that it touches—thus in some sense uniting it with itself—so, too, does the *influentia* of Christ shine down from the Godhead so as unite the uncreated hierarchy of God with every rational creature in the created hierarchies.

In this definition of hierarchy from the *Hexaëmeron*, therefore, Bonaventure uses the word to explain how the uncreated hierarchy of the Trinity, the celestial hierarchy, and the ecclesiastical hierarchy enjoy communion through the person of Christ. It is that which unites different orders of rational being, the ray of light that binds all creatures—whether angelic or human—to one another and to God, the Sun and source of all light. If, as this chapter argues, hierarchy is used by Bonaventure to describe how the created order of reality relates to the *ordo* within the Triune God, then the word *influentia* functions within his theology of hierarchy to indicate that by which the hierarchies are so ordered. It is the divine, Christological "inflowing" that both

---

52. Hellmann, *Divine and Created Order*, 124.

"processes" and "returns" from the uncreated hierarchy so as to engage the created hierarchies in relationships with God and one another. In the same way that the Son is always related to the Father in the uncreated hierarchy through an *influentia*, this *influentia* is the "continuous act with the First Principle" that is always both processing from and returning to the Trinity in order to relate the created *ordo* to the divine.

The Symbol of Jacob's Ladder

Taken together,[53] these definitions from Bonaventure's *II Sent.* and *Hex.* 21 introduce some of the most important vocabulary and themes that characterize the Seraphic Doctor's view of hierarchy, especially in comparison to the original definition of the word put forward by the Areopagite. While the medieval Franciscan certainly borrows mightily from the sixth-century mystic and philosopher, his own adaptation of the concept includes elements that would have been foreign to the Areopagite—most especially his suggestion that God is an uncreated hierarchy. For Bonaventure, "hierarchy" most fundamentally refers to the trinity and unity of God, or the *ordo* of relations within God. When applied to the created *ordo* of reality, the word is likewise used by the Seraphic Doctor as a description of how rational creatures relate to this divine *ordo*, as well as to other rational creatures by way of a continuous activity—an *influentia* that is at once egressive and regressive—which makes them "as like as possible to God."

I here conclude my presentation of the Seraphic Doctor's theology of hierarchy by examining its role in one of his sermons, namely, his first sermon on the subject, "*De sanctis angelis*," or *Sermo 54* from his *Sermones de diversis*.[54] As Jacques Guy Bougerol notes in his intro-

---

53. This section of the chapter has been revised from my article, "Bonaventure on Grace, Hierarchy, and the Symbol of Jacob's Ladder," in *Ordo et sanctitas: The Franciscan Spiritual Journey in Theology and Hagiography. Essays in Honor of J.A. Wayne Hellmann, OFM Conv.*, ed. Michael F. Cusato, Timothy J. Johnson, and Steven J. McMichael (Leiden: Brill, 2017), 207–28. Its revised version is reused with permission here; given the central significance of this symbol throughout this book, however, I am especially grateful to the editors for their invitation to contribute to Hellmann's festschrift. My work in this essay laid a cornerstone of sorts for my continued thinking about this symbol in Bonaventure's doctrine of grace in his other texts, which became foundational for the completion of this book.

54. Within Bougerol's edition of the *Sermones de diversis*, this sermon appears specifically within Bonaventure's collection of *Sermones de sanctis*. Choosing a succinct title for this sermon presents some difficulties since this was not the only sermon that Bonaventure preached on the subject of the angels. Bougerol's edition includes two sermons on this topic,

duction to the critical edition of this sermon collection, "It is impossible to separate the sermons from the whole of Bonaventure's works. There, more than anywhere else, one finds the perfect expression for anyone wanting at the same time to search for a hearing of the Word and an experience of the Spirit."[55] *Sermo 54*, in particular, serves as a helpful text through which to encounter his theology of hierarchy since he describes hierarchy using the symbol of Jacob's Ladder. Jacob's Ladder, as I will argue, "enfleshes" Bonaventure's "discursive speculations"[56] surrounding hierarchy as he defines it in both *II Sent.* and the *Hexaëmeron*. As such, it will also "enflesh" his "discursive speculations" surrounding grace. My examination of the symbol here serves the purpose of both bringing together the themes discussed in this chapter while also paving the final "foundation" for my remarks on grace in *Parts II–III*.

According to Bougerol, *Sermo 54* was delivered at vespers for the Feast of St. Michael on September 29, 1267, about ten years after he was elected Minister General.[57] The theme of the meeting of heaven and earth commands the text, in which Bonaventure uses the symbol of Jacob's Ladder to describe how the celestial hierarchy enjoys continuity with the ecclesiastical hierarchy through the *influentia* of Christ. The sermon opens with a protheme that indeed acknowledges the difficulty of the subject matter at hand: How can humanity know what is in the heavens, which are comprised of *spiritualia, intellectualia,* and the hierarchical orders, since human reason cannot comprehend these

which he presents as "Sermo I" *De sanctis angelis* and "Sermo V" *De sanctis angelis*, but which appear within his edition as *Sermo 54* and *Sermo 55*, respectively. *Sermo 54* ("Sermo 1" *De sanctis angelis*) was preached by the Seraphic Doctor on 29 September 1267. I will be following Bougerol's numeration for this sermon when referring to it throughout the remainder of this chapter. See Bonaventure, *Sermo 54*, in *Sermons de diversis*, vol. 2, ed. Jacques Guy Bougerol (Paris: Les Editions Franciscaines, 1993), 685–713, esp. 685 (hereafter, *SD 2*); and *Sermo 55*, in *SD 2*, 714. I am especially grateful for the editorial comments of Michael Cusato, passed on in a private exchange regarding my "Bonaventure on Grace, Hierarchy, and the Symbol of Jacob's Ladder," in *Ordo et sanctitas*, 207–28, to help clarify this problem. I will comment more extensively on Bonaventure's *Sermones de sanctis* collection as a whole in Chapter 8, where I will examine his theology of sanctity.

55. Bougerol, introduction to *Sermons de diversis*, by Bonaventure, vol. 1 (Paris: Les éditions Franciscaines, 1993), 44 (hereafter, *SD 1*): "Il est impossible de séparer les sermons de l'ensemble de l'oeuvre de Bonaventure. Là parfois, plus ailleurs, on découvre la parfaite expression d'une recherche qui se veut tout à la fois, ecoute de la Parole et expérience de l'Esprit."

56. See again my comments in this chapter's introduction; see also Hammond, "Appendix: Order in the *Itinerarium mentis in Deum*," 198.

57. *SD 2*, 685.

things? How can humanity thus "ascend to eternal and inaccessible light"? Bonaventure opens the sermon with a prayer invoking the Holy Spirit's assistance in leading his hearers to the wisdom by which they can understand such lofty matters.[58]

From the protheme, the sermon unfolds around an extended theological reflection in consideration of the symbol of Jacob's Ladder, taken from Gn 28:12: "And he dreamed that there was a ladder set up on the earth, the top of it reaching to heaven; and the angels of God were ascending and descending upon it." The Seraphic Doctor writes, "This *ladder*, part of which is in heaven and part on earth, signifies the ordering of the hierarchy, which is partly in angelic spirits and partly in humanity and holy souls."[59] From this claim, Bonaventure then continues his sermon by explaining the nine angelic orders from the *CH*. Like the Areopagite, he recognizes three heavenly hierarchies: the highest celestial hierarchy, which consists of the seraphim, cherubim, and thrones; the middle celestial hierarchy, which consists of the powers, virtues, and dominions, and the lowest, which consists of the principalities, archangels, and angels, and he claims "surrounds us and condescends to us."[60]

Notably, however, *Sermo 54* then definitively differs from the teaching of the Areopagite by proceeding to introduce three earthly hierarchies that appear nowhere in Dionysius's extant corpus. The first earthly hierarchy, writes Bonaventure, is the early or the primitive Church (*primitivae Ecclesia*), which consists of what he calls the "patriarchal, prophetic, and apostolic *mentes*"; the second earthly hierarchy is the "promoted" (*promota*) Church and consists of the Martyrs, Confessors, and Virgins; and finally, the third earthly hierarchy is the "enlarged" Church (*Ecclesia dilatata*), or the present-day Church that consists of what he calls the presiding order, the contemplative order, and the active order. According to Bonaventure, the Church itself can be called a "Jacob's Ladder," since it exists partly in heaven and partly on earth insofar as the Church triumphant is connected to the present-day Church.[61] An examination of how he holds that the earthly Church is connected to celestial hierarchy will serve the purpose of illuminating

58. *Sermo 54*, in *SD 2*, 686.

59. *Sermo 54*, in *SD 2*, 687: "Scala ista, cuius pars est in caelo et pars in terra, significat ordinationem hierarchiae, cuius pars est in angelicis spiritibus et pars in hominibus et animabus sanctis."

60. *Sermo 54*, in *SD 2*, 688.

61. *Sermo 54*, in *SD 2*, 688–89.

the meaning of his hierarchical metaphysics, as well as prepare us for encountering that theology within his doctrine of grace.

In attending to Bonaventure's treatment of the ecclesiastical hierarchy from *Hex.* 22 (which does *not* exactly replicate his description of it here in *Sermo 54*), Joseph Ratzinger has observed that the Seraphic Doctor's teaching on the ecclesiastical hierarchy differs from the Areopagite's insofar as the Franciscan's parsing of the concept is deeply tied to his theology of history.[62] While this is certainly true, Bonaventure's division of the ecclesiastical hierarchy into three separate categories here in *Sermo 54*—a trifold division that appears nowhere in the Areopagite's text—also serves another more fundamental purpose. The Seraphic Doctor's understanding of the created hierarchies is rooted within his claim that God is an uncreated hierarchy. His threefold division of the ecclesiastical hierarchy into the primitive Church, the "promoted" Church, and the present-day Church in *Sermo 54*—while certainly adding a historical flare to the Areopagite's text that should not be overlooked—further serves the purpose of again reflecting the threefold order within the uncreated hierarchy. Bougerol has noted that, for Bonaventure, "hierarchy is reality, or rather, reality is hierarchical."[63] If all of created reality is ordered to the intra-divine life of the Triune God, as Hellmann has already demonstrated, then the ordered relationship between the Father, Son, and Holy Spirit provides the exemplar for all creaturely order: All of reality *must* be hierarchical because God *in se* is a hierarchy of three persons. Bonaventure's vision of the cosmos unfolds around this conviction, so that his understanding of reality is comprised entirely of triads: (1) The uncreated hierarchy of the Triune God, which consists of the community of the Father, Son, and Holy Spirit; (2) the celestial hierarchy, which is divided into three subsets of three; and (3) the ecclesiastical hierarchy, or the Church, which Bonaventure also further divides into subsets of three.

Throughout the remainder of *Sermo 54*, the Seraphic Doctor then unfolds his vision of how the created hierarchies relate to the Triune God by employing the notion of *influentia*. The celestial hierarchy, as asserted in the beginning of the sermon, exists partly in heaven and

---

62. See *Hex.* 22 (5, 437–44), and Joseph Ratzinger, *The Theology of History in St. Bonaventure*, trans. Zachary Hayes (Chicago: Franciscan Herald Press, 1971), 47, for a useful charting of the ecclesiastical hierarchy as the Seraphic Doctor presents it in the *Hexaëmeron*.

63. Bougerol, *Saint Bonaventure*, 166: "Pour Bonaventure, la Hiérarchie est la réalité ou plutôt la Réalité est hiérarchique."

partly on earth within "holy souls," namely, souls within the present-day Church. In order to defend this claim, he suggests that the lowest angelic hierarchy inheres in the earthly hierarchy by holding the property of what he calls a freely-flowing and abundant *influentia* (*influentiae copiositate largifluum*).[64] Through this property (*proprietas*), Bonaventure writes, the lowest celestial hierarchy gifts a threefold bread (*triplicem panem*) to the ecclesiastical hierarchy—namely, "guiding bread [*pane manuductivo*], teaching bread [*pane eruditivo*], and supportive bread [*pane supportativo*]."[65] As he explains: "The first bread is that of the principalities, who have to guide us to eternal beatitude through example. The archangels feed us the teaching bread, which teaches hidden things [*arcana*] to us. But the angels feed us the supporting and comforting bread, which guards us in prosperity and against adversity."[66] Later in the sermon, Bonaventure describes how this property of the lowest heavenly hierarchy pertains to the "Church-enlarged," which rather holds the property of being: "watered by the rains of heaven [*caelesti irroratur pluvia*].... This happens when heavenly spirits inflow [*influit*] the gifts of the graces [*charismata gratiarum*] to the lower hierarchies with respect to the Church-enlarged [*Ecclesiam dilatatam*]."[67] According to Bonaventure, these graces that flow down from the lowest celestial hierarchy help the earth produce a threefold "*germinatio*," or fruit, which he identifies as three works through which the whole Church will be saved. These works comprise the activity of the three orders within the "enlarged" or present-day Church: First, the presiding order edifies the Church through example (*aedificationem exemplorum*); second, the contemplative order provides instruction (*exhibitionem documentorum*); and third, those within the active order serve as ministers of temporal things (*per subministrationem temporalium*) for the good of the Church.[68] The function of each order notably corresponds to the threefold bread that flows forth from the *influentia* of the principalities, archangels, and angels that Bonaventure highlighted earlier in the sermon.

Sermo 54 thus presents a short summary of the Seraphic Doctor's hierarchical conception of reality. There, the celestial and earthly

---

64. *Sermo 54*, in *SD* 2, 689 and 693.
65. *Sermo 54*, in *SD* 2, 694.
66. *Sermo 54*, in *SD* 2, 694.
67. *Sermo 54*, in *SD* 2, 699.
68. *Sermo 54*, in *SD* 2, 699.

hierarchies coinhere in one another through a freely-flowing *influentia*, the "fruit" of which is that the present-day Church enjoys a continuous relationship with the celestial hierarchies and the Church Triumphant. In Bonaventure's definitions of hierarchy from *II Sent.*, he had claimed that rational creatures who participate in the hierarchies enjoy a "fruitfulness of plenitude" (*plenitudinis ubertatem*) insofar as the hierarchies "enable them to assist others" through the fullness of charity and grace.[69] Likewise, in his definition of hierarchy in the *Hexaëmeron*, he clearly will also indicate that a hierarchy without activity is "fruitless" (*infructuosa*). Both texts, moreover, stress the simultaneity of the moments of *egressus* and *regressus*, the "procession" and "return" through which all rational creatures relate in an ordered way to the uncreated hierarchy, the Trinity. Here in *Sermo 54*, the inflowing of gifts from the celestial hierarchies into the ecclesiastical hierarchies is similarly described with language reminiscent of "fruitfulness," a *germinatio* through which the Church on the earth below may begin its own return—here, an "ascent"—to the heavenly realm. The Church's "ascent," however, in turn depends on a sort of procession or "descent" of the celestial hierarchies through an *influentia*, so that the hierarchies themselves function just like the ladder in Jacob's dream at Bethel, whereby the created hierarchies are constantly always both "ascending" and "descending," or returning and processing, to one another through an inflowing that unites them all.

Paralleling his discussion of hierarchy from *Hex.* 21, Bonaventure's sermon concludes by implying that these "ascending" and "descending" movements take their precedent in the event of the Incarnation, insofar as Christ's descent to the earth through the Incarnation invites the abundant inflowing of the angelic hierarchies into the present-day Church below, an event that then irrevocably unites the heavens and earth:

And the grace of the body [*gratia corporis*], the grace of the soul [*gratia animae*], and the grace of union [*gratia unionis*] was in Christ. This pact was between God and the earth, since Christ became incarnate, was kept safe, suffered, died, and was buried on the earth, and he was resurrected from the earth and ascended into heaven. And then, the heavens were opened so that we would henceforth be able to enter heaven.[70]

---

69. See again *II Sent.* d. 9, prologue (2, 462).
70. *Sermo 54*, in *SD* 2, 701.

The Seraphic Doctor's theology of hierarchy is a macrocosmic dance of heavenly and created being. For him, "reality is hierarchical," to recall Bougerol's observation, but only because Christ's bodily presence on the earth invites the indwelling of heaven on earth and of earth within heaven. The "fruit" of a rational creature's participation in a hierarchy, whereby she can "descend" to others through acts of charity and grace, is invited by this initial "descent" of Christ to the earth below.

In *La voie de la ressemblance: Itinéraire dans la pensée de saint Bonaventure*, Laure Solignac emphasizes the significance of the Seraphic Doctor's teachings on the Incarnation in this respect, especially when comparing his theology of hierarchy to that of the Areopagite. She highlights the following passage from his *III Sent.* to make this comparison:

For we should say without a doubt that it was fitting [*congruum*] that God would become incarnate; and that it was an eminent showing of his power [*potentiae*], wisdom [*sapientiae*], and goodness [*bonitatis*], which indeed was accomplished in his assumption of human nature [*humani generis assumtione*]. For it was fitting because it was an excellent consummation of the divine works, which was accomplished when the last was joined [*coniunctum*] to the first. For the consummation of perfection [*perfectionis consummatio*] is there, just like would appear in a circle [*circulo*], which is the most perfect of all shapes, since in a circle the same point ends where it began [*punctum terminatur a quo incepit*].[71]

In the flesh of the Incarnate Word, God's "power, wisdom, and goodness"—notably, three of Bonaventure's favorite appropriations for the three persons of the Trinity—are made manifest; or in other words, the uncreated hierarchy itself "descends" to meet the created *ordo* of reality in the event of the Incarnation. Importantly, Solignac argues that this passage is "the point of divergence between Dionysius and the Seraphic Doctor,"[72] because through it, Bonaventure explicitly claims that the Incarnate Word is the consummation of hierarchical perfection. The Incarnation, in other words, is the point at which the "intelligible circle" of created reality achieves the "return." As Solignac suggests, "This perfection does not reside only in the superior (Dionysius) but in the union of the superior with the inferior (Bonaventure),"[73] so that the Seraphic

---

71. *III Sent.* d. 1, a. 2, q. 1, resp. (3, 20).

72. Solignac, *La voie de la ressemblance*, 301: "Le point de divergence entre le Pseudo-Denys et le Docteur séraphique est particulièrement visible dans ce texte."

73. Solignac, *La voie de la ressemblance*, 301–2: "... c'est-à-dire dans la conjonction de

Doctor introduces what she calls a "hierarchical upheaval"[74] in his treatment of the hypostatic union.

What deserves further emphasis here are the ways in which the Incarnation is a "hierarchical upheaval" precisely inasmuch as the image of the "intelligible circle" offered by Bonaventure in both this passage and in his *Sermo 54* is not necessarily a perfect neoplatonic circle. The created *ordo* returns to the divine *ordo* not because it has itself "ascended" to the uncreated hierarchy, but rather because the divine *ordo* has "descended" through the Incarnation to meet the created *ordo*. The circle referenced by the Seraphic Doctor in the above passage from *III Sent.* locates the "point" where the created order of reality "ends where it began" in Christ. The Incarnation, however, is actually something quite new within the created *ordo* of reality—it is itself a "beginning." Were Bonaventure here describing an "intelligible circle" in a purely neoplatonic sense, the point where the created *ordo* "ends where it began" could only be located in the "union of the inferior with the superior," as Solignac has said, or in the intelligible realm. The Seraphic Doctor introduces a "hierarchical upheaval" precisely because he locates the point of "return" in the sensible rather than the intelligible realm: in the Incarnate Christ, "in the union of the superior with the inferior." As with Bonaventure's description of the "return" in his third definition of hierarchy from the prologue to *II Sent.*, d. 9, the point on the circle through which the "return" happens is at once an "end" and a "beginning." It is an "end" because through it, the created *ordo* meets the divine *ordo*, but it is a "beginning" insofar as this meeting takes place by way of a divine "descent" that inaugurates the "ascent" of the created *ordo*.

This, then, is where the image of Jacob's Ladder proffered by the Seraphic Doctor in *Sermo 54* becomes especially useful for "enfleshing" his "discursive speculations" surrounding hierarchy. In the previous chapter, alongside my examination of Dionysius, I also examined the angelic anthropology of the twelfth-century Victorine, Thomas Gallus, as an important source for understanding Bonaventure's doctrine of grace. In his own treatment of this angelic anthropology, as I there

---

premier avec le dernier 'que réside la consommation de la perfection.' La perfection ne réside donc pas tant dans le supériur (Denys) que dans l'union du supérieur avec l'inférieur (Bonaventure)."

74. Solignac, *La voie de la ressemblance*, 302: "bouleversement hiérarchique."

noted, Coolman underscores the fact that for Gallus, "the Dionysian conception of hierarchy in general" is best characterized by "a dynamic ascending-descending structure of inter-related entities that mediates revelation from higher to lower and elevates the lower into the higher," a structure that "can be analyzed in three crucial 'moments' or valences: ascending, descending, and, bringing these together, circling or spiraling."[75] For Gallus, the soul that reaches the seraphic order does not stop moving; rather, the seraphic order fecundates the eight lower orders of the soul, so that "the ascending and descending valences within the hierarchized soul ultimately generate a perpetual 'circulation' within it too."[76] Coolman observes the following point in his summary of this idea in Gallus's *Commentary on the Song of Songs*:

The bride [according to Gallus] says that she "will not cease to go after him—*I will seek his face always* (Ps. 104)—by rising up in unknowing in imitation of God to *circle around the city* (Sg. 3:2)." For *the city* is "the super-infinite fullness of the deity, around which [human and angelic minds] are said to circulate (*circuire*) … by contemplating the invisible divine things with the highest loving, yet not penetrating intimately the divine depths; therefore, [such minds] are said to circle God (*circuire Deum*) or to be *in the circle of God* (*Celestial Hierarchy* 7)." Fittingly, the Victorine compares this circulation to the angels descending and ascending a ladder in Jacob's vision: There is an "inflowing (*influitio*) of his light from the first order all the way to the last and a flowing back (*refluitio*) all the way back to the highest, according to that verse where Jacob saw the *angels ascending and descending* (Gn. 28:12)." In sum, for Gallus, "circular motions" (*motus circulares*) are the signature activity of angelized souls.[77]

These circular motions—this spiraling of angelized souls in Gallus's angelic anthropology, quite notably symbolized by the image of Jacob's Ladder in his commentary on the *Song*—are not quite the same as the neoplatonic image of the "intelligible circle." The angelized soul "circles or spirals" around God perpetually into eternity in a way that can be compared to the "circulation" of the three persons of the Trinity around one another within the intra-divine life.[78] As Coolman thus further

<hr>

75. Coolman, "Medieval Affective Dionysian Tradition," 622; and see his *Knowledge, Love, and Ecstasy*, 232–57, esp. 255–57.

76. Coolman, "Medieval Affective Dionysian Tradition," 622; see also *Knowledge, Love, and Ecstasy*, 255–57.

77. Coolman, "Medieval Affective Dionysian Tradition," 627.

78. Coolman, "Medieval Affective Dionysian Tradition," 627. The notion of spiraling, as it were, is especially apt to describe the hierarchical movements of rational creatures into

comments about this idea in Thomas Gallus's theology: "But this is not a simple circle, not a mere returning to the original point of departure, in order merely to set out on the same course once again ... there is no *static* resting in God, no absolute cessation of the soul's movements. In relation to the pleromatic Trinity, the *affectus* is always pursuing, stretching, expanding.... Never fulfilled, in the sense of filled full, it is always spiraling."[79] Like the angels that are always both "ascending" and "descending" on Jacob's Ladder, according to Gallus, the "hierarchical soul" is a *spiraling* soul precisely inasmuch as these "ascending" and "descending" movements never cease within it, but continue being fecundated by God into eternity: As soon as it ascends, it begins a new descent, and vice versa into perpetuity.

Bonaventure's own use of the symbol of Jacob's Ladder within *Sermo 54* explains his hierarchical metaphysics in this same way, except here extended to a macrocosmic scale—namely, by imaging this circling or spiraling movement of the uncreated, celestial, and ecclesiastical hierarchies with respect to one another. The celestial hierarchy "descends" to the earth below through a freely-flowing and abundant *influentia* of Christ, an abundance which—like the plenitude mentioned by the Seraphic Doctor in his third definition of hierarchy from *II Sent.*—is not self-serving, but rather pours out from the heavens and into those within the present-day Church. The Church is then invited to likewise "ascend," but not without also being called to then "descend" to others within the Church through providing edification, instruction, and serving as ministers of temporal goods.[80] These circular movements, likewise, follow those of the Incarnate Christ, who "descends" from the uncreated hierarchy to the earth below, thus inviting the "ascent" of the created hierarchies to God. Earlier in this chapter, I noted that the plenitude mentioned by Bonaventure within his fourth consideration of the third definition of hierarchy from *II Sent.* relates to his understanding of the Triune God as an overflowing fountain of Goodness. The uncreated hierarchy is a fullness that freely pours itself out in the act of creation. Bonaventure regards a created hierarchy as a means through which the rational creature can be ordered to God,

---

perpetuity. For Gallus, as Coolman notes, these movements never cease: See *Knowledge, Love, and Ecstasy*, 255–57.

79. Coolman, *Knowledge, Love, and Ecstasy*, 256.

80. See *Sermo 54*, in *SD* 2, 699.

especially insofar as the creature's participation in the hierarchy makes him or her "as like as possible to God." To become a divine similitude, the rational creature must similarly become plenitudinous, always "descending" to others whilst not forsaking his or her "ascent" to the Trinity. The symbol of Jacob's Ladder, as it were, provides a symbol through which Bonaventure's hearers in the thirteenth century—and also his readers today—can grasp what it means to thus become plenitudinous: To participate in the hierarchies, for the Seraphic Doctor, is to *spiral* between God and other creatures like the angels that are constantly both ascending and descending on Jacob's Ladder.

The symbol of Jacob's Ladder, as it were, likewise recontextualizes how scholars ought to perceive the "intelligible circle" of reality in Bonaventure's metaphysics in that once the participant has "returned" to the point from which she began her hierarchical procession—namely, the Trinity—she does not stop moving, but begins a new descent, and vice versa into eternity. In this way, the rational creature can remain in the Trinity. Following Gallus, for Bonaventure, to be made as "like as possible to God" through participation in a hierarchy is to be made capable of this perpetual spiraling between God and the rest of the created order of reality. The intelligible circle of reality—if it is to truly be made "as like as possible to God"—must break open into this spiral, so that the "fullness of plenitude" would shape the entire created order of reality into a Jacob's Ladder, a dynamic order of relationships that more closely resembles the Trinity inasmuch as it is never a "standing still." This is what it means to "return" to and then remain in God in Bonaventure's understanding of hierarchical *ordo*.

Conclusion

This chapter has examined the meaning of the word "hierarchy" within the Seraphic Doctor's theology, beginning with his initial presentation of the concept in *II Sent.*, d. 9, continuing with a quick look at its use in the *Hexaëmeron,* and, finally, concluding by examining how the symbol of Jacob's Ladder "enfleshes" his hierarchical speculations in *Sermo 54*. It bears repeating that the critique against hierarchy posed by feminist and liberation theologies in the present day is and must be affirmed as valid: Any social power structure in which "higher" beings oppress and suppress "lower" beings to maintain their own authority must be challenged for the sake of those who, throughout history, have suffered beneath the weight of such structures. In much the same way that Sarah Coakley has called for a reexamination of the meaning of the word "hierarchy" according to the Areopagite's original definition of the word,[81] however, Bonaventure likewise meant something quite different by the notion, as evidenced in all three texts examined here.

First and foremost, hierarchy in the Seraphic Doctor's approximation means the trinity and unity of God, and it refers to the *ordo* that characterizes the perfect communion between the three divine persons within the Trinity. Bonaventure's view of reality is subsequently "hierarchical" in the sense that the created order of reality must reflect this divine *ordo* within God. A rational creature's participation in the hierarchies will order her to the Trinity by making her "as like as possible" to it, a likeness or similitude that for Bonaventure is characterized by notions such as "plenitude" and "fruitfulness." To become "as like as possible to God" for the Seraphic Doctor is an enterprise that necessitates assisting others within the hierarchies as well, so that rational creatures who participate in the hierarchies can be said to circle constantly between the Triune God and the rest of the created order of reality like the angels on Jacob's Ladder. For Bonaventure, the cosmos radiates with relationships that reflect those between the three persons within the Trinity. To behold these hierarchies in the Seraphic Doctor's theology is to behold a macrocosm within which creatures are intimately related to one another and God through the *influentia* of Christ, the light that flows from the Trinity above so as to return all creatures to their divine source. To affirm along with Bougerol that "reality is hierarchical" in Bonaventure's thought is to affirm as well that reality is composed of a complex system of interrelated beings on heaven and earth who are united to one another by way of their perpetual procession from and return to God through this *influentia* that shines upon them all.

While my exposition of Bonaventure's notion of hierarchy has thus introduced us to his perception of the macrocosm, however, it is within his portrait of grace that we will come to appreciate how the microcosm of the human person finds herself situated within this understanding of reality as hierarchical. Just as an *influentia* flows throughout the created

81. Coakley, *God, Sexuality, and the Self*, 319.

order of reality in a way that unites it with God, so too does an *influentia* descend from the Trinity to uplift the human being into this cosmic dance. I turn now to introduce Bonaventure's doctrine of grace so as to underscore the relevance of that doctrine for his hierarchical understanding of reality as I have articulated it here: For the Seraphic Doctor, sanctifying grace is the *influentia* that makes the human soul "as like as possible to God," hierarchizing it for the purposes of relating it to God, neighbor, and the rest of creation. Through grace, the soul "returns" to and then "remains" in God by itself becoming a "Jacob's Ladder," a *spiraling* soul conformed to the Trinity through an inflowing of light from above. In the chapters that follow, we thereby turn from the foundations of Bonaventure's doctrine of grace to the doctrine itself.

Part II

Bonaventure's Doctrine of Grace

Introduction

I am certainly not the first scholar to recognize the indispensability
of Bonaventure's theology of hierarchy within his doctrine of grace.
Previous accounts of this association, however, tend to highlight it with
respect to other topics in the Seraphic Doctor's broader theology and
do not necessarily provide robust accounts of this association in its
own right.[1] As Zachary Hayes nonetheless wrote in his own seminal work on Bonaventure's soteriology, "The structure of hierarchical
thought may well shed light on the question of Bonaventure's theology
of redemption. The broader structures of his thought lend themselves
readily to the use of such a model, and the implications of the model
for soteriology were perceived with greater clarity with the passing of

---

1. For more on this previous scholarship, see especially Chapter 1. As I explained there,
other scholars have indeed noted this association; to my knowledge, however, the present
study is the first to explore this association at length. As I explained in Chapter 1, one of
the most comprehensive treatments of the topic is found in Longpré, "Bonaventure," in
Dictionnaire de spiritualité, col. 1768–1843. Likewise, Guardini's "Die Lehre von der Gnade,"
in *Systembildende Elemente,* 51–69, is a foundational study of Bonaventure's theology of
grace. Guardini's own examination of the subject focuses on the role of grace in the Seraphic
Doctor's theology of divine illumination and thus highlights his metaphysics of light as it
functions within his doctrine of grace. For a selection of other basic introductions to the
Seraphic Doctor's theology of grace, see also Bougerol, "Le rôle de l'*influentia,*" 274–300;
Cullen, "Grace," in *Bonaventure,* 153–64; San Martin Gonzales and José Miguel, "Gratia,"
in *Dizionario Bonaventuriano,* ed. Ernesto Caroli (Milano: Editrice Francescane, 2008),
438–49; Mirabent, *La gloria;* Berard Marthaler, *Original Justice and Sanctifying Grace in the
Writings of Saint Bonaventure* (Rome: Editrice Miscellanea Francescana, 1965); Franz Mitz-
ka, "Die Lehre des hl. Bonaventura von der Vorbereitung auf die heiligmachende Gnade,"
Zeitschrift für katholische Theologie, 50, no. 1 (1926): 27–72; 50, no. 2 (1926): 220–52; and Jean
Pierre Rézette, "Grace et similitude de Dieu chez saint Boaventure," *Ephemerides theologicae Lovanienses* 32 (1956): 46–64.

117

time."[2] The purpose of the next two chapters is to "shed light on the question of Bonaventure's theology of redemption" by providing a systematic account of how his theology of hierarchy explicitly informed his doctrine of grace throughout the course of his career. As Hayes further contends, even though "the element of hierarchy is most fully developed in [his] later writings, particularly in the *Hexaëmeron,* it is by no means peculiar to the late period of his life," so that hierarchy "is an explicit factor in the very earliest literary evidence of the Bonaventurian *corpus.* Evidence is found in virtually all his writings, whether they are early or late, and whether they are of an academic-speculative sort or of a spiritual-mystical nature."[3] The next two chapters will chronologically examine some of the Seraphic Doctor's most important treatments of grace in both sorts of texts in order to bring this evidence to light, beginning, in Chapter 4, with Bonaventure's initial definition of grace in his *II Sent.* as a created *influentia* and his treatise on grace in Part 5 of the *Breviloquium.* Next, Chapter 5 examines Bonaventure's notion of the hierarchical soul as he readapts and reworks it from Thomas Gallus in both the fourth chapter of the *Itinerarium* and in the twenty-second collation of the *Hexaëmeron.*[4]

This methodology of providing chronological textual analyses of key texts that treat grace within the Seraphic Doctor's corpus will be important for providing "proof," as it were, for Hayes's observation above: Although these two chapters affirm that "the element of hierarchy is most fully developed in his later works," they nonetheless also verify the "inner unity"[5] of Bonaventure's doctrine of grace across the course of his theological career. The following two chapters show how—even as early as *II Sent.*—the Seraphic Doctor's hierarchical vocabulary is his vocabulary for grace. Throughout his theological career, Bonaventure defines sanctifying grace as an *influentia* that hierarchizes

---

2. Hayes, *Hidden Center,* 158. See also Chapter 1.

3. Hayes, *Hidden Center,* 158.

4. Readers will here note that Bonaventure's *De don. Spir.,* in which the Seraphic Doctor treats the subject of grace in the prologue, is conspicuously absent in my treatment of grace here in *Part II.* I will treat this text explicitly in Chapter 7 when I turn to the subject of Christology and grace, since the prologue to *De don. Spir.* is focused on a consideration of how the *influentia* of sanctifying grace descends to humanity through the Incarnate, Crucified, and Inspired Word.

5. For more on the scholarly acceptance of the "inner unity" of Bonaventure's thought and accompanying bibliography for this notion, as well as my methodology in treating his doctrine of grace throughout his corpus in a way that respects this uniformity, see again Chapter 1. I borrow the phrase from Hellmann, *Divine and Created Order,* 2.

the soul so that it becomes a divine similitude; or, borrowing the Areopagite's phrasing from *CH*, he defines sanctifying grace as an *influentia* that makes the soul "as like as possible to God."[6]

Within this chronological sweep of Bonaventure's doctrine of grace, both chapters aim to paint a portrait of this similitude. If sanctifying grace hierarchizes the soul, it does so in order to shape the soul into a likeness of the uncreated hierarchy, the Trinity.[7] As Hellmann notes in his study of the concept of *ordo* in Bonaventure's theology, for the Seraphic Doctor: "All that exists comes forth from the ordered First and thereby reflects the divine order.... This means he perceives and interprets everything in light of the Trinity. Bonaventure's theology is Trinitarian because the Trinity is the perfect order, which is the ultimate 'light of understanding' (*lumen intelligendi*) of all things."[8] More recently, Boyd Taylor Coolman has aptly named this characteristic of the Seraphic Doctor's thought his "comprehensive Trinitarianism," whereby, "For Bonaventure, the Trinity is not simply one theological *loci* among others ... nor is it simply the most important in the series of *loci* to be considered subsequently and discretely. Rather, Trinity for him is the meaning of Christian theology, and everything else that he discusses is shaped and framed by it. Bonaventure theologizes trinitarianly...."[9]

Certainly, his doctrine of grace is not exempt from this broader trend. In the previous chapter, I argued that Bonaventure's theology of hierarchy can be symbolized by the scriptural image of Jacob's Ladder: Rational creatures that participate in a hierarchy become a similitude of the Trinity when they become "plenitudinous" and "fruitful," insofar as they are made capable of constantly both "ascending" to God and "descending" to their neighbors into perpetuity.[10] The following two chapters will similarly argue that the soul's *reductio* into the Trinity through sanctifying grace must be understood in this very way, even as it will show how the symbol of Jacob's Ladder is likewise used by the Seraphic Doctor within his doctrine of grace to depict the "shape" of

6. See Dionysius, *CH,* trans. Luibheid, 154; and my discussions of this notion, both in Chapter 2 (with respect to Dionysius's definition of hierarchy) and in Chapter 3 (with respect to Bonaventure's definitions of hierarchy).

7. For my discussion of the Trinity as uncreated hierarchy, see especially Chapter 3.

8. Hellmann, *Divine and Created Order,* 4.

9. Coolman, "Part II: On the Creation of the World," in *Bonaventure Revisited,* 142.

10. For my introduction of this idea, see Chapter 3.

the hierarchical soul that thus remains in God. In so doing, *Part II* elucidates how the *influentia* of sanctifying grace makes the soul "as like as possible" to the Trinity by likewise causing it to become somewhat like a Jacob's Ladder, inasmuch as it will show how, in Bonaventurean thought, sanctifying grace causes the soul to circle between contemplation and action, to constantly participate in hierarchical "ascensions" and "descensions" and never cease doing both.

One brief caveat bears emphasizing before I thus proceed, namely, both chapters will be primarily concerned with defining "sanctifying grace" (*gratia gratum faciens*) in Bonaventure's theology to the detriment of a more focused examination of his teachings on "preparatory" or "helping grace" (*gratia gratis data*).[11] As Alister McGrath has catalogued in his seminal work on the history of the Christian doctrine of justification, thirteenth-century theologians broadly understood "sanctifying grace" or *gratia gratum faciens* "as a supernatural habit within man, while *gratia gratis data* [helping grace] was understood as external divine assistance, whether direct or indirect," a classification that "took place by cataloguing the senses in which *gratia gratis data* could be understood."[12] Bonaventure himself, as McGrath further shows, seemed to broadly define "preparatory or helping grace" as "that of anything which prepares or disposes man toward the gift of *gratia gratum faciens.*"[13] My focus here in *Part II* will be on sanctifying grace because it is in Bonaventure's definition of *gratia gratum faciens*

11. I have chosen to follow Timothy J. Johnson's standard in translating *gratia gratis datum* as "preparatory or helping grace" instead of following what Alister McGrath has called the "widespread tendency" of translating it as "actual grace." Johnson chooses to translate the phrase in the former rather than the latter way "to avoid confusion between Bonaventure's understanding of the term and the more contemporary understanding of actual grace," because "The two should not be identified strictly with each other." See Johnson, *The Soul in Ascent*, 34n60, and his accompanying bibliography in support of this choice. See also McGrath, *Iustitia Dei*, 100; McGrath chooses to follow the widespread practice of translating this phrase as "actual grace"; he admits in the same breath that it "is probably better translated as *prevenient grace*, although even this is not totally satisfactory."

12. McGrath, *Iustitia Dei*, 103. One such catalogue, as McGrath notes, appears in the work of Albert the Great, who distinguished between eight different senses of the term. Bonaventure's own list of distinctions between "helping graces" can be found in *II Sent.* d. 28, a. 2, q. 3 (2, 689), which, as McGrath further notes, differs slightly from Albert's.

13. See McGrath, *Iustitia Dei*, 103. McGrath cites Bonaventure's *II Sent.* d. 28, a. 2, q. 1 (2, 682) as evidence: "Vocatur hic gratia gratis data, quidquid illud sit, quod superadditum est naturalibus, adiuvans aliquo modo et praeparans voluntatem ad habitum vel usum gratiae, sive illud gratis datum sit habitus, sicut timor servilis, vel pietas aliquorum visceribus inserta ab infantia, sive sit etiam aliquis actus, sicut aliqua vocatio vel locutio, qua Deus excitat animam hominis, ut se requirat."

that we will clearly be able to see the association between his theology of hierarchy and his doctrine of grace. For the Seraphic Doctor, it is sanctifying grace that hierarchizes the soul, transforming it into a similitude of the Trinity. I thus turn to unfold what this means in *The Commentary on the Sentences*, the *Breviloquium*, the *Itinerarium*, and the *Hexaëmeron*.

CHAPTER 4

The *Influentia* of Sanctifying Grace in *The Commentary on the Sentences* and the *Breviloquium*

The purpose of this chapter is to introduce Bonaventure's doctrine of grace by examining it in his *Commentary on the Sentences* and in Part 5 of the *Breviloquium*. These two texts are here treated together as suitable sources for my introduction to his theology of grace for four reasons, the first of which is chronological. As a student of theology at the University of Paris beginning in 1245, Bonaventure read the *Sentences* of Peter Lombard under the direction of his teacher, Alexander of Hales. During this time, he followed a program of reading, disputation, and preaching and wrote his *dubia* on the Lombard's *Sentences*.[1] In 1248, he began composition of his *Commentary on the Sentences*, which he completed before he accepted the Franciscan Chair of Theology at the University of Paris in 1253. The massive work represents Bonaventure's

---

1. Bougerol, *Introduction to the Works of Bonaventure*, 100–101: "From 1245 on, Bonaventure worked as a *determinans* under the direction of a master: reading, disputation, preaching, such was the program he followed. Thus, for four years he 'read' the *Sentences* of Peter Lombard. From this period, we have the *Dubia circa litteram magistri*, published by the Quaracchi editors, but from a different manuscript than those in which they found the text of the *Commentaries*. These *dubia* were composed when the future master read the works of the Lombard *cursorie*. It is only in the year 1248 that Bonaventure begins the *Commentaries* proper, being then an informed Bachelor of the Sentences."

"first theological synthesis"[2]: In the same way his definitions of hierarchy from his *Sentences* commentary pave a foundation for his theology of hierarchy in subsequent texts,[3] his presentation of grace in *The Commentary on the Sentences* will likewise frame his teachings on grace as he will rework them throughout his career, both in his academic texts but also in his spiritual treatises and sermons. Bonaventure would write the *Breviloquium* some years later, sometime between 1256 and the early 1260s,[4] as a short compendium to the study of theology which would help train his brothers throughout the Franciscan Order for their vocations as mendicant preachers.[5] Though his treatment of grace in the latter text will be far shorter and less expansive than that of the former, my choice to treat them side by side here will nonetheless show how the latter nonetheless built upon and carried forward the project of the former in important ways as the Seraphic Doctor transitioned from his scholarly role in the University into his pastoral role as Minister General of the Franciscan Order in 1257.

Second, and more importantly, I have chosen to treat these two texts together because—in spite of showcasing some notable developments within his doctrine of grace between his composition of the *Sentences* commentary and the *Breviloquium*—the latter text nonetheless depends upon the former in every respect. As Bougerol astutely once observed, "the *Commentaries* of Bonaventure represent his first theological synthesis. Much later … he was to compose his own *summa*, the *Breviloquium*; but this work would suppose, on every page, the developments and discussions that had appeared in the *Commentaries*."[6] This chapter demonstrates Bougerol's claim to this effect with specific attention to Bonaventure's doctrine of grace: Thematically, these two texts walk hand in hand as his arguments surrounding grace unfold from his *Commentary on the Sentences* into the *Breviloquium*. Taken together, the Seraphic Doctor's treatment of grace in both texts represents his most systematic treatment of the subject in any of his known

2. Bougerol, *Introduction to the Works of Bonaventure*, 99.

3. See Chapter 3.

4. The *Breviloquium* is most commonly dated to 1256/57. Recently, Jay Hammond has argued for a later dating in the 1260s; see Jay M. Hammond, "The Textual Context," in *Bonaventure Revisited*, 29–72.

5. See again Hammond, "The Textual Context," 29–72.

6. Bougerol, *Introduction to the Works of Bonaventure*, 99.

works. To understand what he means by "grace" in any of his writings, we must first begin by unpacking his explanations of the subject, here.

Third, whereas my examination of Bonaventure's doctrine of grace in Chapter 5 will largely consider his revision of Thomas Gallus's angelic anthropology, this chapter's examination of grace in *The Commentary on the Sentences* and the *Breviloquium* looks more toward the Seraphic Doctor's dependence on the Halensian understanding of sanctifying grace. In much the same way that the *Breviloquium*'s treatment of grace will "suppose, on every page, the developments and discussions that had appeared in the *Commentaries*," Bonaventure's treatment of grace in the *Commentaries* will "suppose, on every page, the developments and discussions" of Alexander of Hales and the Halensian school of theology at the thirteenth-century University of Paris. Following Alexander and against the Lombard, Bonaventure will define sanctifying grace as a created gift in both his *Sentences* commentary and the *Breviloquium*, a definition which is not explicit in either the *Itinerarium* or the *Hexaëmeron* but which will nonetheless be presumed when we consider both texts in Chapter 5.

Fourth and finally, and building from these previous observations, Bonaventure's definitions and explanations of grace in these two texts will provide the theoretical foundation from which we can encounter his doctrine of grace throughout his other writings. If, as Hayes has argued, the element of hierarchy "is an explicit factor in the very earliest literary evidence of the Bonaventurian *corpus*," so that evidence for hierarchy within the Seraphic Doctor's soteriology "is found in virtually all his writings, whether they are early or late, and whether they are of an academic-speculative sort or of a spiritual-mystical nature,"[7] then we should indeed expect to find such evidence in these texts inasmuch they represent his most significant theological treatments of grace as a subject in its own right. Thematically, the texts are tied together and walk hand in hand because they both define sanctifying grace as a created *influentia*, or an "inflowing." This word, as I argued in Chapter 3, is part and parcel to the Seraphic Doctor's theology of hierarchy. My task in this chapter, as it were, is to show how Bonaventure's definition of grace as an *influentia* in *The Commentary on the Sentences* and the *Breviloquium* will pave the way forward for his later more explicit

7. Hayes, *Hidden Center*, 158.

assertion that this *influentia* hierarchizes the soul. The element of hierarchy is less explicit in his commentary on the *Sentences* but, as I will argue below, hierarchy is the key to the interpretation of Bonaventure's treatment of grace in *Brev.* 5, which will "suppose, on every page, the developments and discussions of the *Commentaries*." My exposition here will be important for showing how the association between hierarchy and grace is rooted within and grows out of his definition of grace as an *influentia* in *The Commentary on the Sentences*. From the very beginning of his career as a young student, in other words, Bonaventure's vocabulary for hierarchy is his vocabulary for grace. It is by employing this vocabulary, even in his early texts, that the Seraphic Doctor will describe how the soul itself can enjoy its own *reductio* into God and, thereby, become a similitude of the Trinity.

Sanctifying Grace in *The Commentary on the Sentences*

We begin, then, with *The Commentary on the Sentences*, where we encounter the Seraphic Doctor's most expansive treatment of the topic of grace within any of his known works in *II Sent.*, Distinctions 26–27. While certainly not the *only* places where the subject of grace is treated within Bonaventure's *Sentences* commentary,[8] these are nonetheless some of the most important texts for approaching the subject insofar as, in them, he actually defines sanctifying grace as an *influentia*, a created gift within the soul that unites it to the Trinity. The Seraphic Doctor will uphold this definition of sanctifying grace throughout his later writings, so it is crucial here to arrive at a clear understanding of what he means by it.

Though it is the lengthiest treatment of grace in any of his known works, the element of hierarchy as it is associated with his doctrine of grace is less developed here than in any of his other works. As his earliest treatment of the subject, it is also, in some ways, the least mature.

---

8. For example, *I Sent.* d. 14–18 is also a useful place to encounter his doctrine of grace, insofar as these distinctions respond to the Lombard's treatment of grace within the context of his pneumatology. I will treat these distinctions accordingly below, but my focus throughout this section of the chapter will rather be on *II Sent.* d. 26–27 for the reasons outlined above—namely, these present Bonaventure's clearest definition and explanation of sanctifying grace.

Glaringly absent in these distinctions, for example, is an explicit claim that grace hierarchizes the soul or that grace causes the three hierarchical activities of "purification, illumination, and perfection" within it,[9] themes that feature prominently in the *Breviloquium,* the *Itinerarium,* and the *Hexaëmeron.* Notably, moreover, the word "*influentia*" as it was often employed by medieval philosophers and theologians does not always necessarily walk hand in hand with Dionysian hierarchy; the word has neoplatonic roots and was often used in medieval accounts of causality, especially with respect to explaining how a higher cause can act within a lower or secondary cause, a tradition that certainly bears upon the Seraphic Doctor's use of it within his own doctrine of grace, as will be treated below.[10]

Accordingly, my examination of Distinctions 26–27 in *II Sent.* simply aims to underscore the correspondence between the meaning of the word within Bonaventure's definition of sanctifying grace, on one hand, and within his theology of hierarchy, on the other. With respect to the latter, as we saw in Chapter 3, in the words of Hellmann, *influentia* "is Bonaventure's term for indicating the far-reaching and all embracing presence of Christ" that unites the created hierarchies to the uncreated hierarchy of the Trinity, and must be understood as a "continuous act" that ceaselessly processes and returns from the Trinity in order to unite rational creatures to God and one another.[11] On the other hand, Jacques Guy Bougerol argues that, within the specific context of the Seraphic Doctor's doctrine of grace, "This *influentia* is the dynamism of God which, modulated to the measure of the man, communicates the resuscitated life of Jesus Christ in a continuous way to those who believe in his name and receive baptism from salvation

---

9. Bonaventure speaks of purification, illumination, and perfection at various points throughout his discussion of grace in these distinctions, but these three activities never appear together as the neat triad that we would perhaps expect, especially given that he will use this triad in the *Breviloquium* and the *Itinerarium.*

10. For an account of how the word *influentia* was used in neoplatonic and medieval accounts of causality as such, see Jacob Schmutz, "The Medieval Doctrine of Causality and the Theology of Pure Nature (13th to 17th Centuries)," in *Surnaturel: A Controversy at the Heart of Twentieth-Century Thomistic Thought,* ed. Serge-Thomas Bonino, trans. Matthew Levering (Ave Maria, FL: Sapientia Press, 2009), 203–50. Schmutz will accuse Bonaventure of *not* adhering to this tradition and changing it, an accusation which I will address in greater detail below, and again in Chapter 6.

11. See Chapter 3, and Hellmann, *Divine and Created Order,* 126. For Bonaventure's definition of an *influentia* as a "continuous act" that processes and returns, see esp. *Hex.* 21.17–18 (5, 434).

in his Church. Their being-for-God is repaired [through it], they have been recreated into a living participation in the divine nature."[12] My examination of Bonaventure's use of this word in *II Sent.* will show how, within the soul, the *influentia* of sanctifying grace is the "continuous act" that constantly both processes and returns from the Trinity so as to unite the soul to God. Though "less developed" than in the *Breviloquium, Itinerarium,* and *Hexaëmeron* with respect to his theology of hierarchy, his definition and explanation of sanctifying grace as an *influentia* in Distinctions 26–27 nonetheless invites our approach of a more explicit association between hierarchy and grace as it will emerge in his later writings.

My examination of these distinctions will proceed in four parts. I approach Bonaventure's definition of sanctifying grace as an *influentia* in *The Commentary on the Sentences* by first offering a brief word on why he thinks this *influentia* is needed—namely, by introducing his understanding of sin as a defect of the will.[13] I then explore his definition of this *influentia* by dwelling especially on an analysis of *II Sent.,* d. 26, where he follows Alexander of Hales in claiming that grace is a created gift in the soul.[14] Next, we move from this initial definition to formulate an understanding of how this created gift—this *influentia*—functions in the soul. More to the point, my analysis of Bonaventure's definition of grace from his *Sentences* commentary first explores why this *influentia* is needed; secondly, it examines what it is; and thirdly, it explains how it works. Fourth and finally, I provide a general conclusion to Bonaventure's treatment of grace in *The Commentary on the Sentences* that will prepare us to encounter that doctrine in *Brev.* 5.

Why Grace Is Needed: Sin and the Will

Other than *II Sent.,* one of the earliest texts in which the Seraphic Doctor refers to sanctifying grace as an *influentia* is in his *Commentary on the Gospel of John.*[15] In Jn 17:12, Jesus prays for his disciples: "While I was with them, I protected them in your name that you have given me. I guarded them, and not one of them was lost except the one destined

---

12. Bougerol, "Le rôle de l'*influentia*," 299.

13. I will attend to sin in much greater detail in Chapter 6.

14. For my examination of this idea in Halensian theology, see again Chapter 2.

15. See Bougerol's catalogue of Bonaventure's use of this word within his doctrine of grace in "Le rôle de l'*influentia*," 283.

to be lost, so that scripture might be fulfilled." Bonaventure responds to this by writing:

Question 3. Here, we ask about the Lord's petition that keeps his disciples *from evil.* —It seems that he asks this inordinately: 1. Because they were in a state of charity [*caritate*]; but from whatever grace or charity [*gratia vel caritate*] someone has, he can resist any kind of temptation, therefore, etc. 2. And again, no one is able to fall from that grace except through mortal sin [*peccatum mortale*]; but no one can sin unless he wills to sin [*non potest peccare nisi volens*]. Therefore, it is in the freedom of our will [*libertate nostrae voluntatis*] that we are preserved [*conservetur*] in whatever we do; thus, the Lord's petition is superfluous. Let us respond by affirming that, as Augustine said, *to remain* in the good that has been received [*permanere in bono accepto*] happens through the *divine gift* [*divini muneris*] and *our solicitude* [*nostrae sollicitudinis*]. For grace [*gratia*] is preserved [*conservatur*] in us through a continuous inflowing [*continuam influentiam*], and so it is asked by the Lord that it would continuously aid us [*continue adiuvet*]. Whence, if we can fall by our will alone, unless the divine aid intervenes [*inverveniat*], we cannot remain [*permanere*].[16]

Dated tentatively to around 1256,[17] the Seraphic Doctor would have written this *quaestio* and *responseo* about Jn 17:12 shortly after his composition of *The Commentary on the Sentences* and shortly before or simultaneous with his composition of the *Breviloquium,* and indeed, examining his use of the word *influentia* here will shine light on important characteristics of his definition of sanctifying grace as we approach it in the *Sentences.* Most fundamentally, it opens for us a window into the Seraphic Doctor's understanding of sin, which—following Augustine—he defines here and elsewhere as a defect of the will.[18]

According to Bonaventure in the *Breviloquium,* for example, human

---

16. *Comm. Jn.* 17.34 (6, 474).

17. For this dating, see Robert J. Karris, "Introduction," in *Commentary on the Gospel of John,* trans. Karris, Works of St. Bonaventure 11 (St. Bonaventure, NY: Franciscan Institute, 2007), 21.

18. See espcially *Brev.* 3.1 (5, 231): "De qua in summa tenendum est, quod peccatum non est *essentia* aliqua, sed *defecta et corruptela,* qua scilicet corrumpitur *modus, species, et ordo* in voluntate creata; ac per hoc corruptio peccati est ipsi bono *contraria,* nec tamen habet *esse* nisi in bono nec *ortum* trahit nisi a bono, quod quidem est liberum voluntatis arbitrium." I will address Bonaventure's concept of sin and how it taints human nature with respect to the will in greater detail in Chapter 6. For other more extensive treatments of the Seraphic Doctor's teachings on sin, see especially Maurits de Wachter, *Le péché actuel selon Saint Bonaventure* (Paris: Éditions Franciscaines, 1967); Timothy J. Johnson, "Part III: On the Corruption of Sin," 169–93.

persons were created "upright" because they were gifted with a twofold grace in the Garden of Eden:

helping grace [*gratia gratis data*], which was a knowledge illuminating the intellect [*scientia illuminans intellectum*] so that they might know [*cognoscendum*] themselves, their God, and their world, which was created for them; and sanctifying grace [*gratia gratum faciens*], which was a charity enabling their affections [*caritas habilitans affectum*] so that they would love [*diligendum*] God above all things and their neighbors as themselves.[19]

Sin is, then, defined by Bonaventure as a disorder of the will, whereby the first parents of the human race freely chose to love a tangible good instead of loving God above all things. This disordered desire led to the loss of sanctifying grace, which human beings now require if their affections are to be once again made "upright" in the way God created them to be.

This context is important for approaching Bonaventure's teachings on grace in *The Commentary on the Sentences* because it helps explain why he thinks grace is needed in the first place, even as it contextualizes how he will thus describe the effects of sanctifying grace within the soul. Sin is a matter of the will in his theology: Grace must also be understood as a "divine intervention" that works within the will to help set it "upright" so that humanity can once again "love God above all things and its neighbor as itself." And indeed, Bonaventure's definition of sanctifying grace as an *influentia* in *The Commentary on the Sentences* cannot be read apart from this Augustinian understanding of sin as a matter of human volition; by defining grace as an *influentia*, he can specifically explain how this divine intervention within the will takes place.

What Grace Is: A Created *Influentia*

As such, understanding what this *influentia* is—a definition Bonaventure will articulate most clearly in *II Sent.*, d. 26—requires first recalling the scholastic context that produced this definition at the thirteenth-century University of Paris. The Seraphic Doctor's first use of the word *influentia* with respect to grace in his *Sentences* commentary actually

---

19. *Brev.* 2.11 (5, 229–30). Again, I will address Bonaventure's views of pre- and post-lapsarian human nature and the role of grace therein in greater detail in Chapter 6. For more on this particular passage, see also Coolman, "Part II: On the Creation of the World," 157–67.

appears in *I Sent.*, d. 14, there offered as an explanation for how the Holy Spirit processes into the human soul as an "uncreated gift". Following Augustine, as we saw in Chapter 2, Peter Lombard had argued that sanctifying grace is the Holy Spirit, the uncreated gift of charity that forgives sins.[20] Scholastic theologians began rejecting the Lombard's position in this regard because they "wanted more precise distinctions and a clear language of causality in order to explain the interaction between divine and human nature."[21] This scholastic "insistence on logical precision," introduced first by Simon of Tournai in the late twelfth century, "made it unacceptable to deal with the divine presence in humanity along the lines of Peter Lombard."[22] Instead of claiming that grace is the Holy Spirit, Bonaventure's teacher at the University of Paris, Alexander of Hales, followed the precedent set by Simon of Tournai and distinguished between created and uncreated grace. The Seraphic Doctor adhered to the teachings of his master in this respect, asserting against the Lombard that "in all these things he spoke truth, neither did he err, but he was deficient [*defecit*]: because besides this, there is posited a charity [*caritatem*] which is a created habit informing the soul [*habitus creatus animam informans*], in accordance with common opinion [*communem opinionem*]."[23]

As Bonaventure thus argues in *I Sent.*, d. 14, the "uncreated gift" of the Holy Spirit is still given to the soul within this created habit. Bonaventure explains this idea by noting that the Spirit can process "from one into another" (*ab uno in alium*) in two different ways: "either as if into an object [*in obiectum*] into which it is extended [*protenditur*],

---

20. See again also Rydstrøm-Poulsen, *Gracious God*, for a discussion of Lombard's position and a detailed account of this position's rejection, beginning with Simon of Tournai. As detailed in Chapter 2, Poulsen argues that Lombard's position was not new but was rather "firmly rooted in the Augustinian tradition" (483). For more on this, see also J. Patout Burns, "Grace," in *Augustine through the Ages: an Encyclopedia*, ed. Allan D. Fitzgerald, OSA (Grand Rapids: William B. Eerdmans, 1999), 392, who writes that within Augustine's "… Christianized Politinian schema, 'grace' must be conceptualized not as a created disposition or accident but rather as the operation and dwelling of the divine being within the created spirit. Thus Augustine refused to distinguish the divine reality of the Word from the Light shining, dimly or brightly, above and into the angelic or human mind, through which it understands facts and events as instances of foundational principles." See also Peter Lombard, *The Sentences, Book 1: The Mystery of the Trinity*, trans. Giulio Silano (Toronto: The Pontifical Institute for Mediaeval Studies, 2007), d. 14, 73–77; and d. 17, 88–97 (hereafter, *Sent.* 1).

21. Rydstrøm-Poulsen, *Gracious God*, 484.

22. Rydstrøm-Poulsen, *Gracious God*, 484.

23. *I Sent.* d. 17, p. 1, a. 1, q. 1, concl. (1, 294).

or as if into something susceptive [*in susceptivum*] in which it is received [*recipitur*]."[24] The first type of procession refers to the eternal procession of the Spirit whereby the Spirit is said to proceed from the mutual love of the Father and the Son within the intra-divine relationship.[25] The second way, however, refers to the Holy Spirit's temporal procession. According to Bonaventure, this occurs "when the reception of the Holy Spirit is through an inflowing of gratuitous gifts [*influentiam boni gratuiti*]," so that "the Holy Spirit is said to proceed from someone into someone else, not only as if into an object [*in obiectum*], but as if into a home [*sicut in habitaculum*]."[26] We will turn momentarily to examine Bonaventure's definition of the created gift itself as an *influentia* in *II Sent.*, d. 26, but it is necessary to first pause for two observations regarding his first use of the word with respect to grace in *I Sent.*, d. 14.

First, the language of "susceptivity" and "receptivity" is significant. The one in whom the Holy Spirit processes "through an *influentia* of gratuitous gifts" is not only an "object," but a "home," understood as someone who is "susceptive" to this *influentia*. The Seraphic Doctor will later write in *II Sent.* that "there are four elements in the work of salvation: namely, to invite, to assent, to assist, and to persevere: The first belongs to God's inspiration, the second belongs to free will, the third belongs to a divine gift, and the fourth belongs to our solicitude as well as to divine assistance."[27] The notion of "preparatory" or "helping" grace is crucial for understanding the first element, insofar as it is only through God's mercy that the human will, which has been deformed through sin, is urged to pray for the grace that will once again make it "upright." As Johnson comments of this notion, "Preparatory grace includes any number of interior or exterior ways God chooses to invite the soul to conversion. Thus, natural habits, instilled virtues and interior illumination assist the will in responding in an affirmative manner to the divine invitation."[28] Urged toward God by helping grace,

---

24. *I Sent.* d. 14, a. 1, q. 1, concl. (1, 245).

25. *I Sent.* d. 14, a. 1, q. 1, concl. (1, 245): "et primus quidem modus est processione aeterna: quia enim Spiritus sanctus procedit ut amor mutuus, ideo procedit a duobus, ita quod ab uno in alium."

26. *I Sent.* d. 14, a. 1, q. 1, concl. (1, 245).

27. *II Sent.* d. 28, a. 2, q. 1, concl. ad 1 (2, 683); translation used here is that by Johnson, *The Soul in Ascent*, 44.

28. Johnson, *The Soul in Ascent*, 44.

however, the soul will only be made "upright" through the second element Bonaventure identifies in the work of salvation—namely, through the free consent of the will. The Seraphic Doctor, following Augustine, claims, in the *Breviloquium*, that "the one who created you without you, will not justify you without you."[29] In other words, sanctifying grace will only be received by the person who willingly consents to being "susceptive" to it. Bonaventure's explanation of how the uncreated gift of the Spirit "processes" temporally into a "home" within the soul in *I Sent.*, d. 14 implicitly affirms this very idea.[30]

Second, and more importantly for our present purposes, is the Seraphic Doctor's explanation of the *influentia* as that through which the uncreated gift of grace is given. Notably, this *influentia* is not God, but it is the means through which God—the Holy Spirit, the uncreated gift of grace—dwells in the soul that consents to receive it. Bonaventure will subsequently explain this relationship between the "created habit" (the *influentia*) and the "uncreated gift" in detail in *II Sent.*, d. 26–27.

To do so, he opens d. 26 by claiming that grace must be a divine gift that "places something into the one who has been graced."[31] Notably, this largely follows the method of argumentation surrounding the created gift of grace in the *Summa minorum*.[32] Such a gift cannot impart any change in the divine being itself because the divine essence cannot be changed in any way in the act of gifting grace.[33] It therefore follows that "some change happens on the part of the one *receiving* and the one being approved" by grace.[34] In Question 2, Bonaventure

29. See *Brev.* 5.3 (5, 255): "Verum est igitur quod dicit Augustinus, quod 'qui creavit te sine te non iustificabit te sine te,'" quoting Augustine, *Serm. 169*, 11.13 (*PL* 38: 923), trans. Edmund Hill, Works of St. Augustine 3/5 (New Rochelle, NY: New City Press, 1992), 231.

30. This language of receptivity and susceptivity will be crucial when we turn to examine the role of grace within his theological anthropology in Chapter 6. Notably, Shawn Colberg's recent comparative study of merit, grace, and reward in the works of Bonaventure and Aquinas highlights the language of "acception" (*acceptatio*) as being uniquely Bonaventurean; whereas Aquinas prefers the language of ordination (*ordinatio*) in his theology of divine rewards, the Seraphic Doctor prefers "acception," which refers to the human person's capacity to merit divine rewards condignly. Again, the emphasis is on the person's willing "reception" of such rewards in a contractual way. See Colberg, *The Wayfarer's End*, esp. 232–34.

31. *II Sent.* d. 26, a. 1, q. 1, concl. (2, 631): "Gratia divina in gratificato aliquid ponit."

32. See *Summa minorum* 3 (4.2), p. 3, inq. 1, tract. 1, q. 2, a. 1, 956: "Utrum gratia ponat aliquid secundum rem in gratificato"; a. 2, 957: "Utrum gratia sit res creata vel increata."

33. *II Sent.* d. 26, a. 1, q. 1, concl. (2, 631): "nulla cadit mutatio ex parte *Dei acceptantis* vel approbantis…."

34. *II Sent.* d. 26, a. 1, q. 1, concl. (2, 631): "… necesse est, quod aliqua cadat mutatio ex parte *acceptati* et approbati."

next defines what that "something" is by asking "whether that which grace places into the one who is graced is created or uncreated." Unsurprisingly, he follows the "common opinion" of his day in Paris and so affirms the position of Simon of Tournai and Alexander of Hales: He reasons that God is the *causa efficiens* of grace, but cannot be the *causa formalis* of grace since "it is neither possible nor decent [*possibile nec decens*] for God to be the perfecting form [*formam perfectivam*] of any creature."[35] There must be a created gift of grace placed in the soul in addition to the uncreated gift of grace because this created gift of grace is that "something" through which God informs the soul. Read in light of Question 1, in other words, the created gift of grace is that "something" that imparts an ontological change within "the one *receiving*" and "being approved" by grace without nonetheless imparting any change in God.

Bonaventure affirms that this opinion is both "more secure" (*securior*) and "more reasonable" (*rationabilior*) than the other opinions that could be considered in solution to the same question. It is "more secure" because it is supported by the theological masters, the saints, and the theological doctors at the University of Paris.[36] It is within his explanation for why this opinion is "more reasonable," however, that we encounter his most substantive definition for sanctifying grace in any of his works. I here repeat it in full:

It also ought to be preferred because it is *more reasonable*. For just as was shown in the opposing arguments, such acts and effects cannot reasonably be thought to exist within us when they are from something *effective* [*efficiente*], but they are from something that *informs* [*informate*]. For how will a true act of reformation and vivification [*reformationis et vivificationis*] exist in the soul unless there is some completing form [*forma complens*] by which the soul is being informed [*a qua anima informetur*]? And therefore, according to this position, *created grace* [*gratia creata*] should be compared to an inflowing of light [*influentiae luminis*], and its *First Principle* is compared to the sun. Whence also scripture calls God or Christ *the Sun of justice* because, just as corporeal light [*lumen corporale*] from the material sun inflows [*influit*] into the air, through which it is formally illuminating air, so also the spiritual sun, which is God, inflows spiritual light into the soul [*influit lumen spirituale in animam*], from which the soul is formally illuminated

---

35. *II Sent.* d. 26, a. 1, q. 2, concl. (2, 635). See again Rydstrøm-Poulsen's discussion of this idea, which he attributes to Simon of Tournai in *Gracious God*, 435–39.

36. *II Sent.* d. 26, a. 1, q. 2, concl. (2, 635).

[*illuminatur*], reformed [*reformatur*], sanctified [*gratificatur*], and vivified [*vivificatur*]. Whence among all corporeal things, an inflowing of light [*luminis influentia*] is compared to the grace of God. For just as there is a certain kind of inflowing [*influentia*] that assimilates corporeal bodies which receive it to the source of light with regard to quality [*proprietatem*], so also grace is a spiritual inflowing [*spiritualis influentia*] that assimilates and conforms rational minds to the source of light [*mentes rationales fonti lucis assimilat et conformat*]. But this inflowing [*influentia*] is rightly called *grace* [*gratia*], partly because it is given from pure liberality, having been forced by no necessity of nature—for it does not rise from the principles of the subject [*principiis subiecti*], and neither does it proceed from God out of necessity, but from God's own pure benignity; partly also because it makes pleasing [*gratum facit*]— for when it conforms and assimilates the human person to God [*hominem Deo conformat et assimilat*], it returns [*reddit*] the person to God as a friend and causes them to be pleasing and acceptable to God; partly also because it causes that which makes the human person pleasing. For the affect [*affectus*] of the human person turns back in upon itself and is mercenary [*recurvus est et mercenarius*], insofar as it is concerned with itself. So, if the person does anything, they do it by tending to their own benefit. But with divine grace coming in, the whole human person is made pleasing [*hominem totum gratum facit*], so that whether for the advantage of their neighbor or for the honor of God, they will desire to be totally extended through grace [*totum gratis impendere*]. And so it is evident that an inflowing [*influentia*] of this type is reasonably called grace.[37]

Here, then, Bonaventure defines the created gift of grace in contradistinction to the uncreated gift, and he likewise offers a simple explanation of how "the one *receiving* and the one being approved" is changed in an ontological way through that created gift. If sin is a defect of the will, whereby "the affect of the human person turns back in upon itself and is mercenary, insofar as it is concerned with itself," then sanctifying grace must be regarded as that which sets the human person's "affect" in right order, leading her to "desire to be totally extended through grace" rather than concentrated on her own, selfish good. For the Seraphic Doctor, sin is a perverted sort of introversion, the result of a self-absorbed will turned in upon its own good; sanctifying grace, on the other hand, corrects this disordered desire by shaping the human person once again into an "extrovert," namely, by inflowing the affect with the light of God so that the person can once again love God above

---

37. *II Sent.* d. 26, a. 1, q. 2, concl. (2, 635–36).

all things and her neighbor as herself.[38] Bonaventure's explanation of
how the *influentia* of sanctifying grace accomplishes these things within the human soul so that it can "return" to God, especially with respect
to assisting the will in choosing the Good, is the subject of his ensuing
comments throughout the remainder of d. 26–27.

What, though, of hierarchy? There is no mention here of the symbol
of Jacob's Ladder, nor of the hierarchical soul, nor of the three hierarchical activities of "purification, illumination, and perfection" that will
command his later accounts of sanctifying grace. Nonetheless, there
are some striking correspondences between this definition of grace as
that which causes the return of the soul to God and his definitions of
hierarchy from both *II Sent.*, d. 9 and the *Hexaëmeron*.[39] I note here
two such correspondences before turning to consider other characteristics of how this *influentia* works within the soul in d. 26–27.

First, while the triad of Dionysian "purification, illumination, and
perfection" does not explicitly appear here in Bonaventure's definition
of created grace as an *influentia,* the passage above nonetheless refers
to the human person's "assimilation" (*assimiliatur/assimilat*) to God
in two separate instances, always in conjunction with a claim that the
human person is also "conformed" to the First Principle by being thus
"assimilated." This "assimilation," he further notes, is what "returns"
(*reddit*) the human person to God and makes him "pleasing." Sanctifying grace "sanctifies" insofar as it "assimilates" the person to the
Trinity. This language, of course, echoes that used by the authors of the
Summa minorum in their own definition of sanctifying grace as a created gift.[40] Additionally, however, it also echoes his "second definition"
of hierarchy from the prologue to *II Sent.*, d. 9. There, Bonaventure had
interpreted the Areopagite's words from *CH* 3—"a hierarchy is a sacred
order, knowledge, and activity assimilating as much as possible to deiformity, and ascending proportionally into a likeness of God toward

---

38. That grace causes love of God and neighbor belongs to the Augustinian-Lombardian
tradition with which the Seraphic Doctor here wrestles. The Lombard, following Augustine,
holds that grace forgives sins and is "the charity by which we love God and neighbor." That
sanctifying grace makes possible the fulfillment of the double love commandment is a trope
commonly affirmed by medieval theologians, and Bonaventure's assertion as such clearly
stands in line with the Augustinian tradition's longstanding affirmation of the same theological principle. See again Rydstrøm-Poulsen, *Gracious God*, especially his discussion of Augustine's doctrine of grace in 23–27; and Lombard, *Sent.* 1, d. 17, 88.

39. I examined these definitions at length in Chapter 3.

40. See especially my discussion of this in Chapter 2.

the lights have flowed into it from above"—in a twofold way:[41] First, he had claimed that the "sacred order, knowledge, and activity" of a hierarchy refers to the procession (*egressus*) of every rational mind from the uncreated hierarchy, the Trinity, as an image of God. But the second half of the definition, he argued, defines a hierarchy with respect to the "return" of all rational creatures to God and refers to:

> ... the cause of similitude [*ad rationem similitudinis*], when he adds: "assimilated as much as possible through deiformity, and ascending," etc.; and Dionysius is treating that assimilation [*assimilatio*] with regard to habit [*habitum*], when it says: "assimilated as much as possible to God," etc.; and with regard to act [*actum*], when it is further added: "And illuminations coming down from God have been given to it," etc. *For the act of a similitude, or of assimilating grace [gratiae assimilantis], is to lead above [sursum ducere], just as its origin descends from above [desursum descendere] [my emphasis].*[42]

In short, Bonaventure's definition of what it means to be a similitude walks hand in hand with the language of assimilation he borrows from *CH* 3. For him, to "return" to God is to be assimilated to God through this similitude—or, since the Seraphic Doctor himself phrases this same idea in different ways, it is to be made "deiform"; it is to be made "as like as possible to God"; and it is to be "conformed" to the uncreated hierarchy, the Trinity. Bonaventure's use of this language of assimilation within his definition of sanctifying grace is not accidental, but explicitly underscores how sanctifying grace is the *influentia*—the created habit that leads to merit "with regard to act," as we shall see below—that causes the soul to become a similitude of the uncreated hierarchy. By being assimilated to God through this inflowing, humanity can participate in the hierarchical "return" that the Seraphic Doctor has already defined in *II Sent.*, d. 9.

Second, and much more obviously, Bonaventure's explanation of sanctifying grace as an *influentia* also corresponds with his definitions of hierarchy in *II. Sent.*, d. 9 and the *Hexaëmeron*. Where Bonaventure largely borrows from the *Summa minorum* to define the created gift of grace in *II Sent.*, d. 26, his naming of this created gift as an *influentia* in *II Sent.*, d. 26 represents a development from the *Summa minorum*

---

41. For my analysis of this definition, as well as Bonaventure's two other definitions of hierarchy in the prologue to Distinction 9, see Chapter 3.

42. *II Sent.* d. 9, prol. (2, 238).

as well.[43] With respect to his theology of hierarchy, Bonaventure will claim in the *Hexaëmeron* that the created hierarchies ascend to the Trinity "through an *influentiam.*" As he will expound the meaning of this word in that context:

But this *influentia* is not simply something uncreated [*quid increatum*]; nor does it follow that this *influentia* is of an *influentia* [*influentiae sit influentia*], because this *influentia* leads back into God [*reducit in Deum*]; for it means a continuous act [*continuationem*] with the First Principle and a reduction [*reductionem*] into it, not as some distant thing. Whence a true *influentia* is that which processes [*egreditur*] and returns [*regreditur*], just like the Son goes forth from the Father [*exivit a Patre*] and returns [*revertitur*] to him.[44]

In other words, the *influentia* is not God; rather, it is a "created" inflowing that proceeds immediately from the First Principle as a continuous act in a way that can be compared to the Son's eternal procession from and return to the Father in the intra-divine life. Inasmuch as it is always constantly processing from and returning to the First Principle, it is the continuous act by which the created hierarchies enjoy the *reductio* into the Trinity.

His definition of sanctifying grace as an *influentiam* here in his first systematic work of theology functions in precisely the same way. Sanctifying grace is a created gift—notably, not God—in which the uncreated gift is nonetheless still given to the soul, and through which the soul itself can be assimilated to the First Principle when its will is once again made upright. Like a ray of light that is always connected to its source in the sun, uniting everything it illuminates to the source of all light, the *influentia* of sanctifying grace *is* that created gift that both processes and returns from the First Principle and into the human soul so that the soul itself can enjoy its own *reductio* into the Trinity.[45] For Bonaventure, sanctifying grace is that *influentia* that always both "processes" and "returns" from the First Principle, illuminating the soul

---

43. Bougerol's "Le rôle de l'*influentia*," 276–78, helpfully details the development of the Franciscan use of the word in accounts of grace between Alexander and Bonaventure. After the Halensian comparison of grace to light, John of La Rochelle defined this light as an *influentia*, for example.

44. See again my discussion of this passage in Chapter 3. See also *Hex.* 21.17–18 (5, 434).

45. See also Bougerol, "Le rôle de l'*influentia*," 285–86. Romano Guardini and Timothy J. Johnson have both underscored the central role of light in the Seraphic Doctor's doctrine of grace. See esp. Guardini, "Die Lehre von der Gnade," in *Systembildende Elemente,* 53; Timothy J. Johnson, "Dieter Hattrup and Bonaventure's Authorship of the '*De reductione*,'" *Franciscan Studies* 67 (2009): 142.

with the light of God so that the soul can be continuously led back to its source.

How Grace Works: The *Influentia* That Works "in" and "with" Free Will

The soul's "return" to God through this created *influentia* will thus be the subject of the remainder of Bonaventure's *II Sent.*, d. 26–27. Before moving forward, it is helpful here to acknowledge another set of sources behind his use of the word *influentia* in these distinctions so that readers may better understand how the *influentia* assimilates the soul to the Trinity.

For that, Jacob Schmutz underscores the word's neoplatonic roots, especially insofar as medieval theologians borrowed it from neoplatonist accounts of causality in order to explain how God could act within the human person as the first cause of merit through grace.[46] As Schmutz details, theologians from the twelfth and thirteenth centuries who defined grace as an *influentia* understood it literally as a "flowing-in" of a higher cause into a lower cause so that the person could act as a secondary cause for his or her own actions (thus maintaining freedom of the will) while still being influenced by the higher cause, God, with respect to merit. Strikingly, Schmutz accuses Bonaventure of changing the meaning of *influentia* within this tradition. In his own rather brief treatment of the Seraphic Doctor's definition of sanctifying grace in *II Sent.*, he claims that the Franciscan theologian's account of *gratia gratum faciens* as an *influentia* does not leave room for God to act as a first cause within the human person. According to Schmutz, Bonaventure is for this reason a "neo-semi-Pelagian" who can be blamed for the entire downfall of the Catholic teaching on grace leading up to the Reformation.[47]

---

46. See again Schmutz, "The Medieval Doctrine of Causality and the Theology of Pure Nature (13th to 17th Centuries)," 203–50, esp. 217; see also John Milbank's summary of Schmutz's argument in *The Suspended Middle: Henri de Lubac and the Debate surrounding the Supernatural* (Grand Rapids, MI: William B. Eerdmans, 2005), 88–103, and the reaction against Schmutz's account as it is interpreted by Milbank in Cullen's "Bonaventure on Nature before Grace," 161–76. Cullen's account reacts more against Milbank's reading of Bonaventure's teaching on grace and human nature than against Schmutz. I will address these critiques again in Chapter 6 with the attention they deserve.

47. Schmutz, "The Medieval Doctrine of Causality and the Theology of Pure Nature (13th to 17th Centuries)," 217.

Close attention to the Seraphic Doctor's teaching on the *influentia* of sanctifying grace in *II Sent.*, d. 26–27 highlights his dependence on this neoplatonic tradition instead of his divergence from it, however. In d. 26, a. 1, q. 6, for example, he provides an account of how grace moves the will to choose the Good.[48] There, Bonaventure explains this relationship between free will and the *influentia* of grace:

> For grace is like a certain *influentia* proceeding from heavenly light, which always has a connection with its source [*semper habet coniunctionem cum sua origine*], like light with the sun; and because it is always united to its source [*semper suae origini coniungitur*], its work is thus not merely attributable to a cause within the subject *in whom* it exists [*ratione subiecti in quo est*], but also to the cause within the subject *from whom* it exists [*a quo est*]. Whence, just as light not only works *with* air [*operatur cum aëre*], but also works *in* air by reason of a *continuous act* [my emphasis] with its source [*operatur in ipsum aërem ratione continuationis cum suo fonte*], so also grace not only works *with* free will [*cum libero arbitrio*], but also works *in* free will [*in liberum arbitrium*] and moves [*movet*] it.[49]

Contra Schmutz, in other words, Bonaventure defines sanctifying grace as an *influentia* precisely because the neoplatonic meaning of the word as an inflowing of a higher into a lower cause helps him explain the relationship between God, grace, free will, and merit. For the Seraphic Doctor, God acts *in* the human person as a first cause of merit but also acts *with* the person's free will precisely by way of the inflowing of grace, which shines into the soul like a ray of light that acts *in* and *with* the air to illuminate everything it touches. The neoplatonic logic that informs this argument is crucial here to his explanation of how the inflowing of sanctifying grace thus conforms the natural capacities of the human being—including most especially her free will—to God, who acts *in* and *with* those capacities to urge her to choose the Good.

As a result, Bonaventure argues that the soul that is receptive to sanctifying grace can become virtuous. As he writes in d. 27, the habits of the virtues without sanctifying grace are comparable to color without light: Once sanctifying grace flows into the soul and frees the will to choose the Good, these are also "illuminated" and so ordered to their end in God.[50] Sanctifying grace thus also frees the human person

---

48. *II Sent.* d. 26, a. 1, q. 6, concl. (2, 645–46).
49. *II Sent.* d. 26, a. 1, q. 6 concl. (2, 646).
50. *II Sent.* d. 27, a. 1, q. 2 (2, 657).

to act in a meritorious way,[51] so that the person can pass from a state of grace to a state of glory in final beatitude.[52] The neoplatonic meaning of *influentia* is crucial for grasping how Bonaventure conceives the relationship between grace, free will, virtue, and merit in all these respects, since it is through this created gift that God, the higher cause, thus acts *in* and *with* the human being, the lower cause, to lead her to act meritoriously.

Bonaventure's explanation of how the *influentia* of sanctifying grace works *in* and *with* the person's free will as a motive cause in d. 26, moreover, is important for another reason: Crucially, he also asserts that this *influentia* must be a "*continuous act*" (*continuationis*) between the human soul and God. The soul first receives sanctifying grace when, urged by helping grace, it consents to being "susceptive" to it, thus opening itself up in a posture of receptivity rather than closing itself off to it in a self-interested, "mercenary" way. To continue meriting the Good, however, Bonaventure also holds that the soul must remain susceptive to this inflowing throughout its time *in via* until it rests finally in the beatitude of glory.

Such an idea is clarified in d. 26, a. 1, q. 3–4, where the Seraphic Doctor argues that sanctifying grace is not a substance, but rather, a corruptible accident that can be perverted "on account of the aversion of the human mind." Grace, he there writes, cannot be salvific unless it is "from a continuous inflowing from divine goodness over the face of our mind [*ex continuatione influentiae a bonitate divina super faciem mentis nostrae*]"; thus, "when the soul [*anima*] is turned away [*avertitur*] from God, the *influentia* does not continue [*non continuatur*], and consequently, grace is corrupted [*gratia corrumpitur*]." This corruption, he continues, is sin.[53] The *influentia* of sanctifying grace originates in God, the source from which it continuously both processes and returns like a ray of light from the sun, but Bonaventure is quite clear that this

---

51. Bonaventure discusses the habit of grace in relation to merit in *II Sent.* d. 27, a. 2, q. 1–3 (2, 661–68). See also Colberg, *The Wayfarer's End*, 29–59 for a thorough discussion of grace, merit, and reward in Bonaventure's *Commentary on the Sentences* and *Breviloquium*.

52. See *II Sent.* d. 27, a. 1, q. 3, concl. (2, 660) for a discussion of the relationship between grace and glory in Bonaventure's theology. These differ only in name according to the Seraphic Doctor, as he there writes: "It ought to be said that both sanctifying grace and glory names the divine inflowing through which the soul holds God and God dwells in the soul" ("Dicendum, quod tam gratia gratum faciens quam gloria nominat divinam influentiam, per quam anima *habet* Deum, et Deus *habitat* in anima").

53. *II Sent.* d. 26, a. 1, q. 4, ad ob. 5 (2, 641).

inflowing will nonetheless cease immediately if the soul does not thereby hold its face or mind toward God. As soon as the soul begins to turn inward; as soon as it becomes "mercenary"; as soon as it starts to desire its own, tangible good more than it desires the highest Good; then the inflowing will be cut off. Grace is not like a zap of lightening into the soul that instantly ushers the human person from his journey *in via* to his final rest *in patria*; rather, it must be a "continuous act" between God and the soul, whereby the soul must continuously will to receive the gift of grace throughout its time *in via* if it wishes to remain "assimilated" and "conformed" to God before arriving *in patria*. In this way, as Bonaventure writes, "grace not only depends on the one from whom it exists [*a quo est*], but also on the soul in which it exists [*in qua est*], because it will only remain in the soul so long as it turns [*conversam*] its face or mind [*faciem suam sive mentem*] toward God."[54]

Though Bonaventure does not here use the symbol of Jacob's Ladder to describe this continuous activity, the image could perhaps still be useful for helping us conceive this movement of grace in these distinctions. The angels on Jacob's Ladder are always constantly both "ascending" and "descending" between heaven and earth with heaven representing the point from which the "descending" movement begins and the earth representing the point from which the "ascending" movement begins. Similarly, grace "descends" into the human soul from its source in the First Principle, so that the soul itself can here be compared to the earth in Jacob's dream at Bethel, insofar as it is the point from which the *influentia* of grace can then "ascend" or "return" to the Trinity. Were the earth to be closed off to this movement or become incapable of holding the Ladder, the entire system would implode: The structure that unites God to God's creation, namely, the ladder itself, could not stand, and the "descensions" and "ascensions" of the angels would cease. When the soul turns inward instead of turning its face toward God, it is as if the earth in Jacob's dream at Bethel would become as water, and would therefore no longer be capable of stabilizing the ladder upon which the "processing" and "returning" movements of grace should take place. What provides the stable ground for the construction of the ladder—or namely, what invites the *influentia*—is the free consent of the will. For these movements to remain continuous, and for

---

54.*II Sent.* d. 26, a. 1, q. 4, ad ob. 2 (2, 641).

the Trinity to remain united to the soul through these constant "processions" and "returns" of grace, the soul must likewise remain a constant receptacle for grace, comparable to the earth in Jacob's dream. Grace, in other words, is always circling between God and the soul, and it must be a continuous, free act between both God and the soul if this circling is to continue. Its ceaseless procession from and return to the First Principle unites the human person to God *in via,* but this union depends on the person's continued willingness to remain "susceptive" to it.

The *Influentia* of Sanctifying Grace and the Trinity

Whereas I can retroactively use this symbol to describe what the *influentia* of sanctifying grace looks like in Bonaventure's *II Sent.,* however, the Seraphic Doctor's earliest and most expansive treatment of grace nonetheless lacks the explicit hierarchical emphases that will command his teachings on the subject in subsequent texts. In d. 26–27, Bonaventure's definition of grace as an *influentia* follows theological and philosophical precedents in his day insofar as he uses it to describe God's action *with* and *in* the human person's free will by way of the created gift. Despite the fact that the Dionysian triad of purification, illumination, and perfection is not an obvious component therein, his definition of sanctifying grace in d. 26–27 is the foundation upon which he nonetheless constructs and reiterates his teachings on grace in his academic, spiritual, and pastoral texts throughout the remainder of his career as a theologian. His explanation regarding how this *influentia* actually sanctifies the human soul by working *with* and *in* the will to set it "upright" so that it can once again "love God above all things and its neighbor as itself," for example, is presumed in the *Itinerarium* and the *Hexaëmeron,* and will be further clarified and expounded in the *Breviloquium.* Approaching grace in these later texts—as well as in his sermons, as we shall see in Chapter 8—would be impossible apart from attention to this initial definition in *II Sent,* d. 26–27. It's worth reiterating that, despite the lack of explicit references to hierarchy therein, Bonaventure's vocabulary for defining sanctifying grace within these distinctions nonetheless walks hand in hand with his vocabulary for hierarchy. In the same way that Bonaventure defines an *influentia* within his theology of hierarchy as a continuous act that processes and returns between the uncreated and created hierarchies so as to unite them, the *influentia* of sanctifying grace is here defined as a continuous act that constantly processes from and returns to both the Trinity and the human soul, ceaselessly uniting them so long as the soul remains willingly susceptive to it. In this way, sanctifying grace assimilates the soul to the Trinity, transforming it into a divine similitude so that the soul can experience its own *reductio* into God.

With respect to this *reductio,* I here highlight one more crucial characteristic of the Seraphic Doctor's comments on sanctifying grace in *II Sent.* before turning to Bonaventure's development of these teachings in *Brev.* 5. I began this analysis by looking at *I Sent.*, d. 14, where the Seraphic Doctor had claimed that the uncreated gift of the Holy Spirit is gifted *in* the *influentia,* the created gift. Simply put, though the *influentia* of sanctifying grace is not God, Bonaventure nonetheless holds that God is united to the soul in an immediate way through it. In *II Sent.*, d. 29, he reaffirms this thesis by declaring that the result of the soul's reception of this *influentia* is nothing less than an indwelling of the entire Trinity. Here, sanctifying grace causes the soul to become holy and pleasing to God because through it, a "most liberal condescension [*condescensionis liberalissimae*]" of God into the soul can occur. God wants "to dwell [*habitare*] in the soul as if in a temple [*templo*], and again, God wants to consider his servant as a son [*velit servum reputare pro filio*], and … God wants to take up his handmaiden [*ancillam*] in marriage [*coniugium*]."[55] Sanctifying grace, as it were, is the gift through which this threefold condescension takes place within the soul, as he there elaborates:

Neither the consecration nor the adoption nor the union of the soul [*animae*] with God happens through any property of nature [*proprietatem naturae*], but rather through a superadded gift of grace [*donum gratiae superadditum*], which consecrates [*consecret*] the soul so that it would become a temple [*templum*]; which assimilates [*adoptetur*] the soul so that it would be a daughter of God [*Dei filia*]; which adorns the face of the soul [*faciem animae decoret*] so that it would be prepared to be the bride of God [*Dei sponsa*]. But sanctifying

---

55. *II Sent.* d. 29, a. 1, q. 1 (2, 695). Bonaventure offers this description of sanctifying grace in response to a question about whether or not prelapsarian human persons "needed" sanctifying grace in the Garden of Eden. He responds in the affirmative, and in so doing, offers an important distinction between sanctifying grace as a "special influence" and the "general influence" of grace that upholds all things that exist. There are parallels between this passage and the famous fourth question of Bonaventure's *Scien. Chr.* where the Seraphic Doctor similarly considers a "special influence" of grace in contradistinction to a "general influence" of grace. I will address both passages again in Chapter 6 on the role of grace in Bonaventure's theological anthropology.

grace [*gratia gratum faciens*] causes all these things; truly, sanctity [*sanctitas*] is joined with the soul so that it can in no way be stained; truly, conformity [*conformitas*] unites the soul to God so that it cannot be made dissimilar from God in any way; truly, the soul becomes spiritually beautiful so that it cannot be deformed in any way; and for that reason, the soul made pleasing returns [*reddit*] to God.[56]

Bonaventure's definition of sanctifying grace in *II Sent.* does not escape his theology's Trinitarianism, insofar as he here describes how the soul is "made pleasing" through sanctifying grace in a distinctly Trinitarian way. The *influentia* of sanctifying grace "consecrates" the soul, sanctifying it into a home for the uncreated gift of grace, the Holy Spirit. It also causes the soul to be "conformed" to God, assimilating it to the First Principle so that it can be called the "daughter" or "son" of the Father. It likewise makes the soul "spiritually beautiful" so that the soul can thus be taken up in marriage with Christ. Following the intuitions regarding the effects of sanctifying grace put forward by the authors of the *Summa minorum*,[57] Bonaventure here affirms that the entire Trinity dwells within the soul through the created gift. For the Seraphic Doctor, it is only through this Trinitarian indwelling that the soul is thus made capable of its own *redditus*. It is this *redditus* to the Trinity that will be the focus of Bonaventure's treatment of sanctifying grace in Part 5 of the *Breviloquium,* to which I thus now turn.

Sanctifying Grace in the *Breviloquium*

Bonaventure would pick up the pen for the *Breviloquium* at least a decade after he began work on his *Commentary on the Sentences.*[58] As noted in this chapter's introduction, this brief compendium to the

---

56. *II Sent.* d. 29, a. 1, q. 1 (2, 696).

57. See again Chapter 2.

58. This section of the chapter has been revised with permission from the Franciscan Institute from "Part V: On the Grace of the Holy Spirit," in *Bonaventure Revisited,* 215–43. The question of the *Breviloquium's* dating has there also been challenged by Hammond, "The Textual Context," 29–45, esp. 45, who argues that it was most likely written between 1262–1267 at the same time that he was redacting his *Commentary on the Gospel of Luke.* Past scholarship has dated the *Breviloquium* to 1256/57. If further scholarship proves Hammond's argument correct, it would mean that the *Itinerarium* was actually written prior to the *Breviloquium.* (The *Itinerarium* was written in 1259.) If this is the case, I am nonetheless confident that my choice to present the *Breviloquium* immediately *after II Sent.* d. 26–27 works on a thematic level, more so than if I had chosen to treat the *Itinerarium* first. The *Breviloquium* quite clearly presents a simplified—albeit more mature—systematic account

study of theology "would suppose, on every page, the developments and discussions that had appeared in the *Commentaries*."[59] The work itself is divided into seven parts which, as Joshua Benson has already unfolded, outline the Seraphic Doctor's view of salvation history according to seven topics—Trinity, creation, sin, Incarnation, grace, the sacraments, and the Final Judgment. In his article expounding this structure, Benson calls his readers' attention to the text's prologue, where the Seraphic Doctor writes that sacred scripture, "which is called theology," has an *ortus, modus* (or *progressus*), and *fructus* (or *status*): "insinuating that the *ortum* of Scripture applies to the inflowing of the most blessed Trinity; that the *progressum* of Scripture applies to the demands of human capacity; and that the *statum* or *fructum* of Scripture applies to a superabundant and overflowing happiness."[60] Benson's article elaborates how each of these three categories—*ortus, modus,* and *fructus*—can collectively describe the structure of the entire *Breviloquium* both on macro- and microcosmic levels, with Christ positioned as the *medium* or center of the text in Part 4. More recently, Jared Goff has shown how the text is likewise shaped by Bonaventure's Trinitarianism inasmuch as each of the seven parts within the *Breviloquium* relate back to the First Principle—the Trinity—within the text. As Bonaventure writes in Part 1, the Triune God is the "principle and effective exemplar [*principium et exemplar effectivum*] of all things in creation," the "restorative" (*refectivum*) principle in the act of redemption, and the "perfecting" (*perfectivum*) principle in the reward.[61] These three acts of the First Principle notably correspond with the three categories of *ortus, progressus-modus,* and *status-fructus* identified by Benson as the key to understanding the structure of the *Breviloquium,* even as they also correspond with Bonaventure's Trinitarian appropriations for the Father, Son, and Holy Spirit in Part 1 of the text.[62] The very structure

---

of Bonaventure's doctrine of grace from that which appears in his *Sentences* commentary, and they thus fit together well here.

59. Bougerol, *Introduction to the Works of Bonaventure*, 99.

60. See Benson, "Christology of the *Breviloquium*," 247–88.

61. *Brev.* 1.1 (5, 210). See also Jared Goff, "Part I: On the Trinity of God," in *Bonaventure Revisited*, 97–139, and Justin Shaun Coyle's exquisite study, "Appropriating Apocalypse in Bonaventure's *Breviloquium*," *Franciscan Studies* 76 (2018): 99–135, which unfolds how these three categories relate to Bonaventure's Trinitarian appropriations in the *Breviloquium* in beautifully intricate ways. I am especially indebted to Dr. Coyle for sharing his research with me before it was published.

62. See *Brev.* 1.6 (5, 214–15).

of the *Breviloquium,* in other words, narrates the First Principle's work within creation in a Trinitarian way.

Quite strikingly, as we will encounter below, these same three categories—*ortus, modus,* and *fructus*—are similarly useful categories for understanding Part 5, "On the Grace of the Holy Spirit." Bonaventure uses these three categories in *Brev.* 5 to describe how human beings are conformed to the First Principle, the Trinity, through sanctifying grace. Through these same three categories, he likewise begins to more clearly delineate the relationship between grace and hierarchy that had been present but not yet explicit in *II Sent.,* d. 26–27, especially insofar as they map on perfectly to the three hierarchical activities of purification, illumination, and perfection. By exploring these themes, this portion of the chapter will show how *Brev.* 5 defines sanctifying grace in a way that indeed supposes, "on every page, the developments and discussions that had appeared in the *Commentaries,*"[63] as Bougerol once intuited, but it will also expose how the *Breviloquium* in many ways presents a more mature account of sanctifying grace than that which is found in Bonaventure's earlier and lengthier text.

My analysis of this account, like that above, will proceed in four stages. I first provide an introduction to *Brev.* 5 by simply examining Bonaventure's initial comments on grace in the first chapter of Part 5, and then use this to interpret the remaining nine chapters in three sections. This text, as we shall see, serves as a useful bridge for connecting the Seraphic Doctor's early comments on grace in the *Commentary on the Sentences* to his treatment of the subject in both the *Itinerarium* and the *Hexaëmeron* because it so clearly presupposes the content of the former even while more explicitly highlighting hierarchical themes in anticipation of the latter; as such, it will also help us regard the uniformity of his thought with respect to grace and hierarchy across the course of his theological career.

Approaching Bonaventure's Doctrine of Grace in *Breviloquium* 5.1

With respect to the structure of the *Breviloquium* as a whole, Benson has helpfully shown how there are microstructures that reflect the macrostructure of the text within each of the *Breviloquium's* seven parts.

63. Bougerol, *Introduction to the Works of Bonaventure,* 99.

Relatedly, each opening chapter within each of those seven parts serves the purpose of laying out the primary points that "must be believed" regarding each of the seven doctrines treated. *Brev.* 5.1, as it were, is Bonaventure's introduction to the primary points that "must be believed" regarding grace and is the place within the text wherein he lays out his intended structure for the remainder of Part 5. It thus provides a useful point of departure for my examination of the text here.

According to Benson's portrait of the macrostructure of the *Breviloquium,* Part 5 is used by the Seraphic Doctor therein to describe the *modus* of re-creation.[64] Bonaventure concludes Part 4, where Christ was positioned as both the *fructus* of creation and the *ortus* of re-creation, on a Pentecostal note: After his ascension, Christ sends the Holy Spirit so that the disciples would be filled with the spiritual gifts and inflamed by love.[65] From this pneumatological conclusion to Part 4, he then introduces Part 5 by defining grace in a way that is again worth quoting in full:

Thus, considering grace as a divinely given gift, we ought to hold these things, namely, that it is a gift that is immediately given and infused [*immediate donatur et infunditur*] by God. For the Holy Spirit—who is the uncreated gift [*donum increatum*], and *the best and perfect gift descending from the Father of Lights* through the Incarnate Word—is given with it and in it [*cum ipsa et in ipsa*], as John says in the Apocalypse: *A river ... bright as crystal, flowing from the throne of God and of the Lamb.* Likewise, grace is that gift through which the soul is perfected [*perficitur*] and made the bride of Christ [*sponsa Christi*], the daughter of the eternal Father [*filia Patris aeterni*], and the temple of the Holy Spirit [*templum Spiritus sancti*], which can in no way happen except through an ennobling condescension [*dignativa condescensione*] and condescending nobility [*condescensiva dignatione*] of the eternal Majesty through the gift of his own grace. For this is indeed the gift that purifies, illuminates, and perfects [*purgat, illuminat et perficit*] the soul [*animam*]; that vivifies, reforms, and stabilizes [*vivificat, reformat et stabilit*] it; that elevates, assimilates, and joins it to God [*elevat, assimilat et Deo iungit*]; and through which the soul is made acceptable [*facit acceptabilem*] to God. Because of this, a gift of this kind is rightly called and ought to be called sanctifying grace [*gratia gratum faciens*].... No person whatsoever is worthy of arriving at the highest Good, since this is by all means above all the limits of nature, unless he is elevated above himself through God condescending to him. But God does

---

64. Benson, "Christology of the *Breviloquium*," 257.

65. *Brev.* 4.10 (5, 251–52).

not condescend through God's own incommunicable essence, but through an *influentia* flowing forth from God. And neither is the spirit elevated above itself to a fixed place [*situm localem*], but through a deiform habit [*habitum deiformem*]. Therefore, in order for a rational spirit [*spiritui rationali*] to be made worthy of eternal beatitude [*dignus fiat aeternae beatitudinis*], it is necessary for it to become a participant [*particeps*] of this God-conforming inflowing [*influentiae deiformis*]. But this deiform *influentia*, which exists from God [*a Deo*], through God [*secundum Deum*], and because of God [*propter Deum*], thus restores the image of our mind to conformity with the Blessed Trinity not only according to the order of origin [*secundum ordinem originis*], but also according to the rectitude of our free choice [*secundum rectitudinem electionis*] and according to the rest of fruition [*secundum quietudinem fruitionis*].[66]

Here, the Seraphic Doctor indeed offers a short summary of the "developments and discussions" surrounding grace that had appeared in his initial treatment of sanctifying grace from his *II Sent.* Most obviously, his claim that sanctifying grace makes the soul deiform by making it into a "daughter of the Father," the "bride of the Son," and the "temple of the Holy Spirit" echoes almost exactly his previous statement about the effects of sanctifying grace in d. 29. What's more, he again defines sanctifying grace as an *influentia*, a *created* habit infused into the soul by God, which is not God but which nonetheless assimilates the soul to the First Principle. In contrast to his initial definition of this *influentia* from *II Sent.*, d. 26, however, in *Brev.* 5, his description of how this *influentia* is gifted to the soul has a starker Trinitarian accent. Grace descends *from* the Father of Lights, it is given *through* the Incarnate Christ, and it is the gift *with* and *in* which the uncreated gift of the Spirit is given to the soul. The created gift of grace, like the entire created order of reality in the rest of the *Breviloquium*, thus has an *ortus, modus,* and *fructus* that correspond to the three persons of the Trinity: it has its *ortus* in the Father of Lights, its *modus* or *progressus* through the Incarnate Word, and its *status* or *fructus* in the Holy Spirit. Benson's observations concerning the underlying structure of the *Breviloquium*, in other words, inform Bonaventure's initial definition of grace in Part 5.

In addition to including this Trinitarian emphasis that recalls the

---

66. *Brev.* 5.1 (5, 252). See also Colberg, *The Wayfarer's End*, 32–59, for a further examination of Bonaventure's treatment of grace in the *Breviloquium* as it pertains to merit and reward. Colberg helpfully emphasizes the unique role of Bonaventure's use of the language of "*acceptatio*" in his treatment of grace, while likewise underscoring the usefulness of reading *Brev.* 5 alongside Bonaventure's *Sentences* commentaries.

macrostructure of the *Breviloquium* as a whole, however, the Seraphic Doctor develops his definition of grace from *II Sent.*, d. 26–27 in several other rather striking ways. I here highlight two such developments from the passage quoted above, which, when read together, provide an important key to interpreting both the structure and meaning of the remainder of *Brev.* 5.

First, Bonaventure argues that sanctifying grace accomplishes the *reductio* of the soul to the Trinity because it "purifies, illumines, and perfects the soul," "vivifies, reforms, and stabilizes it," and "elevates, assimilates, and joins it to God."[67] In *II Sent.*, d. 26, Bonaventure uses the same language from these three triads to define sanctifying grace, but they do not appear in this particular order; in fact, he there seems to favor a quadrad: "illumination, reformation, sanctification, and vivification." Purification, perfection, stabilization, and assimilation appear there, but these three specific triads are absent. For the first time in *Brev.* 5, in contrast, we see the specific triad of "purification, illumination, and perfection"—the three hierarchical activities that command so much of Bonaventure's treatises on the spiritual life—explicitly associated with his definition of sanctifying grace. An initial reading of this passage in *Brev.* 5.1 might lead readers to conclude that the two triads that appear alongside the Triple Way here are merely poetic devices, an instance in which the Seraphic Doctor waxes eloquently on his subject for no other purpose than to show off his extraordinary command of the written word. A closer examination of the text, however, reveals that all three triads lend themselves to more than mere linguistic flourish.

To understand why this is so, we need only turn to the conclusion of *Brev.* 5.1 where the Seraphic Doctor will argue that sanctifying grace can only conform minds to the Trinity through the "uprightness of free choice" (*rectitudinem electionis*).[68] Following *II Sent.*, Bonaventure asserts in the *Breviloquium* that God does not gift a human person sanctifying grace apart from that person's free will: Humanity fell through an act of their own choice and thus must also freely consent to the gift of sanctifying grace in the act of recreation.[69] In *Brev.* 5.1, Bonaventure

---

67. *Brev.* 5.1 (5, 252).

68. *Brev.* 5.1 (5, 253).

69. See esp. *Brev.* 5.3 (5, 254–56), for a summation of how sanctifying grace works in cooperation with human free choice. Again, Colberg's excellent study of *Brev.* 5 further elaborates this point with respect to merit, divine reward, and grace; see *The Wayfarer's End*, 32–59.

specifies how the gift of sanctifying grace makes the will "upright"—namely, through what he calls "the strength of virtue [*vigorem virtutis*], the beauty of truth [*splendorem veritatis*], and the fervor of love [*fervorem caritatis*]."[70] The Latin word he uses here for "virtue" is *virtutis*, which can also be translated as "power." The double entendre recalls an earlier passage from *Brev.* 1, where he had discussed Trinitarian appropriations and had claimed that divine power can be especially appropriated to the Father, truth to the Son, and love to the Holy Spirit.[71] In other words, his use of the triad in *Brev.* 5.1 indicates that the human will is made "upright" through sanctifying grace in a Trinitarian way.

Even more strikingly, the Seraphic Doctor continues this same passage by writing: "… and the strength of virtue (or power) purifies, stabilizes, and elevates [*purgat, stabilit et elevat*] the soul; the beauty of truth illumines, reforms, and assimilates it to God [*illuminat, reformat, et Deo assimilat*]; and the fervor of love perfects, vivifies, and unites the soul to God [*perficit, vivificat et Deo iungit*], and from these things a human person becomes pleasing and acceptable [*placens et acceptus*] to God."[72] Careful readers will note that this is an exact repetition of the three sets of triads used by the Seraphic Doctor in the beginning of *Brev.* 5.1, albeit rearranged to reflect his Trinitarian appropriations. The work of purification, stability, and elevation is associated with a Trinitarian appropriation of the Father; the work of illumination, reformation, and assimilation with a Trinitarian appropriation for the Son; and the work of perfection, vivification, and union with a Trinitarian appropriation for the Spirit. The Seraphic Doctor thus explicitly identifies which actions of sanctifying grace within the soul can be appropriated to the Father, Son, and Holy Spirit, respectively, as detailed in Table 4.1 below. In short, *Brev.* 5.1 argues that sanctifying grace purifies, stabilizes, and elevates the soul so as to make it the daughter of the Father; it illuminates, reforms, and assimilates the soul so as to make it the bride of Christ; and it finally perfects, vivifies, and unites the soul to God so as to consecrate it as a temple of the Holy Spirit.[73]

---

70. *Brev.* 5.1 (5, 253).

71. See Bonaventure's discussion of the Trinitarian appropriations in *Brev.* 1.6.

72. *Brev.* 5.1 (5, 253).

73. I am indebted to conversations in a course jointly offered by Boyd Taylor Coolman and Stephen F. Brown at Boston College in the Spring 2016 semester, entitled "Bonaventure's *Breviloquium*," for these observations. I am especially indebted to Dr. Coolman, who first highlighted this parallelism.

TABLE 4.1 The Work of Sanctifying Grace within the Soul according to *Breviloquium* 5.1

Father	Purification	Stabilization	Elevation	The Soul becomes the Daughter of God
Son	Illumination	Reformation	Assimilation	The Soul becomes the Bride of God
Holy Spirit	Perfection	Vivification	Union	The Soul becomes the Temple of God

Second, returning to Bonaventure's definition of sanctifying grace cited above, he there also claims that sanctifying grace is a "deiform *influentia*" that "restores the image of our mind to conformity with the Blessed Trinity not only according to the order of origin, but also according to the rectitude of our free choice and according to the rest of fruition."[74] Notably, this yet again easily overlooked statement incorporates all three categories highlighted by Benson within his own examination of the *Breviloquium's* structure, insofar as Bonaventure here implies that sanctifying grace has its *ortus* in the Trinity "according to the order of origin [*ordinem originis*]," its *modus* in the Trinity "according to the rectitude of our free choice [*secundum rectitudinem electionis*]," and its *fructus* in the Trinity insofar as it leads the soul to "the rest of fruition [*quietudinem fruitionis*]." This *ortus, modus,* and *fructus* of grace is what conforms "the image of our mind" to the Trinity and makes us "deiform," or namely, these three activities restore "the image of our mind" to the similitude that had been lost through original sin. This observation becomes significant when one examines the broader structure of Part 5 as a whole. There are ten chapters within *Brev.* 5, whose titles are listed in Table 4.2.[75]

The Latin titles of Chapters 1–3 notably all begin with, "*De gratia*"; those of Chapters 4–6, with "*De ramificatione gratiae*"; and those of Chapters 7–10, with "*De exercitio gratiae.*" Simply put, Bonaventure's own titles delineate his intended structure for Part 5, whereby the first three chapters consider grace as a topic in itself, the next three chapters consider grace as it "branches out" within the human soul, and the final four chapters treat the question of how the human person ought

74. *Brev.* 5.1 (5, 252).
75. *Brev.* 5.1 (5, 552); 5.2 (5, 552); 5.3 (5, 254); 5.4 (5, 256); 5.5 (5, 257); 5.6 (5, 258); 5.7 (5, 260); 5.8 (5, 261); 5.9 (5, 262); 5.10 (5, 263).

TABLE 4.2 Chapter Titles in Part 5 of the *Breviloquium*

Chapter 1	*De gratia, in quantum est donum divinitus datum*	On grace, insofar as it is a divinely given gift
Chapter 2	*De gratia, in quantum iuvat ad bonum meritorium*	On grace, insofar as it aids in the meriting of the Good
Chapter 3	*De gratia, in quantum est remedium peccati*	On grace, insofar as it is a remedy for sin
Chapter 4	*De ramificatione gratiae in habitus virtutum*	On the branching out of grace into the habits of the virtues
Chapter 5	*De ramificatione gratiae in habitus donorum*	On the branching out of grace into the habits of the gifts
Chapter 6	*De ramificatione gratiae in habitus beatitudinum, et per consequens fructum et sensuum*	On the branching out of grace into the habits of the beatitudes, and consequently the [spiritual] fruits and senses
Chapter 7	*De exercitio gratiae respectu credendorum*	On the exercise of grace with respect to what ought to be believed
Chapter 8	*De exercitio gratiae respectu diligendorum*	On the exercise of grace with respect to what ought to be loved
Chapter 9	*De exercitio gratiae respectu agendorum, praeceptorum et consiliorum*	On the exercise of grace with respect to what ought to be practiced in the laws and counsels
Chapter 10	*De exercitio gratiae respectu petendorum et orandorum*	On the exercise of grace with respect to petitions and prayers

to "exercise" the gift of sanctifying grace. Using Benson's previous work as a point of departure, my ensuing analysis of each of these subsets of chapters flows from Bonaventure's claim that sanctifying grace restores the image of the human mind to conformity with the Trinity according to an order of origin (*ortus*), the "rectitude of choice" (*modus*), and the "rest of enjoying God" (*fructus*). Throughout *Brev.* 5, in other words, these three categories and their corresponding chapters serve the purpose of describing *how* sanctifying grace conforms human persons to the Trinity: First, "purifying" the soul so that it can become a daughter of the Father (*ortus*); second, "illuminating" the soul so that it can become a bride of the Son (*modus*); and finally, "perfecting" the soul so that it can become a temple of the Holy Spirit (*fructus*).

The *Ortus* of Grace in Chapters 1–3: Purification

After Chapter 1, the Seraphic Doctor next opens Chapters 2–3 by treating them as a unit, writing: "Second, let us consider the grace of the Holy Spirit that is given to us in its relation to free will [*comparatione ad liberum arbitrium*], and this, in a twofold way: namely, first, inasmuch as it is an aid to merit [*adiutorum ad meritum*]; but second, inasmuch as it is a remedy against sin [*remedium contra peccatum*]."[76] Bonaventure's own titular grouping of these two aspects with Chapter 1 denotes that all three chapters belong together thematically (see again *Table 4.2*, above), but how?

Answering that question requires once again highlighting the Seraphic Doctor's understanding of sin as a defect of the will. This context, which was similarly crucial for reading his definition of sanctifying grace in *II Sent.*, d. 26–27, is once again critical when reading *Brev.* 5.2–3. Sin, for Bonaventure, is a disordered desire, a defect of the will through which the soul places its own selfish desires—its own good—above its desire for God. In this way, the sinful soul is a "mercenary" soul, turned in upon itself to the exclusion of others. In *II Sent.*, d. 26, Bonaventure had claimed that the *influentia* of sanctifying grace assimilates the soul to God insofar as it straightens the will so that it can stop being "mercenary" in this way. Grace sets the soul's desires, or its affect, in right order, helping it to "love God above all things and its neighbor as itself"; or, put differently, it shapes the soul into an "extrovert." Relatedly, *Brev.* 5.2–3 serves the purpose of emphasizing how sanctifying grace sets the will "upright" once the human person thus freely consents to receive the created gift.

In Chapter 2, for example, Bonaventure insists that human persons need the gift of sanctifying grace in order to merit the Good.[77] His reasoning for why this is so includes a lengthy discussion of why the human creature, even in its prelapsarian state, needed this gift to help its will remain upright, writing that the creature was created in such a way that, "because of its own defectability [*defectibilitate*], it would always need [*indigeret*] its Principle, and the First Principle from its own benignity would never cease to inflow [*influere*] the creature."[78] He continues, "Thus, since the rational spirit [*spiritus rationalis*] was created in

<hr>

76. *Brev.* 5.2 (5, 253).
77. *Brev.* 5.2 (5, 253–54). See again Colberg, *The Wayfarer's End*, 32–59.
78. *Brev.* 5.2 (5, 253).

this fashion from nothingness [*de nihilo*], it is *defective* in itself [*in se defectivus*]."[79] Or, in other words, Bonaventure here explains why the soul is mercenary, tending toward its own good: Because it was created from nothing, it tends back toward nothingness, and needs the *influentia* of grace if its will is to turn from being an "introvert" and into an "extrovert." Timothy J. Johnson has called this the notion of "ontological poverty" in Bonaventure's thought, insofar as the human person is "poor in being" simply by virtue of the fact that she is a creature dependent on God for her very existence.[80] Sin results when the person refuses to accept this dependency upon her Creator by choosing to prioritize her own tangible good above God. The person sins when she desires to remain "mercenary" and tends toward her own good rather than submitting herself to the *influentia* of grace that will direct her to love God above all things and her neighbor as herself. Only the person who recognizes her natural deficiency apart from God—the person who freely consents to receive this *influentia* so as to be able to love God above all things and her neighbor as herself—will merit the Good.

In Chapter 3, Bonaventure discusses how graces serves as the remedy to sin by once again making the will upright so that it is ordered to the First Principle in this fashion. Here, Bonaventure presents a summary of his comments concerning the way sanctifying grace works *in* and *with* the free will to free it from sin that he has already expounded at length in *II Sent.* Helping grace urges the will away from evil and prompts it toward the Good, and it is then "for free will to consent or reject it [*consentire vel dissentire*]; by consenting, it receives grace [*gratiam suscipere*]; and thus receiving grace, it cooperates [*cooperari*] with grace so that it might arrive at salvation [*perveniat ad salutem*]."[81] In this way, the will is freed from its mercenary tendencies that distort God's intended order for creation.

Read together, therefore, Chapters 2 and 3 describe the *ortus* of sanctifying grace in the soul insofar as this *influentia* frees the will from sin and helps the human person merit the Good. If Chapter 1 defines grace as an *influentia* that conforms the soul to the entire Trinity, then these chapters show how the soul is "purified" from sin so that it can be conformed to the Trinity through this *influentia*.

---

79. *Brev.* 5.2 (5, 253).
80. See Johnson, *The Soul in Ascent*, 34–35.
81. *Brev.* 5.3 (5, 254).

The *Modus* of Grace in Chapters 4–6: Illumination

From this discussion of the *ortus* of sanctifying grace within the soul, the Seraphic Doctor continues Part 5 by next describing how grace "branches out" or "flowers" into different habits within it. Chapter 4 treats the flowering of grace into the habits of the virtues; Chapter 5, the flowering of grace into the habits of the spiritual gifts; and Chapter 6, the flowering of grace into the habits of the beatitudes, spiritual fruits, and spiritual senses. Through these, grace sanctifies the soul by rectifying (*rectificatur*) it through the habits of the virtues, expediting (*expeditur*) it through the spiritual gifts, and perfecting (*perficitur*) it through the beatitudes.[82]

The key to understanding these three chapters, however, is found toward the end of Chapter 6, where Bonaventure starts to bring them to a conclusion, writing, "From what was said, therefore, it can be clearly gathered that the habits of the virtues principally dispose us to the practices of the active life [*principaliter disponunt activae*]; that the habits of the gifts principally dispose us to the repose of contemplation [*otium contemplativae*]; and that the habits of the beatitudes principally dispose us to the perfection of both [*perfectionem utriusque*]."[83] This triad ought not be read in isolation from the larger context of *Brev.* 5. My above explanation of Bonaventure's definition of grace in Chapter 1 emphasized how he had therein claimed that sanctifying grace makes the will "upright" in three ways: "through the strength of virtue, the beauty of truth, and the fervor of love."[84] I further noted that these three actions directly corresponded with Bonaventure's definition of grace from the beginning of *Brev.* 5.1, even as they also recall his Trinitarian appropriations depicted in Table 4.1. The Seraphic Doctor's statement in Chapter 6, through which he summarizes his presentation of the "branching out" of grace in Chapters 4–6, again corresponds with these previous claims from Chapter 1, as shown in Table 4.3.

This parallelism is not accidental but exposes a purposeful continuation of Bonaventure's claim from Chapter 1 that sanctifying grace makes the human person's will "upright." Sanctifying grace has its "order of origin" in the Trinity, but it also conforms the human person to

---

82. *Brev.* 5.4 (5, 256).
83. *Brev.* 5.6 (5, 259).
84. *Brev.* 5.1 (5, 253).

TABLE 4.3 The Branching Out of Grace in Accordance with Free Choice

Chapter 1: Sanctifying Grace Makes the Will "Upright"	Through the strength of virtue (appropriated to the Father)	Through the beauty of truth (appropriated to the Son)	Through the fervor of love (appropriated to the Spirit)
Chapter 4	Sanctifying grace "rectifies" the soul by branching out into the habits of the virtues, through which the soul is prepared for the active life	————	————
Chapter 5	————	Sanctifying grace "expedites" the soul by branching out into the habits of the spiritual gifts, through which the soul is prepared for the contemplative life	————
Chapter 6	————	————	Sanctifying grace "perfects" the soul by branching out into the habits of the beatitudes, spiritual fruits, and spiritual senses

the Trinity according to "the rectitude of free choice." Read in light of this claim from Chapter 1, Chapters 4–6 explain how sanctifying grace makes the will "upright" through the strength of virtue, the beauty of truth, and the fervor of love. Bonaventure's elegantly symmetrical presentation of the "branching out" of sanctifying grace in these chapters describes the *modus* of grace within the human soul as it flowers into the habits of the virtues, the spiritual gifts, and the beatitudes in accordance with the human person's free will. Moreover, if Chapters 4–6 infer the *modus* of grace within the macrostructure of *Brev.* 5, there is then also here a microstructure to these chapters, as well, insofar as these can also be further subdivided by the three categories of *ortus*, *modus*, and *fructus*. The flowering of grace within the soul has its *ortus* in the "rectifying" habits of the virtues, its *modus* in the "expediting" or advancing habits of the spiritual gifts, and its *fructus* in the habits of the beatitudes, which themselves branch out into the habits of the spiritual fruits and spiritual senses.

With respect to these, Bonaventure's discussion of this "branching out" of grace in Chapters 4–6 concludes by proffering an account of the spiritual sensorium. Once grace has flowered into the habits of the virtues and the spiritual gifts within the human person in Chapters 4 and 5, respectively, it then branches out finally into the habits of the beatitudes, which culminates in the gift of the spiritual senses in Chapter 6. Through the spiritual senses, the Seraphic Doctor writes, the soul:

is made suitable for contemplation and for the mutual beholding and embracing of the Bridegroom and Bride ... through which the highest beauty [*summa pulcritudo*] of the Bridegroom, Christ, is seen because of his Splendor; the highest harmony [*summa harmonia*] is heard because he is the Word; the highest sweetness [*summa dulcedo*] is tasted because he is Wisdom, which includes both, namely, the Word and the Splendor; the highest fragrance [*summa fragrantia*] is smelled because of the Word inspired in the heart; the highest delight [*summa suavitas*] is embraced because he is the Word Incarnate, dwelling among us bodily [*corporaliter*] and giving himself to us in a palpable, kissable, and embraceable way through a most ardent charity [*ardentissimam caritatem*], which causes our mind [*mentem*] to pass beyond this world to the Father through ecstasy and rapture [*ecstasim et raptum*].[85]

In *Brev.* 5.1, Bonaventure had argued that sanctifying grace conforms the soul to the Trinity by making it a daughter of the Father, bride of Christ, and temple of the Holy Spirit. In this discussion of the spiritual sensorium in *Brev.* 5.6, he has concluded this second subset of chapters by vividly recounting how the soul becomes the bride of Christ. The graced soul sees, tastes, touches, hears, and even smells the Incarnate Word, the Bridegroom with whom the soul is conjugally united through the gifts of the spiritual senses. Again, this climactic moment is no accident. It concludes the Seraphic Doctor's presentation of the branching out of grace within Chapters 4–6 in a Christological key that directly recalls his previous claim that sanctifying grace weds the soul to Christ as its bride. This is the *modus* of sanctifying grace according to *Brev.* 5: that grace would branch out into holy habits within our souls in accordance with our free choice so as to unite us in a loving union with the person of Christ.

---

85. *Brev.* 5.6 (5, 259).

The *Fructus* of Grace in Chapters 7–10: Perfection

Perhaps rather strangely, however, the Seraphic Doctor's discussion of grace in the *Breviloquium* does not conclude with this contemplative moment. If Chapters 1–3 treat the *ortus* of grace in the soul, and Chapters 4–6 treat the *modus* of grace insofar as it branches out into the soul in accordance with free choice, we should expect here to arrive at a discussion of the *fructus* of grace, or namely, an argument about how sanctifying grace "perfects" the person so as to bring her to her final "rest" in the Trinity. Three problems challenge this expectation. First, a quick glance back at the chapter titles within Chapters 7–10 reveals that the Seraphic Doctor does not seem to follow the pattern that I argue informs the structure of *Brev.* 5: The subject matter of all four chapters is the "exercise of grace," and the theme of "exercise" seems to be the exact opposite of the expected theme, "the rest of fruition." Second, the Seraphic Doctor's elaborate conclusion to Chapters 4–6 has already described the contemplative rest enjoyed by the soul through the habits of the spiritual senses: Do Chapters 7–10 truly describe the *fructus* of grace? Does not Chapter 6 already achieve this aim? Third, whereas the first two subsets of chapters within *Brev.* 5 each boast three chapters, Bonaventure diverges from this pattern in the conclusion to *Brev.* 5 and instead provides four chapters, signaling that this subsection is indeed structurally different.

Answering these questions first requires surveying the content of Chapters 7–10: How does Bonaventure understand his own project in this final subset of chapters within *Brev.* 5? The Seraphic Doctor concludes Chapter 6 by noting that no one can know the "nocturnal and delicious [*nocturnam et deliciosam*] illumination" of the spiritual senses unless she trains herself for this union. Chapters 7–10, he thus concludes, ought to treat the "exercise" of grace with respect to meritorious actions (*exercitia meritorum*).[86] Bonaventure thus suggests that human persons "exercise" grace through meritorious actions with regard to the articles of faith (Ch. 7); the order of things they should love (Ch. 8); by following the precepts of the divine law (Ch. 9); and with regard to what they pray, or the petitions of the Lord's Prayer (Ch. 10).[87] "The reason for holding these things is this," he writes:

---

86. *Brev.* 5.6 (5, 260).
87. *Brev.* 5.7 (5, 260): "Primo, de exercitatione gratiae in credendis, cuiusmodi sunt

The First Principle in itself is the highest Truth and Goodness; but in its works, it is the highest Justice and Mercy. To the highest Truth is owed firm assent [*firma assensio*]; to the highest Goodness is owed fervent love [*fervens dilectio*]; to the highest Justice is owed universal submission [*universalis subiectio*]; and to the highest Mercy is owed faithful prayer [*fiducialis invocatio*]. And grace is the ordering of our mind [*ordinativa mentis nostrae*] to the worship that is owed to the First Principle: hence it stands that grace directs and regulates us to what is owed [*debita*], and to the meritorious exercises of believing, loving, obeying, and praying [*meritoria exercitia in credendis, amandis, exsequendis et postulandis*], in accordance with what is required of the highest Truth, Goodness, Justice, and Mercy in the blessed Trinity.[88]

The Seraphic Doctor thereby specifies the purpose of Chapters 7–10. Sanctifying grace is "the ordering of our mind to the worship that is owed to the First Principle" insofar as it "directs and regulates us" to this worship through enabling the meritorious acts of believing the Truth, loving the Good, obeying the Law, and praying for Mercy.[89] He has already argued in Chapter 2 that none of these meritorious actions would be possible apart from sanctifying grace. With these claims in mind, we can see how the final four chapters within *Brev.* 5 perfectly correspond to this opening statement. Chapter 7 details how the human person exercises grace through believing the articles of faith as expressed in the Creed. In so doing, he provides "firm assent" to the Truth through grace.[90] Chapter 8 teaches the proper order of what ought to be loved by the human person: God, our souls, our neighbors as much as ourselves, and our bodies.[91] Grace here orders the human person to the Goodness of the First Principle through inspiring a "fervent love." Chapter 9 next explains the precepts of the Law, which boil down to the scriptural commandment to love God above all else and our neighbors as ourselves.[92] Grace thus orders the human mind

---

articuli fidei; secundo, in diligendis, cuiusmodi sunt illa quae spectant ad ordinem diligendi; tertio, in exsequendis, cuiusmodi sunt praecepta legis divinae; quarto in postulandis, cuiusmodi sunt petitiones orationis dominicae."

88. *Brev.* 5.7 (5, 260).

89. More work would be required to draw this out, but it is further notable that these four meritorious actions might roughly correspond with what he claims concerning the fourfold effect of grace in *II Sent.* d. 26, namely, that the *influentia* of sanctifying grace assimilates the soul to the First Principle through "illumination, reformation, sanctification, and vivification."

90. *Brev.* 5.7 (5, 260–61).

91. *Brev.* 5.8 (5, 261–62).

92. *Brev.* 5.9 (5, 262–63).

to obey the just commands of the First Principle. Finally, Chapter 10 teaches the petitions of the Lord's Prayer through which grace orders the human mind to the mercy of the First Principle.[93]

How, though, are these meritorious actions to be understood as the *fructus* of grace in Part 5 of the *Breviloquium*? We first should note that, within the larger context of the *Breviloquium*, the final fruit of grace must always be located within Part 7, where Bonaventure will narrate the events of the final judgment and the elevation of the Church to its final rest in the glory of God.[94] Within the context of *Brev.* 5, however, Chapters 7–10 speak about the *fructus* of grace in a much more immediate sense. First, the very structure of *Brev.* 5 serves as an indication that these chapters consider the fruit of grace. The *ortus* of grace in the soul, as he tells us in Chapters 1–3, is the Trinity, which is gifted to the soul through the *influentia* of sanctifying grace when the will is "purified" from its sinful, mercenary ways. Grace then flowers within the soul in accordance with the person's free choice so as to wed the soul to Christ; in this way, the soul is "illuminated." Read in light of the first two subsets of chapters in *Brev.* 5, Chapters 7–10 explain the result of this "branching out" of grace within the soul: Because her will has been made "upright" through grace in Chapters 4–6, the human person can finally exercise the meritorious acts through which she may worship the First Principle, the Trinity, who gifted her grace and to whom she aims through the meritorious acts enabled by grace. In this way, she will be perfected.

The fundamental point for understanding how Chapters 7–10 function in this way, however, requires turning to the Seraphic Doctor's transition between Chapters 4–6 and Chapters 7–10 at the conclusion of Chapter 6, where he offers these remarks:

And through these steps [*gradibus*] [namely, the branching out of grace into the habits of the virtues, spiritual gifts, and beatitudes], *Jacob's Ladder* is constructed [*consistit scala Iacob*], *whose top touches heaven* and *the throne of Solomon,* upon which sits the most wise and truly peaceful and loving King, who is the most beautiful Bridegroom and *totally desirable; upon whom the angels long to gaze,* and toward whom the desire of holy souls pant *as a deer longs for flowing streams.*[95]

<hr>

93. *Brev.* 5.10 (5, 263–64).
94. See *Brev.* 7 (5, 281–91).
95. *Brev.* 5.6 (5, 260).

To reach an ecstatic union with this fair Bridegroom, he concludes, human persons must train themselves for it through meritorious acts, a claim through which he then transitions to Chapter 7–10. This is the key to interpreting *Brev.* 5.

In the previous chapter, I showed how the symbol of Jacob's Ladder can be used to "enflesh" the Seraphic Doctor's "discursive speculations" surrounding hierarchy insofar as it helps us reimagine what the *redditus* moment in Bonaventure's theology looks like. The rational creature returns to God through hierarchy not because she reaches some sort of stopping-point in a mystical bottom-up journey from the earth to God, but because her participation in a hierarchy makes her fruitful and abundant: The rational creature has "returned" to God when she has been made into a divine similitude, when she has been "made as like as possible to the Divine" by being ordered to ever more fruitful relationships with God and the rest of the created order of reality. In this way, she remains in God. The symbol of Jacob's Ladder helps us understand the *redditus* in Bonaventure's theology because it images how a rational creature circles between God and other creatures through this return, which leads to an "end" that is at once a *status* and a *fructus,* an end and a beginning; or in other words, it helps us envision how the "return" yields to the "remaining."

By employing this specific symbol at the point where he transitions between his discussion of the *modus* and *fructus* of grace in *Brev.* 5, Bonaventure is indeed similarly indicating that the *fructus* of grace—the moment at which the soul "returns" to God after it has been purified and illuminated—is "perfective" precisely insofar as it causes the soul to *remain* in God, to endlessly circle between a contemplative union with Christ and the meritorious actions of believing the Truth, loving the Good, obeying the Law, and praying for Mercy. In other words, by employing this symbol, the Seraphic Doctor suggests that grace makes the soul "deiform" and assimilates it to the Blessed Trinity by hierarchizing it. Throughout *Brev.* 5 thus far, he has detailed how grace shapes the soul by first "purifying" it from sin in Chapters 1–3 (the *ortus* of grace); he then described how grace "branches out" through the habits of the virtues, spiritual gifts, and beatitudes within the soul so as to "illuminate" it from within, preparing it for a contemplative union with Christ in Chapters 4–6 (the *modus* of grace); and he concludes his comments on grace in Chapters 7–10 of the *Breviloquium* by describing the "perfection" of the soul, the *fructus* of grace, as the "exercise" of meritorious acts. The climactic, sensual union with Christ depicted in Chapter 6 is not the "stopping point" of the story of grace within the soul, but rather, a point of departure: It is the moment when the soul—instead of ascending to God so as to never again descend—becomes likened to a "Jacob's Ladder" and is made capable of both "ascending" to God through contemplation and "descending" to its neighbor through perfect virtue. Through the inflowing of sanctifying grace, the soul is conformed to the entire Trinity and can remain there—it is assimilated to the First Principle—precisely insofar as it can now be "fruitful" in both ways.

It bears repeating that this idea expresses the Seraphic Doctor's profound intuition concerning the very nature of the Trinity as a fountain of overflowing goodness. Again, echoing his definition of hierarchy from *II Sent.*, d. 9, Bonaventure holds that to be made "as like as possible" to the uncreated hierarchy—to indeed enjoy the "rest of fruition" in the Trinity while still *in via*—is to be filled with what he there called "the fruitfulness of plenitude [*plenitudinis ubertatem*]," an overflowing charity.[96] The graced person does not ascend to a contemplative union with God so as to never again bend down to the created world around her; rather, sanctifying grace invites her to relate to the created world in a way that can be compared to the descent of the Incarnate Word to creation.[97] In order to enjoy "the rest of fruition" of the Trinity through grace, the human person must be filled with a fruitful plenitude, striving after God through contemplation while yet relating to creation through meritorious acts. This is what it means to be conformed to the Trinity through *gratia gratum faciens*, or to become a similitude of the First Principle, in *Brev.* 5. The *fructus* of grace is that the soul itself becomes like a Jacob's Ladder through God's gracious inflowing from above. In this way, the human person worships the First Principle and truly becomes the daughter of the Father, the bride of Christ, and the temple of the Holy Spirit.

Brev. 5, as it were, likewise gives us important data for how we ought to regard the interaction between the purgative, illuminative, and perfective moments within the soul in Bonaventure's theology. In *Brev.* 5.1, as we saw above, he identifies each of these three hierarchical

---

96. See again *II Sent.* d. 9, prol. (2, 238).
97. See especially my discussion of this in Chapter 3.

activities with the *ortus, modus,* and *fructus* of sanctifying grace within
the soul, even as he also explicitly associates them with a Trinitarian appropriation for the Father, Son, and Holy Spirit, respectively. Notably,
the *fructus* of sanctifying grace does not exclude, but rather includes,
the two earlier moments within it. As already expressed in *II Sent.,*
d. 26–27, Bonaventure understands the *influentia* of sanctifying grace
as a continuous act that circles unendingly between God and the soul.
To continue meriting the Good, the soul must remain willingly receptive to this *influentia* throughout its time *in via.* It must, in other words,
continue to be "purified" and continue to be "illuminated" through it.
If the *fructus* of grace is that the soul is made into a temple of the Holy
Spirit, the soul in no wise ceases to be a daughter of the Father or a
bride of the Son when it arrives at this "perfective" moment. Bonaventure's use of the symbol of Jacob's Ladder to depict the movements of
grace here in Part 5 of the *Breviloquium* highlights how the three hierarchical activities of purification, illumination, and perfection are
dynamically rather than statically ordered to one another within the
soul. These should not be conceived as a "step-ladder" to perfection;
rather, the soul that has arrived at the pneumatic moment—the perfective moment—is only "perfect" insofar as it is also simultaneously the
Father's daughter and the Son's bride, and the soul must continue relating to God in all three ways if it is to remain assimilated to the Blessed
Trinity unto glory. Grace will be "fruitful" within the soul only when
these three hierarchical activities mutually and reciprocally reinforce
one another throughout the person's time *in via.*

Conclusion

Thus, through *The Commentary on the Sentences* and the *Breviloquium,* we are introduced to the foundations of Bonaventure's doctrine of
grace, both insofar as he provides his clearest definitions and explanations of sanctifying grace, but also inasmuch as we can, through them,
affirm that "the element of hierarchy" is indeed an explicit factor in
his soteriology in these, his most significant systematic treatments of
grace. While neither Bonaventure's notion of the hierarchical soul, the
symbol of Jacob's Ladder, nor the three hierarchical activities of "purification, illumination, and perfection" appear overtly in his *II Sent.,*
his definition there of sanctifying grace as an *influentia* that works *in*

and *with* the will to free it from sin nonetheless employs the Seraphic Doctor's hierarchical vocabulary. By defining sanctifying grace as an *influentia* in this, his most expansive treatment of grace in any of his works, Bonaventure emphasizes the fact that it must be a "continuous act" which is always constantly processing and returning between the Trinity and the soul, thus uniting the soul to the "uncreated hierarchy." The Seraphic Doctor's definition of sanctifying grace as an *influentia* of this sort, a created habit in which the uncreated gift is given to the soul, is the foundation upon which he will further construct his doctrine of grace throughout the remainder of his theological career.

That said, though it certainly builds upon the "developments and discussions" from *II Sent.*, *Brev.* 5 in many ways presents a more mature version of the Seraphic Doctor's teachings on sanctifying grace than that which is found in his earlier work. In *Brev.* 5, Bonaventure explicitly claims that sanctifying grace purifies, illuminates, and perfects the soul so as to conform it to the entire Trinity; insofar as he associates these hierarchical activities with Trinitarian appropriations for the Father, Son, and Spirit, his theology of hierarchy becomes a much more central game piece in the *Breviloquium* than it had been in his *Sentences* commentary. Moreover, in the same way that the symbol of Jacob's Ladder is used in his theology of hierarchy to depict how the rational creature becomes "fruitful" in its return to God, so also does he use this symbol here to depict the dynamic ordering of these three hierarchical activities within the graced soul. As such, the *Breviloquium* is an especially useful text through which to bridge our reading of the Seraphic Doctor's early doctrine of grace in the *Commentary on the Sentences* with both the *Itinerarium* and the *Hexaëmeron*. In these two texts, as we shall see in Chapter 5, Bonaventure makes these hierarchical themes within his doctrine of grace even more explicit.

The Hierarchical Soul in the *Itinerarium* and the *Hexaëmeron*

My choice to present these two texts together might, upon first impression, seem rather odd. Written in 1259, two years after the Seraphic Doctor accepted the call to become Minister General of the Franciscan Order, the *Itinerarium* is perhaps his most famous work. As Stephen F. Brown has written, it is "one of the great spiritual books of all times," a claim evinced by the fact that, "In the past half century it has been translated into English more than a half dozen times."[1] The *Hexaëmeron,* in contrast, was one of Bonaventure's final works, begun in 1273 and left unfinished before his untimely death in 1274, and does not enjoy the same widespread popularity as the *Itinerarium.* Moreover, whereas both *The Commentary on the Sentences* and *Brev.* 5 offer us accounts of grace that can be considered systematic in nature, proffering clear definitions of sanctifying grace as a created *influentia* and then explaining how this gift works *in* and *with* the soul to return it to the Trinity, neither the *Itinerarium* nor the *Hexaëmeron* provide such explicit systematic presentations of grace. Despite the years and contextual differences that separate them, however, and also despite the fact that Bonaventure's doctrine of grace is perhaps less clear in these texts than in those I examined in Chapter 4, these two texts are

---

1. See Brown, "Introduction," ix.

nevertheless crucial for unpacking that doctrine for another reason[2]—namely, they both contain an account of Bonaventure's notion of the hierarchical soul as he readapts and revises it from the thirteenth-century Victorine, Thomas Gallus.[3]

My purpose in this chapter is to show how the Seraphic Doctor, as it were, "steals" Gallus's angelic anthropology—albeit with some significant revisions, as will be especially apparent when we turn to the *Hexaëmeron*—within his doctrine of grace. Like Gallus before him, Bonaventure also offers an account of the hierarchical soul. Unlike Gallus, however, he does so entirely within the context of his teachings on grace. Whereas for Gallus, the soul simply is hierarchical, for Bonaventure, sanctifying grace hierarchizes the soul. By attending to this teaching in both the *Itinerarium* and the *Hexaëmeron*, we will clearly be able to see the "evolution" of the association between hierarchy and grace in Bonaventure's theology. As we saw in Chapter 4, this association was latent in *II Sent.* and drawn out explicitly in Part 5 of the *Breviloquium*'s account of the soul's purification, illumination, and perfection through grace. Here in Chapter 5, we will see how the association comes to fruition in the *Itinerarium*, where Bonaventure will for the first time explicitly claim that grace "hierarchizes" the soul, thus borrowing Gallus's angelic anthropology in order to explain how grace restores and repairs the rational soul from sin. The continuity of his doctrine of grace across the course of his career will finally be underscored when we realize that this claim is not only carried forward almost twenty years later in the *Hexaëmeron*, but also therein conceptually expanded. Attention to Bonaventure's own angelic anthropology in both texts will pave the path forward for examining his doctrine of grace with respect to his theological anthropology, Christology, and teachings on sanctity in *Part III*. I begin by looking at the fourth chapter of the *Itinerarium,* continue with an examination of *Hex.* 22, and finally conclude the chapter some general comments to bring *Part II* as a whole to a close.

---

2. Colberg has recently read the *Itinerarium*'s treatment of grace as largely consistent with that of the *Breviloquium*; see *The Wayfarer's End*, 29–76.

3. I introduced Thomas Gallus and his angelic anthropology in Chapter 2. To briefly recap that notion in Gallusian theology, this is essentially the notion that the soul itself *is* hierarchical, or namely, that the soul itself is "shaped" after the nine angelic orders of Dionysius's celestial hierarchy. The seraphic order within the soul in this Gallusian angelic anthropology is the point at which the soul experiences an affective union with God, which then fecundates the lower nine orders of the soul with divine *theoriae*. See also Shelby, "Thomas Gallus' *Explanatio*," 306–14.

Sanctifying Grace in the
Itinerarium mentis in Deum

Approaching Bonaventure's
Doctrine of Grace in the *Itinerarium*

Before turning specifically to Bonaventure's discussion of grace in *Itin.* 4,[4] however, it is first necessary to offer a few comments concerning the structure and meaning of the text itself. This complex text is inspired,[5] as Bonaventure tells his readers in the *Itinerarium*'s prologue, by St. Francis's reception of the wounds of the stigmata. Contemplating St. Francis's "vision of the winged seraph in the likeness of the Crucified"[6] atop Mt. Alverna, Bonaventure structures the *Itinerarium* according to this vision: "through these six wings can rightly be understood the six levels of illuminations, as if by certain steps or roads, through which the soul is prepared to pass over to peace through the ecstatic rapture of Christian wisdom."[7] Each chapter within the *Itinerarium* subsequently unfolds how the soul moves in and through these

---

4. Strikingly, and perhaps problematically, the Seraphic Doctor does not refer to sanctifying grace as an *influentia* in *Itin.* 4. This does not, however, mean that we should read him here as dispensing with his previous definition, especially since he will refer to sanctifying grace as an *influentia* in later texts, such as *De don. Spir.* Bonaventure's explicit reference to the hierarchical soul in the *Itinerarium*, as we shall see below, clearly is in agreement with his treatment of grace in the *Breviloquium*, which, as we have already seen, depends upon his definition of grace in *II Sent.* The lack of reference to an *influentia* is perhaps simply attributable to the "short and sweet" nature of the text. His goal is not to provide an account of what we should hold concerning sanctifying grace according to the orthodox faith, as is the case with both the *Breviloquium* and his *Sentences* commentary, but to show how it works within the soul to lead it to the affective union described in *Itin.* 7. As readers will see below, it certainly stands in continuity with the previous two texts discussed in Chapter 4 and with the *Hexaëmeron*.

5. The question of how to interpret the *Itinerarium* remains a topic of conversation among Bonaventurean scholars. See esp. Jay Hammond's discussion of the text in conjunction with Hellmann's work on the notion of *ordo* in Bonaventure's theology in his "Appendix: Order in the *Itinerarium mentis in Deum*," 191–271. See also the conversation following this appendix between Gregory LaNave and Hammond in *Franciscan Studies*; see first LaNave, "Knowing God through and in All Things: A Proposal for Reading Bonaventure's '*Itinerarium mentis in Deum*,'" *Franciscan Studies* 67 (2009): 267–99; Jay Hammond, "Bonaventure's *Itinerarium*: A *Respondeo*," *Franciscan Studies* 67 (2009): 301–21. See also Regis J. Armstrong, *Into God: Itinerarium mentis in Deum of Saint Bonaventure; An Annotated Translation* (Washington, DC: The Catholic University of America Press, 2020); Colberg, *The Wayfarer's End*, 61–69; and Timothy J. Johnson, "Reading between the Lines: Apophatic Knowledge and Naming the Divine in Bonaventure's Book of Creation," *Franciscan Studies* 60 (2002): 139–58.

6. *Itin.* prol. 2 (5, 295).

7. *Itin.* prol. 3 (5, 295).

steps of contemplation in order to reach a mystical union with the Triune God in Chapter 7. The first two chapters of the text describe how the human person can know God in and through the vestiges of creation. Chapter 3 considers the rational soul as the image of God, whereby the soul can perceive God by inwardly beholding the three powers of memory, intelligence, and will within the mind. Chapter 4 considers how the soul as the image of God is prepared for union with the entire Trinity through grace, by transitioning from being merely an image to also becoming a similitude. The Seraphic Doctor then moves beyond these considerations of created things to consider the Unity and Being of God in Chapter 5, as well as the Goodness of the Triune God in Chapter 6. These considerations culminate finally in Chapter 7, where the soul—like Francis—is carried beyond itself and into the mystical ecstasies of divine union through all these illuminations.

Before providing my own reading of Chapter 4 of the text, which treats the soul as a similitude of the Trinity, two previous readings of the *Itinerarium* in particular can help us elucidate our own understanding of the role of grace within it. First, Jay Hammond's analysis of the text interprets it according to Bonaventure's concept of *ordo* whereby he can conclude that "Bonaventure constructs the text's three paired chapters according to a dialectic between the vertical order of essence … and horizontal order of persons," where "these two orders intricately intertwine to form a grand circular framework of exit and return whereby the *Itinerarium*'s three paired chapters begin at the lowest, proceed through the intermediate, and arrive at the highest."[8] From this observation, however, Hammond further argues that this *ordo* within the structure of the *Itinerarium* ought not be read "in a strictly linear or merely logical manner in isolation from the wider circular framework" that is often so central to the Seraphic Doctor's metaphysics:

Order always has a *primum*, a *medium*, and an *ultimum*. For Bonaventure, this is Christian wisdom. However, there is not a simple linear succession from the *primum* to the *ultimum*. Rather, order follows a circular dynamic whereby each of the levels (*primum*, *medium*, *ultimum*) interpenetrate each other resulting in a multilayered synthesis that integrates everything according to the basic unifying concept of order. The interpenetration of all three comprises the *circumincessio*, both within the divine life of the Trinity and extended to creation in the free act of love that is the Incarnation. In the end

---

8. Hammond, "Order in the *Itinerarium mentis in Deum*," 268–69.

we arrive at the seemingly paradoxical fact that the journey ends where it begins, with the mystery of the *primum principium,* or more specifically, on God who is a community of divine persons. In between, the dialectic of the vertical and horizontal orders brings the beginning, the middle, and the end into a unity. Within this process, all of creation is ultimately caught up in the order of the divine *circumincessio.*[9]

Hammond's argument here concerning the *ordo* of the *Itinerarium,* which should not only be read as a linear sort of "bottom-up" ascent of the soul into God, but rather "circularly" and "dynamically," corresponds well with my own observations concerning Bonaventure's cyclical metaphysics.[10] Similarly, his comments concerning the interpenetration of the *primum, medium,* and *ultimum* within Bonaventure's general concept of *ordo* likewise corroborate my own claims concerning the interpenetration of the *ortus, modus,* and *fructus* of grace—as well as the three hierarchical activities of purification, illumination, and perfection—in *Brev.* 5.[11]

Second, with respect to these, Philotheus Boehner has argued that the entire text of the *Itinerarium* broadly falls within the "second" rather than the "third" moment within the Triple Way:

It has been said that [the *Itinerarium*'s] proper place is in the perfective way, but we believe that it belongs rather to the illuminative way, reaching at the end the contemplation of the unitive way and merging with it. For throughout the six chapters of the *Itinerarium* we are concerned with six *illuminationum suspensiones* (uplifting illuminations) as the Prologue (n. 3) says.... The six steps of the *Itinerarium,* as expressly stated by Bonaventure, precede perfective or unitive contemplation....[12]

In this interpretation of the text, *Itin.* 7 is the point within the text where the soul that has been illuminated through the prior six steps arrives at the moment of perfection, its *fructus* wherein it is joined to the entire Trinity in love.

Building off these previous observations by Hammond and Boehner, I here simply highlight one passage from *Itin.* 1 which can further illuminate for us Bonaventure's intentions for the text and also frame

---

9. Hammond, "Order in the *Itinerarium mentis in Deum,*" 270–71.

10. For these comments, see especially Chapter 3.

11. See again Chapter 4.

12. Philotheus Boehner, introduction to *Itinerarium mentis in Deum,* trans. Zachary Hayes, *Works of St. Bonaventure 2* (St. Bonaventure, NY: Franciscan Institute, 2002), 24.

his comments concerning grace in Chapter 4. Much like his treatment of grace in the *Breviloquium,* the Seraphic Doctor in *Itin.* 1.8 presents the three hierarchical activities of purification, illumination, and perfection as the remedy for sin. If the soul wishes to ascend to God and avoid sin, he argues it must be purified by justice through a holy way of life (*ad iustitiam purificantem*); it must be illuminated with respect to its knowledge (*ad scientiam illuminantem*), which it practices through meditation; and it must be perfected with respect to wisdom (*ad sapientiam perficientem*), which happens in the practice of contemplation. According to the Seraphic Doctor, all three of these hierarchical activities are held together within the soul through constant prayer.[13] From these observations, Bonaventure continues *Itin.* 1 by launching into his description of the soul's mystical ascent into God, a journey that will continue all the way through the text to its conclusion in Chapter 7:

> Thus, since it is first necessary to ascend [*ascendere*] before descending [*descendere*] on Jacob's Ladder, let us place the first step of the ascent at the bottom, putting the whole sensible world itself as a mirror before us, through which we shall pass over into God, the highest Artist. In this way, we will become like the Hebrews, passing from Egypt to the land promised to the Fathers. And we will also be Christians passing with Christ *from this world to the Father.* We will be lovers of that wisdom, which calls and says: *Come to me, all you who desire me, and be filled with my fruits.*[14]

The inclusion of the symbol of Jacob's Ladder here, as at the end of *Brev.* 5.6, provides an important framework for understanding the complexity of the "circularity" and "dynamism" at play throughout the *Itinerarium.* If, as Hammond has already intuited, the text itself ought not be understood linearly, with the multivalent orders that shape the text interpenetrating each other throughout; and if, as Hammond further intuits, the end of the text paradoxically leads us back to the beginning; and also if, as Boehner has argued, the entire text describes how the soul passes from the illuminative way and into the perfective way; then the Seraphic Doctor's inclusion of this symbol here indeed might be playing a rather thick role within the text. Through it, Bonaventure indicates that he knows the end of his mystical treatise will also be a "beginning": Once the soul reaches the "perfective" moment after it has traversed the "illuminative" path of the *Itinerarium,*

---

13. *Itin.* 1.8 (5, 298).
14. *Itin.* 1.9 (5, 298).

it will be *"filled with [divine] fruits."* As has also been implicated in the *Breviloquium*, however, the three hierarchical activities interpenetrate one another within the life of grace. The perfected soul does not cease being purified and illuminated; rather, the perfected soul is "perfect" precisely insofar as it is also still being purified and illuminated, and also insofar as it is made capable of both "ascending" to God through contemplation and "descending" to its neighbor through meritorious action. The clause in Bonaventure's above remarks from the *Itinerarium*—namely, that "it is first necessary to ascend before descending on Jacob's Ladder"—suggests that the entire journey of his most famous spiritual treatise serves the purpose of paving the way forward for the descent, which will once again surely yield to the ascent, and vice versa. The result will truly be a *circumincessio,* as Hammond has already noted, whereby the soul that has thus "ascended" to the perfective way through the illuminative way will in no wise remain still but will continue circling between God and the "vestiges" around it in creation into perpetuity.

The Effect of Sanctifying Grace is a Hierarchical Soul

Neither this ascent nor the descent that follows would be possible, however, apart from sanctifying grace, and thus we arrive at *Itin.* 4. With respect to the overall structure of the text and excluding the prologue, Chapter 4 in one way falls in the center of the treatise's account of the soul's ascent into God and could thus also be regarded as a *medium* that connects the *primum* (Chapters 1–3) with the *ultimum* (Chapters 5–7).[15] Or, if we borrow Benson's observations concerning the structure of the *Breviloquium,* we perhaps might say that *Itin.* 4 describes the

---

15. Recognizing the significance of order and patterns in Bonaventure's thought, it is important to note that my observations here concerning the role of Chapter 4 within the *Itinerarium* are not intended to undermine other structures at work within the text. The Seraphic Doctor obviously lays out his own intended pattern for it with a prologue followed by three ordered pairs—Chapters 1–2, Chapters 3–4, Chapters 5–6—and a clear conclusion in Chapter 7, as I detailed above. My own suggestion that Chapter 4 serves as a *medium* between the text's treatment of knowledge of created realities and knowledge of God is not offered in rejection of that pattern; rather, I simply offer this as an additional way of understanding the role of grace within the text's account of the soul's ascent through illumination. As Hammond has suggested, the order of the text is dynamic and multivalent: We can recognize the "thick" role played by Chapter 4 within the text without negating that Chapters 3–4 are themselves quite obviously an ordered, centered pair between the prologue/Chapters 1–2 and Chapters 5–6/Chapter 7.

modus of the soul's ascent into God within the text. It is here that the Seraphic Doctor details how the soul, having contemplated God in and through the vestiges of creation and in its rational powers in *Itin.* 1–3, receives the grace of Christ through which to contemplate God's unity and trinity in *Itin.* 5–6, finally to pass onto the "perfective" and "unitive" moment in *Itin.* 7.

As Hammond has already well documented, *Itin.* 4 is thus also the Christological center of the text, inasmuch as Bonaventure opens it by pointing to Christ's role in reforming the image of the rational mind that has fallen through sin.[16] Though the "ladder" between heaven and earth was broken by Adam's sin, the Incarnate Christ "himself becomes a ladder" in order to repair what has thus been broken.[17] In order to traverse the fifth and sixth steps on the path of Bonaventure's illuminative way, or namely, in order to pass from knowledge of created realities (*Itin.* 1–3) to a knowledge of and union with God (*Itin.* 5–7), the rational soul needs to be healed by Christ.[18] This, then, is the subject of *Itin.* 4.

There, Bonaventure's theology of hierarchy appears almost immediately in order to describe this reformation of the soul as the image of God. The rational soul will be repaired when "it is clothed over with the three theological virtues, by which the soul is *purified, illuminated, and perfected,*" or, as he further explains, when it has faith in, hopes in, and believes in Jesus Christ, who is the Incarnate, Uncreated, and Inspired Word.[19] Echoing *Brev.* 5, the presence of the three theological virtues within the soul here again lead it to a sensual, nuptial union with Christ, whereby all the soul's spiritual senses are "purified, illuminated, and perfected" through the three theological virtues themselves. According to *Itin.* 4, faith in the Uncreated Word of the Father helps the soul recover its spiritual senses of hearing and sight. Hope in the Inspired Word helps the soul recover its spiritual sense of smell. Finally, when the soul embraces the Incarnate Word in love, it recovers the spiritual senses of taste and touch, so that "With its spiritual senses restored, the soul now sees and hears, smells, tastes and embraces its

---

16. See Hammond, "Order in the *Itinerarium,*" 238–43. Hammond has also here provided a fine analysis of the structure of Chapter 4 as it pertains to and fits within the rest of the *Itinerarium.*

17. *Itin.* 4.2 (5, 306).

18. I will treat the role of Christ in Bonaventure's doctrine of grace more extensively in Chapter 7.

19. *Itin.* 4.3 (5, 306).

Beloved, so that it can now sing like the Bride in the *Song of Songs*, which was written for the exercise of contemplation at this fourth step, which *no one* knows, *unless he receives*."[20]

Existing scholarship tends to accentuate the differences between the Seraphic Doctor's account of the spiritual senses here in *Itin.* 4 from that which appears in *Brev.* 5.6.[21] For the purposes of simply expounding the Seraphic Doctor's doctrine of grace as it functions in both texts, I here rather highlight some similarities. Bonaventure's account of the spiritual senses in *Brev.* 5.6, we recall, was offered at the conclusion of his discussion of the "branching out" of sanctifying grace within the soul in accordance with free will; it there corresponded with the illuminative way, indicating that the soul had been prepared as a "bride for the Son" after it had already been made a "daughter of the Father" through the purgative way. It served as the bridge between Bonaventure's claim that the soul, through this nuptial union, had become like a Jacob's Ladder, capable of circling between contemplation and action so that it could thus remain in perfection and also be called a temple of the Holy Spirit. Moreover, *Brev.* 5.4–6 had a "micro-structure" that narrated the "branching out" of grace in Chapters 4–6: There, sanctifying grace made the will "upright" through the strength of virtue in 5.4, edified it through the spiritual gifts in 5.5, and perfected it in the beatitudes through the fervor of love in 5.6.

Subsequently, in *Itin.* 4, the Seraphic Doctor notably uses a similar microstructure to explain the relationship between the theological virtues and the spiritual senses, whereby faith purifies, hope illumines, and love perfects the soul so that it may embrace the Bridegroom, Christ. Even more strikingly, in the same way that the *Breviloquium* does not conclude with this contemplative embrace in 5.6, Bonaventure likewise then continues *Itin.* 4 by writing:

20. *Itin.* 4.3 (5, 306).

21. As especially demonstrated by a debate between Rahner and von Balthasar; see Karl Rahner, "The Doctrine of the 'Spiritual Senses' in the Middle Ages," in *Theological Investigations*, vol. 18, ed. Edward Quinn (New York: Crossroads, 1983), 173–88 (originally published Karl Rahner, "La doctrine des sens spirituels au Moyen Âge, en particular chez saint Bonaventure," *Revue d'ascetique et de mystique* 14 [1933]: 263–99); Hans Urs von Balthasar, *The Glory of the Lord*, 1:371–73, 2:315–26; and Gregory LaNave, "Bonaventure," in *The Spiritual Senses: Perceiving God in Western Christianity* (Cambridge: Cambridge University Press, 2012), 159–73. The seminal monograph on the subject is that by Fabio Massimo Tedoldi, *La dottrina dei cinque sensi spirituali in San Bonaventura* (Roma: Pontificium Athenaeum Antonianum, 1999). See also Armstrong, *Into God*, 281–82, esp. 281n413.

When we have arrived at these things, our spirit is made hierarchical [*hierarchicus*] for the purpose of rising to conformity with the heavenly Jerusalem, in which no one enters unless through grace [*per gratiam*] descending into his heart, as John saw in his Apocalypse. It then descends [*descendit*] into the heart when through the reformation of the image [*reformationem imaginis*], through the theological virtues, through the delights of the spiritual senses [*oblectationes spiritualium sensuum*], and the ecstasy of rapture [*suspensiones excessum*], our spirit is made *hierarchical* [*efficitur spiritus noster hierarchicus*], namely, purified, illuminated, and perfected [*purgatus, illuminatus, et perfectus*]. For then the nine levels of orders are marked within it, insofar as they are interiorly disposed in our spirit in an ordered way: *announcing* [*nuntiatio*], *dictating* [*dictatio*], *leading* [*ductio*], *ordering* [*ordinatio*], *strengthening* [*roboratio*], *commanding* [*imperatio*], *receiving* [*susceptio*], *revealing* [*revelatio*], *anointing* [*unctio*], steps which correspond to the nine orders of angels, so that the first three of the aforesaid steps consider *nature* [*naturam*] in the human mind [*mente*], the following three steps consider *industry* [*industriam*], and the last three consider *grace* [*gratiam*]. Through these habits, the soul, by entering into itself, enters into the heavenly Jerusalem, where, considering the orders of the angels, it sees in them God, who is dwelling in them and working all things in them.[22]

Once again, in other words, the sensual embrace with Christ the Bridegroom—which Bonaventure likewise identifies with the illuminative way in *Brev.* 5—leads to nothing less than the soul's hierarchization. In the same way that this contemplative union is both an "end" and a "beginning," whereby the soul at this point becomes like a Jacob's Ladder in *Brev.* 5, the contemplative embrace with Christ in *Itin.* 4 is what invites the soul to become "hierarchical," "purified, illuminated, and perfected" so that God is now "dwelling in" the soul and "working all things" within it.

This, then, is also where we begin to see an even sharper development in the association between Bonaventure's theology of hierarchy and doctrine of grace than has yet appeared in either the *Breviloquium* or *II Sent.* For the first time, Bonaventure here explicitly claims that grace causes the soul to become "hierarchical" (*hierarchicus*). Rather than simply identifying the three hierarchical activities of purification, illumination, and perfection with the work of sanctifying grace in the soul, he here suggests that the soul is "purified, illuminated, and perfected" through grace insofar as it has been likened to the nine orders

---

22. *Itin.* 4.4 (5, 307).

named in Dionysius's *CH*. The Seraphic Doctor cites Bernard of Clairvaux in naming the nine orders of Dionysius's angelic hierarchy as they thus appear within the soul, but recognizing the hidden hand of Thomas Gallus here will hold important consequences for how we interpret Bonaventure's teachings on grace in the *Itinerarium*.[23]

Indeed, the Franciscan's description of the function of these orders within the soul—"announcing, dictating, leading, ordering, strengthening, commanding, receiving, revealing, anointing"—directly correspond with Gallus's own description of these orders in the prologue to his commentaries on *Isaiah* and the *Song*.[24] His suggestion that these three levels correspond with nature, industry, and grace, moreover, also corresponds with the Abbot of Vercelli's subdivisions of these orders within those texts as well.[25] I have mapped out these similarities between the respective angelic anthropologies of Gallus and Bonaventure, at least as the latter introduces them in *Itin.* 4, in Table 5.1.

Though the Seraphic Doctor does not directly cite the Victorine in his discussion of these functions of each of the nine angelic orders within the hierarchical soul in the *Itinerarium,* these parallels are too striking to dismiss.[26] Essentially, Bonaventure has here reappropriated Gallus's angelic anthropology in *Itin.* 4 as a way of describing the effects of sanctifying grace within the soul.

Identifying this association is crucial for interpreting the text because Gallus's own angelic anthropology, as Boyd Taylor Coolman has shown,[27] does not itself describe a "bottom-up" mystical ascent to contemplative union with God at the level of the seraph. Rather, according to Gallus, once the soul has "ascended" to the level of the seraph in Dionysius's celestial hierarchy, the divine illuminations received by the

---

23. *Itin.* 4.4 (5, 307): "Unde dicit Bernardus ad Eugenium...." For more on these sources, see Armstrong, *Into God*, 284–91.

24. See my discussion of Gallus's angelic anthropology in Chapter 2. For the Abbot of Vercelli's own parsing of these orders and their functions within the soul, see Gallus, *In Cant.*, 66–67; Gallus, *In Is*.

25. See especially *In Cant.*, 66: "Infima mentis hierarchia consistit in ipsa eius natura, media in industria, que incomparabiliter excedit naturam, summa in excessu mentis. In prima operatur sola natura, in summa sola gratia, in media simul operantur gratia et industria."

26. Gallus's anthropology of the soul, as based upon Dionysius's *The Celestial Hierarchy*, and as explained by Gallus in the prologue to *In Cant.*, 66–67; and in *In Is.*, 154–57. See again my discussion of this angelic anthropology in Chapter 2, and my "Thomas Gallus' *Explanatio*," 306–9, 325–27.

27. See especially Coolman, *Knowledge, Love, and Ecstasy*.

TABLE 5.1 Gallus's Angelic Anthropology in Chapter 4 of the *Itinerarium*

	Thomas Gallus's Angelic Anthropology	Functions of the 9 Angelic Orders in the Hierarchical Soul in *Itin.* 4.4
The Lowest Hierarchy in the Soul: Nature	1. *Angels:* Simple apprehensions that announce something to the soul.	1. Announcing
	2. *Archangels:* The dictations of the simple apprehensions that make judgments about their possible benefit to the soul.	2. Dictating
	3. *Order of Principalities:* The appetites and withdrawals of those apprehensions based on the previous judgments pronounced by the dictations from the Archangels.	3. Leading
The Middle Hierarchy in the Soul: Industry	4. *Powers:* The voluntary motions of both the intellect and affect towards Good or Evil, based on free choice.	4. Ordering
	5. *Virtues:* The infused and acquired virtues that lead the soul to pursue the correct judgment formed from choice made through the Powers.	5. Strengthening
	6. *Dominions:* "The authentic commands of free will" by which the affect and intellect are prepared for the Divine.	6. Commanding
The Highest Hierarchy in the Soul: Grace	7. *Thrones:* The soul is made receptive for God.	7. Receiving
	8. *Cherubim:* The intellect is drawn into God.	8. Revealing
	9. *Seraphim:* The soul experiences an affective union with the Bridegroom, Christ, as the intellect is left behind.	9. Anointing

soul through the affective union it experiences there then likewise "descend" into the lower hierarchical orders of the soul so as to fecundate each of these lower orders with divine light. Just as the divine nature itself can be conceived as an eternal circle, so also, as Coolman observes of Gallus's angelic anthropology, "the ascending and descending valences in the hierarchized soul ultimately generate a perpetual 'circulation' within it too."[28] The Abbot of Vercelli's Seraphic "affective union" is not a stopping point for the soul, but rather, the mode through which

---

28. Coolman, "Medieval Affective Dionysian Tradition," 627; and Coolman, *Knowledge, Love, and Ecstasy,* 232–57.

the entire soul becomes a dynamic, circulating system of interrelated orders enlivened by ecstatic love.

Bonaventure's use of Gallus's angelic anthropology in *Itin.*4, as it were, implicitly brings these same themes to light, especially in anticipation of *Itin.* 7, where he will describe the "perfective" moment as an affective union between the soul and God. Simply put, in the same way that the bridal union with Christ in *Brev.* 5.6 leads the soul to become like a "Jacob's Ladder" so that it can continuously circle between contemplation and meritorious action, so also in *Itin.* 4 does the Seraphic Doctor—by here using Gallus's angelic anthropology—indicate that the bridal union with Christ effectuated by grace will yield to a dynamic ordering within the soul. The soul does not pass from purification, through illumination, and to perfection so as to stop being purified and illuminated; rather, the soul has been hierarchized through grace in *Itin.* 4 inasmuch as all three hierarchical activities have been activated within it. Or in other words, the Seraphic Doctor has in *Itin.* 4 given us a glimpse of what will happen through grace in *Itin.* 7: After it has ascended the "illuminative" way described in the previous six chapters, it will arrive at the level of the seraph—the moment of perfection— where it will be Crucified with Christ. This affective union will not be a stopping point, but will represent the point at which the soul that has been thus illuminated by all six wings of the seraph can then begin its own descent on Jacob's Ladder back to the created order of reality. Positioned in the center of the text in Chapter 4, grace in the *Itinerarium* is the point from which all these "circulations" revolve; through it, the soul can ascend to a union with Christ that will cause it to descend, and vice versa into perpetuity as the grace of the seraph fecundates the whole soul with the light of God throughout the text.

Grace in the *Itinerarium,* therefore, is that which "hierarchizes" the soul. For the first time, following Thomas Gallus, Bonaventure there introduces his own angelic anthropology within his account of grace. While it is in *Itin.* 4 that the association between his theology of hierarchy and his doctrine of grace reaches its most explicit iteration after the *Breviloquium,* his account of sanctifying grace is nonetheless limited there by the brevity of the treatise; though he can assert these ideas in short form, space does not permit their expansion. For that, we must jump ahead roughly twenty years to one of his final texts, which he never quite completed before his untimely death in 1274.

Sanctifying Grace in the *Hexaëmeron*

The Hierarchical Soul in the *Hexaëmeron*

Begun in 1273, Bonaventure's *Collationes in Hexaëmeron* remain some-what of an enigma in certain circles of scholarship: English-speaking scholars are only now beginning to wrestle with and highlight the central importance and meaning of these twenty-three collations on the six days of creation within the Seraphic Doctor's larger *oeuvre*.[29] Treating the Seraphic Doctor's teaching on the hierarchical soul in the *Hexaëmeron* immediately after the *Itinerarium* will here nevertheless be useful insofar as this order of proceeding will clearly highlight the continuity of his doctrine of grace across the course of his career. Whereas Bonaventure could only introduce his angelic anthropology as a "step" within his broader portrait of the illuminative way within the *Itinerarium*, the *Hexaëmeron* gives him space in which to expand and further comment on the *Itinerarium*'s claim that grace hierarchizes the soul.

And indeed, in many ways, we see in the *Hexaëmeron* the convergence of all Bonaventure's teachings on grace from all three texts examined thus far in *Part II*. The *Hexaëmeron*, for example, presumes his definition of sanctifying grace as an *influentia* from his previous explanation of this created gift in *II Sent.* d. 26–27 and the *Breviloquium*.[30]

29. See, for some examples, Davies, *Bonaventure, the Body, and the Aesthetics of Salvation*, 34–75; Jay Hammond, trans., *Collations on the Hexaemeron: Conferences on the Six Days of Creation: The Illuminations of the Church*, Works of St. Bonaventure 18 (St. Bonaventure, NY: Franciscan Institute, 2018); Hughes, "Bonaventure *Contra mundum*?" 372–98. While European scholars have been giving the *Hexaëmeron* its proper due for quite a long time, English-speaking scholars have recently begun to notice a lacuna in English scholarship surrounding this text. I am grateful to private conversations with Jay Hammond, Kevin Hughes, Junius Johnson, and Gregory LaNave for underscoring this lacuna, and for their work in amending it.

30. Unlike the Seraphic Doctor's treatments of grace in both *II Sent.* and *Brev.* 5, Bonaventure's discussion of the hierarchical soul in the *Hexaëmeron* also does not include a definition of grace as an *influentia*. It nonetheless presumes this definition at all points, especially given that his *Collations on the Gift of the Holy Spirit*, one of two "forerunners" to the *Hexaëmeron* that provides a much more explicit "treatise" on grace in its prologue, did define sanctifying grace as an *influentia*, as I mentioned in an above note. See, for example, *De don. Spir.* 1.8 (5, 458–59): "Nobilis *influentia*, quae a Deo incarnato habet originem! ... Istam nobilissimam influentiam impugnat homo per peccatum"; *De don. Spir.* 1.12 (5, 460): "Dionysius determinat nobis usum gratiae in angelica hierarchia et caelesti et dicit, quod si superiores Angeli continerent se et non vellent influere in inferiores Angelos, tunc ipsi clauderent sibi viam influentiae Dei"; and *De don. Spir.* 2.14 (5, 466): "... ad impetrandam divinae gratiae influentiam...." For a selection of Bonaventure's references to the notion of *influentia* in the *Hexaëmeron* that supports my point as such, see *Hex.* 3.19 (5, 346), where he refers to the Christological *influentia* that upholds all things; *Hex.* 14.3 (5, 393), where he

Following his comment from the *Breviloquium,* moreover, the symbol of Jacob's Ladder here becomes the central image through which he will describe the effects of sanctifying grace in the soul. And finally, following the *Itinerarium,* he will here once again employ Gallus's angelic anthropology to describe them.

Unlike in *Itin.* 4, however, the Seraphic Doctor actually names Gallus as a source for this idea in *Hex.* 22. There, he summarizes his hierarchical view of the macrocosm, describing how the nine orders of Dionysius's celestial hierarchy correspond to the ecclesiastical hierarchy.[31] From this, *Hex.* 22 echoes the *Itinerarium* by claiming that these nine orders can also be found within the human soul:

For it is necessary for the hierarchized [*hierarchizata*] soul to have steps corresponding with the heavenly Jerusalem. For the soul [*anima*] is a great thing: The whole world can be described in it. It is called *as beautiful as Jerusalem* because it is likened to Jerusalem through the disposition of the hierarchical levels. But these are disposed in the soul in a threefold way: *according to an ascent* [*secundum ascensum*], *according to a descent* [*secundum descensum*], *and according to a return into the divine* [*secundum regressum in divina*] [my emphasis]. And then the soul sees *angels of God ascending and descending on a ladder,* as Jacob saw in his mind. The Abbot of Vercelli assigned three steps, namely, of nature [*naturae*], of industry [*industriae*], and of grace [*gratiae*]. But it does not seem to be the case that the soul could be hierarchized through nature in any way. And thus let us assign the three levels to industry with nature [*industriae cum natura*], industry with grace [*industriae cum gratia*], and grace above nature and industry [*gratiae super naturam et industriam*].[32]

The Seraphic Doctor's claim against Gallus—namely, that the soul cannot be hierarchized through nature in any way—implies that the Victorine's angelic anthropology should be relegated to the realm of grace, thereby representing a key difference between their accounts.[33] The Franciscan's next move, though, is to name the first level, "industry with nature" (*industriae cum natura*), titularly assigning grace to the

---

very strikingly refers to the "*influentia gratiae Spiritus*" which can be found in the fruitfulness of scripture; and especially *Hex.* 21.17–18 (5,434), which I looked at extensively in Chapter 3. Bonaventure's discussion of the *influentia* in *Hex.* 21 inaugurates his discussion of all created hierarchies, which then extends to his discussion of the hierarchical soul in *Hex.* 22.

31. See again my discussion of this sermon in Chapter 3.

32. *Hex.* 22.24 (5, 441).

33. See Coolman, *Knowledge, Love, and Ecstasy,* 237–38, who similarly notes this difference.

second and third levels while apparently leaving it out in the first. How are we to thereby interpret this amendment? It is useful to read this passage in light of Bonaventure's previous treatment of the hierarchical soul in *Itin.* 4, where he had appeared to more readily affirm Gallus's original schema by suggesting that the three hierarchical levels within the soul simply refer to nature, industry, and grace, respectively. Rather importantly, however, the Franciscan had there also introduced his notion of the hierarchical soul and its orders as an *effect* of grace, quite clearly arguing that sanctifying grace "first descends into the heart" *before* the soul can be "hierarchized" in conformity with the heavenly Jerusalem. Bonaventure's claim that the soul cannot "be hierarchized through nature in any way" here in *Hex.* 22 similarly prefaces his introduction to these three modified Gallusian levels. In both texts, he employs Gallus's angelic anthropology as a way of describing how the inflowing of grace shapes or recreates the soul so as to make it "deiform." This is in stark contrast to the Victorine's original schematic, whereby the soul itself is created as a hierarchy.[34]

Even more importantly, however, is the Seraphic Doctor's subsequent expansion of Gallus's angelic anthropology throughout the remainder of *Hex.* 22 in light of this gentle correction. Indeed, following these remarks, Bonaventure will continue *Hex.* 22 by offering his own quite detailed account of the hierarchical soul, which he strikingly frames here by referring to the symbol of Jacob's Ladder in the same breath as his acknowledgment of Gallus's influence. Attending to the Seraphic Doctor's narrative of how the soul is "hierarchized" in a threefold way—namely, (1) "according to an ascent," (2) "according to a descent," and (3) "according to a return into the divine"—will once again help us reconceive Bonaventure's cyclical metaphysics, and most particularly, the third *redditus* moment to which he here refers. For the time being, I will simply note that Bonaventure's introduction of this threefold movement—with respect to this ascent, descent, and return—does not perfectly map onto the threefold neoplatonic movement of procession, return, and remaining so central to the Dionysian theological enterprise. In Dionysian metaphysics, as for Gallus, the

---

34. See again Coolman, *Knowledge, Love, and Ecstasy,* 237–38: "For Gallus, then, the soul is not 'hierarchized' by saving grace (as Bonaventure will later insist, perhaps in reaction to Gallus); grace does not 'overlay' a hierarchic structure upon a naturally un-hierarchized soul. Rather, the soul itself is created as a hierarchy."

"return" is associated with an "ascending" valence, even as the moment of "procession" is most often associated with a "descending" valence. The "remaining," as Coolman has said of Gallus's angelic anthropology, is comprised of the dynamic relationship between the "descent" and the "ascent," or the procession and the return, so that "The dynamic simultaneity of procession and return establish an *equipoise* described as remaining."[35] Bonaventure's "three valences" as presented here would thereby correspond with a "return," a "procession," and another "return." Neither do these neatly map onto the threefold hierarchical activities of purification, illumination, and perfection, which were so central to Bonaventure's accounts of grace in both the *Breviloquium* and the *Itinerarium.* What, then, is the Seraphic Doctor doing with these three valences?

To thus understand his project with respect to these three movements and how they relate to everything I have already thus laid out here in *Part II,* I here attend to each valence—namely, "ascending," "descending," and "returning"—as Bonaventure summarizes them in the *Hexaëmeron* in order to bring my presentation of sanctifying grace in the Seraphic Doctor's theology to its own fruition. I begin each of these sections by "mapping" his summaries of these valences from *Hex.* 22 in Tables 5.2, 5.3, and 5.4.

The Ascending Pattern of Grace in the Hierarchical Soul

First, we must begin with Bonaventure's account of the "ascending" valence of grace in the *Hexaëmeron.*[36] Depicted in Table 5.2, the Seraphic Doctor lifts this discussion almost verbatim from Gallus, even as he also repeats his own description of the hierarchical soul from *Itin.* 4 (see Table 5.1).[37] In the lowest hierarchy of the soul, he writes, the soul receives information from the senses at the level of the angels. It deliberates or "dictates" (*dictatio*) whether it ought to pursue or reject that which it has perceived at the level of the archangels, and then pursues what it has deliberated through an act of free choice at the level of the principalities.[38] Like Gallus, the Seraphic Doctor understands the

---

35. Coolman, *Knowledge, Love, and Ecstasy,* 23.

36. See *Hex.* 22.25–27 (5, 441).

37. Again, see my discussion of Gallus's angelic anthropology in Chapter 2. See also *Itin.* 4.4 (5, 307), to which I referred, above.

38. *Hex.* 22.25 (5, 441).

TABLE 5.2 The Ascending Pattern of Grace in *Hex.* 22

The Lowest Hierarchy of the Soul: Industry with Nature or Action		The Middle Hierarchy of the Soul: Industry with Grace		The Highest Hierarchy of the Soul: Grace above Nature and Industry	
Dionysian Order	*Function in the Soul*	*Dionysian Order*	*Function in the Soul*	*Dionysian Order*	*Function in the Soul*
Angels	Announcing	Powers	Ordering	Thrones	Receiving
Archangels	Dictating	Virtues	Strengthening	Cherubim	Revealing
Principalities	Leading	Dominions	Commanding	Seraphim	Uniting

lowest hierarchy of the soul here to correspond with what is available to it through human nature: The soul uses its bodily senses to apprehend what is before it, deliberates about that information, and then makes a judgment to pursue what it has apprehended through the faculty of free will.

Unlike Gallus, however, and as we saw above, Bonaventure's account of the hierarchical soul attributes all these activities to "industry with nature" (*industriae cum natura*) instead of to nature alone, a claim that only makes sense if we situate Bonaventure's description of these functions in *Hex.* 22 within his broader doctrine of grace as we have thus far explored it. According to its nature, the soul may certainly use its bodily senses to apprehend what is before it, deliberate the information it receives, and then use its free will to form a judgment about whether or not it should pursue what it apprehends. As the Seraphic Doctor has already made quite clear in the *Commentary on the Sentences*, *Breviloquium*, and *Itinerarium*, however, it is the *influentia* of sanctifying grace that works *in* and *with* these faculties of the soul to enliven them for heavenly industries: The soul will only freely choose to pursue the Good it has apprehended at the level of the angels and thus "ascend" to the middle and highest hierarchies once it has consented to receive the gift of grace that enables its climb. Bonaventure's refusal to ascribe the lowest level to "nature alone" amends the Victorine's angelic anthropology by emphasizing the necessity of grace in aiding the soul's natural faculties—represented in this instance by the angels, archangels, and principalities—to ascend beyond their "mercenary"[39] tendencies and toward God.

39. See again *II Sent.* d. 26, a. 1, q. 2, concl. (2, 635–36): "Affectus enim hominis recurvus

Next, then, Bonaventure describes the middle hierarchy of the soul in this ascending valence, naming this the level of "industry with grace" (*industriae cum gratia*) in another slight amendment to the Victorine. After the lowest levels of the soul have freely chosen to pursue what has been perceived through sense apprehension, the powers next order the soul unto God by removing whatever is disordered in the soul "so that," as Bonaventure writes, "what would be deliberated would be done for God." "Because this is difficult [*difficile*]," he continues, the soul is next strengthened by the virtues and then ruled by the dominions, which lead the soul to the final stage of its "ascent" through grace.[40]

Finally, just like Gallus, Bonaventure can explain the highest hierarchy of the soul in the "ascending" valence as the level of "grace above nature and industry" (*gratiae super naturam et industriam*). Here, he writes, the soul "is lifted above itself [*supra se elevata*] and, deserting itself [*se deserta*], it receives divine illuminations [*suscipit divinas illuminationes*] and gazes upon [*speculatur*] what has been given to it from above; and from this, it rises into the divine and acts through what is above it. These three orders are a receiving [*susceptio*], a revelation [*revelatio*], and a union [*unio*] beyond which the mind does not proceed [*non procedit mens*]."[41] This reception, revelation, and union respectively correspond with the orders of the thrones, cherubim, and seraphim. Bonaventure's explanation of this "highest hierarchy" in the "ascending valence" drips with Gallusian language: "And it is in these things that the entire Song of Songs consists, namely, in the chaste, more chaste, and most chaste receivings [*susceptionibus*]; in the chaste, more chaste, and most chaste speculations [*speculationibus*]; and in the chaste, more chaste, and most chaste unions [*unitionibus*]: and then the soul will be able to say with that Song: *Let him kiss me with the kisses of his mouth!*"[42] This nuptial language also echoes that used by Bonaventure in both *Brev.* 5.6 and in *Itin.* 4 with respect to his descriptions there of the culminating moment in the illuminative way, whereby grace "branches out" into the soul through the virtues, leading the soul to a sensual affective union with Christ.

As in those previous texts written some twenty years prior, however,

---

est et mercenarius …" and my previous discussion of this in Chapter 4. I will expand upon this concept in more detail in Chapter 6.

40. *Hex.* 22.26 (5, 441).

41. *Hex.* 22.27 (5, 441).

42. *Hex.* 22.27 (5, 441).

this affective union between the soul and Christ at the level of the seraph will not be the stopping point of the Seraphic Doctor's narrative of grace in the *Hexaëmeron*. Again, it is necessary to reemphasize the *dynamic* functioning of the nine orders of the soul within Gallus's prior account of this angelic anthropology:[43] According to the Victorine, once the soul has achieved an affective union with God at the level of the seraph, this union fecundates the lower levels of the soul, "descending," as it were, throughout the lower eight orders so that the soul can "spiral" into God through these constant "ascensions" and "descensions" into perpetuity. And while this idea was implicit in Bonaventure's adaptation of Gallus's angelic anthropology in the *Itinerarium*, he continues *Hex.* 22 by affirming this notion explicitly.

The Descending Pattern of Grace in the Hierarchical Soul

Thus echoing Gallus's notion of the affective union experienced by the soul at the level of the seraph, Bonaventure next introduces his discussion of the "descending" valence in the *Hexaëmeron*[44] by emphasizing the fecundity of this union: "It is necessary that the unction on the head of the heavenly hierarchy [*hierarchiae supernae*] would fall onto the beard, or into the middle hierarchy [*mediam hierarchiam*], and onto the vestments, that is, the lowest [*infimam*] hierarchy," he writes, "But this has to happen according to the powers of the soul, which are three according to Dionysius: receiving [*susceptivae*], maintaining [*custoditivae*], and distributing [*distributivae*], so that we might copiously receive [*copiose suscipat*], diligently maintain [*studiose custodiat*], and freely pour out [*liberaliter refundat*], whence, '*freely you have received, so freely give.*'"[45]

First, for the lower orders of the soul to receive these annointings from the seraph, Bonaventure holds that the soul will need "vivacious desire [*vivacitas desideri*], perspicacious scrutiny [*perspicacitas*

---

43. Coolman's discussion of this idea in "Medieval Affective Dionysian Tradition," 622–28, is especially helpful.

44. See *Hex.* 22.28–33 (5, 441–42). See also my discussion of this descending valence in "The *Vir Hierarchicus* and the Goal of Theology according to St. Bonaventure," in *Bonaventure: Friar, Teacher, Minister, Bishop. A Celebration of the Eighth Centenary of his Birth. Conference Proceedings from "Frater, magister, minister, et episcopus: The Works and Worlds of St. Bonaventure," at St. Bonaventure University, July 12–15, 2017*, ed. Timothy J. Johnson, Katherine Wrisley Shelby, and Marie Kolbe Zamora (St. Bonaventure, NY: Franciscan Institute, 2021), 159–71; some of this revised material has been reused with permission here.

45. See *Hex.* 22.28 (5, 441).

TABLE 5.3 The Descending Pattern of Grace in *Hex.* 22

The Highest Hierarchy of the Soul: The Receiving Powers of the Soul		The Middle Hierarchy of the Soul: The Maintaining Powers of the Soul		The Lowest Hierarchy of the Soul: The Distributing Powers of the Soul	
Dionysian Order	*Function in the Soul*	*Dionysian Order*	*Function in the Soul*	*Dionysian Order*	*Function in the Soul*
Seraphim	Vivacious Desire	Dominions	The Authority of the Commands	Principalities	Gives life to neighbor by illustrious example
Cherubim	Perspicacious Scrutiny	Virtues	Strength in the practice of what has been proposed by the commands	Archangels	Gives life to neighbor through the truth of speech
Thrones	Tranquil Judgments	Powers	The nobility of triumph against impediments	Angels	Gives life to neighbor through the humility of following

scrutinii], and tranquil judgments [*tranquillitas iudicii*]." Accordingly, these three activities correspond with the highest hierarchy in the soul in the "descending" way. After having been united to God at the level of the seraph, the soul is then inflamed by desire, since the seraphim are "ardent like fire" (*ardens sicut ignis*). Bonaventure recalls the biblical story of Moses to explain this idea. After seeing this "ardent fire" from the base of Mt. Sinai, Moses ascends the mountain to experience it. This fire, in turn, ignites his desire to an even greater extent, from which he then descends the mountain "for the purpose of teaching the people" (*ad erudiendum populum*). Moses's burning desire, according to Bonaventure, "disposes the soul for the reception of light [*suscipiendum lumen*]," which then overflows from the height of the mountain to pour down upon those below.[46] The soul next "perspicaciously" (*perspicaciter*) perceives the gifts given to it by God and is prevented from "fantasies or occupations that would prevent it from being occupied with or carried into those lights" at the level of the cherubim.[47] Finally,

46. *Hex.* 22.29 (5, 441–42).
47. *Hex.* 22.30 (5, 442).

at the level of the thrones, the passions of the soul are next curbed so that it will have "tranquil judgments" (*tranquillitatem iudicii*) in the act of receiving these lights.[48]

Then, once the soul has received these lights through grace, Bonaventure calls the middle hierarchy of the soul within this "descent" the "maintaining power" of the soul. When the soul "receives from desire and perspicaciously perceives and tranquilly judges what ought to be done, namely, what God wills," Bonaventure writes that it is then ruled by the dominions. It is not enough to simply be ruled, however; the soul must also be strengthened at the level of the virtues so that it can practice and put into action what has been proposed to it by the dominions. By being thus strengthened, even despite tribulations that fall upon it, the soul remains in the Good and so triumphs over all impediments at the level of the powers.[49]

Finally, the Seraphic Doctor asserts that what has been "maintained" in the middle hierarchy of the soul then flows into the lowest hierarchy of the soul, where it is then distributed outward by the soul in three ways: namely, through "the clarity of example [*claritatem exempli*], the truth of speech [*veritatem eloquii*], and through the humility of following [*humilitatem obsequii*]." As Bonaventure writes:

> Thus we ought to give life to our neighbor [*vitam dare proximo*], namely, through example, knowledge, and substance [*per exempla, scientiam, substantiam*]. For the illustriousness of the example corresponds to the principalities, whose it is to lead; the truth of speech, to the archangels; and the humility of following, to the angels. Thus, there is a consummation in humility according to the descent [*consummatio in humilitate secundum descensum*], and a beginning in charity [*inceptio in caritate*]; and vice versa in the act of ascending [*ascendendo*]. So by descending [*descendendo*], we begin from the vivacity of desiring [*vivacitate desiderii*] to the humility of following [*humilitatem obsequii*]. Whence Christ comes to us in humility. So also the soul has angels ascending [*ascendentes*], just as it also ought to have angels descending [*descendentes*]. Whence in John: "For no one ascends into heaven, unless he descended from heaven, like the son of man who is in heaven."[50]

In the same way that soul's union with Christ is not the stopping point of Bonaventure's account of grace in either *Brev.* 5 or in *Itin.* 4, so also

---

48. *Hex.* 22.31 (5, 442).
49. *Hex* 22.32 (5, 442).
50. *Hex* 22.33 (5, 442).

does he here argue that the soul made "hierarchical" through grace truly becomes like a "Jacob's Ladder." The lights it receives through grace at the level of the seraph flow down from atop "Mt. Sinai" to fecundate the lower orders of the soul, with the express purpose of flowing out from the soul in a way that "gives life" to one's neighbor. In the same way that Christ's Incarnation invites the ascending and descending movements of the hierarchies on a macrocosmic level,[51] so also does Bonaventure hold that the graced soul must "descend" from its seraphic union all the way back down to "the humility of following."

Here, then, Bonaventure breaks open Thomas Gallus's angelic anthropology to expand it beyond the realm of contemplation. Gallus himself had described pictorially his own notion of the hierarchical soul with the symbol of Jacob's Ladder. Quite notably, however, the Victorine had confined this dynamism of the "ascending, descending, and circling or spiraling" valences entirely to the realm of contemplation. At one point in his commentary on the *Song*, for example, he had even exclaimed of the "descending" valence: "It is not for the contemplative man to stretch out for the care of others, but only to his own inferior orders."[52] Where Bonaventure's angelic anthropology most fundamentally differs from that of his Victorine predecessor is with respect to this idea. For the Franciscan, the "descending" valence cannot and should not be confined merely to the care of "his own inferior orders," but must necessarily include "the care of others" if the soul is truly to be made "as like as possible to God."[53] The Seraphic Doctor understands the dynamism of the hierarchical soul to *necessarily* extend beyond the soul so as to include one's neighbor. This insight is part and parcel of Bonaventure's Franciscan identity and walks hand in hand with everything we have thus encountered in his treatments of grace in *II Sent.*, the *Breviloquium*, and the *Itinerarium*: The soul that ascends Jacob's Ladder to an affective union with God does not remain there; rather, it must once again "descend" to others through meritorious actions once it has been inflamed by charity.

---

51. For my discussion of this notion, see especially my examination of "Sermo 54 *De sanctis angelis*" in Chapter 3.

52. Gallus, *In Cant.*, 84: "... et nota quod non est viri contemplativi intendere cure animarum aliarum, sed tantum suis inferioribus ordinibus."

53. For more on this notion, see my comments on the similitude and hierarchy in Chapter 3.

The Returning Pattern of Grace in the Hierarchical Soul

Finally, then, we arrive at what Bonaventure calls the "return"—the *redditus*—in *Hex.* 22.[54] According to Bonaventure, this final "hierarchy" within the soul involves three steps of contemplation whereby the soul is enabled to contemplate God in everything that is "outside us" (*extra nos*), "within us" (*intra nos*), and "above us" (*supra nos*).[55] These three steps of contemplation mirror exactly the threefold structure of the *Itinerarium*. In the *Hexaëmeron,* the Seraphic Doctor associates each of these three modes of contemplation with the different powers of the rational soul, writing:

Whence God may be contemplated in those things that are inside us, or outside us, or above us, according to our three faculties [*potentias*], namely, the exterior [*exteriores*], interior [*interiores*], and superior [*superiores*], or the apprehensive [*apprehensivas*], amative [*amativas*], and operative [*operativas*]. And according to the Philosopher, "every noble soul has three operations," namely, the animal toward everything outside it [*animalem ad extra*], the intellectual toward what is inside it [*intellectualem ad intra*], and the divine toward what is above [*divinam ad supra*]. It is therefore necessary that the soul have a hierarchization [*hierarchizationem*] according to these faculties....[56]

Bonaventure's ensuing description of this final hierarchy in *Hex.* 22 is lengthy and in many ways quite convoluted, and I will spare readers with a point-by-point dissection of all that he says therein, which I have nonetheless mapped in Table 5.4. To understand this *redditus*, I here rather turn our attention all the way back to Bonaventure's very first treatments of grace when reading the Lombard's *Sentences* as a young student of theology.

In *II Sent.* d. 26–27, the Seraphic Doctor defines sanctifying grace as an *influentia,* a continuous act between the soul and God through which God acts *in* and *with* the free will to set it "upright" after being deformed by sin. It is here fitting to call attention to an even earlier version of Bonaventure's comments on the Lombard—namely, his *dubia* to the *Sentences*, which he wrote under the direction of Alexander of Hales in 1243–1245. These *dubia* or doubts surrounding the Lombard's text, as Bougerol has observed, and which appear throughout

---

54. See *Hex.* 22.34–39 (5, 442–43).
55. *Hex.* 22.34 (5, 442).
56. *Hex.* 22.34 (5, 442).

TABLE 5.4 The Returning Pattern of Grace in *Hex.* 22, or the Hierarchy of the Soul according to the Three Steps of Contemplation

The Lowest Hierarchy of the Soul: The Exterior/ Apprehensive Powers of the Soul		The Middle Hierarchy of the Soul: The Interior/ Affective Powers of the Soul		The Highest Hierarchy of the Soul: The Superior/ Operative Powers of the Soul	
Dionysian Order	*Function in the Soul*	*Dionysian Order*	*Function in the Soul*	*Dionysian Order*	*Function in the Soul*
Angels	Discerning Scrutiny	Powers	Strict Punishment	Thrones	A Worthy Admission
Archangels	Discerning Choice	Virtues	Strict Consolation	Cherubim	A Worthy Inspection
Principalities	Discerning Execution	Dominions	Strict Calling	Seraphim	A Worthy Induction

the entirety of the Quaracchi edition of Bonaventure's *Sentences* commentary, "are in fact minute questions arising from the text itself. Brief arguments are provided, and a conclusion is offered to enlighten the reading."[57] In short, they are the first foundation from which Bonaventure will go on to write the rest of his commentary on the Lombard's *Sentences* as well as all his other works; they are, simply put, the "wellspring" from which the "inner unity" of his theology flows forth.

In his first *dubium* to *II Sent.* d. 27, Bonaventure argues that the *influentia* of sanctifying grace must be considered from four vantage points: "For grace has to be compared to the First Principle *from which* it exists [*principium a quo*]; to the subject *in whom* it inheres [*subiectum in quo*]; to the thing *against which* it is opposed [*oppositum contra quod*]; and to *the effect* to which it is ordered [*effectum ad quem*]."[58] Sanctifying grace, he continues, can be described variously insofar as it flows from its source in the Trinity (its *principium a quo*); insofar as it opposes the evil of sin (its *oppositum contra quod*); insofar as it has the effect of freeing the human will (its *effectum ad quem*); and insofar as it inheres in the rational soul (its *subiectum in quo*). With respect to the

---

57. See Bougerol, *Introduction to the Works of Bonaventure*, 72, for the dating of these *dubia*; for more on this dating, see also J. A. Wayne Hellmann, Timothy LeCroy, and Luke Davis Townsend, "Historical Introduction," in *Commentary on the Sentences: Sacraments*, Works of St. Bonaventure 17 (St. Bonaventure, NY: Franciscan Institute, 2016), 24. Bonaventure most likely wrote his *dubia* while studying with Alexander between 1243–1245, while he did not begin work on the *Sentences* until around 1250.

58. *II Sent.* d. 27, dub. 1, resp. (2, 669).

"subject in whom" it inheres, Bonaventure claims that sanctifying grace "is divided into the grace of *thinking* [*gratiam cogitationis*], of *willing* [*voluntatis*], and of *perfecting* [*perfectionis*], according to the threefold faculty [*triplicem potentiam*] of the substance in which grace exists [*in qua est gratia*], namely, according to the intellective [*intellectivam*], the affective [*affectivam*], and the operative [*operativam*] power."[59] In other words, sanctifying grace inheres in the intellective power of the rational soul as the grace of thinking; it inheres in the affective power of the soul as the grace of willing; and it inheres in the operative power of the rational soul as the grace of perfecting.

What does any of this have to do with Bonaventure's discussion of the "returning" valence of the hierarchical soul in *Hex.* 22? Simply put, he there repeats this same triad of "how grace inheres in the subject" that he had iterated in his very first treatment of sanctifying grace almost verbatim, albeit exchanging the "intellective" power for the "apprehensive" power with respect to the first faculty. Despite this slight difference (which can perhaps be attributed to the fact that his *dubium* uses the three faculties of the soul as cited by Bernard of Clairvaux in *De libero arbitrio* whereas the *Hexaëmeron* instead uses those named by the author of the *Liber de causis*), this comparison matters because it shows the overwhelming continuity of Bonaventure's position with regard to the third moment—the perfective moment—being operative.

In the *Breviloquium,* the soul is first "purified" by sanctifying grace when it is freed from sin; it is "illuminated" by sanctifying grace when grace branches out within the soul into the virtues, spiritual gifts, and beatitudes, thus preparing it for an affective union with Christ; and it is then "perfected" so as to become a temple of the Holy Spirit when that affective union prepares it for meritorious action. In the *Itinerarium,* likewise, the illuminative way yields to the perfection of the seraph, an affective union which, as he informs us in Ch. 1 of that text, will open up to the "descending" valence after the text concludes. In the *Hexaëmeron,* Bonaventure likewise infers that the soul that "returns" to God through contemplation is the soul in which—echoing his first *dubium* to *II Sent.* d. 27 written so many years beforehand—sanctifying grace inheres in the "apprehensive" power of the soul as the grace of thinking, in the "affective" power of the soul as the grace of willing, and

---

59. *II Sent.* d. 27, dub. 1, resp. (2, 669). Bonaventure in this *dubium* attributes this idea to Bernard of Clairvaux's *On Free Will.*

in the "operative" power of the soul as the grace of perfecting. To be "perfected" through grace in all three texts is to be made capable of "exercising" grace, borrowing Bonaventure's language from *Brev.* 5, whereby the operative powers within the soul are fecundated, enlivened, and inflamed by charity to relate in a holy way to both the Trinity above and the world around it. The soul that "returns" to God in *Hex.* 22, therefore, is the soul in which grace has worked *in* and *with* these three faculties in a way that conforms it completely to the Trinity, as Bonaventure will assert clearly in the opening pages of *Hex.* 23.[60]

Before this, however, Bonaventure concludes his description of this *redditus* in *Hex.* 22 by finally pronouncing that the soul in which each of the three valences are at work—namely, the soul that ascends, descends, and returns—will be like "a woman clothed with the sun, and the moon under her feet, and on her head a crown of twelve stars."[61] The soul will be crowned in this fashion because, as he continues, "in this life we cannot stand in one place [*non possumus stare in uno*], so the soul has twelve subjects like twelve lights surrounding it, which are always moving [*semper moveatur*] as in a certain circle [*in quodam circulo*]."[62] In other words, the soul that has been made hierarchical through this ascent, descent, and return does not stand still. It has not "processed" from some point on a neoplatonic circle to which it "returns" through grace and then stops moving. Again, it is helpful to repeat that the three movements of the hierarchical soul in *Hex.* 22 do not map on perfectly to the neoplatonic triad of procession, remaining, and return. Rather, what he has essentially described here is a return, a descent, and then another return. The hierarchical soul he describes is a Jacob's Ladder inasmuch as its ascent leads to a descent and then back up again: The hierarchical soul in the *Hexaëmeron*, following Gallus's original intuitions in his own angelic anthropology, is a soul that ceaselessly continues "circling" into perpetuity by way of these ascensions and descensions, these returns and processions. Bonaventure can open his discussion of the three valences of the hierarchical soul in

---

60. *Hex.* 23.1 (5, 444–45): "Dictum est, quomodo anima hierarchizatur in consideratione lucis solaris, secundum quod sol ille est vigens, splendens, calens; Pater et Filius et Spiritus sanctus est origo omnium illuminationum vel irradiationum in ratione excellentiae, influentiae, praesidentiae; et secundum quod illa assimiliatur soli secundum conformitatem et propter integritatem hierarchicae dispositiones et propter triformem aspectum…."

61. *Hex.* 22.39 (5, 443).

62. *Hex.* 22.40 (5, 443).

Hex. 22 by employing the symbol of Jacob's Ladder because the symbol is intended to describe this continuous dynamism, or in other words, the hierarchical soul's remaining in God. The soul that thus ascends in the final *redditus* moment described here has, yet again, not arrived at some sort of "stopping point" in a mystical journey; rather, Bonaventure uses this valence in *Hex.* 22 to designate that soul in which the purgative, illuminative, and perfective moments have all been perpetually activated. The soul does not *cease* "ascending" or "descending," but will continue to circle or spiral through all these holy activities even unto glory.

Quite strikingly, when summarizing these three valences in the opening sentences of *Hex.* 23, Bonaventure will simply refer to this third of the three "movements" of the hierarchical soul, or the second *redditus* moment, as a "*re*-ascension (*reascensum*)."[63] The symbol of Jacob's Ladder fittingly describes the hierarchical soul because it images, for Bonaventure, the perpetual activities of the soul that has thus been influenced by the light of grace through all these hierarchical ascensions and descensions.

Though the Seraphic Doctor never completed his *Hexaëmeron,* he nonetheless concludes *Hex.* 23 by reiterating these same themes. With respect to the text's larger structure, *Hex.* 20–23 all fall within Bonaventure's discussion of the "Fourth Day" of creation and collectively narrate how human understanding can be uplifted through contemplation.[64] After expounding his angelic anthropology in *Hex.* 22, he continues *Hex.* 23 to consider how the soul that has been thus "hierarchized" can thus remain in God throughout its time *in via.* At the end of *Hex.* 23, he quite strikingly brings all his collations on the "Fourth Day"—which have all been concerned with the theme, "understanding uplifted by contemplation"—with the following remarks:

And he was saying: I wanted to lead you to this *tree of life. King Solomon hath made him a litter of the wood of Libanus. The pillars thereof he made of silver, the seat of gold, the ascent of purple: The midst he covered with charity.* The seat of gold is contemplative wisdom [*sapientia contemplativa*]. And no one has this, except he who has the pillars of silver, which are the virtues, which

---

63. *Hex.* 23.1 (5, 445): "Postea dictum est, quomodo anima hierarchizatur in contemplatione *sui* secundum *ascensum* et *descsensum* et *reascensum.*"

64. Bonaventure provides a "roadmap" for his project in the *Hexaëmeron* in *Hex.* 3.24–30 (5, 347–48).

stabilize the soul [*virtutes stabilientes animam*]. The ascent of purple is charity [*caritas*], which causes the soul to ascend [*ascendere*] to things above it and to descend [*descendere*] to those below.[65]

Bonaventure's unfinished *Hexaëmeron* leaves us squarely in the realm of his doctrine of grace. The contemplative soul, the *hierarchical* soul, has here been led to the "tree of life," where it too will be filled with "plenitude" and will become "fruitful" through the charity that will cause ceaseless ascensions and descensions to take place within it. To remain in God through grace in the *Hexaëmeron* is to be made capable of such fruitful circling or spiraling whereby the ascent will yield to the descent, and surely back up again into eternity.

Conclusion

To conclude, I return to where my introduction to *Part II* began—namely, with Hayes's observation in *The Hidden Center* that "The structure of hierarchical thought may well shed light on the question of Bonaventure's theology of redemption. The broader structures of his thought lend themselves readily to the use of such a model, and the implications of the model for soteriology were perceived with greater clarity with the passing of time," noting further that hierarchy is thus "an explicit factor in the very earliest literary evidence of the Bonaventurian *corpus*. Evidence is found in virtually all his writings, whether they are early or late, and whether they are of an academic-speculative sort or of a spiritual-mystical nature."[66]

Both Chapter 4 and Chapter 5 have tried "to shed light on the question of Bonaventure's theology of redemption" by providing a systematic and chronological account of how his theology of hierarchy indeed explicitly informed his teachings on sanctifying grace throughout the course of his career. This account began with my examination of Bonaventure's definition of sanctifying grace as a created *influentia* in his *Commentary on the Sentences*. Though the association between hierarchy and grace is less explicit there than in any other text treated here, this definition provided the foundation upon which I could nevertheless construct Bonaventure's doctrine of grace in *Brev.* 5, the

---

65. *Hex.* 23.31 (5, 449).
66. Hayes, *Hidden Center*, 158.

Itinerarium, and the *Hexaëmeron*. In *Brev.* 5, for example, he expounds his previous definition of sanctifying grace from his *Sentences* commentary and there explicitly shows how grace conforms the human person into a likeness of the entire Trinity by purifying, illuminating, and perfecting it from within. Bonaventure's theology of hierarchy becomes a central game-piece in this shorter, albeit more mature, treatment of grace, insofar as these three hierarchical activities take center stage within the text. Through explaining the *ortus* of grace in the purgative way, the *modus* of grace in the illuminative way, and the *fructus* of grace in the perfective way, *Brev.* 5 suggests that the soul itself can become like a "Jacob's Ladder" through this *influentia*. The clear emergence of this association between hierarchy and grace becomes even more explicit in the *Itinerarium*, where Bonaventure will for the first time borrow Thomas Gallus's angelic anthropology in order to claim that grace hierarchizes the soul, and also in *Hex.* 22, where he will expand on this notion in greater detail. I here conclude my own presentation of his teachings on sanctifying grace with three general observations.

First, as Hayes intuited, Bonaventure's theology of hierarchy is indeed an explicit factor in all four texts examined here. Were the Seraphic Doctor's doctrine of grace to be summed up in a single sentence, we could perhaps simply say that, for him, "Sanctifying grace is a created gift, an *influentia* that hierarchizes the soul so as assimilate it to the Trinity."

Second, and closely following upon this first point, while Bonaventure indeed expressed the relationship between grace and hierarchy with greater and greater clarity with the passing of time, the "inner unity" of his doctrine of grace between all four texts is nonetheless staggering. Bonaventure develops and sharpens his thoughts on grace between his commentary on the *Sentences* and the *Hexaëmeron*, but he does so in such a way that builds upon and finds indispensable the definitions and presuppositions put forward in his very first work of systematic theology.

Third and finally, it is worthwhile to conclude by simply underscoring what it is, exactly, that highlighting this association between "hierarchy" and "sanctifying grace" accomplishes in our reading of the Seraphic Doctor's doctrine of grace. Most fundamentally, this association illuminates how scholars ought to approach the threefold movement of procession, return, and remaining within that doctrine. In the same way that the "return" in his theology of hierarchy must not be understood as reaching some sort of "end point" on a neoplatonic circle, but rather, as leading the rational creature to a point that is both an end and a beginning—or phrased differently, as the point to which the rational spirit ascends so that it may once again descend to its neighbor through grace and charity through a "fruitfulness of plenitude"—so also does Bonaventure's account of the hierarchical soul in the *Breviloquium*, the *Itinerarium*, and the *Hexaëmeron* involve a dynamic ordering that causes the soul to "descend" as soon as it "ascends" so that the soul remains in God. For the Seraphic Doctor, the soul becomes like God insofar as it becomes "fruitful" and is characterized by "plenitude" through sanctifying grace. This likeness or "similitude" of the soul to God is symbolized over and over again throughout these texts by the symbol of Jacob's Ladder. The soul's *reductio* into the Trinity through grace, just as in Bonaventure's theology of hierarchy, does not describe a "stopping point" at which the soul can be said to have "finally arrived"; rather, grace is perpetual, a continuous activity, an "inflowing" to which the soul must be continuously receptive—and thus continuously purified, illuminated, and perfected—if it is to remain "as like as possible to God." The perfective moment in Bonaventure's doctrine of grace in all these texts is always operative. The soul that ascends to God is made "like" the Trinity not because the soul is content to rest in contemplative perfection in a selfish way, but because it must then likewise bend down from this union to invite others to participate in its *circumincessio* as well. This is what it means to "remain" in God and be "perfected" in Bonaventure's doctrine of grace—namely, it is to be filled with the "fruitfulness of plenitude" that orders us to ever more abundant relationships with God and the entire created order of reality as we spiral through charitable ascensions and descensions even unto glory.

Part III

Theological Implications of Bonaventure's
Doctrine of Grace

Introduction

Whereas *Part II* provided an account of what grace is in Bonaventure's theology, we turn now to a more focused examination of why it matters: How does this definition of sanctifying grace as an *influentia* that hierarchizes the soul play into the Seraphic Doctor's broader systematic theology? Here in *Part III*, I answer this question by exploring his doctrine of grace with respect to three distinct but nonetheless interrelated theological topics. First, in Chapter 6, *Grace in Bonaventure's Theological Anthropology*, I examine Bonaventure's teachings on the relationship between grace and human nature. Recent scholarship on this topic has criticized him for supposedly suggesting that human nature is not ordered to beatitude in his theology; building from my previous exposition of his definition of sanctifying grace in *Part II*, I challenge this critique by showing how Bonaventure built the need for grace not only into his theological anthropology, but also into his very doctrine of creation. In so doing, Chapter 6 narrates the role of the *influentia* of sanctifying grace in both his teachings on pre- and postlapsarian human nature. Next, in Chapter 7, *Grace and Christ the Hierarch*, I show how this *influentia* is always sourced to creation through the Word in Bonaventure's theology. Previous scholarship on the subject has debated various ways of articulating a unified theory surrounding Christ's role in his soteriology; the purpose of Chapter 7 will be to situate Bonaventure's Christology within my own narrative of grace, which I argue provides this long sought-after unified theory. Finally, in Chapter 8, we will arrive at the "climax" of the book—namely, the Seraphic Doctor's teachings on sanctity. This chapter will examine Bonaventure's hagiographical literature to definitively tie together his systematic doctrine of grace as I have thus far expounded it with his teachings on the saints. Dwelling especially on his treatments of St. Francis and the Virgin Mary, we will here explore what it means to be made hierarchical through grace in the fullest possible way.

Admittedly, I have chosen these three theological topics in particular—Bonaventure's theological anthropology, his Christology, and his theology of sanctity—inasmuch as they narrate a story of grace in their own way. Chapter 6 shows us why humanity needs the *influentia* of sanctifying grace in the first place; Chapter 7, how, after losing the *influentia* of sanctifying grace, Christ restores that *influentia* to the created order of reality; and Chapter 8, how this restoring work of Christ "purifies, illuminates, and perfects" the saints as "hierarchical persons." Or, to borrow a schema from the Seraphic Doctor himself, I here tell my own story regarding the *ortus, modus,* and *fructus* of grace in Bonaventure's theology.

Chapter 9, *General Conclusion: Further Implications,* finally concludes the entire study with some general remarks for further consideration. Here, I discuss holes that I will not be able to adequately address with respect to other theological topics in the Seraphic Doctor's thought within the present study, such as his pneumatology and ecclesiology, while also offering a selection of subjects for which my work here might nevertheless still be useful in contemporary theological conversations. Most importantly, I will finally return to a question raised in my Introduction from Chapter 1: What is the role of grace in Bonaventure's understanding of theology as *sapientia*?

CHAPTER 6

Grace in Bonaventure's Theological Anthropology

Approaching the subject of grace in Bonaventure's theological anthropology is, unfortunately, a task fraught with controversy. This is due in large part to a critique leveled against the Seraphic Doctor by Jacob Schmutz, who sees in his theology the cornerstone for the later development of a doctrine of pure nature, a criticism that John Milbank also champions in his book, *The Suspended Middle*.[1] Milbank has summarized Schmutz's project, which he adopts in his own text without any citations to Bonaventure's writings,[2] in the following way:

1. See Schmutz, "Medieval Doctrine of Causality and the Theology of Pure Nature," 203–50, esp. 217.

2. See Milbank, "Aquinas and the Radicalization of de Lubac's Account of the Supernatural," in *The Suspended Middle*, 88–103, in which Milbank does not provide a single footnote to any of Bonaventure's works. Milbank's critique of Bonaventure is simply a repetition of Schmutz's earlier argument. His argument builds upon that provided by Schmutz, although Milbank cites an earlier version of the same chapter as it originally appeared in the French publication of the same text (see 89n1). For more robust accounts of the Seraphic Doctor's theological anthropology, see especially Davies, *Bonaventure, the Body, and the Aesthetics of Salvation*; J. F. Quinn, *The Historical Constitution of St. Bonaventure's Philosophy* (Toronto: Pontifical Institute of Medieval Studies, 1973), esp. 101–320; Chavero Blanco, *Francisco de Assis, Imago Dei: Aproximación a la antropologia teológica de san Buenaventura* (Murcia: Espigas y Azucenas, 1993); Giuseppe Rocco, *L'antropologia in San Bonaventura* (Vicenza: Editrice Veneta, 2009); Solignac, "L'homme, ressemblance du Fils," in *La voie de la ressemblance*, 289–358; Coolman, "Part II: On the Creation of the World," 141–67. See also Johnson, *The Soul in Ascent*, whose treatment of prayer also includes a succinct and helpful account

Jacob Schmutz has suggested—with exhaustive documentation—that we should now see the transition in the understanding of the supernatural as but one aspect of a vaster change in the comprehension of all causality and particularly divine causality. This thesis concentrates round a shift in the meaning of the word *influentia*. Until 1250 or so *influentia* was linked with neoplatonic notions of *processio* and remained true to its metaphorical base. Divine influence (but also finite influence) was literally an *in-fluentia*, a "flowing in" of something higher to something lower to the degree that it could be received. On this model, the 'general' divine activity is indissociable from God's 'special' activity, his overall from his particular providence.[3]

Schmutz and Milbank both claim that Bonaventure changes the meaning of the word, *influentia*, in the fourth question to his *Scien. Chr.*, inasmuch as he introduces a general *influentia* that can be dissociated from the special *influentia* of grace mentioned by Milbank above.[4] According to them, this general influence of Bonaventure's acts *with* a human subject, the secondary cause, rather than *in* the human subject as a first cause. In their reading, this move leads to the later development of a doctrine of pure nature because, by suggesting that God acts *with* rather than *in* secondary causes, as Christopher Cullen has since summarized: "Bonaventure emerges as a pivotal figure in the rise of a secularized rationality, i.e., a view of human reason as no longer intrinsically ordered to the transcendent final end of union with God."[5]

Cullen, then, has responded to this critique by affirming that Bonaventure does indeed put forward a doctrine of pure nature in his teachings on prelapsarian nature, but he likewise argues that the Seraphic Doctor does this solely to show how human nature is "orderable" to God in the state of innocence. This doctrine, as Cullen also contends, is important because through it, Bonaventure indicates that prelapsarian human beings were orderable to beatitude in the state of innocence while simultaneously allowing for the possibility of the person's free assent to grace, following the Augustinian maxim, "He who created you without you, does not justify you without you." For Cullen, in other words, prelapsarian human nature in Bonaventure's theology

---

of Bonaventure's views on the ontological and moral poverty of human nature, which are indispensable considerations when thinking about his theological anthropology as well.

    3. Milbank, *Suspended Middle*, 89–90.

    4. Schmutz, "Medieval Doctrine of Causality and the Theology of Pure Nature," 215–17, esp. 216nn37–39; Milbank, *Suspended Middle*, 96–97.

    5. Cullen, "Bonaventure on Nature before Grace," 164.

remains incomplete apart from grace working within it.[6] Despite seeing what he calls a "historical moment of pure nature" in Bonaventure's account of the prelapsarian human person, Cullen argues that the Seraphic Doctor would have deemed it inconceivable for the human person to achieve beatitude apart from grace, against the argument put forward by both Schmutz and Milbank.[7]

His response to their critique, however, is limited since he does not entirely address the heart of that critique—namely, that the Seraphic Doctor changes the meaning of the word *influentia* in his doctrine of grace from its neoplatonic definition as a "flowing-in" of a higher into a lower cause. I have already addressed this critique in part in my treatment of Bonaventure's definition of sanctifying grace as an *influentia* of this sort in his *II Sent.*: This *influentia*, as the Seraphic Doctor indicates, is the created gift in which the Trinity dwells within the soul that consents to receive that gift, so that God acts *in* and *with* the human subject as a first cause for merit through the created *influentia*. In other words, against Schmutz, Bonaventure certainly defined sanctifying grace as an *influentia* in a way that remained true to the neoplatonic meaning of the word as a "flowing-in" of a higher into a lower cause.[8]

Nonetheless building off Cullen's previous reflections, my purpose in this chapter is to examine more closely the role of this "inflowing" within Bonaventure's theological anthropology in order to argue that human nature indeed remains "incomplete" without it. If the Seraphic Doctor defines sanctifying grace as an *influentia* that hierarchizes the soul into a likeness of the Trinity by purifying, illuminating, and perfecting it, then he likewise holds that the soul was *created* to be thus hierarchized by this *influentia*. Moreover, since Bonaventure further argues that the entire created order of reality relates to the divine *ordo* through this similitude, examining the role of sanctifying grace within Bonaventure's theological anthropology will also serve the purpose of showing how all of creation is likewise "incomplete" apart from this *influentia*. The human person was created to be "receptive"

---

6. This incompleteness in prelapsarian human nature, Cullen argues, is comparable to that of an infant in limbo, who does "not know the pain of fire, which is the punishment of sinners; but [who also does] not receive the reward of the just, namely, the vision of God.... Thus they are neither sad nor in joy." See Cullen, "Bonaventure on Nature before Grace," 174.

7. Cullen, "Bonaventure on Nature before Grace," 166–67.

8. For this, see my previous treatment of his definition of sanctifying grace in his *II Sent.* in Chapter 4.

or "susceptive" of the *influentia* of sanctifying grace through which it could transition from merely being an image of God to becoming a deiform similitude of the Trinity, and humanity's choice to close itself off to that inflowing in sin subsequently causes the disruption of *ordo* throughout the macrocosm. Acknowledging the recent critique against it, this chapter analyzes the role of grace in the Seraphic Doctor's theological anthropology in order to prove that, for him, the *influentia* of sanctifying grace is indubitably indispensable for humanity's—and accordingly, the entire created order of reality's—achievement of beatitude.

With respect to methodology, this chapter diverges somewhat from Chapters 3–5 inasmuch as it will not provide an overview of Bonaventure's theological anthropology by attending to its development through an *explicatio* of several key texts treated chronologically. In Chapters 3–5, this methodology was helpful for demonstrating the consistency of his thought with respect to his definitions of hierarchy and sanctifying grace throughout the course of his theological career. This chapter also assumes this consistency with respect to his theological anthropology, even as it also presumes everything I have already argued regarding hierarchy and grace in the previous three chapters. My argument here, however, will be comprised of conceptual building blocks that will help us arrive at a clearer understanding of the role of grace in his theological anthropology with regard to the critique against this teaching. First, since the distinction between a "general *influentia*" and a "special *influentia*" comprises the heart of this critique, I consider what these terms mean in Bonaventure's theology, especially looking at his use of this distinction in Question 4 of his *Scien. Chr.* Building from this analysis, I then examine the role of the "special *influentia*" within the Seraphic Doctor's teachings on prelapsarian human nature, underscoring how in his doctrine of creation, the entire created order of reality was related to the Trinity through it. Finally, I conclude by reflecting on the nature of sin and the loss of this *influentia* in his teachings on postlapsarian human nature, showing how this loss also leads to the disruption of the entire created *ordo* of reality.

The General *Influentia*, the Special *Influentia*, and the Image Between

What, then, of the critique against Bonaventure posed by Schmutz and Milbank? In his original article detailing how the Seraphic Doctor might be the culprit behind the "systematization" of a "theology of pure nature," Schmutz rightly notes that the Franciscan theologian introduces a distinction between a "general *influentia*" and a "special *influentia*" within the context of *Scien. Chr* 4. There, while treating the question of human certitude as it pertains to the knowledge of Christ,[9] Bonaventure discusses a "general *influentia*" on one hand, which "accompanies every act of the creature" and "upholds us in all our acts," as well as a "special *influentia*," on the other hand, "which God must voluntarily grant to go beyond what is naturally possible for man" and which the Seraphic Doctor identifies as "grace."[10] Schmutz then argues concerning this distinction:

The primacy of the divine influence, without which no secondary agent can act, is thus still affirmed, but this influence is merely "general" and belongs to a natural concurrence necessary for the conservation of man's powers, without which he would not have been able to resist the temptation of the devil.... It took no more than this for Protestant dogmatics at the end of the nineteenth century to see in Bonaventure himself the throes of a dangerous neo-semi-Pelagianism, the harbinger of later "dissolutions."[11]

---

9. Pertinently, Joshua Benson has recently shown how this question is often misinterpreted inasmuch as the context of the rest of the treatise is ignored when scholars treat it. As he writes: "in an effort to contextualize question four, many scholars have abstracted this question from the rest of the disputation.... Though these scholarly essays clarify Bonaventure's teaching on human knowledge, they tend to obscure the meaning of the *Scien. Chr.* as a whole...." The criticisms of Schmutz and Milbank certainly belong to the type of inquiry with which Benson here takes issue. The argument against Bonaventure's doctrine of human nature made by Schmutz and Milbank stems from an isolated reading of a question that has too often been read out of context. Question 4 of *Scien. Chr.* is devoted to the question of human cognition as it relates to the knowledge of Christ and is not necessarily the best text for understanding Bonaventure's doctrine of grace as it relates to human nature more broadly speaking. I will address Benson's own parsing of the structure of the text as it pertains to my argument below. See Joshua Benson, "Structure and Meaning in St. Bonaventure's *Quaestiones Disputatae de Scientia Christi*," *Franciscan Studies* 62 (2004): 67–68. See also Schmutz, "Medieval Doctrine of Causality and the Theology of Pure Nature," 215–17, esp. 216; and Milbank, *Suspended Middle*, 96–97. Schmutz does provide two citations to Bonaventure's *Commentary on the Sentences*, but these are read in service of his own reading of Questions 4 of *Scien. Chr.*

10. Schmutz, "Medieval Doctrine of Causality and the Theology of Pure Nature," 216.

11. Schmutz, "Medieval Doctrine of Causality and the Theology of Pure Nature," 217.

By underscoring this "general *influentia*" in Bonaventure's theology, Schmutz faults the Seraphic Doctor for suggesting that God only acts *with* humanity's "natural capacities" in a concurrent way rather than acting *in* the human subject as the first cause of merit.[12] Before turning to examine the role of grace in Bonaventure's accounts of both pre- and postlapsarian human nature, it is here important to arrive at a clearer understanding of this distinction between a "general" and "special" *influentia* as the Seraphic Doctor himself describes it and which Schmutz here criticizes. Attending to Bonaventure's explanation of both types of *influentia* in *Scien. Chr.* 4 will serve the purpose of both (a) responding to Schmutz's critique regarding Bonaventure's introduction of a general *influentia* while (b) preparing us to encounter how both these "inflowings" work within his broader teachings on theological anthropology in subsequent sections of this chapter.

With respect to the text as a whole, *Scien. Chr.*—much like the *Breviloquium* and the *Itinerarium*—is structured in seven parts, or seven Disputed Questions, which correspond with the Seraphic Doctor's metaphysics of remaining, procession, and return.[13] Building from his previous analysis of the structure of the *Breviloquium*, Joshua Benson has noticed how these seven parts are similarly structured according to Bonaventure's "triadic" way of thinking: Questions 1–3 of *Scien. Chr.* treat divine knowledge; Question 4 treats the question of human certitude; and Questions 5–7 treat the wisdom of Christ's soul. As Benson argues, these groupings are important "not only in terms of what they concern individually, but in terms of how they are sequentially ordered in the text," so that "The disputation moves *from* the divine, *through* humanity, and *into* the soul of Christ."[14] It also thereby moves from *scientia*, through *cognitio*, and into *sapientia*, even as it reflects the three movements of Bonaventure's metaphysics (emanation, exemplarity, and consummation).[15] Question 4 of the text, which asks "whether that which is known by us with certitude is known in the eternal reasons themselves,"[16] is positioned in the middle of this threefold

---

12. I have already addressed this particular aspect of Schmutz's critique in Chapter 4, especially with respect to Bonaventure's original discussion of this *influentia* in *II Sent.* d. 26–27.

13. See especially Benson, "Structure and Meaning," 67–90.

14. Benson, "Structure and Meaning," 70–71.

15. Benson, "Structure and Meaning," 70–71.

16. *Scien. Chr.* q. 4 (5, 17).

structure as the point where "divine knowledge" (q. 1–3) and Christ's wisdom (q. 5–7) meet in human knowledge.

For Bonaventure, as Benson observes, "Human knowing stands in stark contrast to divine knowing. It is not marked with simplicity and perfection, but with mutability and uncertainty. These limitations can only be remedied when the human mind attains to eternal reasons." Thus, according to the Seraphic Doctor in Question 4: "To attain certainty, the human mind requires the presence of the eternal reasons, which impart infallibility to the knower and immutability to the known."[17] Crucially for our purposes, Benson shows how the Seraphic Doctor concludes his discussion of human certitude in Question 4 with a notable "flourish," transitioning between Question 4 and Questions 5–7 by writing, "But that truth which is absolutely immutable can be seen only by those who are able to enter into that innermost silence of the soul, and to this no sinner is able to come, but only one who is supremely a lover of eternity."[18] According to Benson, Bonaventure's conclusion to Question 4 with this "flourish" is important because "the above statement brings into one phrase God—humanity—Christ. It also brings into unity the meanings I suggest this text can have as a whole," so that, as Benson continues, "the structure of [the Questions as] 3–1–3 has been unified in its center without compromising its beginning or end but synthesizing both in itself. This is the consummation of the entire text, the point at which it finds its own repose but also the center from which all meaning [in the text] flows."[19] Question 4 is the "center" of *Scien. Chr.*, the point at which the human person is called to imitate Christ's wisdom in order to pass from *scientia* to *sapientia* as well as the point around which the entire text revolves. It is within this larger context as already elaborated by Benson that we can now approach the content of Question 4.

There, returning to Schmutz's critique, Bonaventure does indeed distinguish between a "general *influentia*" and a "special *influentia*" when arguing that the presence of the eternal reasons are required for certitude in human knowledge. In accordance with a common opinion of other theologians in his day, he affirms that such certitude must be

---

17. Benson, "Structure and Meaning," 75.

18. Benson, "Structure and Meaning," 76. The translation here is that provided by Benson in his article. See *Scien. Chr.* q. 4, ad ob. 26 (5, 27).

19. Benson, "Structure and Meaning," 89.

acquired through an "influence of light";[20] what must be clarified in his conclusion to Question 4, then, is *what* this *influentia* is and *how* the human mind attains the certitude of the eternal reasons through it. In consideration of these questions in particular, he argues:

that inflowing of light [*lucis influentia*] is either general [*generalis*], through which God inflows into all creatures [*influit in omnibus creaturis*], or it is special [*specialis*], as that which God inflows through grace [*influit per gratiam*]. If it is general, then we ought no more call God the giver of wisdom than we should say that God is the cause of earthly fertility; it would mean no more to say that knowledge [*scientia*] comes from God than wealth. If it is a special *influentia*, of the type that is in grace, then we would have to say that all knowledge [*cognitio*] would be infused, and that none is acquired or innate. But all these things are absurd. And so there is a third way [*tertius modus*] of understanding this, like a middle position between each way [*medium tenens inter utramque viam*], namely, that for certain knowledge, the eternal reason is necessarily required as a regulative and motive cause [*regulans et ratio motiva*], but indeed not as a sole cause nor in the fullness of its clarity. But along with created reason [*ratione creata*], it is contuited by us in part in accordance with the state of the wayfarer.[21]

Notably, where Schmutz and Milbank accuse Bonaventure of splitting the *influentia* into two distinct categories—namely, the "general" and the "special"—the Seraphic Doctor here in *Scien. Chr.* 4 actually discusses a "third" interpretation, something between the "general" and the "special" by which the human mind attains the eternal reasons so as to arrive at certitude. How are we then to understand all *three* of these ways of knowing?

Answering this question requires, first of all, turning to Bonaventure's subsequent explanation later in his conclusion to Question 4. He continues his response by claiming that the human mind is capable of attaining the eternal reasons—and thus arriving at certitude—because the human mind is an image of God. As he further explains in a passage that is quite lengthy but is nonetheless worth repeating in full:

For a creature is disposed to God by means of the vestige [*vestigii*], image [*imaginis*], and likeness [*similitudinis*]. Insofar as it is a vestige, it is related to God as to its principle [*ad principium*]; insofar as it is an image, it is related

---

20. See Bougerol's succinct and helpful introduction to the history of the word "*influentia*" in these respects in "Le rôle de l'*influentia*," 274–300.

21. *Scien. Chr.* q. 4, concl. (5, 23).

to God as to its object [*ad obiectum*]; but insofar as it is a similitude, it is related to God as to an infused gift [*ad donum infusum*]. And therefore every creature which is from God [*a Deo*] is a vestige; every creature that knows God [*cognoscit Deum*] is an image; and every creature in whom God dwells [*in qua habitat Deus*], and that creature alone, is a similitude. And there are three levels of the divine cooperation [*divinae cooperationis*] corresponding with these degrees of relationship. In a work which is performed by a creature that is a vestige, God cooperates as a creative principle [*principii creativi*]; but in any work that is meritorious or pleasing to God [*opus meritorium et Deo placitum*], which is accomplished by the creature who is a similitude, God cooperates by way of the infused gift [*doni infuse*]; but in any work accomplished by a creature who is an image, God cooperates as a motive cause [*rationis moventis*]. And this is the work of certain knowledge [*opus certitudinalis cognitionis*], which the lower reason cannot accomplish apart from higher reason. Thus, since certain knowledge pertains to the rational spirit [*spiritui rationali*] inasmuch as it is the image of God, it therefore attains the eternal reasons [*aeternas rationes attingit*] in this kind of knowledge. But because it is never fully made deiform [*plene deiformis*] in the state of the viator, it thus does not attain to them clearly, fully, and distinctly, but only to a greater or lesser degree as it approaches deiformity to a greater or lesser degree, but it always attains to them in some way, since the rational spirit can never be separated from the image. Whence, because the image was free from the deformity of guilt [*sine deformitate culpae*] in the state of innocence, it nevertheless did not yet have the full deiformity of glory [*plenam deiformitatem gloriae*]; it therefore was attaining the eternal reasons only in part [*ex parte*], but not enigmatically [*non in aenigmate*]. But in the state of postlapsarian nature, it lacks deiformity and has deformity, so it now attains to them in part and enigmatically [*ex parte et in aenigmate*]. But in the state of glory, it will lack every deformity and have the fullness of deiformity [*plenam deiformitatem*], so it will attain them fully and clearly.[22]

I will attend to the role of grace and the state of the "image" in the Seraphic Doctor's teachings on prelapsarian nature momentarily, but for now, I merely highlight how Bonaventure's distinctions between (1) a "general *influentia*," (2) a "middle" way of understanding how the human mind arrives at certitude, and (3) a "special *influentia*" of grace correspond perfectly with his teaching concerning the vestige, image, and similitude.[23]

Simply put, these three distinctions must be read with respect to

22. *Scien. Chr.* q. 4, concl. (5, 24).
23. For my previous introduction to these three orders of being, see Chapter 3.

Bonaventure's interest in explaining all of reality in a Trinitarian way. As we already encountered in Chapter 3, everything in creation can be called a "vestige" that reflects God's power, wisdom, and goodness inasmuch as the Trinity is the efficient cause of everything that exists. Because every "vestige" depends on God for its creation and continued existence, Bonaventure holds that everything that exists is upheld by a "general *influentia*." Second, as we also already saw in Chapter 3, a creature can be called an "image" of God when it possesses a rational soul—namely, a memory, an intellect, and a will—capable of knowing God as an object. The Seraphic Doctor's discussion of the "middle" or third way of understanding human certitude surrounding the eternal reasons in *Scien. Chr.* 4 pertains to the image, insofar as this relates specifically to the rational soul's capacity for knowing God. The image can "know" the eternal reasons with certitude when God acts as a motive cause for this knowledge. According to Bonaventure, helping grace, or *gratia gratis datum*, is that which moves the will to pray for sanctifying grace: Here in *Scien. Chr.* 4, this "middle way" rather notably functions in much the same way. As Bonaventure writes in the passage above, "the nature of the image is never absent from the rational spirit, it always attains to the reasons in some way." The image will always attain to the eternal reasons because its rational powers reflect the Trinity itself. It is always capable of knowing God (*capax Dei*) as an object in its very composition as a rational creature, but it cannot know God with complete certainty apart from a divine motive cause, much like helping grace moves the will to desire the Good before it prays for sanctifying grace. And indeed, as the Seraphic Doctor indicates above, for the image to be conformed to the Trinity, it must yet possess the "special *influentia*" of sanctifying grace that works *with* and *in* it in order to transform it into a similitude of God.[24]

Bonaventure's project in *Scien. Chr.* 4, as it were, primarily considers the "image." With respect to the larger structure of the text as already expounded by Benson, this is the point through which Bonaventure shifts from his discussions of God's *scientia* and human *cognitio* to Christ's *sapientia*. Or in other words, he is here transitioning from talking about the image's capacity for knowledge to discussing the wisdom of the similitude. Beatitude, for Bonaventure, belongs only to the

---

24. For my comments regarding this function of sanctifying grace, see Chapter 4.

image that has become a deiform similitude, or in other words, to the rational mind that has been conformed to the Trinity through sanctifying grace after helping grace has moved its will to pray for this gift as a motive cause. With Cullen, we can recognize a "moment of pure nature" here, but also with Cullen, and building upon Benson's previous observations concerning the structure of the text as a whole, it is crucial to note that the image in *Scien. Chr.* 4 remains indisputably "incomplete" apart from the special *influentia.* Complete certitude in beatitude, as Bonaventure there makes quite clear, is impossible for the rational mind to reach apart from sanctifying grace, which can only be imparted through the wisdom of Christ to which the conclusion of Question 4 ushers us forward.[25]

These distinctions between different ways of knowing God in *Scien. Chr.* can be further corroborated by comparing this text from Question 4 to *II Sent.* d. 29. This is the Distinction in which, paving the way forward for his treatment of grace in *Brev.* 5, the Seraphic Doctor claims that sanctifying grace "sanctifies" precisely insofar as it unites the soul to the entire Trinity, causing it to become a daughter of the Father, a bride of the Son, and a temple of the Holy Spirit.[26] In *II Sent.*, Bonaventure makes this claim in response to a question about whether or not prelapsarian souls "needed (*indiguit*)" the *influentia* of sanctifying grace in the Garden of Eden, asserting that the human person in the state of innocence indeed "needed sanctifying grace (*indiguit gratia gratum faciente*) so that he might be consecrated into the temple of God, adopted as a Son, and taken up in a conjugal union."[27] To explain this assertion, Bonaventure considers two ways in which a creature can be "received" by God. First, there is a "general" kind of reception (*acceptatione generali*), which applies to every created thing insofar as God created everything that exists and thus upholds everything that exists. Second, however, there is a "special" kind of reception (*acceptatio specialis*), "by which God is said to receive those who are worthy of eternal beatitude; and God does not accept a reception of this sort unless it is a rational creature [*creatura rationalis*]; for only the rational creature is one who is 'capable of God and can be a participant in God

---

25. See Benson's comments concerning this conclusion as noted above; "Structure and Meaning," 89.

26. I treated this triad at length and introduced d. 29 in Chapter 4.

27. *II Sent.*, d. 29, a. 1, q. 1 (2, 695).

[*eius capax est et particeps esse potest*].'"[28] "For holy souls which please God are called the temple of God, the daughter of God, and the bride of God,"[29] he writes, "because the infinitely great God wished to dwell in the soul as in a temple; and again, because God wished to consider his servant as a son; and because he wanted to take up his handmaid in marriage."[30] This second type of "special" reception, he continues, is always the result of a gratuitous condescension of God and always exceeds the natural capacities of the creature.

Here, the distinctions between the two different modes of "inflowing" (*influentiae*) in Question 4 of Bonaventure's *Scien. Chr.* are given counterparts with respect to the different modes of God's "receiving" (*acceptatione* or *acceptatio*) the different orders of existence within the created *ordo* of reality. God "receives" all of creation in a "general" way, simply because God created everything that exists and upholds all of existence; every vestige is thus upheld by a "general *influentia*." God can only receive a creature in a "special" way, however, when that creature receives sanctifying grace, through which God dwells in the creature as a temple, adopts the creature as a son, and weds the creature as a bride; the Trinity thereby dwells within the creature through the "special *influentia*." Between both modes of "reception" stands the rational creature, the "image" who is *capax Dei*: It is only the "image" who possesses a memory, intelligence, and will, and it is thus only the rational creature who is capable of first knowing God as an object in the mind, and then being moved by helping grace to freely consent to receiving sanctifying grace through such knowledge. Prelapsarian human persons "needed" (*indiguit*) the special *influentia* in the Garden of Eden because, without it, they would have remained merely at the level of the image and could have never become a similitude apart from it. In the same way that human certitude is not the *end* of Bonaventure's narrative of grace in *Scien. Chr.* 4, his distinctions between a "general receiving" and a "special receiving" in *II Sent.* d. 29 propose how the human person as the "image" of God indeed remains bereft of beatitude and the similitude apart from the "special *influentia*."

I highlight these two texts in particular to show how Schmutz's critique of Bonaventure fails to provide a nuanced account of what the

---

28. *II Sent.* d. 29, a. 1, q. 1 (2, 695).
29. *II Sent.* d. 29, a. 1, q. 1 (2, 695).
30. *II Sent.* d. 29, a. 1, q. 1 (2, 696).

Seraphic Doctor means by both the "general *influentia*" and the "special *influentia*." The Seraphic Doctor does indeed introduce a "general *influentia*" that upholds every vestige in its existence in contradistinction to the "special *influentia*" of grace, but Schmutz's account highlights and focuses on the "general *influentia*" without at all attending to what Bonaventure says regarding either the "special *influentia*" or the "third way of understanding this, like a middle position between each way."[31] Bonaventure does not distinguish between these three "modes" in a way that would suggest that God no longer acts *in* the human subject as a first cause of merit; he is quite clear that the human person, the image of God, cannot achieve the beatitude of the similitude at all apart from the special *influentia,* sanctifying grace, working in it.[32] Rather, these three distinctions are part and parcel to his "comprehensive trinitarianism."[33] Each "way" describes how the different modes of existence in the created order of reality relates to the Trinitarian order within God: The vestige through a "general *influentia*," the image through a divine motive cause urging it toward certitude, and the similitude through the "special *influentia*." To single out the "general *influentia*" is to misinterpret entirely Bonaventure's very clear position concerning the role of the "special *influentia*" in gifting the similitude to the image. It is to fail also to grasp the progressive character of how the created *ordo* of reality relates to God in his theology. Bonaventure's concept of the "general *influentia*" only applies to a consideration of how God acts or cooperates with the human person inasmuch as the human person—like everything else that exists in the created order of reality—is a creature, a vestige completely dependent on God for her very existence. Every vestige, every created thing, whether rational or irrational, is upheld by the Trinity through this general inflowing. To suggest that Bonaventure's introduction of this concept in some way leads to a view of human nature as no longer intrinsically ordered to God is to fail to recognize that this is actually Bonaventure's term for describing how every created thing is ordered to God and is dependent upon this "general inflowing" for its creation and continued existence.

That the human person as an "image" of God is indeed dependent

31. *Scien. Chr.* q. 4, concl. (5, 23): "Et ideo est tertius modus intelligendi, quasi medium tenens inter utramque viam...."

32. For a more detailed explanation of how this occurs, see again my discussion of this *influentia* in my treatment of *II Sent.* d. 26–27 in Chapter 4.

33. Coolman, "Part II: On the Creation of the World," 141–67.

upon this "general *influentia*" is underscored by Bonaventure in *Brev.* 5.2.[34] There, the Seraphic Doctor argues that all rational creatures were created by the Triune God from nothingness, and so they naturally tend back toward the nothingness from which they came. As he reasons there:

The human person was created in this way so that, because of his own defectiveness [*sua defectabilitate*], he would always need [*indigeret*] his First Principle, and the First Principle would never cease to inflow its own goodness to the creature. Therefore, because the rational spirit is defective in itself [*se defectivus*] insofar as it came from nothingness [*de nihilo*], so also its very nature is limited and poor [*egena*], insofar as it tends to turn back in on itself [*se recurvus*], loving its own good. Hence, because it owes its existence entirely to God, it is totally dependent upon God; and because it is defective, it tends back to non-being [*non-esse*] on its own.... Because he is totally dependent upon God, and God does not need any good from the person, he can do nothing by his own power to make God indebted to him—most especially the eternal reward which is God—unless through a divine condescension [*divinam condescensionem*]. This, then, is why—in order for his existence to be maintained in his deficiency—he always needs the help of the divine presence [*divinae praesentiae*], the divine upholding [*manutenentiae*], and the divine inflowing [*influentiae*] to be maintained in being [*manuteneatur in esse*]. And while this is in each and every creature [*universalis in creaturas omnes*], it is nevertheless called by the name of grace [*nominatur tamen nomen gratiae*], because it does not proceed from anything owed, but from the liberality of the divine goodness.[35]

Like every other vestige in creation, the human person is fundamentally "poor" in being because she is "totally dependent upon God" for her creation and continued existence. Timothy J. Johnson has aptly called this the concept of "ontological poverty" or the "poverty of being" in Bonaventure's theology, noting how humanity can never escape it.[36] For the Seraphic Doctor, humanity can never pass from indigence to some sort of "wealth" of being whereby it ceases to be dependent on the "divine presence, the divine upholding, and the divine inflowing." Like every other vestige in creation, the human person is entirely dependent upon the "general *influentia*" of God's grace, the "liberality of the divine

---

34. See Chapter 4.
35. *Brev.* 5.2 (5, 253–54).
36. Johnson, *The Soul in Ascent*, 35.

goodness" that condescends to all God's creatures in their ontological indigence.

Unlike every other vestige in creation, however, this passage from *Brev.* 5 underscores a crucial difference between the ontological poverty of the vestige and that of the rational creature. The rational creature, as one who was created in the image of the Trinity, possesses a memory, intelligence, and will with which it may choose "to turn back in on itself, loving his own good" instead of recognizing its radical dependence upon its Creator. By virtue of its very existence as a "creature," and thus as a vestige of the Trinity, the human person as the "image" of God will never cease being upheld by the "general *influentia*." Because it was created from nothing, however, its will tends naturally back in upon itself in a "mercenary (*mercenarius*)"[37] way: What the image needs, then, is something further to help it continuously desire to be upheld by God. What it needs, in short, is the "special *influentia*," which will gift it with the similitude that sets its desires "upright" despite its mercenary ways.[38] The human person as the "image" of God stands between the "vestige" and the "similitude." She will never cease being dependent upon the "general *influentia*," but she also requires the "special *influentia*" if her will is to thus remain continuously desirous of God. Recognizing this "betweenness" of the image, as it were, is the perfect point from which to begin contemplating the role of sanctifying grace in Bonaventure's teachings on prelapsarian human nature.

The Special *Influentia* in Prelapsarian Human Nature

Having clarified the difference between the "general" and "special" inflowings as the Seraphic Doctor presents them in *Scien. Chr.* 4, my purpose here will be to examine the role of the "special *influentia*" within his teachings on prelapsarian human nature. Building on my above remarks, this portion of the chapter argues that prelapsarian human nature in Bonaventure's theology remains incomplete apart from this

---

37. The word "mercenary" is used by the Seraphic Doctor in his definition of sanctifying grace from *II Sent.* d. 26, a. 1, q. 2, concl. (2, 635–36): "Affectus enim hominis recurvus est et mercenarius.…" I borrow it here and throughout this chapter since it is Bonaventure's own word for describing this concept.

38. See my discussion of this function of the *influentia* of sanctifying grace in Chapter 4.

"special *influentia*," since it is through this special inflowing that the human person progresses from merely being an image capable of God to becoming a similitude in whom God dwells. Because the Seraphic Doctor holds that the entire created order of reality is likewise ordered to the Trinity through this similitude, moreover, here we will also see how creation itself—and not only human nature—likewise remains incomplete apart from the "special *influentia*" of sanctifying grace.

Understanding both levels of incompleteness, however, requires first arriving at a basic understanding of what it means to be called a human person in Bonaventure's theological anthropology. As Boyd Taylor Coolman has recently noted, the Seraphic Doctor's theological anthropology, as well as his doctrine of creation in general, is "unabashedly anthropocentric."[39] My below comments begin by exploring this anthropocentricism; for Bonaventure, the entire created order of reality—which is comprised of both sensible and intelligible natures—relates to God through the human person, who has both a body through which it can relate to the sensible realm and a rational soul through which it can relate to the intelligible realm. Human nature mediates between different orders of being in Bonaventure's thought. This idea will be deeply significant when I then turn to consider the role of the special *influentia* of grace within his account of prelapsarian human nature: If the human person needs sanctifying grace in order to pass from being merely capable of God as an image to actually possessing God as a similitude, then so too does the entire cosmos need sanctifying grace inasmuch as it relates to God through this similitude, as well.

"Ensouled Bodies" between Sensible and Intelligible Creation

We begin, then, by examining Bonaventure's understanding of what it means to be a human person. Thus far in this book, my comments on his doctrine of grace have been mostly limited to a consideration of the soul and the effects of sanctifying grace within it, since the Seraphic Doctor defines sanctifying grace as an *influentia* that hierarchizes the soul by purifying, illuminating, and perfecting it for the purposes of shaping it into a similitude of the Trinity.[40] The human

---

39. Coolman, "Part II: On the Creation of the World," 164.

40. See Chapter 5 for my description of Bonaventure's notion of the hierarchical soul as such.

person for Bonaventure, however, is more than a soul. It is here in our consideration of his theological anthropology that his doctrine of grace must therefore be extended to include his portrait of the entire human person, both soul and body. To approach Bonaventure's theological anthropology is to approach both. As other scholars have already well noted, his various discussions of human nature do not adhere to a platonic notion of the body as the prison of the soul, but rather follow Aristotle in referring to human persons as "embodied souls," or "ensouled bodies."[41] For the Seraphic Doctor, as Giuseppe Rocco has noted, the soul and body will always remain "incomplete" apart from one another,[42] an idea highlighted and summarized by Bonaventure in a succinct way in *Brev. 7*, where he writes that "the completion of human nature (*completio naturae*) requires that humanity be constituted simultaneously with both a body and a soul (*simul ex corpore et anima*), just as matter and form have a mutual appetite and inclination toward one another."[43] Inasmuch as I will here argue that prelapsarian human nature remains incomplete apart from the special *influentia* of sanctifying grace, this concurrently means that the entire human person as an "ensouled body" is thus also "incomplete" apart from this *influentia*.

Relatedly, this introduction of the body in my account of Bonaventure's doctrine of grace is significant for another reason. Whereas the Areopagite's own consideration of "hierarchy" is considered by many scholars to be limited to the intelligible realm, Bonaventure's account of hierarchy presents what Laure Solignac has called a "hierarchical upheaval" precisely because the "perfective" moment in his theology is characterized by the Uncreated Word's descent from "superior things" to "inferior things" in the event of the Incarnation.[44] For Bonaventure, the "point" whereby the created *ordo* of reality returns to the Divine *ordo* is not located in the ascent of creation to the Divine, as is the case in the *Corpus Dionysiacum*, but rather, in the descent of the Divine to

41. See Rocco, *L'antropologia in San Bonaventura*, esp. 46; as well as Solignac, *La voie de la ressemblance*, esp. 292–302. For more on how the soul and body are united in Bonaventure's theology, see also Quinn, *The Historical Constitution of Bonaventure's Philosophy*, 120–35; and Thomas M. Osborne, "*Unibilitas*: The Key to Bonaventure's Understanding of Human Nature," *Journal of the History of Philosophy* 37, no. 2 (1999): 227–50.

42. Rocco, *L'antropologia in San Bonaventura*, 48: "Il corpo e l'anima sono due sostanze incomplete che si completano l'un l'atra allo stesso modo che la materia e la forma si completano a vicenda."

43. *Brev.* 7.5 (5, 286).

44. See again Solignac's discussion of these themes in *La voie de la ressemblance*, esp. 301–2, and my treatment of them in Chapter 3.

creation. In stark contrast to the theology of the Areopagite, Bonaventure's understanding of hierarchy locates the point of the created order of reality's "return" to God in the sensible rather than in the intelligible realm—namely, in the Incarnate Christ, "in the union of the superior with the inferior."[45] In the same way that the "image" stands between the "vestige" and the "similitude" in Bonaventure's theology, the human person is unique within his account of the created order of reality because the human person stands between the intelligible and sensible realms as a creature who possesses both a rational soul and a body. It is within the Seraphic Doctor's theological anthropology that the sensible and intelligible orders of creation meet, thus providing the circumstances for his "hierarchical upheaval," or namely, the return of the created *ordo* of reality to God through the Incarnate Word.

Any consideration of Bonaventure's view of prelapsarian human nature must therefore begin by considering the body. The Seraphic Doctor describes the body's composition in *II Sent.* d. 17. There, in agreement with most of his medieval peers, he affirms that the human body is an earthly nature comprised of the four elements: earth, water, air, and fire. Additionally, however, he further insists that the human body also shares in "heavenly natures (*natura caelestis*)" for two reasons: first, according to "quality," because he claims that the four earthly elements within the human body are held together by an "inflowing" (*influentia*) of power from "superior bodies (*corporum superiorum*)," i.e., the stars and planets;[46] and second, according to "conformity (*conformitatem*)," because he also claims that the luminosity and heat of human bodies conform to heavenly natures in a way that distinguishes them from other physical bodies within earthly creation.[47] In all these ways, Bonaventure holds that the human body shares something in common with natures from every level of the sensible creation, or in other words, with every irrational vestige in creation—whether earth,

---

45. Solignac, *La voie de la ressemblance*, 301–2: "… c'est-à-dire dans la conjonction de premier avec le dernier 'que réside la consommation de la perfection'. La perfection ne réside donc pas tant dans le supérieur (Denys) que dans l'union du supérieur avec l'inférieur (Bonaventure)."

46. *II Sent.* d. 17, a. 2, q. 2, resp. (2, 422–23). See also Solignac, *La voie de la ressemblance*, 293–95, esp. her French translation of this same passage on 294–95n15. Bonaventure says something quite similar in the second part of the *Breviloquium*; see, for example, *Brev.* 2.4 (5, 221–22).

47. *II Sent.* d. 17, a. 2, q. 2, resp. (2, 423). See also Solignac, *La voie de la ressemblance*, 293–95.

air, water, fire, or the matter that comprises the physical composition of the stars and planets in the heavens. While this admittedly very medieval account of the composition of the human body will seem strange from the perspective of a modern scientist, its scientific implausibility ought not distract us from the fundamental theological point he here underscores: Since the body is composed of materials from both earthly and heavenly natures, it is thereby capable of relating to every vestige in the cosmos as a physical being composed of both earthly and heavenly matter.[48] Before it even mediates between the sensible and intelligible realms, the human body itself also mediates between different grades of the physical creation, thus making it the only suitable vehicle through which all irrational creation—both earthly and heavenly—may enjoy its own *reductio* into God.

Unlike every other irrational vestige in creation, however, and as we already saw above in my discussion of the "general *influentia*" in Bonaventure's theology, the human body stands out since it was created for a union with a rational soul. He describes this union at length in *Brev.* 2:

According to the orthodox doctrine of faith, let us hold the following points about the human body in its first state, namely, that the body of the first man, formed from *the slime of the earth*, was created so that it would be subject and proportionable to the soul in its own way. It would be "proportionable [*proportionabile*]" to the soul with respect to its level complexion, a beautiful and variegated structure, and the uprightness of its stature. But it was "subject" [*subiectum*] to the soul so that it would be obedient without rebellion, capable of propagating without lust, capable of growth without defect, and also immutable to every kind of incorruption, not even through death intervening.[49]

Because the body was created thus "proportionate" and "subjected" to the soul, Bonaventure continues *Brev.* 2 by then arguing that the power, wisdom, and goodness of the Trinity were all especially made manifest in the prelapsarian human person. First, the Father's "power [*potentia*]" was made manifest in human nature because "God created him from two natures that were the greatest distance from one another, joined in

---

48. A succinct discussion of the "physical creation" in Bonaventure's doctrine of creation can be found in *Brev.* 2.3–5. See also Coolman, "Part II: On the Creation of the World," 148–52.

49. *Brev.* 2.10 (5, 227–28).

one person and nature; these are the body and soul [*corpus et anima*], one of which is a corporeal substance, but the other of which—namely, the soul—is a spiritual and incorporeal substance; so these are the greatest distance from each other in the genus of substance [*in genera substantiae*]."[50] Next, the Son's "wisdom [*sapientia*]" was also manifested in the prelapsarian human person because the body also "had to be proportionate in its own way to the soul," whereby "the body is united to the soul, which uplifts the body to beatitude by perfecting, moving, and holding it." In this way, Bonaventure asserts, the body was created upright with respect to its organs, its physique, its face and hands, and its "straight stature and uplifted head," which all "attest to the rectitude of its mind." [51] He then finally concludes that prelapsarian human nature also manifested the Spirit's "goodness (*bonitas*)" inasmuch as it was created completely innocent and free from sin. In prelapsarian creation, the human body was so obedient and conformed to the soul that it "would have within it no fight of rebellion, no propensity to lust, no lack of strength, and no corruption of death."[52]

This perfect union between the body and soul in prelapsarian creation was thus the crown of all sensible creation because:

Human bodies are disposed to receiving the noblest form [*nobilissimam formam*], which is the rational soul [*anima rationalis*], to which the desire [*appetitus*] of every sensible and corporeal nature is ordered and brought to an end [*ordinatur et terminatur*], so that by means of that which is a form having existence, life, sense, and intelligence, every nature would be led back [*reducatur*] to its Principle in the manner of an intelligible circle [*ad modum circuli intelligibilis*], in which it is perfected and beatified [*perficiatur et beatificetur*].... And for this reason, it is undoubtedly true that we are the end [*finis*] of everything that exists; and all corporeal things [*corporalia*] were created for serving humanity [*ad humanum obsequium*], so that from all these things humanity would be enkindled for the purposes of loving and praising the Creator of the universe, whose providence disposes all.[53]

Though the human body shares something in common with every vestige in the sensible order of creation, it nonetheless differs from earth, air, fire, water, and the stars and heavenly spheres because it was created for a union with the rational soul through which it is *capax Dei*

---

50. *Brev.* 2.10 (5, 228).
51. *Brev.* 2.10 (5, 228).
52. *Brev.* 2.10 (5, 228).
53. *Brev.* 2.4 (5, 221–22).

in a way that merely sensible and irrational creation is not. As Laure Solignac has noted of all these ideas, for Bonaventure, "the body is a union (a joining of the celestial nature and the terrestrial nature), and it is created for a union (with the soul),"[54] so that the body itself "is explicitly identified as the principle *of achievement* for the corporeal world, that is to say as the principle in which the universal *reductio* of sensible being is achieved." [55] Coolman's comment that Bonaventure's theological anthropology is "unabashedly anthropocentric" here comes into clear focus: Human nature is the crown of all sensible creation because it is comprised of both a body and a soul, and is thus the locus through which sensible creation can be uplifted to its Creator.

We should here note, however, that this anthropocentricism in Bonaventure's theology is not merely confined to a consideration of the sensible sphere of reality. In the *Breviloquium,* the Seraphic Doctor identifies the human person as "the principle in which the universal *reductio* of sensible being is achieved," but this same idea is mirrored with respect to human nature and all intelligible being as well. In addition to sharing something in common with irrational created natures in the sensible sphere, the prelapsarian person also shares something in common with angelic natures in the intelligible sphere: a rational soul. The prelapsarian human in Bonaventure's theology straddles both levels of reality. It is at once an intelligible and a sensible nature, an "ensouled body" that is capable of relating to every kind of nature within the created order. In the same way that the image stands between the vestige and the similitude, and in the same way that its physical body mediates between earthly and heavenly physical natures, human nature likewise stands between sensible natures and intelligible natures. Bonaventure therefore identifies human beings as the crown of all prelapsarian creation, intelligible creation (or angelic natures) included. Human nature stands at the center of his portrait of the hierarchical macrocosm as the locus wherein earth meets heaven,[56] whereby the sensible is uplifted into the intelligible through the human person's rational soul, but also

---

54. Solignac, *La voie de la ressemblance,* 297: "En d'autres termes, le corps est une union (conjonction de nature céleste et de nature terrestre), et il est fait pour une union (avec l'âme)."

55. Solignac, *La voie de la ressemblance,* 310: "L'âme humaine est explicitement identifiée au principe *d'achèvement* du monde corporel, c'est-à-dire au principe dans lequel s'achève la *reductio* universelle des êtres sensibles."

56. See again my discussion of this theme in Chapter 3.

vice versa, since it is through the human person's body that the intelligible likewise "descends" into the sensible. Or in other words, the human person is identified by Bonaventure as "the principle of achievement" for the corporeal and the intelligible world, since the human person as an "ensouled body" is the principle in which the universal *reductio* of all being finds its center, which will eventually be brought to fruition in the fullest possible way through the Incarnation.[57]

In sum, Bonaventure defines a human person as an "ensouled body," a being that—unlike every other irrational vestige in the sensible realm, and also unlike every other rational image in the intelligible realm—was created with both a body and a soul. Though the former is ordered to the latter in his theology, he is quite clear that these remain "incomplete" apart from one another with respect to human nature. Because it thus straddles the sensible and intelligible orders of creation, human nature is the locus through which the entire created order of reality will enjoy its *reductio* into God. What, though, of grace? What is the role of the special *influentia* in the Seraphic Doctor's description of these prelapsarian "ensouled bodies" that mediate between the sensible and intelligible realms of the created order?

Traversing the Distance between the Image and
the Similitude through the Special *Influentia*

Understanding the role of grace in the Seraphic Doctor's prelapsarian theological anthropology, as it were, requires looking beyond a consideration of the person as simply a vestige and an image to consider her as a similitude of the Trinity as well. For him, the human person is upheld by the same "general *influentia*" that upholds all creaturely existence inasmuch as that person is a "vestige" of the Trinity; she is ontologically poor and dependent upon this general inflowing for her creation and continued existence as a creature. As we also saw above, however, she is yet distinguished from every irrational vestige in creation inasmuch as she is also an "image" of the Trinity, and thereby possesses a rational soul with a memory, intellect, and will capable of knowing the Truth and choosing the Good. Her will is nonetheless described

---

57. Bonaventure intimates this in *Brev.* 2.11 (5, 229), where he discusses how human nature completes the universe inasmuch as it is the only type of being that can have a knowledge of both the "inner" and "outer" books of creation, which will ultimately be fulfilled in Christ, who is the book written "within" and "without."

by Bonaventure as being naturally mercenary. Because the person was created by God from nothing, she tends back to the nothingness from whence she came and is liable to love her own good rather than choosing to "love God above all things and her neighbor as herself."[58] The prelapsarian human person therefore needs something in addition to her natural faculties if she is to continuously desire to submit herself to God's "general *influentia*" rather than bow to these selfish, mercenary tendencies. Instead of merely remaining at the level of the image, she also needs to become a *similitude* of the Trinity.

In the *Breviloquium*, Bonaventure directly addresses this problem, asserting that the prelapsarian human soul was gifted with four aids to help it from giving in to its selfishness:

And since humanity could fall by reason of its defective nature [*naturae defectivae*], formed from nothing and not yet confirmed in glory, the most merciful God conferred to humanity a fourfold aid [*quadruplex adiutorium*]: Two of nature [*naturae*] and two of grace [*gratiae*]. For God instilled a twofold rectitude [*duplicem rectitudinem*] in that nature: one for the purpose of rightly judging, and this is the rectitude of conscience [*rectitudo conscientiae*]; and another for rightly willing, and this is *synderesis*, which murmurs against evil and urges human nature toward the good. Additionally, God also added a twofold perfection [*duplicem perfectionem*] of grace: helping grace [*gratiae gratis data*], which is a knowledge illuminating the intellect [*scientia illuminans intellectum*] so that they might know themselves, their God, and their world, which was created for them; and sanctifying grace [*gratiae gratum facientis*], which is a charity enabling their affections [*caritas habilitans affectum*] so that they would love God above all things and their neighbors as themselves.[59]

Here, Bonaventure hints that "helping grace" might indeed pertain to the "middle" path of illumination between the "general" and "special" *influentiae* to which I alluded in my earlier analysis of *Scien. Chr.* 4. In the Garden of Eden, helping grace (*gratiae gratis data*) was gifted to humanity as a "knowledge enlightening the intellect so that they might know themselves, their God, and the world that made them." In addition to this, however, Bonaventure further insists that prelapsarian human persons were also gifted with sanctifying grace (*gratiae gratum faciens*)—the "special *influentia*"—which "made them pleasing" in the

58. See my discussion of humanity's dependence on the "general *influentia*" and its "mercenary" will above.

59. *Brev.* 2.11 (5, 229–30).

Garden of Eden by gifting a charity "which enabled their affections so that they might love God above all things and their neighbors as themselves." Sanctifying grace thus served the very important purpose of keeping the prelapsarian human person's will from being mercenary, from turning back to its own good and tending toward the nothingness from which it was created.

Just as importantly, however, Bonaventure further insinuates that the presence of sanctifying grace within the prelapsarian affect in this way served another crucial purpose—namely, by thus setting the prelapsarian will "upright" so that it could love God above all things and its neighbor as itself, sanctifying grace is also the superinfused gift through which the prelapsarian person can thereby become a similitude of the Trinity in addition to being called an image. As he there argues, the entire created order of reality "is a certain kind of book in which its Creator, the Trinity, shines out, is represented, and is read through three levels of expression, namely, in the manner of a vestige, an image, and a likeness."[60] In what should by now be a familiar pattern, he claims that the aspect of the vestige is found in every creature; that only intelligent or rational creatures can be called an image of the Trinity; and finally, that the similitude can only be found in those creatures who are "God-conformed." As he writes, "Through these successive levels, comparable to steps, the human intellect is designed to ascend gradually to the supreme Principle, which is God," so that

The rational spirit stands in the middle between the first and last [*medius inter primam et ultimam*], so that the first is below it, the second within it, and the third above it. And so in the state of innocence, when the image was not yet spoilt, but was made deiform through grace, the book of creation [*liber creatura*] sufficed to enable humanity to contemplate the light of divine wisdom. They were then so wise that when they saw all things in themselves, they saw them in their proper genus, but also in their art, because this corresponds with the threefold way things exist, namely, in their own matter or nature, in a created intelligence, and in the Eternal Art.... For this triple vision, humanity received a threefold eye, as Hugh of St. Victor says, namely, the eye of the flesh [*carnis*], the eye of reason [*rationis*], and the eye of contemplation [*contemplationis*]: The eye of the flesh, by which they would see the world and those things that are in the world; the eye of reason, by which they would see the soul and those things that are in the soul; and the eye of contemplation,

---

60. *Brev.* 2.12 (5, 230).

by which they would see God and those things that are in God. And so, with
the eye of the flesh, humanity could see all those things which were outside
itself [*extra se*]; with the eye of reason, all those things which were inside itself [*intra se*]; and with the eye of contemplation, all those things which were
above it [*supra se*]. But indeed, the eye of contemplation does not function
perfectly unless in glory, which humanity dismissed through their culpability,
although they may recover it through grace and faith and the understanding
of scriptures, by which the human mind is purified [*purgatur*], illuminated
[*illuminatur*], and perfected [*perficitur*] for the purposes of contemplating
heavenly things.[61]

Recently, Coolman has highlighted a key observation with respect
to the above passage. The Seraphic Doctor here "introduces a subtle,
but crucial diastema in this framework" for prelapsarian human nature.[62] The vestige and the image, as Coolman notes, are "givens" in
creation "and cannot be forfeited"; "the third and last, however, the
God-conformity or divine likeness, remains to be attained and maintained or enacted. There is a 'distance' to be traversed between image
and likeness, a contemplative ... 'exercise' that must be enacted in order to enact this divine likeness."[63] As Bonaventure himself indicates,
these three levels of being are "successive levels" or "stages" that the
human intellect was created to "gradually ascend." Coolman calls this
"a *prescription* or prescriptive *telos*" with respect to prelapsarian human nature, in that by introducing this "diastema" between the levels
of the image and the similitude, the Seraphic Doctor argues that "the
human creature should not remain merely at the level of the image, but
propelled by grace should strive for likeness, and once attained, should
preserve it."[64]

We need not necessarily go farther than these observations to recognize the indispensable role of the "special *influentia*" in Bonaventure's teachings regarding prelapsarian human nature. The role of sanctifying grace in prelapsarian creation was to gift human nature with
the similitude through which the entire Trinity would dwell within the
human soul and conform it to God above its natural powers as a vestige
and an image. As he previously argued in *II Sent.* d. 29, prelapsarian
human nature "needed" this special *influentia* in order to enjoy this

61. *Brev.* 2.12 (5, 230).
62. See Coolman, "Part II: On the Creation of the World," 162.
63. Coolman, "Part II: On the Creation of the World," 162.
64. Coolman, "Part II: On the Creation of the World," 162.

conformity with the Trinity, or in order to become the daughter of the Father, the bride of the Son, and the temple of the Holy Spirit.[65] Apart from this *influentia*, the prelapsarian human person could not traverse the diastema between its natural capacity for knowing God and the supernatural contemplative end for which it was created—namely, loving God above all things and loving its neighbors as itself. The special *influentia*, as we saw above, is needed if the soul is to pass from *scientia* and *cognitio* to *sapientia*, and Bonaventure is abundantly clear in the *Breviloquium* and *II Sent.* that the prelapsarian human person required this gift to be conformed to God. These texts, paired with my above discussion of the difference between the "general" and "special *influentia*" in *Scien. Chr.* 4, should leave no question regarding the Seraphic Doctor's understanding of the role of grace in his teachings on human nature. There is certainly a "moment of pure nature" here in *Brev.* 2 and in *II Sent.*, d. 29 with respect to his teachings regarding the image, but, for Bonaventure, for the human person to achieve beatitude—conformity or "assimilation" with the Trinity—she must traverse this diastema between the image and the similitude. She can only do so through the "superinfused gift," the special *influentia* of grace that purifies, illuminates, and perfects her natural faculties from within to make her capable of "loving God above all things and her neighbor as herself."

What deserves further emphasis here, however, is how the rest of the created order of reality was likewise ordered by this similitude in prelapsarian creation as well. As Coolman further argues of Bonaventure's conclusion to *Brev.* 2 in a lengthy passage that nonetheless merits repetition:

All this sets the stage for a remarkable climax to Bonaventure's doctrine of creation … in order for creation to be what the Creator intended, there must be creatures who possess not only the divine vestige and image, but also the divine likeness. But, as seen, in order for the rational creature to possess the divine likeness it must traverse the diastema between image and likeness. But traversing this distance is a function of contemplative vision, a function of seeing the Trinity at all three levels of created expression, that is, of reading rightly the book of creation. But that vision is a function of divine likeness; without deiformity, the eye of contemplation is blind and cannot read rightly and correctly the Trinitarian "book" of creation. But the creature itself is part of this 'book' and does not stand apart from it as some neutral observer-reader.

---

65. See my above remarks in this chapter.

Rather, coming full circle, the rational creature's deformity is itself constitutive of the book of creation. Thus, without human deformity, not only is the reader defective, but a crucial 'chapter' of the book is missing as well.... The mutual entailments of Bonaventure's theology are thus dizzying: the goal of creation is to reflect or express the Trinity. That requires that human possess divine likeness.... The universe is not a complete Trinitarian expression unless it contains rational creatures who contemplate it precisely as such, and in so doing achieve and maintain its (pneumatic) pinnacle, namely, divine likeness. Knowing, loving, and praising the Trinity in and of itself perfects the Trinitarian expressiveness of the created order. In short, Bonaventure has built the contemplative vocation of the rational creature into the very Trinitarian fabric of creation. Stepping back, what also becomes apparent here is how, for Bonaventure, the human creature's own state and fate is wholly and intimately bound up with that of the cosmos itself ... insofar as rational creatures achieve divine likeness, thus far the cosmos achieves its *telos*; to the extent that rational creatures fall short or even decline from divine likeness, to that extent does the whole creation suffer. The well-being of the macrocosm is indexed to the health of the microcosm.[66]

What Coolman's text very importantly highlights for our purposes is how, in thus building "the contemplative vocation of the rational creature into the very Trinitarian fabric of creation" with respect to the similitude, Bonaventure has also built the need for sanctifying grace into "the very Trinitarian fabric of creation" as well.

This is because the human person, an "ensouled body" who stands between the intelligible and sensible spheres of reality as both a vestige and an image, needs the special *influentia* of sanctifying grace to "traverse the diastema" between the image and the similitude. It needs this special *influentia* in order to become a "likeness" of the Divine—to become a daughter of the Father, a spouse of the Son, and a temple of the Holy Spirit. It needs this special *influentia* in order for its will to be set "upright" from its mercenary ways, so that it can turn away from its selfish love of its own good and toward God. It needs this special *influentia* if—in addition to "knowing" the Trinity as an object through helping grace and also in addition to being upheld by the general *influentia* that maintains all of creation in existence—it is to "love God above all things and its neighbor as itself" and thus merit the Good. It needs this special *influentia* if it is to be gifted with the eye of contemplation through which it can behold God "above" it in addition to the

66. Coolman, "Part II: On the Creation of the World," 162–63.

eye of the flesh and the eye of reason to see everything "without" and "within" it.

What's more, since Bonaventure holds that the intelligible and sensible spheres of reality meet through the "ensouled bodies" of prelapsarian human nature, the human person's need for this special *influentia* entails that all intelligible and sensible creation "needs" this *influentia* as well. Irrational creation is not capable of the similitude, even as angelic rational creatures lack a body that would share something with sensible natures. The human person's reception of the similitude, on the other hand, effectively invites the indwelling of the Trinity across all levels of creation since it is in the human person's "ensouled body" that these two disparate orders of reality meet, and also since it is in the human person's "ensouled body" that the rest of the created order of reality can enjoy its own *reductio* into the Trinity. If the "contemplative vocation of the rational creature" is built into the Trinitarian fabric of creation in Bonaventure's theology, then so is the need for sanctifying grace.

Where this argument can be carried even further, moreover, is through a consideration of what it is exactly that this "contemplative vocation" entails in Bonaventure's description of prelapsarian human nature. We have seen repeatedly how the *redditus* moment in his teachings on hierarchy and grace ought not be regarded as merely some sort of static end through which the human creature "ascends" to a contemplative union with God so as to never again "descend"; rather, the special *influentia* of sanctifying grace "returns" the human soul to God precisely inasmuch as it causes the soul to then remain in God, to perpetually circle between a contemplative union with God and meritorious action with respect to the created order of reality. The soul is made hierarchical through grace because this "remaining" always constantly includes both the ascending and descending movements to and from contemplation. The soul that has arrived at a contemplative union with God at the level of the seraph in Bonaventure's schema of the hierarchical soul does not and never was meant to simply stop moving there; rather, its contemplative union with God inflames it to once again "descend" so that it may share the light of God with others in the sensible realm.[67] This idea is not left out of Bonaventure's portrait of the role

---

67. For my discussion of this notion in Bonaventure's theology of hierarchy, see especially Chapter 3; for my discussion of this notion with respect to Bonaventure's notion of the hierarchical soul, see Chapter 5.

of sanctifying grace in prelapsarian human nature, but rather, it provides the key to understanding how the human person—and indeed, the entire created order of reality—can actually traverse the diastema between the image and the similitude. The image is *capax Dei*, but will remain selfish and mercenary apart from sanctifying grace. It needs the "special *influentia*" if it is to become a similitude whose contemplative vocation includes relating to both God and the rest of the created order of reality in a holy way.

As a somewhat obscure but nonetheless still helpful example, this idea is evident in one passage from the Seraphic Doctor's *II Sent.* d. 16, where he explicitly discusses a "diastema" of this sort in prelapsarian human nature. There, he asks whether or not the characteristic of the image can be "more principally"[68] (*magis principaliter*) found in an angel than in a human soul, declaring in response that a rational creature can be called an image of God in two different ways based upon two different levels of *ordo*. In a certain way, a rational creature is ordered to God according to its *esse* or existence; in another way, however, a rational creature is ordered to God according to its *bene esse* or its "well-being."[69] This distinction notably harkens back to an argument made by Hugh of St. Victor in his *De Sacramentis Christianae fidei*, who had distinguished between what he calls the *esse* and *pulchrum esse*, or "beautiful being," of a rational creature. As Coolman has noted of this Hugonian insight, "In some sense, the burden of human being in Eden was to discern the relation between *esse* and *pulchrum esse* in the visible creation so that the same progressive pattern of formation might be replicated within itself.... For him, the Fall is, in a sense, a failure to perceive and attain beautiful being [*pulchrum esse*]."[70] Bonaventure's own reference to *esse* and *bene esse* within his explanation of what it means to be an image of God inherits this Hugonian distinction, albeit using slightly different terminology. Importantly for our purposes, like Hugh, the Seraphic Doctor also uses it within *II Sent.* with respect to his description of prelapsarian rational souls. For one familiar with the Hugonian background behind it, his assertion that rational souls can be ordered according to both *esse* and *bene esse* in their prelapsarian

---

68. *II Sent.* d. 16, a. 2, q. 1, conc. (2, 400).

69. *II Sent.* d. 16, a. 2, q. 1, conc. (2, 401).

70. See Boyd Taylor Coolman, "'In whom I am well pleased': Hugh of St. Victor's Trinitarian Aesthetics," *Pro Ecclesia* 23, no. 3 (2014): 334–35. See also Hugh of St. Victor, *De sacramentis* b. 1, p. 1, ch. 3 (*PL* 176, 188C-189A).

state connotes a progressive diastema within his definition of the rational soul as the image of God. Like Hugh, the "being" of the image is only the first step of order within the rational creature; to achieve the "well-being," or beautiful being, of the image, the rational creature must progress farther.

How, then, does the rational creature progress from "being" to "well-being" as the image of God? Bonaventure continues his explanation by claiming that a rational creature is "immediately ordered to God [*immediate ordinetur ad Deum*]" through the *esse* of the image. Additionally, he writes, it is ordered from the *bene esse* of the image "when the creature, which is the image, is placed in charge of others who hold the cause of the vestige [*praeponatur aliis, quae tenent rationem vestigii*], so that others are ordered [*ordinentur*] to it as to an end [*finem*]."[71] Bonaventure then describes three different ways in which a rational creature can thus be "ordered" as the image of God:

And thus, there is a threefold *ordo* in a rational creature, according to which it may be conformed to God. First, because it is born immediately conformed to God; and this is the essential image [*essentialis imagini*], and this is found equally in an angel and the human soul, because with each, "the mind is immediately formed from the first truth." Second, there is the image by which one creature is placed in charge [*praeponitur*] of other creatures; and angels excel [*praecellunt*] in this, because they are rightly appointed over not only animals, but also humanity.... Third, there is an order by which irrational creatures are ordered to rational creatures as to an end [*ordinantur tanquam in finem*], for whom they were created ... and accordingly, this order applies more fittingly to humanity with God than an angel; for corporeal and sensible creatures were created more for human persons than for angels. And thus, it is obvious that the cause of the image [*ratio imaginis*], as it is attended to in the fittingness of order [*convenientia ordinis*], is found equally [*aequaliter*] in humanity and in the angel with regard to that which is from *esse*, because both are immediately ordered to God. With regard to that which is from *bene esse*—namely, an order with respect to creatures—they hold themselves in an *excessive* or *ecstatic* way [*per modum excedentis et excessi*]. For it is more fitting for the angel to be characterized as a ruler [*regiminis*] with respect to order; but it is more fitting for humanity to be characterized as an end [*finis*] with respect to order.[72]

71. *II Sent.* d. 16, a. 2, q. 1 (2, 401).
72. *II Sent.* d. 16, a. 2, q. 1 (2, 401).

In this admittedly rather odd passage, it is precisely the human person's affinity with sensible created reality which permits her to pass from her simple "being" as a rational creature to "well-being," an existence whereby the human person—the only created nature that shares in both sensible and intelligible creation—likewise orders other creatures to their end in God as well. To be created in the image of God, for Bonaventure, implies an immediate ordering to God inasmuch as the human person is naturally capable of knowing God as an object in her mind; to achieve a truly "beautiful existence," however, the human person must exceed herself in an ecstatic way for other creatures. Quite strikingly, the diastema between "being" and "well-being" can only be traversed in this ecstatic moment, when the "image" becomes capable not only of relating to God, but of leading the sensible order of reality to its end in God as well.

As we have already seen, however, it can only become capable of serving as this "end" for sensible creation when it consents to receiving the *influentia* of sanctifying grace, which will gift it with the similitude that will open the "eye of contemplation" in human nature. The role of grace in Bonaventure's doctrine of prelapsarian human nature is indeed "dizzying,"[73] inasmuch as sanctifying grace is the gift through which the prelapsarian person becomes capable of passing from "being" to "well-being," from being an introverted, selfish, and mercenary creature concerned only with her own good to becoming an extroverted, selfless, and ecstatic creature who relates to God and the rest of the created order of reality. Prelapsarian human nature would remain "incomplete" apart from the special *influentia* of sanctifying grace because apart from it, human nature would be unable to traverse all these "diastemas," between the image and the similitude, between mere "being" and *beautiful* being." This "well-being" is characterized, we should further note, not only by the rational creature's capacity for God, but also by the rational creature's capacity to relate to the entire created order, both with respect to her "neighbors"—namely, other rational creatures—but, rather importantly, to sensible and irrational creation, as well.

This *reductio* of the created order into the divine order cannot and should not be understood in a simply linear way. The human person's

---

73. See Coolman, "Part II: On the Creation of the World," 163.

achievement of the similitude, which it can only enjoy through sanctifying grace, has truly cosmic implications since this achievement ensures that every created thing in the created *ordo* of reality relates to God and other creatures in the way God intended. The "eye of contemplation" that is opened by the similitude does not close "the eye of the flesh" or "the eye of reason"; rather, these are also provided their clearest sight in Bonaventure's theology when the "eye of contemplation" is functioning properly. In the same way that the order of the seraph "enlivens" the lower orders of the soul in his notion of the hierarchical soul,[74] the "eye of contemplation" is similarly that which illuminates the lower natural faculties within the human person. Strikingly, these three "eyes" even parallel his various descriptions of how grace hierarchizes the soul according to three levels—namely, in accordance with "nature" (corresponding with the level of the vestige and the eye of the flesh), in accordance with "industry" (corresponding with the level of the image and the eye of reason), and solely through grace (corresponding with the level of the similitude and the eye of contemplation)! The person whose "eye of contemplation" is opened enjoys a relationship with God "above" in a way that opens the door to more fulfilling relationships with that which is both "without" her in the sensible order of reality and "within" her in the intelligible. The prelapsarian person's *reductio* into God through the similitude should in this way, once again, not be conceived as a "bottom-up" ascent whereby the person is then removed from the rest of the created order: Rather, the similitude is the means through which the prelapsarian human person could relate to every image in the intelligible order of reality and every vestige in the sensible sphere of reality in the fullest and most meaningful possible way. For Bonaventure, to be united to God through the similitude is to be made capable of all these relationships, of passing from "being" to a "well-being" through which all of creation might similarly be drawn into the "contemplative vocation" that threads together the tapestry of Bonaventure's rich and "dizzying" portrait of prelapsarian creation.

In all these ways—again revisiting the recent critique against Bonaventure pitted by both Schmutz and Milbank—every order of being within prelapsarian creation remains "incomplete" apart from the special *influentia* of sanctifying grace that thus gifts this similitude to

---

74. See again my discussion of the hierarchical soul in Chapter 5.

it. The prelapsarian human person remains "incomplete" apart from it because it is only through this special *influentia* that she will traverse the diastema between the image and the similitude in order to become capable of "loving God above all things and her neighbor as herself." The entire created order of reality likewise remains "incomplete" apart from it since it is only through this special *influentia* that the "contemplative vocation" that was woven into the very fabric of creation could be achieved; it is also only through this special *influentia* that all created things—whether sensible or intelligible—can return to the Trinity. Had the primogenitors of the human race remained receptive to this *influentia,* the created *ordo* would have been illuminated by "the eye of contemplation" that enlightens all of reality even into glory. Our first parents would, nevertheless, choose a different path.

Freely Denying the Special
Influentia through Sin

In his *Disputed Questions on Evangelical Perfection*, Bonaventure alludes to the "general *influentia*" that maintains everything that exists in the created order of reality in a way that highlights the ontological poverty of every created nature that depends on it:

For every nature, because it is from nothingness [*de nihilo*], holds a certain defect in itself and declares itself defective [*defectivam*]. For a nature is maintained [*conservatur*] when it preserves a unity in its component principles and also in its quantitative parts for its own powers [*viribus suis*]. It is also maintained when it expels everything that induces division inasmuch as is possible. But nature is perfected [*proficit*] when it desires to receive [*appetit suscipere*] an *influentiam* from a superior nature [*a natura superiore*], to which it subjects itself, so that it can be completed [*compleri*] by it. This, therefore, is humility: to recognize one's own defect; to reduce oneself to a certain unified littleness [*parvitatem unitivam*]; to repel the divisive spirit of being puffed up and of pride; and to subject and offer oneself to the *influentiae* of heavenly grace [*supernae gratiae*].[75]

As a whole, *Perf. Evang.* responds to theologians at the University of Paris who began to loudly object to the growing mendicant presence at the University in the mid-thirteenth century. Reacting especially to

---

75. *Perf. Evang.* q. 1, conc., sec. 1 (5, 122).

the arguments against the Franciscans posed by the theologian and canon lawyer, William of St. Amour, Bonaventure aims through it to defend the Franciscan way of life against his detractors at the University.[76] The above quotation is taken from the Seraphic Doctor's response to a question about whether or not the virtue of humility—or namely, the act or habit of "demeaning oneself for the sake of Christ"—"pertains to Christian perfection." Bonaventure obviously responds in the affirmative, and his above remarks were offered in service of providing justification for that position against William of St. Amour.

Though written in defense of the virtue of humility, these comments nevertheless also open for us a window into the nature of sin in his theology. The Seraphic Doctor here implicitly refers to the "general *influentia*" that upholds everything that exists: "Every nature, because it is from nothingness, holds a certain defect in itself and declares itself defective," he writes. Every creature is ontologically poor inasmuch as it depends on God for its creation and continued existence. Human nature, he further asserts, can only be "perfected" and "maintained" when it acknowledges this "defect," reducing "itself to a certain littleness" and subjecting and offering itself to a superior *influentia*, or namely, as Bonaventure writes, "when it *desires* [my emphasis] to receive an *influentia* from a superior nature, to which it subjects itself, so that it can be completed by it." This capacity for desiring to be upheld by a superior *influentia*—for recognizing one's ontological poverty and resting in it—is a unique characteristic of those creatures who can be called an image of God, as we have already seen in this chapter. It is the unique vocation of prelapsarian human nature, likewise, to remain desirous of this *influentia*, which it cannot do on its own. Since its will is mercenary and tends back in upon itself and to the nothingness from which it came, it needs—as we have also seen—the special *influentia* of sanctifying grace to help it thus remain desirous of heavenly grace, of willingly accepting its ontological poverty in humility so that it might be perfected in all its powers by a "superior nature."

For Bonaventure, human nature can never escape the poverty of its creaturely being as such. Simply put, and building off everything I have argued thus far in this chapter, the human person will always be

---

76. Robert J. Karris, introduction to *The Disputed Questions on Evangelical Perfection*, trans. Robert J. Karris and Thomas Reist, Works of St. Bonaventure 13 (St. Bonaventure, NY: Franciscan Institute, 2008), 7–28.

dependent upon such "heavenly grace": Human nature in Bonaventure's theological anthropology is always needing to be filled by the "inflowings" of grace with respect to each and every level of its existence. It is always radically dependent on the "general *influentia*" as a vestige. As the image of the Trinity, moreover, it needs helping grace to assist its rational powers in knowing God and attaining to the certitude of the eternal reasons, as the Seraphic Doctor asserts in *Scien. Chr.* 4. Most especially, it always needs the "special *influentia*"—sanctifying grace—if its will is to remain "upright" so that it may love God above all things and its neighbor as itself, thereby also becoming a similitude and providing the clearest possible "sight" to both the "eye of the flesh" and the "eye of reason" as well. The virtues of humility and poverty are part and parcel to the Christian vocation in Bonaventure's theology because these are part and parcel to what it means to be human.[77] If God is an overflowing "plenitude," an overflowing fountain of goodness and love, then human nature must continuously remain open and receptive to God's gracious and overabundant inflowings. Or, phrased differently, if God is comparable to a fountain from which these inflowings pour forth, then we can perhaps compare human nature in Bonaventure's theology to a basin or cup into which the Trinity's graces must continuously flow. Human nature was created to be willingly "receptive" and "susceptive" of grace in this way,[78] a posture which in turn invites the similitude through which the entire created order of reality can be uplifted into God.

We arrive, then, at sin. Simply put, sin in Bonaventure's theology is the willing refusal to be receptive of grace. It is a rejection of this ontological poverty, and it is rooted in the human person's refusal to

---

77. Like humility, Bonaventure also argues that poverty is part and parcel of human nature in *Perf. evang.* q. 2, a. 1, concl. (5, 129): "But nature itself—whether in its original or in its fallen state—was created especially for this way of poverty. For man was created naked, and if he had remained in that state, he would have appropriated nothing for himself; truly, the fallen man is born naked and will die naked. And so this way is straightest when, not straying from the ends of the path, human nature advances along this path as poor and naked as long as it can suffer it. And this is what is said in 1 Tm 6:7: 'We carry nothing into this world, and certainly we can carry nothing out.' And from this, the Apostle concludes: 'But having food and sufficient clothing, with these we are content.' But there is nothing more constrictive or poorer than to be content with simple food and clothing, which the Apostle describes as good and perfect from his teaching on human nature."

78. I borrow the language of "receptivity" and "susceptivity" here from Bonaventure's definition of the inflowing of sanctifying grace from *II Sent.* d. 26; see my previous discussion of this in Chapter 4.

recognize his need for grace at all three levels of his existence as a vestige, image, and similitude of the Trinity.

The Seraphic Doctor defines sin in a succinct way in *Brev.* 3, where, following Augustine, he says sin is not any sort of thing, but is rather a corruption or a defect of the human will. "And besides, the corruption of sin is contrary to the good as such," he suggests, "nevertheless, it does not have any existence except in something good, nor does it come from anything unless from a good, which is the free choice of the will."[79] According to Bonaventure, God gifted our first parents with free choice because this was the condition for merit; the rational soul is *capax Dei*, as he indicates in *Brev.* 2, "but it does not arrive at the glorious reward of beatitude unless through merit; but something cannot contain merit unless it is done voluntarily and freely."[80] The only way in which the first parents could have passed from "being" to "well-being," from the image to the similitude, in other words, was by remaining in a posture of willing receptivity to the inflowing of grace that would uplift them—and likewise, the whole created order of reality—into a union with the Trinity and one another. Prelapsarian human persons, however, were mercenary, created from nothing and tending toward the nothingness from which they came. For their wills to remain "upright" despite their tendency to turn back in upon themselves, for the entire human person to remain upright in both soul and body (since the prelapsarian body's "uprightness" was proportionate to that of the soul), and, in fact, for the entire created order of reality to enjoy its *reductio* into the Trinity through the human person's "upright" state, God gifted prelapsarian human nature with sanctifying grace. Had the primogenitors remained willingly receptive of that gift, the "special *influentia*" would have continued to inflow their natural faculties in a way that would have helped them traverse the diastema between the image and the similitude, thus also leading them to fulfill the contemplative vocation that tied together the fabric of Bonaventure's tapestry of the entire created macrocosm. The fate of the entire macrocosm depended upon Adam and Eve's free choice to remain like "basins" that were thus always being filled by the inflowings of grace.

Because the first parents were created with free will, however, the Seraphic Doctor continues to explain sin in *Brev.* 3 by writing:

79. *Brev.* 3.1 (5, 231).
80. *Brev.* 2.9 (5, 227).

But because this creature was made from nothing and thus imperfect by nature, it could fail to act out of this intrinsic relationship with God. It could instead act for itself rather than for God, by failing to act with God as its source, according to God's norms, or with God as its end. This is precisely what sin is: a corruption of measure, of form, and of order. As a defect, sin has a cause that is not "efficient," but "deficient," for it is nothing other than a defect of the created will. Now corruption can only be the corruption of something good, and only a corruptible being is subject to corruption; therefore, sin can exist only in some corruptible good. And so free will, by falling away from the true Good, corrupts its own measure, form, and order; hence, all sin as such proceeds from the will as its source, and resides in the will as its proper subject. This occurs whenever the will, because of its imperfection, mutability, and fickleness, rejects the Good that is unfailing and immutable, and clings to one which is changeable.[81]

Sin happened, in other words, when the primogenitors of the human race "rejected the Good" and thus also rejected the panoply of relationships with God and the created order of reality that sanctifying grace enabled. As soon as the will acted "for itself" and began to cling to a changeable good; as soon as it became an "introvert" rather than letting grace work within it to transform it into an extroverted similitude; as soon as it turned inward rather than remaining willingly receptive to the "special *influentia*"; as soon as it sought certitude of its own and denied the assistance of helping grace in its rational powers; as soon as it began to think that its own, defective nature was the highest good rather than recognizing its dependence on the "general *influentia*" that upholds its existence as a vestige—*it sinned*. Bonaventure in this way describes the Fall of Adam and Eve in the Garden of Eden as a disordering of desires: Through choosing a changeable good over God, both persons turned inward through an act of pride rather than remaining in an open posture of humility, which, as we saw above, is part and parcel to an ontologically poor human nature.[82] "So both," as he writes of Adam and Eve, "by inordinately lifting themselves above themselves, fell miserably below themselves from the state of innocence and grace to the state of guilt and misery."[83] The result of this disordered desire,

---

81. *Brev.* 3.1 (5, 231). I have chosen here to use Dominic Monti's translation of this text, which is much more eloquent than that which I could provide, found in *Breviloquium*, trans. Monti, Works of St. Bonaventure 9 (St. Bonaventure, NY: Franciscan Institute, 2005), 100–101.

82. See *Brev.* 3.3 (5, 232–33).

83. *Brev.* 3.3 (5, 233).

this corrupt choice of the free will, was nothing less than the disorder of the entire created order of reality.

The first result of this sin, according to Bonaventure—and thus also the first step in this disorder that is introduced into the macrocosm through it—is that human nature loses the gift of sanctifying grace. The Seraphic Doctor's claim in the above passage that the primogenitor's free choice to sin was a failure to act (1) with God as its source, (2) according to God's norms, and (3) with God as its end, which therefore results in a corruption of (1) measure, (2) form, and (3) order, should be framed by an earlier comment within *Brev.* 3 that appears a few lines prior in the text. The human creature was fashioned by the First Principle, he there suggests, so that, "proceeding from the supreme good and inwardly conformed to that Triune cause," it "should have in its substance and in its will measure, form, and order. It was meant to accomplish its works with God as their source, in accordance with God's norms, and with God as their end."[84] Why is this important? These threefold patterns correspond with what he will later say about the *influentia* of sanctifying grace in the postlapsarian person in *Brev.* 5, where he will detail at length how this inflowing has its "source" or *ortus* in the Father, its *modus* in the Son, and its *fructus* in the Holy Spirit. As he there describes, by purifying, illuminating, and perfecting the soul so as to make it the daughter of the Father, the bride of the Son, and the temple of the Holy Spirit, sanctifying grace orders the postlapsarian soul in a hierarchical way so that it can become a similitude of the entire Trinity.[85] Bonaventure's definition of sin as a corruption of "measure," "form," and "order" in human nature through which the human person fails to act with God as its "source," "according to God's norms," and "with God as its end" in *Brev.* 3 foreshadows his comments on sanctifying grace in Part 5. Sin removes the similitude from the human person. Since she no longer receives the inflowing of sanctifying grace that works *in* and *with* her free will, the person is no longer "inwardly conformed to that Triune cause"; she is no longer constantly being "purified, illuminated, and perfected" by grace. Instead of possessing a dynamic soul with "measure, form, and order," the human person's free choice to turn inward causes the hierarchical order within her soul to become *disordered*

---

84. *Brev.* 3.1 (5, 231), trans. Monti, 100.
85. See my discussion of Part 5 of the *Breviloquium* in Chapter 4.

instead. Sin thus causes the soul to lose the "hierarchical" shape enabled by sanctifying grace.

This idea is further highlighted, for example, in the Seraphic Doctor's description of the "disorder" that occurs within Adam and Eve as a result of sin later on in *Brev.* 3:

Thus both the man and the woman commonly transgressed the command, but for different reasons, since it was not the man, but *the woman who was seduced.* Nevertheless, in both the man and the woman, there occurred a disordering [*deordinatio*] from the highest to the lowest, because it began first in the mind or in reason [*in mente sive in ratione*], then in their senses [*sensualitate*], and finally in their works [*opere*]. For both were brought low through disobedience and enticed by their appetite, since both had risen up in pride: The woman by desiring and embracing what she could not take, and by all means the man as well, who loved and prized what he already had.[86]

This "disordering" of the faculties from "highest to lowest" within our primogenitors has implications for the three "eyes" discussed above: The "eye of contemplation" is closed, the "eye of reason" becomes clouded so that humanity can no longer perceive the image of God within itself, and the "eye of the flesh" instead becomes dominant. This "top-down" infection of sin, as it were, corresponds perfectly with the Seraphic Doctor's use of Gallus's angelic anthropology to describe the effects of grace within postlapsarian human nature. The hierarchical soul, we recall, "revolves around" the order of the seraph, the "perfective" moment wherein the soul is united to God in an affective embrace that fecundates the lower orders of the soul so that it can remain always "purified, illuminated, and perfected" in all its interior orders and exterior actions. For Bonaventure, the soul ascends through sanctifying grace to a contemplative union with God at the level of the seraph so that it can then "descend" to its neighbor through meritorious action, and vice versa into perpetuity. This is how the postlapsarian soul remains in God in his teachings on the effects of sanctifying grace. Sin, in turn, disrupts this order. The human person's free choice to sin results in her being "cut off," as it were, from the "special inflowing" of sanctifying grace: Sin begins in the affective power and in the free will, and it then filters down into the rest of the soul from "the highest to the

---

86. *Brev.* 3.3 (5, 233).

lowest" faculties, finally infecting the human person's actions so that she can no longer relate in an ordered way to God and her neighbor.

Indeed, because the soul has thus been "disordered" and is no longer capable of remaining "upright" through the "special *influentia*" of sanctifying grace, the human body in postlapsarian human nature likewise also now becomes crooked and bent. Like the soul, the body becomes "disordered." Because it is no longer ruled by the similitude and the "eye of contemplation," "the eye of the flesh" becomes dominant and subsequently starts to rebel against the soul.[87] Because it is no longer perfectly "proportionate" and "subjected" to the soul, moreover, the postlapsarian human body is now subjected to decay, suffering, pain, and death. The whole human person—the crown of creation, the "ensouled body" to whom all sensible and intelligible reality was ordered through the similitude gifted by *gratia gratum faciens*—is now corrupt, crooked, and disordered. As Johnson has noted, our first parents have now become "morally impoverished" in addition to their ontological poverty, and this moral poverty disrupts their entire being.[88] The "measure, form, and order" within them have been corrupted, and every part of them suffers, both soul and body.

This havoc wrought by the primogenitor's free choice to sin, however, does not simply conclude when it has tainted human nature.[89] Working backwards through my comments on Bonaventure's teachings on prelapsarian human nature above, we know that all of creation was meant to be illuminated by the "eye of contemplation" gifted in the similitude. Human nature was to be the crown of creation inasmuch as it was in humanity that the sensible and intelligible natures could meet, so that the entire created order of reality could be drawn into relationships with God and one another. Because humanity lost the gift of sanctifying grace through its free choice to sin, the contemplative vocation that was woven by the First Principle into the very fabric of creation has not been fulfilled. Because the human body has been corrupted along with the soul, the sensible can no longer enjoy its *reductio* into the Trinity. The human person as an image of God can no longer pass from "being" to "well-being" by serving as an "end" for the sensible order of reality. The intelligible order of reality, likewise, can

---

87. *Brev.* 3.6 (5, 235).
88. Johnson, *The Soul in Ascent*, 35–42.
89. See also Johnson, "Part III: On the Corruption of Sin," 171.

no longer "descend" through the similitude to meet the sensible. In all these things, by damaging humanity, sin damages the order that characterizes the Seraphic Doctor's rich and "dizzying" portrait of the macrocosm with respect to all these relationships. The vestiges and images remain, but these are not the locus of hierarchical perfection: For that, the cosmos need the similitude restored to it once again. It needs, in other words, the "special *influentia*" of grace. Only then will the entire created order of reality—every vestige in the sensible realm as well as every image in the intelligible—be able once again to participate in the full *reductio* into the Trinity for which all things on heaven and earth were created.

Conclusion

Against a recent critique of the Seraphic Doctor's teachings on the role of grace in human nature, this chapter has examined the role of the inflowing of sanctifying grace in Bonaventure's theological anthropology, arguing that human nature effectively remains "incomplete" apart from it. I began by attending to the heart of this critique—namely, that by introducing the notion of a "general *influentia*" in addition to a "special *influentia*" of sanctifying grace in *Scien. Chr.* 4, the Seraphic Doctor thereby suggests that human nature can in some way achieve an "end" apart from beatitude. I showed how Bonaventure's introduction of a "general *influentia*" as such in no wise lends itself to this argument, but was rather proffered by him as a means of describing how every vestige in creation is dependent upon God for its creation and continued existence. I further introduced Bonaventure's theological anthropology to argue that the entire created order of reality, including prelapsarian human nature, "needs" the "special *influentia*" of sanctifying grace to relate to the Trinity through the similitude. Prelapsarian human persons needed to remain willingly receptive to sanctifying grace if they were to fulfill the contemplative vocation woven into creation, and if they were to traverse the diastema between the image and the similitude and thus pass from their purely natural state to the rest of supernatural beatitude in God. Finally, I showed how the free choice to deny this "special *influentia*" led to sin and the disruption of order throughout the entire macrocosm. This narrative of the role of the "special *influentia*" of sanctifying grace in Bonaventure's theological anthropology has shown the indispensability of that *influentia* within both his teachings on human nature and creation writ large: Apart from sanctifying grace, both human nature and the entire created order of reality would fail to achieve its end in beatitude.

It is fitting to conclude by repeating Bonaventure's warning that we already saw above in my discussion of *Brev.* 2 concerning the closure of the "eye of contemplation" in human nature:

But indeed, the eye of contemplation does not function perfectly unless in glory, which humanity dismissed through their culpability, although they may recover it through grace and faith and the understanding of scriptures, by which the human mind is purified [*purificatur*], illuminated [*illuminatur*], and perfected [*perficitur*] for the purposes of contemplating heavenly things.[90]

Notably, Dominic Monti's English translation of this passage renders the final clause in this passage thusly: "By these means, the human soul is cleansed, enlightened and perfected for the perfection of heavenly things."[91] I here simply note that highlighting the triad of "purification, illumination, and perfection" is key to connecting everything I have presently claimed regarding the role of sanctifying grace in the Seraphic Doctor's theological anthropology to everything I previously argued concerning the effects of sanctifying grace in Chapters 4–5. Human persons return to and then remain in the Trinity inasmuch as sanctifying grace hierarchizes the soul by purifying, illuminating, and perfecting it. These three hierarchical activities must be understood dynamically within Bonaventure's account of the hierarchical soul as such; the soul is made "as like as possible" to the Trinity through all three activities, so that the soul can circle endlessly between a contemplative union with God and the rest of creation through meritorious action. The hierarchical soul, as it were, describes the soul that has ceased merely being an image of the Trinity and has instead become a similitude, a "fruitful" creature capable of "loving God above all things and its neighbor as itself" through the plenitude of sanctifying grace.

Human nature, as it were, was created to be thus hierarchized, to constantly remain receptive to the continuous inflowing of sanctifying grace that would work within it to purify, illuminate, and perfect it,

---

90. *Brev.* 2.12 (5, 230).
91. *Brev.* 2.12, trans. Monti, 98.

thereby shaping it into a similitude of the Trinity. Its failure to remain receptive, its choice to close itself off to God's gracious inflowing, and the subsequent introduction of sin into the macrocosm that would disrupt the *redditus* of the entire created order of reality into God requires that the similitude be thus restored to both human nature and creation. For that, as we shall see in the next chapter, creation needed the "Hierarch"—the Word who would "descend" from "the superior to the inferior" so that human nature could once again be purified, illuminated, and perfected in a way that would ensure the entire created order of reality could once again remain in God.

CHAPTER 7

Grace and Christ the Hierarch

In his *Commentary on the Gospel of Luke*, the Seraphic Doctor provides an allegorical, moral, and anagogical interpretation of Jesus's words in Lk 13:33: "Yet today, tomorrow, and the next day I must be on my way, because it is impossible for a prophet to be killed outside of Jerusalem."[1] His anagogical interpretation of the text interprets each of these "days"—namely, "today," "tomorrow," and "the next day"—as follows:

The first day is purgation [*purgatio*]; the second, illumination [*illuminatio*]; and the third, perfection [*perfectio*]. Lk 2:46 says above: "And it came to pass that after three days they found him in the temple." —Or, another interpretation is that the first day is the contemplation of God in his vestiges; the second day is the contemplation of God in his image or in a mirror [*speculo*]; the third day, in God Himself. Nm 10:33: "The ark of the Lord went before them, for three days providing a place for the camp." —Or, another interpretation is that the first day is the contemplation of the subcelestial hierarchy [*hierarchiae subcaelestis*]; the second day, of the heavenly [*caelestis*] hierarchy; and the third day, of the supercelestial [*supercaelestis*] hierarchy. In the first is the casting out of demons. In the second is the perfection of health, but in the third, there is the consummation of every good. And of this *triduum*, Jos 2:22 says: "The explorers came to the mountains and remained there for three days." —This ark is Christ, who in whatever of these hierarchies is the

---

1. *Comm. Lc.* ch. 13, v. 33, par. 70 (7, 355).

highest Hierarch [*hierarcha altissimus*] and our leader, so that we might come to the land of promise which has been re-promised to us. As a figure of this he says that he walks through the *triduum,* because he makes us always ascend on high [*sursum ascendere*] through this triple hierarchy, unless, as luck would have it, we would descend to actions [*descendamus ad actiones*]. As a figure of this, Gn 28:12 says that "Jacob saw the angels of God ascending and descending on the ladder." No one saw them standing still [*nullus vidit eos stantes*]. By this, it is signified that we always ought to be doing good works. For this is to draw near the heavenly Jerusalem, which we do not approach by the steps of the body, but through the affections of our heart and mind [*affectibus cordis et mentis*].[2]

While the topic of grace is not explicitly mentioned here, the Seraphic Doctor's words nonetheless offer a useful summary of all the subjects covered so far in this book. Here, for example, his hierarchical portrait of the macrocosm—comprised of the earthly, celestial, and supercelestial hierarchies (treated in Chapter 3)—is presented side by side with his notion of the hierarchical soul, a microcosm that must be "purified," "illuminated," and "perfected" by grace to be called a "temple" of God (Chapters 4–5). His suggestion, moreover, that God can be contemplated in the divine vestige, image, and likeness parallels my discussion of his theological anthropology in light of these same themes (Chapter 6). He even employs the symbol of Jacob's Ladder to describe how these hierarchies function: For Bonaventure, as I have argued throughout the preceding chapters, one does not become "as like as possible to God" through grace by "standing still," but rather one becomes conformed to the uncreated hierarchy of the Trinity through constant "ascents" and "descents," by "circling" always between God and the rest of creation and thereby "remaining" in the Trinity.

What I have not yet underscored, however, and as this passage from his *Comm. Lc.* highlights quite well, is the way in which all these themes are brought together in Christ. For the Seraphic Doctor, Christ *is* the similitude of the Father, the "highest Hierarch," and a "Ladder" whose descent from the uncreated hierarchy through the Incarnation gifts the *influentia* of sanctifying grace throughout creation.[3]

---

2. *Comm. Lc.* ch. 13, v. 33, par. 72 (7, 356).

3. I have already introduced this idea to some extent in my examination of Bonaventure's theology of hierarchy in the third section of Chapter 3, where I briefly introduced his Christology in relation to his hierarchical metaphysics. This chapter expands my previous remarks in these respects.

Accordingly, the purpose of this chapter is to highlight Christ's central role within Bonaventure's doctrine of grace in all these respects, particularly in light of his claim that Christ is the "Hierarch." Much like in the above passage from his *Comm. Lc.*, I claim that the themes explored throughout this study come together in Bonaventure's Christology, particularly insofar as Christ mediates grace on both micro- and macrocosmic levels in his soteriology. For the Seraphic Doctor, Christ's redemptive role in creation involves both levels: The story of grace cannot simply be the story about the forgiveness of my sins, but must instead involve the whole tapestry of relationships that characterize his hierarchical understanding of reality. If, for Bonaventure, the *influentia* of sanctifying grace hierarchizes the soul into a similitude of the Trinity, it does so only because Christ is the first "Hierarch," the one who descends from the uncreated hierarchy and into creation so that the entire created order of reality can then begin its own ascent into God through sanctifying grace.

My examination of Christ's role in Bonaventure's soteriology will proceed in three parts. First, since the topic of Christology in Bonaventure's soteriology has already been widely treated, I begin with a brief recap of previous scholarship on this subject. Scholars who have already explored the relationship between the Seraphic Doctor's Christology and soteriology have largely struggled to articulate how, exactly, Bonaventure perceives Christ's soteriological role in creation. Here, I will show how my own argument regarding the relationship between grace and hierarchy in Bonaventure's thought might help resolve some of these interpretive problems. Second, I turn to a more focused examination of Bonaventure's explanation of Christ's salvific work in creation, specifically with respect to his claim that the *influentia* of sanctifying grace is gifted to creation through the Uncreated, Incarnate, Crucified, and Inspired Word. Third and finally, I argue that the name "Hierarch" throughout his writings corresponds to the movements of the Word throughout salvation history as I described them in the second section of the chapter. The very logic of Bonaventure's doctrine of grace—especially insofar as we have read that doctrine in light of his hierarchical metaphysics—is rooted within his Christology, which can be illuminated when we arrive at an understanding of what this particular name for Christ means.

Christology in Bonaventure's Soteriology

The Christocentricity of the Seraphic Doctor's theology is already widely affirmed to be a definitive characteristic of his thought. The Christological emphases within his writings are part and parcel to his Franciscan identity and follow the Poverello's own devotion to "nakedly following the naked Christ."[4] That Christ would play a central role within his doctrine of grace is not a striking claim; the question of how Christ actually redeems the human person within his soteriology, however, has nonetheless been a continued point of conversation among scholars throughout the twentieth century.[5] A brief introduction to the *status quaestionis* surrounding Bonaventure's Christology and soteriology will here serve the purpose of showing how my own reading of his doctrine of grace might contribute to that conversation.

Usefully, to that effect, Zachary Hayes's now classic treatment of Christology and soteriology in *The Hidden Center* summarizes in a succinct way the various models utilized by twentieth-century

---

4. Scholarship underscoring this aspect of St. Francis's charism is too extensive to list here. For a small selection, see Michael W. Blastic, "Prayer in the Writings of Francis of Assisi and the Early Brothers," in *Franciscans at Prayer*, ed. Timothy J. Johnson (Leiden: Brill, 2007), 3–29; Michael F. Cusato, "Francis and the Franciscan Movement (1181/2–1226)," in *The Cambridge Companion to Francis of Assisi*, ed. Michael J. P. Robson (Cambridge: Cambridge University Press, 2012), 17–33; and Damian McElrath, ed., *Franciscan Christology* (St. Bonaventure, NY: Franciscan Institute, 1980). Studies of Bonaventure's Christocentricism are likewise almost too numerous to count; one of the most useful studies remains Hayes's *Hidden Center*, upon which I will heavily depend here. Other notable treatments include those by Werner Dettloff, "'*Christus tenens medium in omnibus*': Sinn und Funktion der Theologie bei Bonaventura," *Wissenschaft und Weisheit* 20 (1957): 28–42, 120–40; Alexander Gerken, *Theologie des Wortes: Das Verhältnis von Schöpfung und Inkarnation bei Bonaventura* (Düsseldorf: Patmos-Verlag, 1963); Werner Hülsbusch, *Elemente einer Kreuzestheologie in den Spätschriften Bonaventuras* (Düsseldorf: Patmos-Verlag, 1968); Pietro Maranesi, *Verbum inspiratum: Chiave ermeneutica dell'Hexaëmeron di San Bonaventura* (Rome: Instituto Storico dei Cappuccini, 1996); and Ambroise Nguyen van Si, *La théologie de l'imitation du Christ d'aprés Saint Bonaventure* (Rome: Editizione Antonianum, 1991). While not titularly devoted to the subject of Christology, Solignac's *La voie de la ressemblance* makes a very convincing argument concerning Bonaventure's Christocentricism using the logic of *ressemblance* to which I shall also gesture repeatedly in my own ensuing remarks.

5. See Hayes, *Hidden Center*, 152–55, for a very concise analysis of these debates, which concern most especially the theories of Alexander Gerken, Romano Guardini, Werner Hülsbusch, Julian Kaup, and Rufin Silic; see Gerken, *Theologie des Wortes*; Romano Guardini, *Die Lehre des Heil: Bonaventura von der Erlösung: ein Beitrag zur Geschichte und zum System der Erlösungslehre* (Düsseldorf: L. Schwann, 1921); Hülsbusch, *Elemente einer Kreuzestheologie*; Julian Kaup, "Christus und die Kirche nach der Lehre des hl. Bonaventura," *Franziskanische Studien* 26 (1939): 333–44; and Rufin Silic, *Christus und die Kirche, ihr verhältnis nach der lehre des heiligen Bonaventura* (Breslau: Müller and Seiffert, 1938).

Bonaventurean scholars to explain the Seraphic Doctor's soteriology. Hayes has helpfully underscored the fact that the question surrounding how to approach Bonaventure's theology of redemption and Christ's role within it is largely a question of consolidating what appear to be alternative methodologies for approaching the subject within the Bonaventurean *corpus*. Romano Guardini, for example, identified three theories used by the Seraphic Doctor to explain Christ's role in redemption—namely, what he called "the moral-legal theory, the physical-mystical theory, and the personalist theory."[6] Through the moral-legal theory, Bonaventure—honoring the Anselmian theory of satisfaction and broadly reflecting the Western theological tradition's approach to the subject—affirms that humanity is redeemed through Christ's sacrifice on the cross.[7] On the other hand, the Seraphic Doctor also affirms a theology of redemption that pays tribute to the theology of the Greek Fathers: According to this perspective, which Guardini calls the "physical-mystical theory," sin is a disorder that must be set right rather than an injustice to be satisfied. Christ redeems human persons by sanctifying them and setting them in right "order," so that the question of redemption is ultimately a question of deification rather than one of justification or satisfaction.[8] Finally, Guardini made note of the "personalist theory" of redemption in Bonaventure's writings. As Hayes summarizes, this theory "emphasizes the fact that sin involves a loss of God's friendship which is restored by redemption and grace," so that "God appears pre-eminently in personal terms, seeking the creature and lifting it up so as to lead it back to Himself."[9] In Guardini's view, these three theories—albeit seemingly at odds—are held by the Seraphic Doctor in his soteriology simultaneously.[10]

His identification of these three theories, however, faced problems when placed under scrutiny by later scholars. As Hayes notes, "The satisfaction-theory raises the question of the meaning of the incarnation; the

---

6. Guardini, *Die Lehre des Heil*, 72ff.; Hayes, *Hidden Center*, 152–53.

7. Guardini, *Die Lehre des Heil*, 72–118; Hayes, *Hidden Center*, 152–53. Guardini treats the didactic aspects of Christ's soteriological work under this category as well.

8. Guardini, *Die Lehre des Heil*, 119–56; Hayes, *Hidden Center*, 152–53.

9. Hayes, *Hidden Center*, 153; see also Guardini, *Die Lehre des Heil*, 21. Whereas the moral-legal theory and the physical-mystical theory receive extensive treatment at the hand of Guardini, this final theory is mentioned by him with very little elaboration. Guardini notes that the personalist-theory is most often treated by the Seraphic Doctor in his scriptural commentaries, ascetical-mystical, and homiletic works.

10. Guardini, *Die Lehre des Heil*, 20.

physical-mystical theory raises the question of the meaning of the life and death of Jesus," so that "While Guardini sees no contradiction between the two in the case of Bonaventure, he did not succeed in demonstrating their inner harmony convincingly."[11] Scholars after Guardini had to find their own ways of articulating how these multiple theories could fit together in their interpretations of Bonaventure's soteriology. For example, Rufin Silic, instead of trying to demonstrate the inner harmony of these three theories, emphasizes the "satisfaction-theory" as the fundamental model for understanding redemption in Bonaventure's writings; Silic claims that the Incarnation derives its meaning from Christ's salvific work on the cross in the Seraphic Doctor's theology.[12] Crucially for our present purposes, Silic also argues that Bonaventure increasingly favored the name "Hierarch" for Christ in his later works, a development Silic uses to claim that the Seraphic Doctor's Christology and accompanying soteriology changed in a significant way over time.[13]

Alexander Gerken criticizes both these approaches. He surmises, first of all, that Silic emphasized the "satisfaction-theory" too much over the "physical-mystical theory," while, secondly, Guardini's explanation of the "physical-mystical theory" did not enough take into account the Seraphic Doctor's theology of the cross.[14] Nonetheless sympathetic to Guardini's view that Bonaventure upheld both theories simultaneously, Gerken proposes a new way of trying to harmonize them by proposing two new theories—namely, the "reparation-theory" and the "completion-theory," incorporating both of Guardini's previous two models within the former.[15]

Reacting especially to Guardini, Silic, and Gerken, Hayes suggests that scholars cease speaking of "a multiplicity of theories" surrounding Bonaventure's theology of redemption and instead approach it "in light of some broader insights into the genesis of his thought."[16] As Hayes contends:

---

11. Hayes, *Hidden Center*, 153.

12. Silic, *Christus und die Kirche*, 91–92; Hayes, *Hidden Center*, 153–54.

13. See Silic, *Christus und die Kirche*, 34–35; Hayes, *Hidden Center*, 154.

14. Gerken, *Theologie des Wortes*, 256–72; Hayes, *Hidden Center*, 154. After Gerken and Hayes, Ilia Delio has argued that the Crucified Christ is the center around which Bonaventure's mystical theology revolves; see Delio, *Crucified Love: Bonaventure's Mysticism of the Crucified Christ* (Quincy, IL: Franciscan Press, 1998).

15. Gerken, "Die Reparationstheorie," in *Theologie des Wortes*, 225–72; "Die Kompletionstheorie," in *Theologie des Wortes*, 273–98; Hayes, *Hidden Center*, 154–55.

16. Hayes, *Hidden Center*, 157.

It seems preferable to emphasize that he has but one theory which he has created out of a multiplicity of sources. Since he himself does not designate this theory—nor any other theory—with a convenient term, we shall call it the theory of redemption-completion, thereby underscoring the two principal factors involved: The world is both incomplete and fallen; and the work of Christ relates to both of these dimensions simultaneously.[17]

Hayes determines that both these dimensions of Bonaventure's soteriology are brought together by his theology of the Incarnation. The Seraphic Doctor's theology of redemption is centered always on the mystery of Christ, whose Incarnation is "addressed to the world in both its incompleteness and in its fallenness."[18] Against Silic, moreover, Hayes argues that the "element of hierarchy" was central to Bonaventure's theology of redemption in even his earliest literary output.[19] Though he increasingly favored the name "Hierarch" for Christ in his later works, the Seraphic Doctor's theology of hierarchy was always important in the context of his soteriology. According to Hayes, Christ's salvific role involves "completion" as well as "redemption" precisely insofar as Bonaventure perceives the structure of the universe in a hierarchical way, whereby the Incarnation "completes" that structure by uniting God to human nature "as the fullest realization of the most noble potency of creation."[20]

As such, Hayes's observation regarding the "inner harmony" of Bonaventure's soteriology, especially inasmuch as he affirms "the element of hierarchy" to be an "explicit" factor across the course of his theological career against Silic, has been a foundational insight behind my argument throughout this book. His "redemption-completion" theory is certainly helpful for conceiving Christ's role in Bonaventure's account of soteriology, especially inasmuch as it emphasizes the idea that the Seraphic Doctor has "but one [soteriological] theory which he has created out of a multiplicity of sources," which nonetheless all revolve around Christ, and also inasmuch as this theory can fittingly describe Christ's salvific work in both the microcosm and the macrocosm, which, according to Hayes, are both in need of "redemption" and "completion."

17. Hayes, *Hidden Center*, 156–57.
18. Hayes, *Hidden Center*, 178–79.
19. Hayes, *Hidden Center*, 158.
20. See Hayes, *Hidden Center*, 157–62, at 162.

However, we should note that Hayes's theory does not necessarily neatly tie together all the loose ends that hang down from previous scholarship on the same subject. For one example, Hayes's "one theory" is nonetheless still *two*fold, even as it does not necessarily solve the problem of demonstrating the inner harmony of Guardini's original *three* theories: "redemption" corresponds well with Guardini's "moral-legal" theory, while "completion" corresponds with Guardini's "physical-mystical theory," but what of the "personalist" theory, or the idea that Christ saves humanity by restoring it to a "friendship" with God which had been lost through sin? In emphasizing these two elements as definitive of Bonaventure's soteriology, what happens to the other pieces of the puzzle as highlighted by other Bonaventurean scholars?

I propose that our explorations of the Seraphic Doctor's doctrine of grace here might contribute to the *status quaestionis* surrounding Christology and soteriology in his thought since it might provide a unified theory that could connect all these disparate elements. More specifically, I hold that Hayes's intuition concerning the central role of hierarchy in Bonaventure's theology of redemption needs to be pressed further to tie all of these loose ends together.

For one rather poignant example in demonstration of this idea, we are given a possible method for perhaps even convincingly demonstrating the "inner harmony" of Guardini's original three theories if we attend to the "element of hierarchy" in Bonaventure's doctrine of grace. As we have repeatedly witnessed, the Seraphic Doctor defines sanctifying grace as an *influentia* that hierarchizes the soul. Frequently, he describes this angelic anthropology by highlighting the three hierarchical activities of purification, illumination, and perfection within it. As he explicitly argues in Part 5 of the *Breviloquium,* the soul is "purified" by sanctifying grace when it becomes a "daughter" or "son" of the Father; it is "illuminated" by sanctifying grace when it becomes a "bride" or spouse of the Son; and it is finally "perfected" by sanctifying grace when it becomes a "temple" of the Holy Spirit. Strikingly, these three hierarchical activities and their corresponding relations with the three persons of the Trinity correspond with Guardini's original three "theories" for interpreting Christ's role in Bonaventure's soteriology. The Anselmian "moral-legal theory" coincides with the activity of purification, whereby the soul is freed from sin to become a daughter of the Father. The Eastern "physical-mystical theory" of deification also seems to walk hand in hand with Bonaventure's claim that sanctifying grace "illuminates" the soul from within to wed it to Christ. And last but certainly not least, the "personalist" theory also corresponds to Bonaventure's suggestion that the soul is "perfected" when it is made into a temple of the Holy Spirit, so that it can become a "friend" of God through grace.

Where Hayes had insightfully suggested against Silic that the "structure of hierarchical thought may well shed light on the question of Bonaventure's theology of redemption" throughout the course of his theological career, my exploration of this "structure" within Bonaventure's doctrine of grace throughout the preceding chapters has shown how this insight must be carried even further to reach its fullest potential within the context of his Christology. Inasmuch as Bonaventure's theology of hierarchy is the key to interpreting his doctrine of grace, it is also the key to interpreting Christ's role in his soteriology. And indeed, where Hayes rightly intuits that we should interpret *one* soteriological theory that brings together a multiplicity of sources in his theology, his suggestion that Bonaventure "himself does not designate this theory ... with a convenient term" will here be challenged: Could the Seraphic Doctor's designation of Christ as the "Hierarch" fulfill this very purpose?

Though Silic astutely observed that the Seraphic Doctor used this designation with increasing frequency in his later career, Bonaventure himself names Christ the "Hierarch" as early as the *Breviloquium*. When treating the Christology of that text, Corey Barnes also recognizes the potential importance of this name in Bonaventure's soteriology:

Bonaventure's dedication to an Anselmian satisfaction theory represents a foundation for his own soteriological reasoning rather than a ceiling. Among the diverse approaches to soteriology embraced by Bonaventure is a stress on Christ's exemplarity and how that exemplarity respects the basic constitution of humanity and its order toward the First Principle. Phrased in more Dionysian terms, Bonaventure presents Christ, the one true hierarch, as restoring the cosmic hierarchy by restoring the order or hierarchy within human beings.[21]

As Barnes here intuits, Bonaventure's naming of Christ as the "Hierarch" can potentially weave together all these different threads of his

---

21. Corey Barnes, "Part IV: On the Incarnation of the Word," in *Bonaventure Revisited*, 213.

soteriology—his use of the Anselmian "moral-legal" theory,[22] his favoring of the Eastern teachings on deification and the "physical-mystical theory," as well as the presence of the "personalist" theory in his writings—into a common tapestry. The remainder of this chapter will be devoted to an explanation of how the name "Hierarch" brings all these threads together in Bonaventure's soteriology. For that explanation to make sense, however, it is first necessary to turn to the question of how Christ redeems the macrocosm by redeeming the microcosm—namely, by "restoring the order or hierarchy within human beings." This hierarchical order within human beings, as we have seen in the preceding chapters, is gifted to them by the *influentia* of sanctifying grace. What I must therefore demonstrate below is how, according to Bonaventure, this *influentia* is always Christologically sourced.

The Christological Source of Sanctifying Grace

The Seraphic Doctor explicitly states as much in the first conference from his *Collations on the Seven Gifts of the Holy Spirit* (*De don. Spir.*). There, before proceeding with his explanation of the seven spiritual gifts in the remaining six conferences, Bonaventure begins his lectures to his brothers at the University of Paris by providing "An Introductory Treatment of Grace: According to Its Origin, Use, and Fruit."[23] After *II Sent.* and Part 5 of the *Breviloquium*, his ensuing remarks represent

22. Barnes's suggestion here that the "Anselmian satisfaction theory" represents a "foundation" for Bonaventure's "soteriological reasonings" agrees with my above association of the hierarchical activity of purification with Guardini's "moral-legal theory." It is useful to recall that in Part 5 of the *Breviloquium*, the three hierarchical activities within the soul build up from the level of purification, leading secondly to illumination, and finally to perfection. The soul that has been perfected through sanctifying grace does not stop being purified nor illuminated, but rather becomes likened unto a "Jacob's Ladder" inasmuch as all three activities must be continuously "activated" within the hierarchical soul, all building from the level of purification. That the "Anselmian satisfaction theory represents a foundation" for Bonaventure's "soteriological reasoning rather than a ceiling" is affirmed by the Seraphic Doctor in his explanation of how sanctifying grace hierarchizes the soul: The element of satisfaction is needed before the soul can be illuminated and perfected, but this does not mean that the element of purification is any less important.

23. For more on the historical context, purpose, and content of Bonaventure's *De don. Spir.*, see Hayes, introduction to *Collations on the Seven Gifts of the Holy Spirit*, trans. Zachary Hayes, Works of St. Bonaventure 14 (St. Bonaventure, NY: Franciscan Institute, 2008), 7–25. See also *De don. Spir.* (5, 457), for the title of the first collation: "Praemittitur tractatio de gratia secundum eius ortum, usum et fructum."

one of his three most significant treatments of the subject of grace in any of his works. Indeed, his discussion of the "use" (*usum*) and "fruit" (*fructum*) of grace in this text echoes themes I already explored at length in my examination of the previous two texts in Chapter 4.[24] What he claims concerning the "origin" (*ortum*) of grace from the first conference of *De don. Spir.* clearly connects his Christology with his soteriology. "From whence does grace thus originate?" he queries; he responds: "I say that it has its source from the Father of Lights through the Incarnate Word, through the Crucified Word, and through the Inspired Word."[25]

In his book *Verbum Inspiratum: Chiave ermeneutica dell'Hexaëmeron di San Bonaventura*, Pietro Maranesi extensively examines what the Seraphic Doctor means by referring to Christ as the "Uncreated Word," the "Incarnate Word," and the "Inspired Word" within the context of his soteriology. Though the Seraphic Doctor's most mature understanding of the "Inspired Word" will not appear until the *Hexaëmeron*, Maranesi has convincingly shown how Bonaventure's use of this "triplex Verbum" always refers to the historical work of the Word in "narrating" the speech of the Father in creation. The Father creates all things through the "Uncreated Word," while the "Incarnate Word" is the historical expression of the "speech" of the Father in creation. The "Inspired Word," as it were, is the "subjective" expression of the Word within the individual, which illuminates the rational creature from within; in this way, the Word does not *cease* acting within history but rather continues enabling

---

24. Grace, he explains, is useful insofar as it directs us in our progress, since it helps human beings "be faithful with respect to God, strong in ourselves, and generous with respect to our neighbor"; *De don. Spir.* 1.9 (5, 459). Its fruit, likewise, is threefold, since the person in possession of grace will enjoy the remission of guilt, the fullness of justice, and the continuance of the happy life; see *De don. Spir.* 1.13 (5, 460). Though space does not permit my treating these two topics here, what Bonaventure claims concerning the "use" and "fruit" of grace in the first conference provides further support for my argument in Chapter 4: Sanctifying grace is, once again, defined as an "*influentia*" and compared to a fountain of water or ray of light that has a continuous connection with its source in the Trinity. It strengthens human persons by flowering into the virtues, and then makes them generous in relation to their neighbors by making them capable of descending to others like the angels in Dionysius's heavenly hierarchy. See, for example, Bonaventure's discussion of the "use" of grace in *De don. Spir.* 1.9–12 (5, 459–60), especially 1.12 (5, 460): "Dionysius determinat nobis usum gratiae in *angelica hierachia* et *caelesti* et dicit, quod si superiores angeli continerent se et non vellent influere in inferiores Angelos, tunc ipsi clauderent sibi viam influentiae Dei." It is noteworthy, as well, that Bonaventure's discussion of the "fruit" of grace in *De don. Spir.* 1.13–16 (5, 460–61), can be seen as corresponding with the structure of Part 5 of the *Breviloquium*, which I examined at length in Chapter 4.

25. *De don. Spir.* 1.8 (5, 458).

the *reductio* of all creation back to the Father through its relationship with each individual rational creature. As Maranesi deduces, "the three definitions are the three successive modalities of the single nature of the Word, who is 'the expression of the Father.'"[26]

Importantly for our present purposes, in his expansive treatment of the development of Bonaventure's theology of the "triplex Verbum" in these respects, Maranesi has also convincingly shown how Bonaventure's discussion of the "origin" of grace in his *De don. Spir.* likewise narrates three historical "moments" of the Word's actions in salvation history with respect to the gift of sanctifying grace. First, Bonaventure's claim therein that grace "has its source from the Father of Lights" implicitly refers to the "Uncreated Word," who, "with the Father," creates humanity in such a way that human beings are capable of receiving the gift of grace. Second, grace is given by the "Incarnate-Crucified Word," whereby the Word appears in the "flesh" and so is the mediator of grace in history. Third and finally, the "Inspired Word" gifts grace in the human mind, making possible the individual's subjective experience of grace.[27]

In other words, Maranesi's work on the "triplex Verbum" has already shown how Bonaventure's discussion of grace with respect to these successive modalities of the Word in *De don. Spir.* serves the purpose of narrating the Word's soteriological role throughout the horizontal order of salvation history. For the Seraphic Doctor, sanctifying grace is always given to creation through the Word, whether before the Fall (and thus in reference to the Uncreated Word) or after the Fall (and thus in reference to the Incarnate, Crucified, and Inspired

---

26. See Maranesi, *Verbum inspiratum*, 25: "Le tre definizioni sono le tre modalità successive dell'unica natura del Verbo di essere 'expressio Patris.'"

27. See especially Maranesi, *Verbum inspiratum*, 109: "La scansione storico-salvifica dell'uso del 'triplex Verbum' fatto nel *De donis* conferma tale determinazione dei tre momenti, offrendo, pero, di essi il contesto storico-salvifico nascosto in quelle relazioni. La convergenza tra le due serie di dati e il loro reciproco completarsi possono essere evidenziate mediante il seguente schema, in cui si porranno insieme gli elementi constitutivi dei *Sermoni* e del *De donis*: 1. Il *Verbo increato*, che è 'apud Patre', rende l'uomo strutturalmente capace di ricevere la grazia; 2. Il *Verbo incarnato-crocifisso*, che è 'in carne', è la mediazione e il datore storico della grazia; 3. Il *Verbo inspirato*, che è 'in mente', rende possibile soggettivamente all'uomo un incontro personale con la grazia." Maranesi's reference to the Sermons here refers to an earlier chapter of his text, in which he had explored Bonaventure's theology of the "Inspired Word" in some of Bonaventure's sermons. His exploration of the term in *De don. Spir.* underscores how Bonaventure's theology of the Inspired Word enjoyed continuity with and was developed from these sermons, which was then carried to its most mature form in the *Hexaëmeron.*

Word). Subsequently, Bonaventure's discussion of grace's "Christological" source in *De don. Spir.* provides a useful structure through which we can also come to understand Christ's role in his doctrine of grace. In the pages that follow, I provide an account of how grace is gifted to creation through each of these "modalities" of the Word, which will lay the foundation for finally encountering Bonaventure's naming of Christ as the "Hierarch" in the final section of this chapter: Through this name, as I will argue, the different threads of Bonaventure's Christology as it pertains to his soteriology—and therefore also these different modalities of the Word—can all be woven together.

The Uncreated Word as the Source of Grace

First, Bonaventure begins his discussion of the "origin" of grace in *De don. Spir.* by declaring that grace descends to humanity from the "Father of Lights." As Maranesi has already noted, this declaration is rooted in Bonaventure's conviction that Christ's role in gifting sanctifying grace is intimately connected with his role in the intra-Trinitarian life as the Uncreated Word, as the similitude of the "Father of Lights" within the uncreated hierarchy, the Trinity. Maranesi's text rightly emphasizes the importance of Bonaventure's theology of the "Uncreated Word" in his unfolding of the narrative of salvation history, whereby the Seraphic Doctor's teachings on the Uncreated Word are especially attached in that narrative to the act of creation. For Bonaventure, as Maranesi details, all things in creation "proceed" from the Father through the Uncreated Word. My focus here will rather be on the significance of this idea for the Seraphic Doctor's doctrine of grace— namely, on how in order to understand how Christ gifts the *influentia* of sanctifying grace as the Incarnate and Crucified Word, it is first necessary to establish that this gift was given to creation (even in its prelapsarian state) through Christ the Uncreated Word. A careful reflection regarding the role of the Uncreated Word in gifting grace before the Fall will here lay the foundation for encountering how grace is also given through the Incarnate, Crucified, and Inspired Word below.

The Uncreated Word: The *Medium* of the Uncreated Hierarchy   To understand how the Uncreated Word thus gifts grace to prelapsarian creation in Bonaventure's theology, however, we first must step back to appreciate the broader contours of his Trinitarian theology. The Seraphic Doctor's Trinitarian theology, as we have now seen repeatedly throughout this book, stands at the center of his doctrine of grace. The Trinity is, for him, the "uncreated hierarchy" from whom all things process and to whom all creatures must return through their participation in the created hierarchies. Sanctifying grace causes the soul itself to become "hierarchical" inasmuch as it conforms the soul to the uncreated hierarchy, the Trinity. If the Trinity as the "uncreated hierarchy" is at the center of Bonaventure's doctrine of grace, however, we must similarly note that it is Christ—and more specifically, the Uncreated Word—who stands at the "center" of his doctrine of the Trinity.

In the prologue to *II Sent.* d. 9, the Seraphic Doctor describes the uncreated hierarchy as a perfectly ordered relationship of three equal but distinct persons.[28] Within his broader Trinitarian theology, his consideration of that relationship begins always with a consideration of the Father, the "Unbegotten One" and "fountain-fullness" of goodness who is always "first" in Bonaventure's understanding of the *ordo* within the intra-Trinitarian life.[29] As the "first," the Father is characterized by his *fecunditas,* which is, as Hellmann notes, "so rich that He communicates all of himself, except the character of his firstness," when he produces the Son in an act of overflowing love.[30] The communicative love of the Father and Son then together spirate the person of the Holy Spirit, the third person of the Trinity.[31] Within Bonaventure's account of the intra-Trinitarian life, in other words, the Father is purely productive,

28. For my discussion of Bonaventure's definition of hierarchy in light of this description of the uncreated hierarchy in *II Sent.* d. 9, see Chapter 3.

29. See my discussion of the concept of *ordo* within Bonaventure's theology, especially with respect to the Trinity, in Chapter 3. For a discussion of the Father's "firstness," see Hellmann, *Divine and Created Order,* 60.

30. Hellmann, *Divine and Created Order,* 59. See also Bonaventure, *I Sent.* d. 7, a. 1, q. 2, resp. (1,139): "... quia fecunditas ad generandum, est in Patre, quia principium, et ideo principium, quia primum. Impossibile autem est, quod primum communicet alii primitatem." For more on the role of the Father in Bonaventure's theology of the immanent Trinity, see especially *I Sent.* d. 27, p. 1 (1, 466–80); for the production of the Son within the immanent Trinity, see especially *I Sent.* d. 9 (1, 179–93), *I Sent.* d. 27, p. 2 (1, 480–92); for the spiration of the Spirit within the immanent Trinity, see especially *I Sent.* d. 10–11 (1, 192–218). Bonaventure's discussion of the Trinity in *Brev.* 1 also provides a usefully concise general introduction to his Trinitarian theology; see *Brev.* 1 (5, 210–18). See of course also Bonaventure's *Myst. Trin.* (5, 45–115).

31. Again, see especially *I Sent.* d. 10–11 (1, 192–218). Following Richard of St. Victor, Bonaventure holds that the Spirit proceeds from the Father and the Son as the mutual charity between them; see especially d. 10, a. 1, q. 3, resp. (1, 199) and d. 11, a. 1, q. 1, resp. (1, 211–13).

completely *giving* Himself in a self-communication of love so as to produce both the Son and Spirit; the Spirit, then, is purely receptive, completely *receiving* the self-communication of both the Father and the Son.[32] The Son stands in the middle of both persons as one who is both produced (insofar as the Father "begets" him), and producing (insofar as he, together with the Father, produces the Spirit). In this way, the Son is the *medium* within Bonaventure's conception of the intra-Trinitarian life, since he is both a receiver and a giver of the divine life. Hellmann notes that by referring to the Uncreated Word as the *medium* in this way, Bonaventure does not mean to say that the Spirit is somehow not immediately connected to the Father, and vice versa. Rather, "*Mediatio* is the dynamic ordering of one person to another thereby effecting a real unity in a communion of persons," whereby: "*mediatio* does not destroy immediacy.... The Father produces the Spirit '*mediante Filio*,' and the Spirit is reduced to the Father '*per Filium*.' This in no way means that there is distance, separation, or difference. Rather, it means that the Spirit and the Father are one in perfect unity. For Bonaventure, the divine order is perfect *mediatio*."[33] Grace does not hierarchize the soul so that it would "stand still" or become "static," but "hierarchizes" it so that it would become capable of relating to God and the rest of creation in an ordered way. These ordered relationships cause a soul to become "deiform" because God's being, as Hellmann also intuits of Bonaventure's theology, is not a "standing still," but an ordered relationship—a *circumincessio*.[34] Even before sanctifying grace inflows through the Incarnate, Crucified, and Inspired Word and into rational creatures to conform them to God through these ordered relationships, the Uncreated Word is itself the "center" of these relationships within the uncreated hierarchy of the Trinity. The Trinity is not static, not a "standing still," but a divine dance whose holy *ordo* must be understood, as Hellmann further notes, as "*circular* [my emphasis], with the elements of coming forth and the return ... accomplished by the *medium*."[35] Inasmuch as

---

32. Bonaventure sums this up succinctly in the *Breviloquium*, wherein he discusses the temporal missions of the Son and Spirit in relation to their modes of procession in the intra-Trinitarian life; see *Brev.* 1.5 (5, 214).

33. Hellmann, *Divine and Created Order*, 64.

34. Hellmann, *Divine and Created Order*, 16: "Within the inner life of the divine order in God, the Son comes forth from the Father and in the Spirit the Son becomes one with the Father in a return. This is *circumincessio* in which the circular movement of the *egressio-regressio* is complete."

35. Hellmann, *Divine and Created Order*, 66.

the three movements of procession, return, and remaining characterize the Seraphic Doctor's understanding of how rational creatures relate to God and one another through grace, they also characterize his description of the intra-Trinitarian life. The Uncreated Word is identified by Bonaventure as the *medium* within the uncreated hierarchy of the Trinity around whom these intra-Trinitarian "processions" and "returns" constantly revolve.

Laure Solignac has similarly highlighted the significance of the Seraphic Doctor's notion of the similitude with respect to this very dynamic regarding the Word's role in the immanent Trinity. She highlights Part 1 of the *Breviloquium* in demonstration of this idea, where Bonaventure writes:

Similarly, the Son is also the Image, Word, and the Son. 'Image' designates that person as the expressed likeness [*similitudinem expressam*]; 'Word,' as the expressive likeness [*similitudinem expressivam*]; and 'Son,' as the hypostatic likeness [*similitudinem hypostaticam*]. Again, 'Image' refers to the conformed likeness [*similitudinem conformem*]; 'Word,' to the intellectual likeness [*similitudinem intellectualem*]; and 'Son,' to the connatural likeness [*similitudinem connaturalem*].[36]

Commenting on this passage, Solignac shows how the logic of the similitude informs the Seraphic Doctor's presentation of these three names for Christ within the intra-divine relationship. As an "expressed likeness," the Son is the "Image" of the Father, whereby "the accent is thus set on … the receptivity of the Son with respect to the Father."[37] The "Word," as the "expressive likeness," alternatively emphasizes the *activity* of the Son in relation to the Father, since the Son as the Word expresses the Father's own self-communicative goodness to the Spirit.[38] From this, Solignac notes how the "Son" is thus the "similitude personified, that is to say, *the person who is properly the similitude*,"[39] and is thus also the "hypostatic likeness" of the Father.

36. *Brev.* 1.3 (5, 212). See Solignac's presentation of this passage in *La voie de la ressemblance*, 104.

37. Solignac, *La voie de la ressemblance*, 107: "avec le nom *Image*, l'accent est donc mis sur … la passivité ou la réceptivité du Fils par rapport au Père.…"

38. Solignac, *La voie de la ressemblance*, 107–8.

39. Solignac, *La voie de la ressemblance*, 108: "… la seconde personne est la ressemblance personnifiée, c'est-à-dire la *personne dont le propre est d'être ressemblance*." Solignac highlights how these three names are also presented by Bonaventure in a progressive way in light of her work's larger argument that the similitude walks hand in hand with the Seraphic Doctor's understanding of the concept of "*itinerarium*."

Her work demonstrates how Bonaventure's teaching on the role of the "similitude" in his doctrine of grace is firmly rooted in both his Christology and Trinitarianism. The *influentia* of grace can conform human beings—and indeed, all rational creatures within the created hierarchies—to the uncreated hierarchy of the Trinity only insofar as Christ is the "expressed," "expressive," and "hypostatic" likeness of the Father. The Son, the One who is "properly" the similitude of the Father, is also named the "Image" and the "Word" because these names refer to the different modes of this similitude within the intra-Trinitarian life: As the "Image," the Son is receptive of the Father's similitude, and as the "Word," the Son actively expresses it to the Spirit. Bonaventure's understanding of how the Son is thus the "likeness" of the "Father of Lights" within the uncreated hierarchy of the Trinity walks hand in hand with his view of Christ's role as the *medium* therein, inasmuch as he is both the passive "receiver" of the Father's expression of love, proceeding from the Father as His Image, as well as the active expression of the Father's love to the Spirit as the Word. To refer to the "Uncreated Word" within the context of Bonaventure's Trinitarian theology is to refer to his role as this *medium* between the divine relationships, as the one who actively expresses the Father's love to the Spirit. The name "Word," then, will also be the most fitting name through which to understand the Son's active role in mediating the relationship between the economic Trinity and the created order of reality too.

The Uncreated Word: The *Medium* Between the Trinity and Creation

The Word's salvific activity in the economic Trinity is derived from his role in the immanent Trinity. Because the Uncreated Word is the *medium* within the intra-Trinitarian life, the Seraphic Doctor also holds that the Uncreated Word is thus properly the *medium* between God and the created order of reality as well.

Indeed, in the same way that the *ordo* within the intra-divine life is "circular," with both a "coming forth" and a "return" mediated by the Uncreated Word, Hellmann has noted that all of creation bears a special relation to the Word through these same two movements in Bonaventure's thought: "The first aspect is the center in the exit (*medium in egressu*), and here the *medium* is called the exemplar. In the second, the center in the return (*medium in regressu*) is called the mediator (*mediatorem*)."[40] For Bonaventure, the created order of reality both processes from and returns to God through the Word.

The role of the Uncreated Word is, as such, central to the Seraphic Doctor's hierarchical metaphysics as we have seen it work throughout this book. This metaphysics is characterized by the three neoplatonic movements of procession, return, and remaining: According to Bonaventure, a human being "remains" in God through the *influentia* of sanctifying grace when she constantly is both ascending and descending between God and her neighbor, or namely, when the *influentia* of sanctifying grace orders her to right relationships with God and the rest of creation. What I have not yet noted, and what deserves further emphasis here, however, is how all these movements as they apply to human beings within his teachings on grace are foregrounded in his Trinitarian theology and Christology. The Uncreated Word is the *medium* around which the movements of procession and return revolve in the uncreated hierarchy itself. Similarly, within the created order of reality, the processing and returning movements of all creation from and to the uncreated hierarchy will thereby be enabled through the Uncreated Word, who is named by Bonaventure as the "Exemplar" in the procession (*egressus*) of all creation from the Trinity and the "Mediator" in its return (*regressus*).

With respect to the former movement, the procession (*egressus*), Bonaventure's teachings on exemplarity have already been treated *ad nauseam* by Bonaventurean scholars, and space does not permit my dwelling on it in an extensive way here.[41] Relying on Hellmann's usefully succinct definition of the notion, the doctrine of exemplarity "teaches that the second person is the *medium* for the creation of the world."[42] Hayes's summation of exemplarity in *The Hidden Center* accentuates the relevance of this notion with respect to Bonaventure's doctrine of grace:

40. Hellmann, *Divine and Created Order*, 66n27; Bonaventure, *Red. Art.* 23 (5, 325): "Necesse est etiam ponere medium in egressu et regressu rerum; sed medium in egressu est, quod plus teneat se a parte producentis, medium vero in regressu, plus a parte redeuntis: sicut ergo res exierunt a Deo per Verbum Dei, sic ad completum reditum necesse est, *Mediatorem Dei et hominum* non tantum Deum esse, sed etiam hominem, ut homines reducat ad Deum."

41. The most cited study on Bonaventure's exemplarism remains Gilson's *The Philosophy of St. Bonaventure*, esp. Chapter IV, "The Ideas and Divine Knowledge," 139–61. For a more recent introduction to the topic, see Solignac, "La ressemblance divine, l'un et le multiple," in *La voie de la ressemblance*, 139–208.

42. Hellmann, *Divine and Created Order*, 66.

In the most basic sense, it is God in His own self-knowledge who is the Exemplar of all else; and since God exists only as a trinity, exemplarity refers at one level to the entire trinity. However, in a special manner, the mystery of the trinity itself is reflected in the mystery of the second person. As the full and total expression of God's primal fruitfulness, the Son is simultaneously the expression of all that God can be in relation to the finite. The triune structure of God Himself is expressed in the Son. The relation between the Father and the Son is the first and primal relation, and the basis for all other relation. As the Word is the inner self-expression of God, the created order is the external expression of the inner Word. Whatever created reality exists possesses in its inner constitution a relation to the uncreated Word. Since the Word, in turn, is the expression of the inner trinitarian structure of God, that which is created as an expression of the Word bears the imprint of the trinity.[43]

According to Bonaventure, everything in creation is either a vestige, image, or similitude of the Trinity. The entire created order of reality—including all the hierarchies that comprise the Seraphic Doctor's hierarchical portrait of the macrocosm—bears the "imprint" of the Trinity in these ways precisely because they process from the Trinity through the person of the Word. As the expressive similitude of the Father, the Uncreated Word is the *medium* between the Father and the Spirit in the immanent Trinity. As the expressive similitude in the economic Trinity, therefore, the Uncreated Word is similarly the *medium* between the uncreated hierarchy and the rest of creation. He is the Exemplar from whom all things "process" in the act of creation so that they, too, can be created as "an expression of the Word" and "[bear] an imprint of the Trinity."

Because all things thus process from the Word in the procession (*egressus*), it is the Uncreated Word who will thus also serve as the *medium* between the uncreated hierarchy and the created order of reality in the return (*regressus*) as well. According to Bonaventure, all rational creatures within the hierarchies both process and return to God through an *influentia*,[44] and as Hellmann has observed, "In holding this position, Bonaventure identifies *influentia* with the twofold role of Christ the *medium*."[45] In the *egressus*, the entire created order of reality processes from the Father through the Uncreated Word as the

---

43. Hayes, *Hidden Center*, 14.

44. See again Bonaventure's definition of an *influentia* in *Hex* 21.18 (5, 434): "Unde vera est influentia, quae egreditur et regreditur, ut Filius exivit a Patre et revertitur in ipsum."

45. Hellmann, *Divine and Created Order*, 133.

Exemplar; in the *regressus,* it returns to the Father through a Christological *influentia,* understood as "that power that orders all humans back to the unity of the Father where there is the final and perfect order."[46] We have already seen this particular logic at work in the Seraphic Doctor's teachings on sanctifying grace, which he defines as an *influentia* of this sort and which he says returns the soul to God by conforming it to the Trinity. Through the *influentia* of sanctifying grace, the soul itself is made hierarchical, and is thus made capable of "returning" to God when it is purified, illuminated, and perfected from within. What deserves to be underscored here is the central significance of the Word in pouring forth that inflowing so as to invite the *regressus* of the entire created order of reality to the Trinity.

Most significantly for our purposes, according to the Seraphic Doctor, the created order of reality has always related to the uncreated hierarchy through this Christological *influentia,* even in its prelapsarian state. As he writes in the first collation of *De don. Spir.*: "It is certain that God, who is the original *principium* of all things, by creating humanity to his own image and likeness in the state of innocence, created humanity so near to God that humanity could be informed by grace through the Uncreated Word."[47] Even before the Fall, the Uncreated Word served as the *medium* between creation and God because prelapsarian humanity received the gift of the similitude—the *influentia* of sanctifying grace—directly from the Uncreated Word.

This is indispensable when we consider Christ's role in Bonaventure's soteriology because, for him, the entire created order of reality is led back to the Trinity in the *regressus* through humanity, the bearers of the similitude in the corporeal world. We should recall that he regards humanity as the crown of creation precisely inasmuch as human beings were created to receive the similitude through the gift of sanctifying grace.[48] Humanity was created to be the *medium* between intelligible reality (the angelic and uncreated hierarchies) and the sensible creation, inasmuch as human beings were created with both a body (so that they share in sensible reality) and a rational soul through which they were created *capax Dei* (so that they share in intelligible reality).

---

46. Hellmann, *Divine and Created Order,* 133.

47. *De don. Spir.* 1.5 (5, 458).

48. See esp. *Brev.* 2.11–12 (5, 229–30); see also Coolman, "Part II: On the Creation of the World," 141–67. See also Chapter 6.

The human body "is disposed to receive the noblest form, which is the rational soul, to which is ordered and brought to completion the desire of every sensible and corporeal nature," as Bonaventure writes in the *Breviloquium*,[49] so that through the soul, "every nature may be led back to its beginning, in which it is perfected and beatified, as if in the manner of an intelligible circle."[50] Crucially, this "intelligible circle" can only be completed in Bonaventure's thought—even in his description of prelapsarian creation—inasmuch as our prelapsarian primogenitors received the *influentia* of sanctifying grace directly from the Uncreated Word. Even before the Incarnation, the Uncreated Word poured forth the *influentia* of sanctifying grace into human nature that would thus unite the intelligible to the sensible, and so conform the entire created order of reality to the Trinity.

Of course, humanity's free choice to sin led to its being cut off from this inflowing. As a result, human beings are no longer united to the Uncreated Word through it: They are, rather, broken "ladders" who are no longer capable of relating in an ordered way to the Trinity and the rest of creation through the *medium* of the Word. The *regressus* through the Uncreated Word is no longer possible. Since the entire created order of reality was "completed" through the *influentia* of the Uncreated Word before the Fall through prelapsarian human nature, moreover, this free choice to sin leads in a much broader way to the disruption of the *ordo* throughout all creation. Because humanity no longer possesses the similitude, all of the postlapsarian creation similarly cries out for redemption, for the *influentia* through which it can return to the Trinity. The role of the Word in Bonaventure's soteriology is illuminated by this insight: To return to the uncreated hierarchy, the macrocosm requires the restoration of the similitude to the microcosm; it longs for the *influentia* of the Word through which all creation can thus return to and then remain in the Trinity.

The Incarnate Word as the Source of Grace

Thus, Bonaventure claims that sanctifying grace must be gifted to creation through the Incarnate Word in his *De don. Spir.* In Part 4 of the *Breviloquium*, the Seraphic Doctor attributes the unique suitability of

49. *Brev.* 2.4 (5, 221).
50. *Brev.* 2.4 (5, 221).

the Incarnate Word in restoring the similitude to postlapsarian creation to the fact that the Incarnate Word enjoyed "the fullness of grace" in three ways—namely, he enjoyed "the plenitude of grace in his affection [*plenitudo gratiae in affectu*]," "the plenitude of wisdom in his intellect [*plenitudo sapientiae in intellectu*]," and "the plenitude of merits in his deeds or effects [*plenitudo meriti in opere vel effectu*]."[51] An exploration of each of these three "plenitudes" as Bonaventure explains them in Part 4 of the *Breviloquium* will help me offer my own "brief word" about his theology of the Incarnation, while also helping us behold how the Incarnate Word thereby serves as the source of grace in his theology.

The Plenitude of Grace in Christ's Affection   First, according to the Seraphic Doctor, the Incarnate Word experienced a fullness of grace in his affections because, "from the moment of his conception, he was filled with every grace: the grace of the particular person [*gratiam singularis personae*], the grace of headship [*gratiam capitis*], and the grace of union [*gratiam unionis*]."[52] Because of the first *gratiam singularis personae*, Bonaventure recounts, the Incarnate Word was full of a grace that sanctified and strengthened him so that he could be free from sin, thus making him capable of providing satisfaction for all human persons, following the argumentation of Anselm's *Cur Deus homo*.[53] Next, Christ enjoyed the "grace of union [*gratiam unionis*]" because in him there was a union of the divine and human natures. This union of natures was necessary, according to Bonaventure (again recalling Anselm), because "nothing can serve as a medium of reconciliation unless it possesses in itself both natures, the higher and lower, that which is adored and that which adores."[54] Finally, the "grace of headship [*gratiam capitis*]" refers to the fact that the Incarnate Word

51. *Brev.* 4.5 (5, 245). For more on the Christology of Part 4 of the *Breviloquium*, see especially Benson, "The Christology of the *Breviloquium*," 247–88; and Barnes, "Part IV: On the Incarnation of the Word," 195–214.

52. *Brev.* 4.5 (5, 245).

53. *Brev.* 4.5 (5, 245). See also Anselm, *Cur Deus homo* (*PL* 158, 359); and Barnes, "Part IV: On the Incarnation of the Word," 198n8, for a bibliographical sketch of the influence of the *Cur Deus homo* on Bonaventure's Christology. Barnes rightfully acknowledges Bonaventure's great indebtedness to Anselm's classic text, but also underscores how the Seraphic Doctor puts forward his own unique Christology in the *Breviloquium*; notably, Barnes highlights Bonaventure's notion of the "Hierarch" as one such sign of the Seraphic Doctor's uniqueness. See my comments on Barnes's suggestion to this effect above.

54. *Brev.* 4.5 (5, 246), trans. Monti, 148.

is "efficacious for the purpose of inflowing [*ad influendum efficax*]," possessing in himself a "fontal and original plenitude" through which all who are united to him through grace can receive the *influentiam* of movement and sense (*motus et sensus*).[55]

What, though, do these three types of grace have to do with "the fullness of affection" in Christ? Admittedly, this association will seem rather forced for the modern reader. They play a key role in Bonaventure's doctrine of grace, however, by indicating the Incarnate Word's unique suitability for reintroducing the *influentia* of sanctifying grace to postlapsarian creation. For Bonaventure, the affection is intimately associated with the notion of the similitude in the context of his theological anthropology: The human being is the *image* of God because he possesses an intellect capable of knowing the Trinity as an object, but he can only be called a likeness of God when his affection is completely conformed to the Trinity in love.[56] It is not accidental that Bonaventure would begin his discussion of "the fullness of grace" in the Incarnate Word by considering affection. Rather, this emphasizes the point that the divine similitude has been restored to postlapsarian humanity through Christ. By claiming that the Incarnate Word enjoyed the fullness of grace in his "particular person," Bonaventure indicates that Christ himself possesses the sanctifying grace relinquished by all other human beings through their free choice to sin. Because he also enjoys the "grace of union," moreover, the Incarnate Word is yet still

---

55. *Brev.* 4.5 (5, 246). Bonaventure discusses the "grace of headship (*gratiam capitis*)" in *III Sent.* d. 13, a. 2 (3, 283–93), a concept borrowed from his theological master, Alexander of Hales. Romano Guardini's work on the *influentia sensus et motus* in Bonaventure's theology remains the most expansive treatment of the concept; see his *Systembildende Elemente*, 125ff. Guardini shows with great precision how this concept works on both physiological and mystical levels in Bonaventure's theology. Physiologically, Bonaventure's notion of the *influentia sensus et motus* brings together his reading of Aristotelian physics with his neoplatonic metaphysics; more specifically, the concept is used to describe how the human body is enlivened by the spiritual soul (see Ch. 10, "Die Lehre von der Influentia sensus et motus," 125–45). Guardini then shows how this principle—of life flowing throughout the body—is used in the same way by the Seraphic Doctor in his theology of hierarchy to describe how the "mystical" body is held together by the *influentia* of Christ (see Chapter 11, "Die Theologische Bedeutung der Lehren von der Gradatio Entium und Der Influentia sensus et motus," 146–83). Insofar as Christ possesses the "grace of headship" from which the *influentia sensus et motus* enlivens the hierarchies, he is also the head of the Church; the mystical body is held together, in short, through the *influentia sensus et motus* that flows from Christ (see Chapter 12, "Das Corpus Mysticum," 184–205). As Guardini notes, the concept shows how, in Bonaventure's theology, the mystical body of Christ is held together by "a system of operative grace" ("ein System von Gnadenwirkungen," 192).

56. See again Chapter 6.

the "expressive likeness" of the Father in the hypostatic union: Through the Incarnation, the similitude is restored to humanity because the Uncreated Word—the "expressive likeness" of the Father—is united to a human nature. Through pointing to the "grace of headship," the Seraphic Doctor then shows how this union between the Incarnate Word and the Father is not closed to others, but rather can reunite all human beings who receive grace from him as members of one body.[57] Bonaventure's claim that the Incarnate Word enjoys "the fullness of grace in his affections" indicates how Christ is the expressive similitude in creation, the only human person capable of being fully conformed to the Trinity in love.

The Plenitude of Wisdom in Christ's Intellect   Second, Bonaventure moves from this discussion of the fullness of grace in Christ's affections to next consider the fullness of wisdom in Christ's intellect. As he writes, "In the Word Incarnate, namely, Christ our Lord, was the fullness of wisdom not only according to his knowledge, but also with respect to the different types and manners of his knowledge."[58] From this, the Seraphic Doctor then explains how the Incarnate Word possessed an "eternal knowledge [*cognitio sempiternalis*]" on the part of his divinity, a "sensible knowledge [*cognitio sensibilis*]" on the part of his sensuality and his flesh, and a threefold "abstract knowledge [*cognitio scientialis*]" on the part of his mind and spirit—namely, a knowledge of nature, grace, and glory.[59] Joshua Benson has shown how this discussion of the fullness of Christ's wisdom walks hand in hand with his argument concerning the fullness of grace in Christ's affection:

"Just as the Principle of our restoration redeems us by a most generous grace," Bonaventure begins his explanation, "it also redeems by a most provident wisdom. For what was created according to the order of Wisdom cannot be restored except by the light and order of that same wisdom." This wisdom cannot be lacking at all in Christ, just as he could not lack the fullness of grace. Thus, just as Christ is free from all sin, so Bonaventure believes that Christ is free from all ignorance.[60]

---

57. This notion is crucial for understanding Bonaventure's ecclesiology. See especially Guardini, "Das Corpus Mysticum," in *Systembildende Elemente*, 184–205. See also my discussion of these themes in my treatments of the Crucified Word below.

58. *Brev.* 4.6 (5, 246).

59. *Brev.* 4.6 (5, 246).

60. Joshua Benson, "The Christology of the *Breviloquium*," 273. Outside of the *Breviloquium*, the question of Christ's knowledge in Bonaventure's theology remains a topic

In other words, the Seraphic Doctor's discussion of the "fullness of wisdom" in Christ's intellect is intended to show, once again, the particular suitability of the Incarnate Word in restoring creation to its original purpose. In the same way that the fullness of grace in Christ's affection indicates that the gift of the similitude has been restored to creation, the fullness of wisdom in his intellect likewise indicates that the human intellect has once again been made capable of knowing the Trinity as an object after it had been "darkened" by the ignorance of sin. The Incarnate Word is both the perfect similitude and the perfect image of God.

The Plenitude of Christ's Meritorious Actions   Third, in addition to being filled with grace in his affections and wisdom in his intellect, the Incarnate Word also enjoyed "the plenitude of merits in his deeds or effects." As Bonaventure concludes in Part 4 of the *Breviloquium*:

And it is in Christ's merit, then, that all our merits are rooted [*radicata*], whether those that are satisfactory for the penalty, or those that are meritorious of eternal life, because we are neither absolved from our offenses against the highest Good, nor are we made worthy to gain the immensity of the eternal reward, which is God, unless through the merit of the God-Man [*per meritum hominis-Dei*], of whom we are able and ought to say: *Lord, all we have done, you have done for us.* Indeed, he is the Lord of whom the Prophet spoke: *I say to the Lord, 'You are my God, for you have no need of my goods.'*[61]

In Part 5 of the *Breviloquium*, the Seraphic Doctor will later unpack how sanctifying grace redeems fallen human beings by conforming them to the entire Trinity. As he will detail there, grace first "purifies" the soul by making it into a daughter of the Father, freeing the human will to choose the Good. Second, grace "illuminates" the soul by wedding it to the Son as grace flowers into the virtues, spiritual gifts, and beatitudes. Third, sanctifying grace "perfects" the soul so that it becomes a temple of the Holy Spirit. The *fructus* of grace in Part 5 of the *Breviloquium* is that the human soul is thus made capable of relating both to God and to neighbor through contemplation and meritorious

---

of lively conversation among scholars of the Seraphic Doctor, insofar as his text, *Scien. Chr.*, has often been examined with respect to the particular problem about the extent of certitude in human knowledge. As Benson has elsewhere argued, however, Bonaventure's central concern in *Scien. Chr.* is to show how the knowledge of God and the knowledge of humanity meet in the person of Christ, so that "Christ is the ultimate center of what is and what is known." See Benson, "Structure and Meaning," 67–90, at 67 and 90.

61. *Brev.* 4.7 (5, 248).

actions when it has thereby been purified, illuminated, and perfected—or in other words, when it has been made hierarchical.

That Bonaventure would conclude his comments on the fullness of grace in the Incarnate Word in Part 4 of the *Breviloquium* on this same key is crucial for understanding how the Incarnate Word serves as the source of grace in his theology. Indeed, when read alongside Part 5, we see that the three "plenitudes" discussed by the Seraphic Doctor in Part 4—namely, (1) the fullness of grace in the Incarnate Word's affections; (2) the fullness of wisdom in the Incarnate Word's intellect; and (3) the fullness of the Incarnate Word's merit—correspond exactly with his discussion of the movements of grace in the next part of his brief compendium to the study of theology. For Bonaventure, human beings can only experience the *ortus, modus,* and *fructus* of sanctifying grace within their souls because the Incarnate Word expresses the *ortus, modus,* and *fructus* of grace in himself.[62] Postlapsarian humanity can become hierarchical through sanctifying grace only insofar as the Incarnate Word is himself the "fullness of grace": He is purified in his affections, illuminated by wisdom in his intellect, and is perfect through the fullness of his merit. He is hierarchical.

Inasmuch as the microcosm of the postlapsarian human being needs the *influentia* of sanctifying grace to become a similitude of the uncreated hierarchy, the Incarnate Word is therefore responsible for restoring this similitude to creation. Indeed, if sanctifying grace is primarily understood as that which hierarchizes the soul in the Seraphic Doctor's theology, it does so only because it makes the soul like the Incarnate Word, the "expressive similitude" of the Father. In Christ, therefore, human nature truly finds its completion insofar as the similitude is restored to it through the Incarnation. The relationships that comprise the hierarchical *ordo* within the macrocosm are likewise "completed," since the Incarnate Word reintroduces the similitude to human nature through which sensible reality can once again be related to the intelligible in an ordered way. Through the Incarnate Word, all of creation can once again experience "the fullness of grace" through the similitude, and thus also be restored to the deiformity for which it was created.

---

62. See also Benson, "The Christology of the *Breviloquium*," 272–77.

The Crucified Word as the Source of Grace

The Crucified Word as the Source of Grace for the Individual   If the Incarnate Word restores the similitude to postlapsarian creation, it is nonetheless through his passion on the cross that he pours forth the *influentia* of sanctifying grace that will effectively redeem it. Bonaventure writes in the first collation *De don. Spir.* that grace comes down to us through the Crucified Word "in order to heal our feebleness."[63] As he argues, "We have been brought to life in Christ through Christ, because Christ triumphed over death," so that "death was not able to devour him, rather the font of life devoured death.... So Christ has died, so that the dead would be resuscitated for the reception of life and grace [*ad susceptionem vitae et gratiae*]."[64] For Bonaventure, if the Incarnate Word is himself the fullness of grace, it is nonetheless the Crucified Word whose bleeding wounds inflow sanctifying grace down from the cross so as to actually redeem postlapsarian human beings: "And a river of grace is flowing forth from his side, who has the power to heal us."[65]

Notably, the Seraphic Doctor even implicitly associates this redemptive work of the Crucified Word with his notion of the hierarchical soul in his sermon for the *Second Sunday after Easter* in his *Sermons de diversis*, where he provides an extensive exegesis of 1 Pt 2:21: "Christ also suffered for us, leaving you an example that you should follow in his steps." Bonaventure writes:

This word is taken from 1 Pt 2, in which the mystery of the Passion of the Lord is described, and is thus recited in Church during the present time, lest we should become forgetful or ungrateful for the Passion of our Lord. And it is described in a threefold way, namely, by way of the reward of redemption, when it says, "Christ also suffered for us," that is, for our redemption; by way of directing us through his example, when it is added, "leaving you an example," namely, for our direction; and by way of leading us in his footsteps, when it is said, "that you should follow in his steps," namely, in perfect imitation. *And so this threefold passion of Christ has in us a threefold hierarchical effect [triplicem effectum hierarchicum], since the Lord is the foundation of the ecclesiastical hierarchy, namely, the effect that we are purified, illuminated, and perfected [purgandi, illuminandi, et perficiendi]* [my emphasis]. For the Passion of Christ purifies insofar as he suffers for redemption; it illuminates inasmuch

---

63. *De don. Spir.* 1.6 (5, 458).
64. *De don. Spir.* 1.6 (5, 458).
65. *De don. Spir.* 1.6 (5, 458).

as the Passion is the example that directs us; and it perfects and consummates insofar as it is leading us in his footsteps. For Christ purifies us by way of the reward: "Who gave himself for us, that he might redeem us from all iniquity and might cleanse to himself a people acceptable, a pursuer of good works" (Ti 2:14). He gives himself for us by way of providing an example; for his particular example is taught when Prv 24 says: "I laid it up in my heart, and by the example I received instruction" (Prv 24: 32). But that the example of the Passion illuminates in the highest way is spoken about in the song of Habbakuk: "His brightness shall be as the light: horns are in his hands" (Hab 3:4), that is, in the arms of the cross. But he perfects or consummates us by way of his footsteps, just as it says in Lk 7: "but everyone shall be perfect, if he be as his master" (Lk 6:40), that is, if he is following his master's footsteps, and this was entreated by the Psalm: "Perfect thou my goings in thy paths, so that my footsteps would not be moved" (Ps 16:5). Here, with these brief but nevertheless pithy words, Saint Peter insinuates this threefold effect in the proposed theme when he says, "Christ suffered for us," etc., as if he were saying: Christ's passion is purifying us from our iniquity, and it is leaving us an example by illuminating us in every truth, so that we might follow his footsteps into every perfection and all holiness.[66]

Bonaventure will continue his sermon by unfolding for his brothers how each of these threefold hierarchical effects are wrought by Christ's suffering on the cross. If sanctifying grace is a deiform *influentia* that hierarchizes the soul by purifying, illuminating, and perfecting it from within, then it is from the wounded flesh of the Crucified that this inflowing bursts forth like a spring of water, nourishing human persons by purifying them, illuminating them, and bringing them finally to the perfection of sanctity. The threefold hierarchical effect that pours forth from the wounds of the Crucified Hierarch is the threefold hierarchical effect of sanctifying grace, through which we are finally brought to conformity with the Incarnate Word—who is himself perfectly purified, illuminated, and perfected, as we saw above. By becoming likened unto the Incarnate Word through the sacrifice of the Crucified Word,

---

66. "Dominica secunda post Pasha," in *SD* 2, 321–22. See also Hayes, *Hidden Center*, 185–86, who also cites this sermon with respect to expounding Christ's role in Bonaventure's soteriology: "Thus, clearly, this statement in homiletic form reflects the theory of satisfaction within the hierarchical framework. It seems equally clear that the element of satisfaction, which corresponds to purgation, is but the point of departure for a process that far transcends what can be said in the legal categories native to the satisfaction-theory." In short, Hayes sees in this sermon further proof for his claim that Bonaventure's use of his theology of hierarchy within his soteriology plays a "thick" role.

human beings can also be united to the Uncreated Word so as to be drawn into the Trinitarian life and be made "deiform."[67]

The Crucified Word as the Source of Grace for the Church   Turning from the microcosm to the macrocosm, it is in this way that Bonaventure can also regard the cross as a "Tree of Life," "whose roots are watered by an ever-flowing fountain, which then expands into a living and great river with four channels for the purposes of watering the garden of the whole Church."[68] Even as sanctifying grace pours forth from the wounds of the Crucified so as to purify, illuminate, and perfect human beings, the wounds of the Crucified are also the locus through which the *influentia* that holds together Bonaventure's hierarchical portrait of the macrocosm can once again flow throughout creation so as to redeem it as well.

This is because, for the Seraphic Doctor, Christ's passion establishes the ecclesiastical hierarchy through which the Crucified inflows "life and sense" to all those who receive sanctifying grace through him. Bonaventure's sermon for the third Sunday of Advent in his *Sermones dominicales* elaborates upon this theme.[69] There, the Seraphic Doctor

67. For more on the centrality of the Crucified Word in Bonaventure's theology, see Delio, *Crucified Love*. See also Hellmann, *Divine and Created Order*, 73–74, where Hellmann associates the "circular" movements of the Incarnate Word's restorative work in creation with the Crucifixion: "Decent [sic] and ascent (*descensio et ascensio*) unfold the mystery of the one who holds the middle place (*tenens medium*). Later it will be seen that the middle place is ultimately achieved on the cross because here the *descensio* arrives to the lowest point possible and there the *ascensio* begins. Bonaventure places the development of his spiritual and mystical theology on these two aspects of the *medium*. The Christian must identify with the *medium* in both the *descensio* and *ascensio*. Only in this way does the human come to the final *reductio ad Patrem* whereby the vertical order converges into the horizontal order closing the intelligible circle, thereby accomplishing all things."

68. Bonaventure, *Lignum vitae*, prol. 3 (8, 68–69).

69. For the historical context of Bonaventure's *Sunday Sermons* collection, see Timothy J. Johnson, introduction to *The Sunday Sermons of Saint Bonaventure*, trans. Timothy J. Johnson, Works of St. Bonaventure 12 (St. Bonaventure, NY: Franciscan Institute, 2008), 11–58. See especially Johnson's comments regarding the broad purpose of these sermons: "The *Sunday Sermons* are representative of Bonaventure's conscious attempt to utilize the sermon genre to call the *viri spirituales*, that is, those called to evangelical perfection and the ministry of preaching within the Minorite Order through the rhythm of the liturgical year. While the *Sunday Sermons* can be considered a model sermon collection, Bonaventure [intends] this unified text to be used primarily to shape the identity of his confreres as they reflect on scripture, and preach among themselves and to likeminded religious and clerics" (14). For the Latin edition, see *Dominica tertia adventus*, in *Sermones dominicales*, ed. Jacques Guy Bougerol, Sancti Bonaventurae Opera 10 (Rome: Città Nuova Editrice, 1992), 70–78. English translations of this sermon here are by Timothy J. Johnson, "Sermon 4: Third Sunday of

highlights the role of Christ as the *medium* between the Trinity and creation, underscoring the above-mentioned idea that the Word has always fulfilled this role, both before and after the Fall: "He who was the medium in the way of creation, would be the medium in the way of recreation. Consequently, the world might be restored through the Word through whom it was made."[70] The sermon argues that Christ is the most "appropriate" *medium* in this sense in three ways: first, in regard to the fact that he is the *medium* in the hypostatic union, since he is both fully God and fully human;[71] second, in regard to the fact that he is the *medium* in "the regular discipline of conduct, never straying from the medium of truth when speaking nor from the medium in every type of virtue and perfection"[72]; and finally, in regard to the fact that he is the *medium* in "the powerful influence of his passion."[73] The first two reasons correspond with my above discussion of the role of the Incarnate Word as the source of grace; the third reason, however, rather expands this so as to include a consideration of the grace that flows from the Crucified Word as well. Again, Bonaventure's expansion of this third point here warrants our full attention:

Christ was the medium of powerful influence in the passion where *he wrought salvation in the midst of the earth.* Just as the heart, which is the medium of life-giving warmth in the senses, by means of mediating spirits, influences the life of the other members of the material body, so Christ, crucified in the midst of thieves, he who is the *tree of life* planted by God *in the midst of paradise* of the Church, by means of mediating sacraments, influences the life of the other members of the mystical body. This is what Rv 22:1–2 says: *He showed me a river of the water of life, clear as crystal, coming forth from the throne of God and the Lamb, in the midst of the city street. River* refers to the dispensation of the sacraments; in fact it is *as clear as crystal* because of the clarity and beauty given to the souls cleansed in this water. It is called *river of the water of life* because of the efficacious grace that enlivens souls; and it *proceeds from the throne of God and the Lamb* because it proceeds from God, as from an author and efficient cause, but from Christ, as from a mediator and one who merits. Therefore, all sacraments are said to receive their efficacy from the passion of Christ. Whence, according to Augustine: "The sacraments flowed from the

---

Advent," in *Sunday Sermons,* The Works of Bonaventure 12 (St. Bonaventure, NY: Franciscan Institute, 2008), 91–99.

70. "Sermon 4: Third Sunday of Advent," in *Sunday Sermons,* trans. Johnson, 92.

71. "Sermon 4: Third Sunday of Advent," in *Sunday Sermons,* trans. Johnson, 93.

72. "Sermon 4: Third Sunday of Advent," in *Sunday Sermons,* trans. Johnson, 93.

73. "Sermon 4: Third Sunday of Advent," in *Sunday Sermons,* trans. Johnson, 91.

side of the sleeping Christ." The blood and water flowed *into the midst of the city streets*, that is, into the Church which is the mystical body, so that it might be brought back to life through him.[74]

Why is this important? As we saw above, Bonaventure holds that the Incarnate Word possesses a "plenitude of affection" in part because he possesses the "grace of headship" (*gratiam capitis*), otherwise known as "capital grace." This means that the Incarnate Word is full of an over-flowing *influentia* that provides "movement and sense" (*motus et sensus*) to all those who receive sanctifying grace from him. They receive this *influentia* in a way that can be compared to a human body receiving "movement and sense" from the head:[75] By possessing "the grace of headship," the Incarnate Word is "the efficacious source of life [*influere sensus et motus*] for all its members," who together comprise the ecclesiastical hierarchy, the Church.[76] Notably, the above excerpt from Bonaventure's fourth sermon for the third Sunday of Advent associates this notion of the "grace of headship" with the Crucified Word as well. Indeed, this *influentia sensus et motus* flows forth from the "Tree of Life," or the cross, inasmuch as the "blood and water" that spill out from Christ's side produce the sacraments, by means of which "the life of the other members of the mystical body" are "influenced."[77] The efficacious grace that redeems postlapsarian human beings from sin here flows together with the efficacious grace through which the Church is established, the "body of Christ" in which all who have thus been redeemed can be bound together through the "grace of headship."

74. "Sermon 4: Third Sunday of Advent," in *Sunday Sermons*, trans. Johnson, 94–95.

75. *Brev.* 4.5 (5, 246).

76. See Peter D. Fehlner, *The Role of Charity in the Ecclesiology of St. Bonaventure* (Rome: Editrice Miscellanea Francescana, 1965), 58. Fehlner here depends upon the scholarship of Guardini, whose extensive treatment of Bonaventure's notion of the *influentia sensus et motus* remains the most useful introduction to the topic. (Again, see Guardini, *Systembildende Elemente*, 125ff.) Fehlner's work, likewise, remains the most useful treatment of the Seraphic Doctor's rich ecclesiology.

77. Scholars wishing to explore the fruitfulness of Bonaventure's sacramental theology will be greatly aided by a recent flurry of publications regarding the topic, including two English translations of his treatments of the sacraments from his *Commentary on the Fourth Book of Sentences*. See *Commentary on the Sentences: Sacraments*, trans. J. A. Wayne Hellmann, OFM Conv., Timothy R. LeCroy, and Luke Davis Townsend, Works of St. Bonaventure 17 (St. Bonaventure, NY: Franciscan Institute, 2016); and *Bonaventure on the Eucharist: Commentary on the Sentences, Book IV, dist. 8–13*, trans. Junius Johnson, Dallas Medieval Texts and Translations (Louvain: Peeters, 2017). For an introduction to Bonaventure's sacramental theology, see also J. Alexander Giltner and J. A. Wayne Hellmann, "Part VI: On the Sacramental Remedy," in *Bonaventure Revisited*, 273–95.

As Peter D. Fehlner has argued, and as the Seraphic Doctor's sermon shows us, Christ's role as the head of the Church when understood in this way cannot be divorced from a consideration of his role as the heart of the Church as well: "As the efficacious influence which Christ exercises through the sacraments and hierarchy over his mystical members is best described in terms of the grace of headship, so the unity which such an efficacious influence effects and within which it is operative is best described in relation to Christ under the figure of heart of the Church."[78] The Word who is crucified upon the Tree of Life is the *medium* between the Trinity and creation because, like a heart that pumps blood throughout the body, the *influentia* of grace that pours forth from Christ's wounds enlivens the body of Christ, the Church, from within. In Bonaventure's ecclesiology, this efficacious movement of the *influentia sensus et motus*—this inflowing of sense and life through which the Incarnate Word breathes life throughout his Church—is the means through which individual persons within the Church can be bound together in a charitable union, and thus also relate in an ordered way to all those in the angelic hierarchy as well.[79] If it is as the Incarnate Word that Christ possesses "the grace of headship," it is as the Crucified Word that Christ can be rightly called the heart of the macrocosm, because this *influentia sensus et motus* pours forth from the wounds of the bleeding Christ to vivify the Church and effect its unity in love.

The Inspired Word as the Source of Grace

Finally, it is as the "Inspired Word" that Christ personally influences the individual who consents to receive sanctifying grace. In *De don. Spir.*, Bonaventure writes that "grace rises within us through the Inspired Word," because "even though 'God sent his Son' in human flesh, still, unless you believe in him crucified, you shall not have grace." Ti 3:5–7 underscores this idea: "It is not because of the works of justice which we have done, but because of God's mercy that he has saved us through the bath of regeneration and renewal by the Holy Spirit, who is poured out abundantly on us through Jesus Christ, our Savior."[80]

Pietro Maranesi's study of the Seraphic Doctor's teachings on the

---

78. Fehlner, *The Role of Charity*, 68.
79. Fehlner, *The Role of Charity*, 69.
80. *De Don. Spir.* 1.7 (5, 458).

"Inspired Word" in *Verbum inspiratum: Chiave ermeneutica dell'Hexaëmeron di San Bonaventura* provides an important context for how readers of Bonaventure ought to understand this notion in his theology. Maranesi's book chronologically details the Seraphic Doctor's various treatments of the Inspired Word across the course of his theological career, beginning with *The Tree of Life*, the *Breviloquium*, and the *Itinerarium*, moving through Bonaventure's sermons, then continuing with the Seraphic Doctor's claim that grace is sourced through the Inspired Word in *De don. Spir.*, and concluding finally with an examination of the *Hexaëmeron*. With respect to the latter, Maranesi argues that the "Inspired Word" is the key to the interpretation of the entire text. Though the *Hexaëmeron* boasts by far the Seraphic Doctor's most mature account of the Inspired Word, Maranesi's catalogue of Bonaventure's use of the concept within the context of his theology of the "triplex Verbum" underscores certain key characteristics through which we can nonetheless broadly summarize what he means by the phrase. When he refers to the "Uncreated Word" and the "Incarnate Word," as Maranesi argues, Bonaventure refers to two objective movements of the Word in salvation history: All things are first created by the Uncreated Word, through which they are related to the Father in the prelapsarian creation, and then all things must be re-created through the "Incarnate Word" in a postlapsarian world. The work of the "Crucified Word" is wrapped up with that of the Incarnate Word in this reading of salvation history since it is through the Crucifixion that the Incarnate Word redeems the fallen cosmos through his death on the cross. These modalities of the Word are "objective," according to Maranesi, because they refer to definite historical moments in which the Uncreated and Incarnate-Crucified Word acts in history for the sake of all creation.[81]

As Maranesi has convincingly shown in his lengthy analysis of Bonaventure's own development of the concept, the Inspired Word must be understood as referring to the third modality of the Word's action in history—namely, as the means through which Christ "subjectively" participates in the salvation of each individual.[82] Whereas the salvific work of the Uncreated and Incarnate Word applies to the entire macrocosm, the salvific work of the Inspired Word is addressed

---

81. See especially Maranesi, "Il Verbum Increatum e il Verbum Incarnatum," in *Verbum Inspiratum*, 31–56.

82. Maranesi, *Verbum Inspiratum*, 57ff.

to individual human beings on a personal basis. More specifically, Bonaventure's teachings on the Inspired Word often appear alongside his teachings on illumination theory: Once the Uncreated and Incarnate Word have "objectively" acted within history, the Inspired Word inwardly instructs the individual from within through grace, illuminating the intellect in a way that, as Maranesi argues, "always terminates in an affective experience of the Uncreated and Incarnate Word."[83] This interior illumination through the Inspired Word leads the individual to an ecstatic assimilation with the Truth,[84] or namely, to beatitude. More simply put, the role of the Inspired Word in the Seraphic Doctor's theology is illuminative, whereby the Inspired Word inwardly instructs the individual to prepare her for assimilation with the Incarnate and Crucified Word.

Notably, Maranesi's conclusions regarding the meaning of the Inspired Word in Bonaventure's theology relegate these themes to the Seraphic Doctor's Christology, and not to his pneumatology. When Bonaventure writes about the Inspired Word, he is not referring to the Holy Spirit.[85] At first glance, the opposite would seem to be true in his discussion of the Inspired Word as the "source" of grace in his *De don. Spir.* But according to Maranesi, close attention to the text—especially when it is read next to Bonaventure's references to the Inspired Word in his other writings—rather suggests that the Inspired Word is the source of grace in *De don. Spir.* because the Inspired Word illuminates the individual from within to prepare the individual for his reception of the uncreated gift of grace, the Holy Spirit.[86]

Such observations are important within the context of Bonaventure's doctrine of grace because they show how, for the Seraphic Doctor, the role of Christ in bestowing grace does not simply end on the cross. The individual who consents to receive the gift of sanctifying grace through the urging of helping grace will enjoy a personal relationship with Jesus through the Inspired Word.

Moreover, the association of the Inspired Word with intellectual

---

83. Maranesi, *Verbum Inspiratum*, 379: "In esse è emerso che il processo intellettivo è terminato sempre in un'esperienza affettiva con il Verbo increato e incarnato...."

84. Maranesi, *Verbum Inspiratum*, 382: "La rivelazione del Verbo, incontrato intellivamente e affettivamente 'per Verbum inspiratum,' produce un'assimilazione 'eccessiva' alla Verità stessa, cioè con il Verbo."

85. See Maranesi's reasoning for this in *Verbum Inspiratum*, 112–16.

86. Maranesi, *Verbum Inspiratum*, 115–16.

illumination as highlighted by Maranesi situates Bonaventure's theology of the "triplex Verbum" within the narrative of grace as I have been describing it throughout this book. In Bonaventure's angelic anthropology, sanctifying grace hierarchizes the soul into a similitude of the Trinity specifically through the three activities of purification, illumination, and perfection. Quite notably, the Christological moment within his angelic anthropology is always attached to the second of these activities—namely, to illumination. This is clearly underscored, for example, in Part 5 of the *Breviloquium*, where Bonaventure describes how sanctifying grace illuminates the soul by branching out into the habits of the virtues, spiritual gifts, and beatitudes, leading finally to the soul's bridal union with Christ. The Seraphic Doctor's angelic anthropology in the *Itinerarium* then reiterates this same theme. Maranesi's own examination of the third modality of the Word in salvation history also specifically shows how, throughout his theological career, Bonaventure seems overwhelmingly to associate the Inspired Word with interior illumination. This Christological movement within the individual's soul yields, of course, to the pneumatological, the moment of perfection in Bonaventure's angelic anthropology, but the latter cannot take place apart from the former: The Inspired Word is the source of grace in Bonaventure's theology precisely inasmuch as the Word interiorly illuminates the soul to lead it to an "affective union with the Incarnate and Crucified Word," which will then yield to pneumatological perfection. As Maranesi intuits, the soul that has thereby been gifted with the uncreated gift of the Holy Spirit through sanctifying grace will not cease being thus inwardly illumined by the Inspired Word; rather, so long as it continuously submits itself to the *influentia* of sanctifying grace that flows into it through the Crucified Word, it will remain open to the Inspired Word, which will continue to illuminate it from within so that it can remain constantly purified, illuminated, and perfected unto glory.

The Movement of the Word throughout Salvation History

Through all these modalities, sanctifying grace always inflows to creation through the Word in Bonaventure's theology. Though all grace ultimately flows first from the "Father of Lights," the Word is nonetheless always the *medium* of grace between "the Father of Lights" and creation, and thus also between the Trinity and the created order of reality. Before the Fall, the *influentia* of sanctifying grace immediately flowed into prelapsarian human nature through the Uncreated Word. Inasmuch as all prelapsarian creation was ordered to the similitude provided by sanctifying grace, all prelapsarian creation was also ordered to the Trinity through the Word. After the Fall, the Incarnate Word descended from the uncreated hierarchy and into creation, so that the "fullness of grace" in his affection, intellect, and merit would restore the similitude of the Trinity to the created order of reality. The Crucifixion of the Incarnate Word then poured forth the *influentia* of sanctifying grace that would effectively redeem the entire cosmos, while the Inspired Word continues to illuminate individuals in a "subjective" way from within. The Seraphic Doctor's doctrine of grace in these ways is thoroughly Christological: To follow the movements of grace throughout his narrative of salvation history is to follow as well the movements of the Uncreated, Incarnate, Crucified, and Inspired Word in thereby gifting that *influentia* to creation.

Christ the Hierarch in Bonaventure's Soteriology

What thus remains to be demonstrated, however, involves my contention at the beginning of this chapter that Bonaventure's naming of Christ as the "Hierarch" weaves together all these different movements of sanctifying grace through the Word in his soteriology. In what follows, I will show how the very logic of Bonaventure's doctrine of grace—particularly insofar as I have been reading it throughout this book in light of his theology of hierarchy—is rooted within his Christology, and more specifically, within this particular name for Christ.

To address an important caveat, much like the word "hierarchy" itself, this name for Christ will rightly be repugnant to modern theological sensibilities. My intention here is not to suggest that contemporary theologians ought to reclaim this name for Christ. Where "hierarchy" is understood as an oppressive power structure, then a "Hierarch" will similarly be perceived as the person of authority most at fault for oppressing those below them within that system. Inasmuch as I have been arguing throughout this book that "hierarchy" itself meant something quite different for Bonaventure than it does for us, we can expect the word "Hierarch" to be functioning here in a very different way than we would perhaps expect as well.

Indeed, my aim here is simply to explain what the Seraphic Doctor meant by it, especially insofar as I see it as helpful for understanding the role of Christology in his soteriology. "Hierarchy," for Bonaventure, simply means the trinity and unity of God. A rational creature's participation in a hierarchy conforms her to God when it causes her to become a similitude of the Trinity. The Seraphic Doctor's very earliest definition of hierarchy claims that a rational creature will be conformed to the Trinity when the creature bends down to her neighbor through what he calls the *"fruitfulness of plenitude."*[87] Hierarchical perfection in his doctrine of grace is not located in an "ascent" of the rational creature to God that takes place at the expense of other creatures. Neither does the creature that ascends to God through grace simply "stop moving" once she has thus arrived at a contemplative union with God. Rather, for the Seraphic Doctor, hierarchical perfection consists in the rational creature's ascent to God that leads her to descend to the created order of reality, and vice versa in perpetuity. In this, the rational creature shall be truly filled with "the fruitfulness of plenitude" (*plenitudinis ubertatem*) through which she will be conformed to the Trinity. The rational creature can only pass from "being" to "well-being" or from the image to the similitude[88] when she continuously ascends and descends between God and creation.

What remains to be seen below, however, is how Bonaventure's view of hierarchical perfection as such is rooted in his Christology, especially inasmuch as he names Christ as the "Hierarch" who activates all these movements within creation—these ascents and descents and reascents—not by remaining in the Uncreated Hierarchy and in intelligible reality as a figure of authority who is content to watch his creation suffer, but *by himself descending* into the sensible realm through the Incarnation, and by descending also to death on the cross, and even into hell for the sake of his creatures. Quite simply, grace makes us "hierarchical" in Bonaventure's theology because it conforms us to Christ the "Hierarch"—the Uncreated, Incarnate, Crucified, and Inspired Word whose own "movements" throughout salvation history we are meant to emulate through grace.

---

87. See again my discussion of this theme in Chapter 3. See also *II Sent.* d. 9, prol. (2, 238).
88. See my discussion of this concept in Chapter 6.

Proving this requires, first and foremost, attending to a few instances in which Bonaventure actually refers to Christ as the "Hierarch." Even if he does use the appellation more frequently in his later writings than in his earlier works, as Rufin Silic observed and as Zachary Hayes affirmed, nonetheless, a quick survey of Bonaventure's use of the word across the course of his career underscores the fact that it means much the same thing wherever it appears. Attending to three passages from the *Breviloquium*, the *Itinerarium*, and the *Hexaëmeron* will suffice to introduce us to the meaning of this name in the context of Bonaventure's soteriology while also exposing this continuity.

First, the Seraphic Doctor refers to Christ as the Hierarch within a discussion of theology and scripture in the prologue to the *Breviloquium*. Whereas philosophy is concerned only with things as they exist in nature, he contends, theology—as the study of sacred scripture—considers grace, glory, and eternal Wisdom.[89] Because theology is the science that thus treats "higher things," philosophical knowledge is always subjected to theological knowledge. So, as he continues:

It is as if [theology] erects a ladder, the bottom of which touches earth, but whose height touches heaven. And this is all done through that one Hierarch [*per illum unum hierarcham*], Jesus Christ, who is not only the Hierarch in the ecclesiastical hierarchy insofar as he assumed human nature, but is also the Hierarch in the angelic hierarchy, and is the middle person in the supercelestial hierarchy of the most blessed Trinity itself. Through him, from the height of God, the grace of unction *descended* [*descendit unctionis gratia*] not only *upon the beard,* but also *on the edge of his robes* [Ps 132:2]: not only in the heavenly Jerusalem, but also in the Church militant.[90]

Here, the Seraphic Doctor uses the word "Hierarch" to underscore Christ's role as a *medium* between the Uncreated Hierarchy of the Trinity and the rest of creation, as discussed above. Christ is the "one Hierarch" because he is the *medium* of relationships within *each* of the three hierarchies that comprise Bonaventure's vision of the cosmos, including even the uncreated hierarchy of the Trinity. Grace "descends" through this Hierarch from the uncreated hierarchy and into the created hierarchies below in a way that irrevocably unites them in relationships with one another and with God.

89. *Brev.* prol. 3 (5, 205).
90. *Brev.* prol. 3 (5, 205).

Similarly, in *Itin.* 4, immediately after describing the soul's hierarchization through grace,[91] Bonaventure again highlights the role of scripture in aiding the person who has thus been sanctified.[92] Because scripture primarily treats the works of restoration, it is mainly concerned with the virtues of faith, hope, and charity, "virtues through which the soul [*anima*] has to be reformed … especially through charity [*caritate*]."[93] He continues:

The Apostle says that this charity *is the end of the law,* insofar as it is *from a pure heart and good conscience and an unfeigned faith* [1 Tm 1:5]. It is the *fulfillment of the law,* as the same Apostle says. And our Savior says that the whole Law and the Prophets hang on these same two precepts, namely, love of God and neighbor. These two things are intimated in the one spouse of the Church, Jesus Christ, who is at once [*simul*] our neighbor and God, at once brother and master, at once also king and friend, at once the Uncreated and Incarnate Word, our Creator and Restorer, as the *Alpha and Omega*; who is also our highest Hierarch [*summus hierarcha*], purifying and illuminating and perfecting his spouse [*purgans et illuminans et perficiens sponsam*], namely, the whole Church and every holy soul [*animam sanctam*].[94]

In *Itin.* 4, sanctifying grace hierarchizes the soul so that it can perpetually ascend and descend between God and other creatures—so that it can be transformed into a "Jacob's Ladder" capable of ascending to God while simultaneously descending to others through perfect virtue, thus fulfilling the double love commandment.[95] Notably, Christ here actually enfleshes the double love commandment and, in so doing, makes possible these ascending and descending movements of the hierarchical soul: Christ is both neighbor and God, the Uncreated Word and the Incarnate Word, the "Hierarch" who embodies the charity to which all scriptures point and through which all hierarchical souls can be purified, illuminated, and perfected to become a similitude of the Trinity. Here, as in the *Breviloquium,* Bonaventure names Christ as the "Hierarch" because this designation fittingly describes Christ's role as the *medium* between the Uncreated Hierarchy and "holy souls" within the Church below.

---

91. See Chapter 5.

92. Within the specific context of the *Itinerarium*, Bonaventure suggests that scripture will aid "the image reformed through grace" in the same way that philosophy had aided the mind on its journey to God in the first three chapters of the text. See *Itin.* 4.5 (5, 307).

93. *Itin.* 4.5 (5, 307).

94. *Itin.* 4.5 (5, 307).

95. Again, see my previous discussion of this in Chapter 5.

This passage from *Itin.* 4, moreover, perfectly parallels a previous passage from *Itin.* 1 wherein the Seraphic Doctor had described how human nature is "deformed through guilt" and thus must also be "reformed through grace." The powers of the soul, he there wrote, must be "purified by justice, cultivated through knowledge, and perfected through wisdom."[96] Of course, these correspond to the three hierarchical activities of purification, illumination, and perfection. Bonaventure indeed continues *Itin.* 1 by claiming that the soul is purified, illuminated, and perfected through the Incarnate Word of God, the source of grace and truth who "pours into us the *grace of charity* which, since it is *from a pure heart and good conscience and unfeigned faith* [1 Tm 1:5], sets the soul upright according to the threefold consideration mentioned above."[97] The Seraphic Doctor's reference to 1 Tm 1:5 in *Itin.* 1 foreshadows his use of this same verse with respect to grace in *Itin.* 4 quoted above, wherein Bonaventure refers to Christ as the Hierarch. In other words, Chapters 1 and 4 of the *Itinerarium* quite explicitly associate these three salvific hierarchical activities of grace within the soul to Christ the Hierarch.

This observation is important when we recall the *status quaestionis* surrounding the relationship between Christology and soteriology in Bonaventure's thought as I introduced it in the first section of this chapter. The question surrounding Christ's role in Bonaventure's soteriology is largely a question of consolidating what appear to be alternative methodologies for approaching the subject throughout his writings, beginning with Guardini's original identification of three such theories—namely, the "moral-legal theory," the "physical-mystical theory," and the "personalist theory." Post-Guardini, scholars have variously attempted to articulate how these three theories hang together in Bonaventure's soteriology, since Guardini did not "demonstrate their inner harmony convincingly."[98] I previously noted a correspondence between these three theories and the three hierarchical activities according to which "purification" seems to fall within Guardini's "moral-legal theory"; "illumination" within the "physical-mystical theory"; and "perfection" within the "personalist theory." I mention this correspondence again since Bonaventure *explicitly* attributes these three

---

96. *Itin.* 1.6 (5, 297).
97. *Itin.* 1.7 (5, 298).
98. Again, see Hayes, *Hidden Center*, 153.

hierarchical activities to the work of Christ the "Hierarch" in the *Itinerarium*. Simply put, this name could itself potentially "demonstrate … [the] inner harmony" of Guardini's three soteriological theories convincingly.

The significance of this name for Christ in the Seraphic Doctor's soteriology indeed continues to be corroborated when we turn to the *Hexaëmeron*, where it appears in the third collation.[99] As within both the *Itinerarium* and the *Breviloquium*, he uses the name in the context of a discussion of scripture. In *Hex.* 3.10–11, Bonaventure argues that the Incarnate Word is the key to understanding scripture, insofar as the Incarnate Word is "he who is principally concerned with the works of restoration. For unless you understand the order and origin of restoration, you cannot understand scriptures."[100] As he continues to explain, "It was he who restored the heavenly hierarchy and the hierarchy below heaven, which had totally fallen. Thus, it was necessary that he touch [*tangeret*] both heaven and earth. This Hierarch had to be most high, wise, acceptable to God, victorious, generous in a freely-flowing way [*largifluus*], and just."[101]

The Seraphic Doctor's explanation of the "Hierarch" in *Hex.* 3 elaborates upon all six attributes. First, as one who is "most high in power," he argues that the Hierarch is the "only one who is able to save."[102] Second, the Hierarch has a threefold wisdom as one who is endowed with intelligence—namely, innate wisdom, through which the Hierarch "knows all things which we are able to know by habit"; infused wisdom, through which "he comprehends gloriously and infinitely because *of his wisdom there is no number*"; and eternal wisdom, through which

---

99. Werner Dettloff provides an extensive analysis of Bonaventure's naming of Christ as the "Hierarch" in this passage from the *Hexaëmeron*, especially as it applies to his reading of scripture. See Dettloff, "*Christus tenens medium in omnibus*," 124–27.

100. *Hex.* 3.10–11, at 3.11 (5, 345).

101. *Hex.* 3.12 (5, 345): "Iste reparavit hierarchiam caelestem et subcaelestem, quae tota corruerat. Ergo necesse fuit, ut tangeret caelum et terram. Iste hierarcha debuit esse praecelsus, sensatus, Deo acceptus, victoriosus, largifluus, iustus." The word "largifluus," which is translated by de Vinck in his translation of the *Hexaëmeron* as "most generous," is a difficult word to translate (see *Collations on the Six Days,* trans. José de Vinck [Paterson, NJ: St. Anthony Guild Press, 1970], 48). I have chosen to translate it as "a freely-flowing generosity" to coincide with my translation of Bonaventure's use of this same phrase in *Sermo* 54 "*De sanctis angelis*" from his *SD* 2, 689 and 693. As I examined at length in Chapter 3, in that sermon, the Seraphic Doctor uses this phrase to describe Christ's "freely-flowing *influentiam*," by which Christ holds together the hierarchies in communion with one another.

102. *Hex.* 3.13 (5, 345).

he "knows all things." "For," he writes, "it was necessary that the One who would restore the whole universe would know the conditions of the whole universe."[103] Third, as one "acceptable to God," the Hierarch enjoys the fullness of grace so that he could properly reconcile humanity to God.[104] Fourth, as one who is "totally victorious," the Hierarch triumphs over death and sin.[105] Fifth, as one who is "freely-flowing on account of his great *influentiae*," Christ ascends to heaven so that the Holy Spirit can then descend, pouring forth the gifts that will purify, illumine, and perfect the world below.[106] Sixth, as one who is "supremely just," Bonaventure claims that the Hierarch will serve as a just judge during the final judgment at the end of time.[107] Two observations are here warranted.

First, read alongside his references to the "Hierarch" in both the prologue to *Breviloquium* and *Itin.* 4, we can see how the meaning of the word "Hierarch" did not change in any major way between Bonaventure's earlier texts and his later description of these six attributes in the *Hexaëmeron.* In all three texts, Bonaventure names Christ as the "Hierarch" within the specific context of Christ's soteriological role as narrated by scripture.[108] To refer to Christ as the "Hierarch," for the Seraphic Doctor, is to refer to his salvific work in creation, and even more specifically, to his role in gifting the created hierarchies with the grace through which the "microcosm" of the soul can once again become "purified, illuminated, and perfected" after the Fall. By thus redeeming the microcosm, the Hierarch redeems the fallen macrocosm, as well. Indeed, the word as Bonaventure employs it also generally refers to Christ's role as a cosmic *medium.* To borrow a phrase from Ewert Cousins, Christ is the "Hierarch" for the Seraphic Doctor because he is also a "coincidence of opposites," both God *and* man, Alpha *and* Omega, the Uncreated *and* Incarnate Word.[109] In all three of these texts, Bonaventure does not refer to Christ as the Hierarch because he views him as a figure of authority

103. *Hex.* 3.14 (5, 345).
104. *Hex.* 3.17 (5, 346).
105. *Hex.* 3.18 (5, 346).
106. *Hex.* 3.19–20 (5, 346).
107. *Hex.* 3.21 (5, 346–47).
108. Again, Dettloff's work is here important with respect to connecting the "Hierarch" in Bonaventure's theology with his reading of scripture; see especially Dettloff, "*Christus tenens medium in omnibus,*" 124–27.
109. Ewert H. Cousins, *Bonaventure and the Coincidence of Opposites* (Chicago: Franciscan Herald Press, 1978).

who oppresses those below him in an unjust system of power; rather, he calls Christ the Hierarch precisely because Christ descends from the uncreated hierarchy through the Incarnation to meet humanity in an act of humility, thereby inviting the ascent of all created things to God.

Second, we should also note that these "attributes" of the Hierarch as described by the Seraphic Doctor in *Hex.* 3 are strikingly similar to the movements of grace through the Uncreated, Incarnate, Crucified, and Inspired Word that we encountered in our above discussion of the Christological source of grace in Bonaventure's theology. The Hierarch is "most high in power" because he is one with the Father; or, in other words, he is the only one able to save because he is God, the Uncreated Word (the first attribute). The Hierarch then "descends" from the uncreated hierarchy as the Incarnate Word. As one who is both fully God and fully man, the Incarnate Word enjoys the fullness of both knowledge and grace (the second and third attributes). Because he is one who is preeminent in power, full of knowledge, and full of grace—in short, because he is the God-Man who restores the similitude to creation after the Fall—the Hierarch can conquer death and sin as the Crucified Word (the fourth attribute). He "ascends" to heaven so that the Holy Spirit can "descend" with the gifts of grace (the fifth attribute), and then will finally serve as judge of humanity during the end times (the sixth attribute).

In other words, Bonaventure's lengthiest explanation of what he himself means by the name "Hierarch" within the context of his soteriology in the *Hexaëmeron* is a summary of the historical movements of the Word from heaven to earth and then back to heaven within the horizontal order of salvation history. The Seraphic Doctor has already identified the Uncreated, Incarnate, Crucified, and Inspired Word as the source of grace in *De don. Spir.*: Here in his later text, he gives us a name through which to tie all these "movements" of grace in salvation history through the Word together—that of "*Hierarch.*" His explanation of this name in the *Hexaëmeron*, moreover, is not at odds with his previous references to Christ the Hierarch in his earlier works, but rather expands the implications of those previous texts in a more pronounced way.

This observation becomes even more important when we compare what Bonaventure says about these "attributes" in *Hex.* 3 to a passage from *Hex.* 8. There, he uses the image of the six-winged seraph as a way of presenting what those who have faith "ought to believe" about the Incarnate Christ. This seraph has six wings:

> ... three according to the descent [*tres secundum descensum*], and three according to the ascent [*tres secundum ascensum*]; in the order of descent, coming from the wing above the head through the middle to the wing above the feet. These are the three articles concerning the incarnation, crucifixion, and the descent into hell according to the soul [*secundum animam*]. For it begins at the top, because it was necessary that he would be united to a nature in which he himself would become visible and through which he would descend, because he himself is from an immutable nature. Finally he came to the cross; and at last to hell. These are the wings on the left.[110]

He continues:

> Similarly, there are three in the ascending: His resurrection from hell into the world, his ascension from the world into heaven, and his coming from heaven to the judgment so that there would be an ascension from the Church Militant into the Church Triumphant. But first happens the plundering of hell in the resurrection, the opening of the door in the ascension, and the consummation of the kingdom in the judgment; and nothing is more certain than these things.[111]

The six wings of the seraph notably again describe the movements of the Word throughout salvation history. They also correspond, albeit imperfectly, to Bonaventure's six "attributes" of the Hierarch from *Hex.* 3.

It is necessary to pause here and recall again Laure Solignac's thesis that the Seraphic Doctor's teachings on the Incarnation are the point of divergence between Dionysius's and Bonaventure's respective theologies of hierarchy.[112] According to her, Bonaventure presents a "hierarchical upheaval" in his teachings on hierarchy precisely inasmuch as he claims that the "intelligible circle" of reality is brought to completion in Christ, not when the sensible is uplifted into the intelligible (Dionysius's teaching), but rather, when the intelligible descends to the sensible through the event of the Incarnation (Bonaventure's teaching).[113] She cites a passage from *III Sent.* in demonstration of this idea, worth repeating here:

---

110. *Hex.* 8.15 (5, 371).
111. *Hex.* 8.17 (5, 371).
112. See again my discussion of this in Chapter 3.
113. See again Solignac, *La voie de la ressemblance*, 301–2.

For we should say without a doubt that it was fitting that God would become incarnate; and that it was an eminent showing of his power, wisdom, and goodness, which indeed was accomplished in his assumption of human nature. For it was fitting because it was an excellent consummation of the divine works, which was accomplished when the last was joined to the first. For the consummation of perfection is there, just like would appear in a circle, which is the most perfect of all shapes since in a circle the same point ends where it began.[114]

This is the point of divergence between Dionysius and Bonaventure, Solignac argues, precisely because through it, Bonaventure explicitly claims that the Incarnate Word is the consummation of hierarchical perfection. As Solignac suggests, "This perfection does not reside only in the superior (Dionysius) but in the union of the superior with the inferior (Bonaventure),"[115] so that the Seraphic Doctor introduces a "hierarchical upheaval" in his treatment of the hypostatic union.

As I have already argued, and as I have shown throughout this book with respect to his teachings on the soul's hierarchization through grace, this Bonaventurean "hierarchical upheaval" is an "upheaval" because the "intelligible circle" offered by him in this passage from *III Sent.* is not necessarily a perfect neoplatonic circle. The created order of reality here returns to the Divine order—namely, the uncreated hierarchy, the Trinity—not because it has itself ascended to the Divine in the intelligible realm, but rather because the Divine has descended through the Incarnation to meet it in the sensible realm. Bonaventure's "intelligible circle of reality" locates the Incarnation as the "point" where the created order of reality returns to God in Christ, but the Incarnation is actually something quite new within creation. It is also a beginning. Unlike Dionysius, Bonaventure does not identify the point of return as a union of the inferior with the superior, as Solignac has observed, but rather, in the union of the superior with the inferior. There is no neoplatonic escape from the sensible here: The Seraphic Doctor introduces a "hierarchical upheaval" in his teachings on the Incarnation when he locates "hierarchical perfection" in the sensible rather than in the intelligible realm—or namely, in the descending movement of God to the

114. *III Sent.* d. 1, a. 2, q. 1, resp. (3, 20).

115. Solignac, *La voie de la ressemblance*, 301–2: "... c'est-à-dire dans la conjonction de premier avec le dernier 'que réside la consommation de la perfection'. La perfection ne réside donc pas tant dans le supériur (Denys) que dans l'union du supérieur avec l'inférieur (Bonaventure)."

created order of reality in the horizontal-temporal order of salvation history rather than in the ascending movement of the rational creature to God.

His description of Christ the Hierarch in the *Hexaëmeron* proffers an even more robust account of this "hierarchical upheaval." Whereas the rational creature must "ascend" the six wings of the seraph to enjoy a contemplative union with God in the *Itinerarium*,[116] his use of this same image in the *Hexaëmeron* locates the beginning of all hierarchical ascents and descents in the descending movements of Christ from the uncreated hierarchy and into the created, horizontal order of reality—into history itself—as the Incarnate Word.

We should further note, moreover, that this descent is carried beyond a mere consideration of the Incarnate Word and is actually threefold: The Incarnation restores the similitude to the created order of reality, but this is only the first stage of the Word's descending movements in creation. Indeed, it is only as the Crucified Word that the *influentia* of sanctifying grace actually pours forth from Christ so as to effectively redeem every fallen soul to a likeness of the Trinity, so that the "hierarchical upheaval" wrought by the Incarnation is "upheaved" to an even greater extent in the wounds of the Crucified Word. As Peter D. Fehlner has also observed:

In the depths of his humiliation, in his sleep on the cross, in death which is the final rupture of the unity and existence of the microcosm and therefore of creation, Christ enters into the depths of creation, and being exalted in death provides for men and for the world a new center of unity. All creation can now point to Christ as the heart of the world.[117]

It is from the "depths of his humiliation" that the Crucified Word can become the heart of the world through the Church, as we saw above, pouring forth the *influentia* of sanctifying grace that will in turn invite the entire cosmos to be conformed to the Trinity: The microcosm of the human person who has been hierarchized through sanctifying grace; the ecclesiastical hierarchy, which will receive its own life and sense through Christ's open wounds by way of the sacraments; and the celestial hierarchy, which will be restored to the integrity for which

---

116. See my discussion of the *Itinerarium* in Chapter 5.
117. Fehlner, *The Role of Charity*, 71.

it was created when brought into communion with the Church through this *influentia* as well.[118]

But these first two "descents" of the Word are followed by yet a third: The *true* "depths of his humiliation" are considered when we reflect upon the Word's descent into hell after his death. Not only does Christ "descend" to human flesh through the Incarnation; not only does the Word suffer and die on the cross. As the Seraphic Doctor recounts in the *Hexaëmeron*, the Word descends far below what the human being *in via* can even comprehend by descending to hell.

After the Seraphic Doctor has detailed this "descending" valence of the Word's movements through salvation history, he likewise names three "ascending" movements as we read in the aforementioned passage: "[1] his resurrection from hell into the world, [2] his ascension from the world into heaven and [3] his coming from heaven to the judgment." Comparable to his later description of the hierarchical soul in the *Hexaëmeron*, which will describe an "ascent," a "descent," and a "reascension" of the soul through grace,[119] the final ascending movement here with respect to the Word can perhaps be regarded as another "re*descension*." Christ does not ascend from hell and the earth into heaven in such a way that he will stop influencing creation. As we saw above, he will continue to work within individual rational souls through grace as the Inspired Word. In addition to this "subjective" work within the soul, moreover, Bonaventure affirms in *Hex.* 8 that Christ will also again "objectively" act within salvation history as the Judge during the Eschaton: For this to happen, he will again "*come from heaven*," descending for the sake of the created order of reality.

In these ways, the movements of the Hierarch throughout the Seraphic Doctor's account of salvation history perfectly mirror the movements of the created hierarchies, including that of the hierarchical soul in his account of the effects of sanctifying grace. In his angelic anthropology, a graced soul first ascends to a Seraphic, contemplative union with God that will then fecundate the lower orders within the soul in a descending valence. This descent will yield to another ascent to the seraph, and vice versa, so that the sanctified soul remains in God precisely

---

118. See again my examination of Bonaventure's *Sermo* 54 on "De sanctis angelis" in Chapter 3.

119. See again *Hex.* 23.1 (5, 445): "Postea dictum est, quomodo anima hierarchizatur in contemplatione *sui* secundum *ascensum* et *descsensum* et *reascensum*."

inasmuch as these constant ascents and descents conform it to an ever greater likeness to God throughout eternity. Oppositely, the Uncreated Word first descends to the created order of reality through the Incarnation, Crucifixion, and his descent to hell, and then ascends back to earth through the Resurrection, back to heaven through the Ascension, but will then again descend for the sake of his creatures during the Final Judgment. Inasmuch as the created hierarchies "spiral" toward an ever greater likeness of the Trinity through grace, these spiraling movements are all foregrounded in those of the Word throughout salvation history since he "descends," "ascends," and then "redescends." Bonaventure's cyclical metaphysics is indeed "dizzying,"[120] inasmuch as it does not at all describe a journey that begins on one point at the "top" of a circle which then travels the circumference merely to end up right back where it began.[121] Rather, based upon the movements of Christ the Hierarch in his account of soteriology, to "remain" in God through grace for Bonaventure is to be always moving toward new and fuller relationships with that which is both above and below.

Inasmuch as his Christology thereby grounds and informs his hierarchical metaphysics, we should further note that this emphasis on the *kenotic* movements of the Uncreated Word into the created order

---

120. Again, I borrow this phrase from Coolman, "Part II: On the Creation of the World," in *Bonaventure Revisited*, 162–63.

121. See also Hellmann's comments comparing the movements of Christ to a circle in *Divine and Created Order*, 73: "In this greatest of miracles [namely, the Incarnation], the image of the circle appears. For Bonaventure, the circle illustrates every aspect of the mystery of Christ. His eternal generation from the bosom of the Father, his birth, death, resurrection and ascension all reveal the glory of the *medium*. Here, the two dimensions of the circular movement are clearly seen. The first aspect is described by Christ's eternal generation from the Father, entrance into the world and ultimate identification with it in his death. This is the *egressio*, where the *primum* turns to the *ultimum*, namely, God turns to the creature. Bonaventure also aptly describes this aspect by the term *descensio*. The second aspect closes the circular movement through the resurrection and ascension, the *redditio*. Here the created *ultimum* turns to the uncreated *primum*, namely, the creature turns to God. This is the *ascensio*. For Bonaventure, this is the great circle of coming forth and returning." See also Hayes, *Hidden Center*, 172: "With obvious reference to the question of sin and satisfaction, Bonaventure describes the incarnation as the mystery which provides the price of our salvation to a superabundant degree. The second and fourth arguments are clearly related to each other. The second argument makes use of the symbol of the circle, so eminently fit to express the mystery of *egressio-regressio*, to argue that the incarnation is a mystery of cosmic completion in which the circle of reality is brought to perfection by the conjunction of the first and the last." For more on Bonaventure's use of this symbol of the circle as it pertains to his doctrine of the incarnation, see especially Hayes, *Hidden Center*, 172n65, where Hayes notes Bonaventure's indebtedness to Alan of Lille in this respect (cf. *Theol. Reg.*, reg. 7 [*PL* 210, 627]).

of reality—or namely, on the implication that hierarchical perfection is actually located in the descent of the intelligible to the sensible in an act of divine humility—is a deeply Franciscan insight. Since Bonaventure was a follower of the Poverello, he was also a follower of the "naked" Christ. It is no secret that Bonaventure's devotion to the Crucified saturated his work: That hierarchical perfection—that sanctity—for him would be reconceived in accordance with his commitment to "nakedly following the naked Christ" ought to surprise no one. For him, the "Hierarch" is the "Hierarch" precisely because it is the image of the Crucified fixed to the San Damiano cross that informs his way of doing theology, which includes, of course, all the different contours that shape his doctrine of grace.

Conclusion

This chapter has highlighted the central importance of the Seraphic Doctor's Christology within his doctrine of grace, especially as I have interpreted that doctrine through his theology of hierarchy throughout this book. The chapter began by offering a very brief introduction to the *status quaestionis* surrounding the role of Christ in Bonaventure's soteriology. Whereas previous scholarship has struggled to articulate one theory by which to understand Christ's soteriological role in his thought, I offered the suggestion that approaching the question of redemption through his theology of hierarchy might be helpful for articulating a unified picture of his theology of redemption, building especially on an insight from Zachary Hayes. The second part of the chapter then narrated how, in the Seraphic Doctor's teachings on grace, the Word is always the *medium* between the Trinity and creation who gifts the *influentia* of sanctifying grace. For Bonaventure, sanctifying grace always inflows to creation through the Uncreated, Incarnate, Crucified, and Inspired Word. Finally, I attended to the name "Hierarch" in his soteriology. As we saw above, this word can be viewed as Bonaventure-an "shorthand" for capturing how the different modalities of the Word hang together in his doctrine of grace: The Hierarch is the Hierarch precisely inasmuch as this name connotes the movements of the Uncreated, Incarnate, Crucified, and Inspired Word throughout salvation history. Insofar as it is associated with these modalities of the Word, moreover, the name tells us how interpreters of the Seraphic Doctor ought to conceive his hierarchical metaphysics, as well as his accompanying notion of hierarchical perfection. As Laure Solignac has already intuited, Bonaventure's Christology truly does present a "hierarchical upheaval" to the thought of Dionysius by identifying the point of created reality's return to the Trinity in the descending movements of the Word in creation. Bonaventure clearly grounds the hierarchical logic that informs his doctrine of grace within his Christology, especially within this name, "Hierarch."

I return, therefore, to the quote from Bonaventure's *Comm. Lc.* with which I began this chapter:

This ark is Christ, who in whatever of these hierarchies is the highest Hierarch and our leader, so that we might come to the land of promise which has been re-promised to us. As a figure of this he says that he walks through the *triduum*, because he makes us always ascend on high through this triple hierarchy, unless, as luck would have it, we would descend to actions. As a figure of this, Gn 28:12 says that "Jacob saw the angels of God ascending and descending on the ladder." No one saw them standing still [*nullus vidit eos stantes*].[122]

As we have seen throughout the preceding chapters, the dynamism inherent within the Seraphic Doctor's theology of grace is rooted within his Trinitarian theology, his suggestion that the uncreated hierarchy itself is not a "standing still," but a perfectly ordered relationship between the Father, Son, and Holy Spirit. In light of this, the present chapter has shown how, for Bonaventure, we only become likened to this Trinity through the grace of the Hierarch, Christ, whose salvific work in creation invites the entire macrocosm to participate in this holy dynamism. In the next chapter, we turn to an examination of Bonaventure's understanding of sanctity in light of these same themes. For the Seraphic Doctor, sanctifying grace conforms the entire human being—both soul *and* body—to Christ the Hierarch, so that we can truly say of those who have been thus sanctified, "no one saw them standing still."

---

122. *Comm. Lc.* ch. 13, v. 33, par. 72 (7, 356).

CHAPTER 8

The Hierarchical Person

Bonaventure's Theology of Sanctity

The grace of God our Savior has appeared in these last days in his servant Francis to all who are truly humble and who are friends of holy poverty, who, venerating God's overflowing mercy in him, are taught by his example to *reject* completely *impiety and worldly desires,* to live in conformity with Christ and to thirst after blessed hope with indefatigable desire.... First overcome by the gifts of heavenly grace, which were then increased by the merit of unconquerable virtue, he was filled with the prophetic spirit and also assigned to an angelic ministry and was totally inflamed by a Seraphic fire. And like a hierarchical man [*vir hierarchicus*] lifted on high *in a fiery chariot,* as should be made brilliantly apparent running through the course of his life, it may be reasonably confirmed that he came *in the spirit and power of Elijah....* This messenger of God, worthy to be loved by Christ, to be imitated by us, and to be admired by the world, was Francis.[1]

Thus the Seraphic Doctor begins his hagiographical portrait of the Poverello, the "hierarchical man" (*vir hierarchicus*) in whom "*the grace of God our Savior* has appeared," whose extraordinary sanctity completely conformed him to Christ. Previous accounts of Bonaventure's theology of sanctity have tended to treat the topic within the context of his "wisdom theology."[2] As a result, the question of what it

---

1. *Leg. Maj.,* prol. (8, 504–5).
2. See Timothy J. Johnson, "*Wisdom Has Built Her House; She Has Set Up Her Seven*

means to be called a saint in the Seraphic Doctor's thought has become intimately bound with the question of what it means to be a theologian. In *Hex.* 19.3, for example, he writes, "Therefore, passing from *knowledge* [*scientia*] to *wisdom* [*sapientia*] is not assured; it is thus necessary for a *medium* be placed between them, namely, *holiness* [*sanctitatem*]. But passing over is an *exercise* [*exercitium*]: The exercise of passing from the study of science to the study of holiness, and from the study of holiness to the study of wisdom."[3] Gregory LaNave uses this passage from the *Hexaëmeron* as the textual evidence for his book's central argument—namely, that holiness is a pathway to theological wisdom in Bonaventure's thought, and that Francis—as one who possesses wisdom—can properly be called a "theologian."[4] Similarly, Christopher Carpenter has argued that for Bonaventure, theology itself is a pathway to sanctity.[5] Studies such as these underscore the inseparability of Bonaventure's doctrine of holiness from his view of theology while, at the same time, prompting some further questions: Are all theologians holy? Are all saints, in turn, theologians? This chapter will momentarily, as it were, sever these two topics. While I will return to the question of Bonaventure's doctrine of grace and view of sanctity with respect to his "wisdom theology" at the conclusion of this study, this present chapter aims simply to examine his teaching on sanctity as a topic in its own right. How does Bonaventure understand sanctity? What does it mean, according to the saint from Bagnoregio, to be holy?

It is my contention that such questions cannot be answered apart from the themes outlined in the preceding chapters of this book. If sanctifying grace, as I have argued, is consistently presented by the Seraphic Doctor as an *influentia* that "hierarchizes" the soul, shaping it after the nine orders of Dionysius's celestial hierarchy so as to "make it as like as possible" unto the Triune God, then Bonaventure's claim in

---

Pillars: Roger Bacon, Franciscan Wisdom, and Conversion to the Sciences," in *The English Province of the Franciscans (1224–c.1350)*, ed. Michael Robson (Leiden: Brill, 2017), 294–315. For more on this question and accompanying bibliography, see especially my introduction to the "Bonaventurean Question" in Chapter 1. As I indicated in the introduction, I will not address this issue until my general conclusion in Chapter 9.

3. *Hex.* 19.3 (5, 420).

4. See especially Gregory LaNave, introduction to *Through Holiness to Wisdom*, 26–28; see also his discussion of Francis's wisdom on 123–45.

5. See Carpenter, *Theology as the Road to Holiness in St. Bonaventure*. LaNave provides a helpful overview of the differences between his account and that of Carpenter, as well as several other theologians who treat the same subject, in *Through Holiness to Wisdom*, 14–26.

the prologue to the *Legenda maior* that Francis is a hierarchical man (*vir hierarchicus*) bears great significance. This chapter will examine Bonaventure's hagiographical texts and sermon literature, especially the *Legenda maior* and his *Sermones de sanctis*, to show how his view of sanctity is indeed characterized by these same themes.

In *Part II*, we saw how Bonaventure defines sanctifying grace as an *influentia* that hierarchizes the soul. In the same way that the angelic and ecclesiastical hierarchies are conformed to the uncreated hierarchy through a Christological *influentia* (Chapter 3), so too does the Seraphic Doctor hold that the "whole human person" can be conformed to the Trinity through this divine inflowing.[6] In Chapter 4, I examined this idea as Bonaventure unfolded it in his *II Sent.* and the *Breviloquium*, and I then introduced his notion of the hierarchical soul in the *Itinerarium* and the *Hexaëmeron* in Chapter 5. As I noted in my "story" of Bonaventure's doctrine of grace in *Part II*, Bonaventure frequently utilizes the symbol of Jacob's Ladder to describe what the soul made "hierarchical" through sanctifying grace looks like. For example, as we already saw in Chapter 5, he employs this symbol at length in *Hex.* 22:

For it is necessary for the hierarchical soul to have steps corresponding with the heavenly Jerusalem. For the soul is a great thing: The whole world can be described in the soul. It is called *as beautiful as Jerusalem* because it is likened to Jerusalem through the disposition of the hierarchical levels. But these are disposed in the soul in a threefold way: According to an *ascent,* according to a *descent,* and according to *a return* into the divine. And then the soul sees *angels of God ascending and descending on a ladder,* as Jacob saw in his mind.[7]

I proceeded in Chapter 5 to present each of these three "valences" within the hierarchical soul as Bonaventure explains them in *Hex. 22*. To refresh readers' memories, the Seraphic Doctor there describes how the soul ascends through grace to the charity of the seraph, which then "gives life" to the rest of the soul in the descending valence. Here, the charity of the seraph overflows throughout the soul in such a way that the descending valence culminates in the "humility of following,"

---

6. This phrase, "the whole human person," is lifted from Bonaventure's definition of sanctifying grace in *II Sent.*, which I discussed at length in Chapter 4. See again *II Sent.* d. 26, a. 1, q. 2, concl. (2, 636): "... but with divine grace coming in, the whole human person is made pleasing, so that whether for the advantage of her neighbor or for the honor of God, she will desire to be totally *expended* through grace."

7. See also my discussion of this passage in Chapter 5. See again *Hex.* 22.24 (5, 441).

understood as the descent of the soul to its neighbor through works of virtue. In this way, the soul is then prepared for another "return" or "reascent" to God, so that the soul remains in God when it is constantly both ascending and descending between a contemplative union with God and meritorious action. In this text and elsewhere throughout his writings on grace, the symbol of Jacob's Ladder is more than merely an image; rather, it plays a rather thick role in the *Hexaëmeron* inasmuch as it serves the purpose of describing what it is exactly that grace does within the human soul in Bonaventure's thought. If the "hierarchical soul" is the effect of sanctifying grace, then the symbol of Jacob's Ladder for him functions on a conceptual level to explain what this means.

In Chapter 7, I showed how these ascents, descents, and re-ascents as therefore symbolized by this image—and indeed, Bonaventure's entire hierarchical metaphysics—are also rooted in Bonaventure's Christology. For the Seraphic Doctor, Christ is the Hierarch, whose descent from the uncreated hierarchy (insofar as he is the Uncreated Word) and into creation as the Incarnate, Crucified, and Inspired Word gifts the sanctifying grace that will shape human souls in this fashion.

What I would like to argue here, then, is that Bonaventure regards the "saint" as one who has been thus transformed: Sanctity has a definite shape in the Seraphic Doctor's theology, and this shape is hierarchical. The saint, for Bonaventure, *is* a Jacob's Ladder. The saints have been perfectly "hierarchized" inasmuch as they have fully opened themselves up for the purposes of receiving the inflowing of grace that will animate the ascending and descending valences within their souls by purifying, illuminating, and perfecting them. The saints are those who have been made capable of "remaining" in God, those in whom grace inheres in the rational soul in such a way that it has traversed the diastema between the image and the similitude. If, for Bonaventure, human nature was created to receive the similitude; if human nature was created with the gift of sanctifying grace so that it could willingly receive the similitude by which and through which the whole macrocosm could be ordered to the Trinity;[8] and if human nature lost this similitude through the primogenitor's free choice to sin—then the saints are emblematic of what human nature can look like once it has been

---

8. See again Coolman, "Part II: On the Creation of the World," in *Bonaventure Revisited,* 162ff.

fully restored to the similitude through the *influentia* of Christ's grace. What's more, whereas Thomas Gallus's angelic anthropology was confined purely to a consideration of the soul, we also see in Bonaventure's discussions of the saints a crucial expansion of the Victorine's notion of the "angelized mind." For the Franciscan, unlike for his Victorine predecessor, the body is a crucial component within the Seraphic Doctor's discussions of sanctity.[9] According to Bonaventure, the saint is a hierarchical person, one who has been transformed into a divine similitude through grace in both soul and body, a theme especially underscored by his treatment of Francis's stigmata but which also emerges quite explicitly in his treatments of the Virgin Mary. In short, my purpose in this chapter is to show how the saints themselves *embody* Bonaventure's systematic doctrine of grace.[10]

My argument as such will serve two crucial purposes. First, it will demonstrate the continuity of these themes within Bonaventure's various portrayals of different saints: What do these persons share, according to Bonaventure, so that they can all be called "holy"? Second, and even more importantly, this discussion will also establish continuity between his presentations of sanctity as they are articulated in his hagiographical, liturgical, and sermon literature and his doctrine of grace as found within his more systematic, academic texts. With a few exceptions, the previous chapters in this book have all been devoted

---

9. For more on the significance of the flesh in Bonaventure's theology, see especially Emmanuel Falque's discussion of Bonaventure in his "The Conversion of the Flesh (Bonaventure)," in *God, Flesh, and the Other*, trans. William Christian Hackett (Evanston, IL: Northwestern University Press, 2015), 167–201. For more on this theme, see also Falque, Laure Solignac, "Penser en Franciscain," 299.

10. It is important to note as well that the significance of the flesh in Bonaventure's theology also walks hand in hand with the Franciscan understanding of and appreciation for *locus*; the relationship between this Franciscan appreciation for *locus* and the Seraphic Doctor's expansion of Gallus's angelic anthropology beyond the soul and into matter deserves further study. For more on this, see especially Timothy J. Johnson, "Place, Analogy, and Transcendence: Bonaventure and Bacon on the Franciscan Relationship to the World," in *Innovationen durch Deuten und Gestalten: Klöster im Mittelalter zwischen Jenseits und Welt*, ed. Gert Melville, Bernd Schneidmüller, and Stefan Weinfurter (Regensburg: Verlag Schnell and Steiner, 2014), 83–96; Timothy J. Johnson, "Dream Bodies and Peripatetic Prayer: Reading Bonaventure's *Itinerarium* with Certeau," *Modern Theology* 21, no. 3 (2005): 413–27; Timothy J. Johnson, "Prologue as Pilgrimage: Bonaventure as Spiritual Cartographer," *Miscellanea Francescana* 106–7 (2006–2007): 445–64. I am also grateful to Dr. Johnson for sharing with me his unpublished paper on this subject in relation to the thirteenth-century Franciscans before Bonaventure, "Place and Prayer in the *Summa Halensis*: Preliminary Reflections," which has now been revised and published as "Place, Person, and Prayer in the *Summa Halensis*," in Schumacher, ed., *The Summa Halensis: Doctrines and Debates*, 325–42.

primarily to expounding the latter. My present task is to show how Bonaventure's teachings on grace and hierarchy as I have examined them thus far definitively play out in his more pastoral works.

Methodologically, I rely upon the Seraphic Doctor's hagiographical literature, especially the *Legenda maior* and the *Sermones de sanctis*, to show how these themes play out across his various portraits of the saints. While Bonaventure's concern in these texts is obviously with the saints and can thus broadly fall within the category of hagiography,[11] scholars have often underscored reasons why these texts also extend beyond this category in rich and diverse ways. For example, Regis Armstrong has argued that the *Legenda maior* is a work of "spiritual theology," a biography of Francis aimed at nothing less than "rekindling the dynamic spirit of Francis" for his confreres as the Order both flowered and faced controversy in the mid-thirteenth century.[12] I focus on Bonaventure's portrayal of Francis in the *Legenda maior* rather than that of the *Legenda minor* because, as I will explore in greater detail below, the threefold structure that informs the "spiritual theology" of the longer *legenda* lends itself readily to a discussion of hierarchy in Bonaventure's doctrine of sanctity. More recent scholarship has also emphasized the fact that the *Legenda maior*, like the *Legenda minor*, was originally composed by Bonaventure for a quasi-liturgical context. In particular, it was meant "for refectory reading during Francis' octave"[13] and presented a "prayed Francis, who is the example, even the 'exemplar of all Gospel perfection,' whom the brothers should imitate so they become conformed to Christ just as Francis conformed to him."[14] Bonaventure's portraits of the saints in the *Sermones de sanctis*, similar to his portrait of the "prayed Francis" in the *Legenda maior*

11. For Bonaventure's sermons on the saints as "hagiographical," see Timothy J. Johnson, "Bonaventure as Preacher," in *A Companion to Bonaventure*, 417: "As Carlo Delcorno points out, the medieval sermon, more than any other literary genre, succeeded in conveying hagiographical models to the faithful, and Bonaventure, who willingly turns to narrative when preaching, regards the saints as both resplendent with wisdom and gladdened with desire." See also Carlo Delcorno, *Exemplum e letterature: tra Medievo e Rinascimento* (Bologna: Mulino, 1989), 25.

12. Regis Armstrong, *The Spiritual Theology of the* "Legenda major" *of Saint Bonaventure* (PhD diss., Fordham University, 1974), esp. 15.

13. Jay M. Hammond, "Bonaventure's *Legenda maior*," in *A Companion to Bonaventure*, 460. For the context and purpose of the *Legenda minor*, see Timothy J. Johnson, "*Item ordinetur de Legenda Beati Francisci*: A Prolegomena to the Study of Bonaventure's *Legenda minor*," *Frate Francisco* 76, no. 1 (2010): 225–39.

14. Hammond, "Bonaventure's *Legenda maior*," 465.

and *Legenda minor*, were likewise intended as exemplars of holiness that would urge his brothers to spiritual reform.[15] Of these sermons, Timothy J. Johnson observes:

> If grace informs and, indeed, reforms the spiritual-material world, then the saints, as proclaimed and performed in sermons and hagiographical accounts, have agency in the dynamic of reform. To speak of them as 'models of holiness' to be imitated is certainly true, but as incarnate 'forms' of divine grace, the saints are far more.... Often translated as 'model,' the term 'exemplar' includes an effective dimension that can be obscured when the word is rendered as 'model.' Sharing in grace understood as *influentia*, the saints, together with the angels, manifest hierarchical agency in the distribution of the gifts from on high within the Church.[16]

In other words, these texts are especially suited for showcasing Bonaventure's doctrine of grace because they present the saints as "incarnate 'forms' of divine grace," whose example the Friars Minor can follow if they likewise hope to traverse the diastema between the image and the similitude.[17]

The chapter will first attend to these themes as they apply within the Seraphic Doctor's hagiographical examinations of Francis. It will then survey these same themes by considering a selection of sermons from his *Sermones de sanctis*, beginning with Mary and continuing with some of Bonaventure's sermons on Sts. Andrew and Agnes and

---

15. See especially Timothy J. Johnson, "Reform, Hagiography, and Sanctity: Bonaventure's Sermons on the Saints," in *Ordo et sanctitas*, 186–206. For more on medieval sermons, hagiography, and the genre of "*Sermones de sanctis*" in general, see also Delcorno, "Agiografia e predicazione," in *Exemplum e letterature*, 25–77; George Ferzoco, "The Context of Medieval Sermon Collections on Saints," in *Preacher, Sermon, and Audience in the Middle Ages*, ed. Carolyn Muessig (Leiden: Brill, 2002), 279–92; and Beverly Mayne Kienzle, ed., *Models of Holiness in Medieval Sermons: Proceedings of the International Symposium (Kalamazoo, 4–7 May 1995)*, Textes et études du Moyen Âge 5 (Louvain-La-Neuve: Fédération Internationale de Instituts d'Études Medievales, 1996), and especially Kienzle's introduction at xi–xx. In his introduction to medieval *Sermones de sanctis*, Ferzoco notes that Bonaventure has comparatively few sermons on the saints in comparison to other thirteenth-century collections; while this is certainly true, these nonetheless remain a rich source for exploring his doctrine of grace, as this chapter intends to demonstrate. The edition of Bonaventure's *Sermones de sanctis* upon which I will be depending here is that provided by Jacques Guy Bougerol; as will be discussed below, this is the definitive edition of Bonaventure's sermons on the saints, since Bougerol has here culled down the collection that appears in the Quaracchi edition to those that are definitively authentic Bonaventurean sermons. See Jacques Guy Bougerol, ed., *Sermones de sanctis*, in *SD* 2.

16. Johnson, "Reform, Hagiography, and Sanctity," 189.

17. Again, for more on this diastema, see Coolman, "Part II: On the Creation of the World," 162; and my Chapter 6.

on the Feast of All the Saints. The chapter will conclude by considering those who have received sanctifying grace but who have not been perfectly "hierarchized" like the saints. Obviously, from Bonaventure's perspective, not everyone who receives the gift of sanctifying grace can be called a saint in the same way as Francis, Mary, Andrew, and Agnes: How can one who is not a saint be made "as like as possible to God" through the inflowing of grace? Insofar as Bonaventure's teachings on sanctity in the *Legenda maior* and the *Sermones de sanctis* provided a prescription for the spiritual reform of his Franciscan brothers whom he encouraged to follow Francis's path to holiness, I close by considering how we might gather from them a prescription for how those *in via* might likewise become "as like as possible to God."

St. Francis: The *Vir hierarchicus*

Nowhere is the claim that the saints embody Bonaventure's theology of grace more apparent than in his hagiographical literature and sermons surrounding St. Francis. This is apparent, first of all, in the words of Bonaventure's prologue to the *Legenda maior* with which I began this chapter.[18] In his 1974 dissertation devoted to a study of the *Legenda maior* as a work of "spiritual theology," Regis J. Armstrong set an important precedent for all subsequent studies of the text by noting how the Seraphic Doctor's introductory remarks establish a "threefold rhythm" upon which the entire text is structured. As Armstrong observes, for Bonaventure, "*The grace of God our Savior*" has appeared in Francis and can serve as an example to be imitated because those who follow Francis will learn through him how: (1) "to reject completely impiety and worldly desires"; (2) "to live in conformity with Christ"; and (3) "to thirst after blessed hope with indefatigable desire."[19] Armstrong proceeds to construct his reading of the *Legenda maior* atop this observation:

This threefold pattern, we maintain, forms the triangular structure of the *Legenda Major*. Thus chapters one and two, three and four, and fourteen and fifteen, which are historical in character, correspond to the three phases which have been outlined. And, we believe, this same pattern emerges in

---

18. See again *Leg. Maj.*, prol. (8, 504–5), and above, n. 1.
19. Armstrong, *The Spiritual Theology of the Legenda maior*, 52.

the analysis of the virtues of Saint Francis, chapters five to thirteen, which may be divided in a threefold manner according to the same approach. This pattern of development suggests Bonaventure's perception of spiritual growth according to the hierarchical ways of purgation, illumination and unification. This approach, which is the subject of the *De triplici via*, characterizes much of the Seraphic Doctor's spiritual writings as he describes man's journey to God through rising above the things of this world. The Prologue's reference to Francis as 'a hierarchical man taken above in a chariot of fire' indicates this structure in this study of the inner life of the saint. In addition to this manner of procedure, Bonaventure's use of the Biblical images of light, darkness, clouds and rainbows implies another methodology which may be applied to the *Legenda major* and which is more philosophical in nature. 'This is our entire metaphysics,' Bonaventure writes in his *Collationes in Hexaëmeron*, 'emanation, exemplarity, and fulfillment: to be illumined by spiritual rays and to be led back to the highest reality.' The application of this principle provides an insight into Bonaventure's attempt to move from the historical data of the earlier biographies to a more profound understanding of the spiritual men. The manner in which Bonaventure presents the biographical material emerges as deeply symbolic.[20]

More recently, Jay Hammond has noted how Armstrong's observations here have become "standard in modern scholarship" on the *Legenda maior*.[21] On a macrolevel, as Hammond observes following Armstrong, "the *beginning* historical narrative of Francis's life (chs. 1–4) refers to purgation, the *progress* of his life according to the virtues (chs. 5–13), which follow a 'more thematic order' instead of a strict 'chronological order,' refers to illumination, and the two historical chapters at the *end*, which narrate Francis' death and canonization (chs. 14–15), refer to perfection."[22] On an intermediate level, again following Armstrong, Hammond confirms that the chapters which follow the "more thematic order" (chapters 5–13) follow the same pattern when read on their own (with chapters 5, 8, and 11 referring to purgation; chapters 6, 9, and 12 referring to illumination; and chapters 7, 10, and 13 referring to perfection), while those that follow "a strict chronological" or historical order likewise are structured in the same way (with chapters 1–2 referring to purgation, chapters 3–4 referring to illumination, and chapters 14–15 referring to perfection). Extending Armstrong's argument even

---

20. Armstrong, *The Spiritual Theology of the Legenda maior*, 53–55.
21. Hammond, "Bonaventure's *Legenda maior*," 483.
22. Hammond, "Bonaventure's *Legenda maior*," 484.

further, however, Hammond also notes that this threefold pattern informs the *Legenda maior* on microlevels, as well, suggesting that "the triple way provides the interpretive key for understanding the narrative within of [*sic.*] each chapter."[23] Hammond provides extended analyses of chapters 4 and 13 to show how the threefold way indeed works on these microlevels within these specific chapters.[24] As he concludes, echoing Armstrong's previous work on the subject: "Taken together, the macro, intermediate, and micro structures help explain how Bonaventure organizes, interprets and redacts his sources as he constructs his hagiography of Francis according to a theology of grace that manifests itself through the repetitive activities of purgation, illumination, and perfection."[25]

This previous scholarship on the *Legenda maior* importantly underscores how the very structure of Bonaventure's *Legenda maior* lends itself to my present claim that the Seraphic Doctor conceives of grace in a hierarchical way. We have already repeatedly heard the beat of this "threefold rhythm," as Armstrong has called it, resounded throughout Bonaventure's writings on grace. Part 5 of the *Breviloquium* is structured according to this threefold rhythm, whereby sanctifying grace "purifies" the soul, freeing the will so that the soul can become the daughter of the Father; it "illuminates" the soul by strengthening it in virtue, thus making it the spouse of the Son; and it "perfects" the soul by causing it to become a temple of the Holy Spirit and a "Jacob's Ladder."[26] These three hierarchical acts appear again in the *Itinerarium*, where Bonaventure claims that sanctifying grace conforms the soul to Christ by "purifying, illuminating, and perfecting" it, therefore shaping it after the nine orders of Dionysius's *CH*.[27] In the *Hexaëmeron*, likewise, Bonaventure describes the soul as a "Jacob's Ladder" which can return to God only insofar as grace causes the soul to both ascend to a Seraphic union with God and descend to its neighbor in "the humility of following" (*ad humilitatem obsequii*).[28]

---

23. Hammond, "Bonaventure's *Legenda maior*," 485.

24. For Hammond's discussion of these micro-structures, see "Bonaventure's *Legenda maior*," 487–503.

25. Hammond, "Bonaventure's *Legenda maior*," 485.

26. See my discussion of these themes with respect to Part 5 of the *Breviloquium* in Chapter 4, as well as my discussion of these themes in "Part V: On the Grace of the Holy Spirit," 215–44.

27. See my discussion of these themes in the *Itinerarium* in Chapter 5, as well as *Itin.* 4.4.

28. See my discussion of these themes in *Hex.* 22 in Chapter 5, as well as *Hex.* 22.33 (5, 442).

Notably, in addition to the threefold rhythm of (1) "rejecting impiety," (2) living in conformity with Christ, and (3) "thirsting" after hope which has already been underscored by Armstrong in the above selection from the prologue to the *Legenda maior*, Bonaventure's claim that Francis is a "hierarchical man" (*vir hierarchicus*) is likewise preceded by this same threefold rhythm. As Bonaventure writes, (1) Francis was "first overcome by the gifts of heavenly grace," which were then (2) "increased by the merit of unconquerable virtue," so that finally, (3) "he was filled with the prophetic spirit and also assigned to an angelic ministry and was totally inflamed by a Seraphic fire." These three attributes, which directly precede the Seraphic Doctor's claim that Francis is a "hierarchical man" in the prologue to the *Legenda maior*, also correspond perfectly with the "shape" of grace as we have seen him mold it throughout his theological career. In Table 8.1, I provide a brief summation of the structure of Part 5 of the *Breviloquium* (Column 1) so as to compare it with Bonaventure's reasons pertaining to why Francis is a "hierarchical man" in the prologue to the *Legenda maior* (Column 2). Strikingly, these also correspond with Armstrong's and Hammond's previous observations concerning the macro-, intermediate, and microlevels of the threefold structure within the *Legenda maior* (Column 3).

The threefold rhythm that forms the macro-, intermediate, and microstructures within the *Legenda maior*, as both Armstrong and Hammond have already intuited, reflects "the structure ... of the inner life of the saint."[29] Francis can be called a "hierarchical man" because he himself has been purified, illuminated, and perfected in the ways described by Bonaventure throughout his systematic treatments of grace in *II Sent.*, the *Breviloquium*, and the *Itinerarium*, and which he will expand further in the *Hexaëmeron*.

We must here attend to how these hierarchical activities "of the inner life of the saint" should be understood. In much the same way that this threefold rhythm informs the entire text of the *Legenda maior* on macro-, intermediate, and microlevels, the "hierarchical activities" of purification, illumination, and perfection in Francis ought not to be understood in only a linear way. Or, to phrase it differently, they should not be understood only with respect to the ascending valence in his hierarchical soul. Rather, as the complex structures of the *Legenda*

---

29. See again Armstrong, *The Spiritual Theology of the Legenda maior*, 54, quoted above.

TABLE 8.1 Hierarchical Activities and the Saint

The Hierarchical Activities that Structure Part 5 of the *Breviloquium*			The Reasons Why Francis Is a "Hierarchical Man" in the Prologue to the *Legenda Maior*	The Hierarchical Activities that Structure the *Legenda Maior*
(a) Chs. 1–3	Treat the *Ortus* of sanctifying grace: purification	Consider grace as a divinely given gift that helps the soul merit the Good and remedies sin	(a) He was "first overcome by the gifts of heavenly grace";	(a) purification
(b) Chs. 4–6	Treat the *Modus* of sanctifying grace: illumination	Consider how grace strengthens the soul by branching out into the habits of the virtues, gifts, beatitudes, etc.	(b) which were then "increased by the merit of unconquerable virtue";	(b) illumination
(c) Chs. 7–10	Treat the *Fructus* of sanctifying grace: perfection	Consider how grace is "exercised" when the soul becomes a Jacob's Ladder	(c) "he was also filled with the prophetic spirit and assigned to an angelic ministry and was totally inflamed by a Seraphic fire."	(c) perfection

maior reveal, Francis can be called a saint precisely because this three-fold rhythm is always at work within him.

This idea finds support when we look closely at Column 1(c), Column 2(c), and Column 3(c) in Table 8.1, above. The *fructus* of grace according to Part 5 of the *Breviloquium* is that the soul is "perfected" when it becomes a "Jacob's Ladder." The contemplative embrace of the soul with Christ in *Brev.* 5.6 should not be regarded as a stopping point of the soul's journey through grace, but rather must be understood as the point from which the soul can thus descend through grace to meritorious actions while still *in via*. In this way, the soul made hierarchical through grace is "made as like as possible" to the plenitude of the uncreated hierarchy, the Trinity. Comparing Columns 1 and 2 in Table 8.1, especially given that the *Breviloquium* was either written in the years immediately preceding Bonaventure's composition of the *Legenda maior* or was written simultaneously with it,[30] we see a striking correspondence between the reasons provided in the prologue to the *Legenda maior* concerning why Francis can be called a "hierarchical man" with the Seraphic Doctor's discussion of the *ortus*, *modus*, and *fructus* of grace in Part 5 of the *Breviloquium*. Francis is first endowed with the gifts of divine grace, which enable him to merit the Good and frees him from sin (purification); he is then strengthened by grace for the life of virtue, so that he can become the Spouse of Christ (illumination); and he is finally perfected so that he may act meritoriously (perfection).

Indeed, looking specifically at Column 3(c), this perfective moment itself has three moments in the prologue to the *Legenda maior*: (1) Francis was "filled with the prophetic spirit"; (2) he was "assigned to an angelic ministry"; and (3) he was "inflamed by a Seraphic fire." Just like in Bonaventure's discussion of the spiritual sensorium within Part 5 of the *Breviloquium*, this threefold "perfective" moment within the inner life of Francis would seem upon first reading to denote a sort of climax, understood as the culmination of the ascending movement of grace within the hierarchical soul. This is most certainly true, but—just like in Bonaventure's discussion of the spiritual sensorium within Part 5 of the *Breviloquium*, as well as in his discussion of the hierarchical soul in *Hex.* 22—it is not the end of the story with respect to Bonaventure's account of Francis's inner perfection.

Attending to these three perfective "moments" underscores this idea in three ways. First, his claim that Francis was filled with a "prophetic spirit" means in this example that the Poverello was filled with a spirit that encouraged him to teach others divine truths. Second, in the same way that the angels within Bonaventure's portrayal of the celestial hierarchy are said to be "fruitful" and achieve the divine likeness when they bend down to others in ministry,[31] Bonaventure's claim that Francis was "assigned to an angelic ministry" subtly but clearly recalls both the ascending and descending valences of hierarchical activity. Francis, Bonaventure here explicitly writes, was hierarchically elevated to such

---

30. Jay Hammond has recently argued for the latter position with respect to the dating of the *Breviloquium*; see Hammond, "The Textual Context," 29–45.

31. See again my discussion of this in Chapter 3, and *II Sent.* d. 9, prol. (2, 238). I will refer to this passage again throughout this chapter, since, as we will see below, the word "*ubertatem*" appears several times across the Seraphic Doctor's various treatments of sanctity.

an extent that he was ennobled to minister to others. Third, we saw in *Hex.* 22 that, following Thomas Gallus, Bonaventure understands the seraphic order within the hierarchical soul to be both a beginning and an end. The ascending valence within the hierarchical soul culminates in the charity of a contemplative union with God, but the fecundity of the seraph then descends throughout the rest of the orders within the soul to end finally in "the humility of following" (*ad humilitatem obsequii*), or the descent of the hierarchical soul to its neighbor. Similarly, Francis's inner perfection must not be understood as a stopping point, or the point at which the hierarchical activities within his soul cease; rather, he is perfect because his ascent to God has so inflamed him with holiness that his "descent" to his neighbor through prophecy, ministry, and charity has been enabled. Francis, according to Bonaventure, can thus be called "perfect" because he "remains" in God through these constant ascents and descents, or processions and returns.

This observation becomes especially important when we turn from the prologue to Chapter 13 of the *Legenda maior*, where the Seraphic Doctor treats the miracle of St. Francis's sacred stigmata. Within the macrostructure of the *Legenda maior*, as observed already by both Armstrong and Hammond, Chapter 13 represents a thematic bridge between the illuminative and perfective ways since Bonaventure's account of the stigmata miracle represents both the climax of Francis's life of virtue (chs. 5–13) as well as the beginning of his perfection in sanctity (chs. 14–15).[32] For the Seraphic Doctor, the wounds of the stigmata signify that Francis was completely conformed to the Crucified Christ. Addressing Francis, Bonaventure concludes Chapter 13 with a laudatory prayer that emphasizes this theme. "Now, finally, *near the end*, both the sublime similitude of the seraph and the humble likeness of the Crucified is shown to you at the same time, interiorly inflaming you and exteriorly signing you as *the other Angel ascending from the rising sun*, so that you might have in you *the sign of the living God*,"[33] he writes:

For the cross of Christ—first offered to you and taken up by you in your conversion and thereafter continuously carried in you through your proven

<hr>

32. See my discussion of Armstrong and Hammond above; see also Armstrong, *The Spiritual Theology of the* Legenda maior, 53–55; Hammond, "Bonaventure's *Legenda maior*," 483–85.

33. *Leg. Maj.* 13.10 (8, 545).

way of life, both in the progress of your way of life and in its demonstrated example to others—shows with such clarity of certainty that you have finally arrived at the height of evangelical perfection, so that no truly devout person would debase this demonstration of Christian wisdom that has been plowed into the dust of your flesh.[34]

The stigmata, in other words, are a sign from God that Francis has achieved the perfective moment within the threefold way. As the outward expression of his inward sanctity, his bodily wounds imprinted "into the dust of [his] flesh" provide a visible sign of Francis's purified, illuminated, and perfected spirit. As Bonaventure writes earlier in Chapter 13, "Thus, it is evident to certain witnesses that those sacred signs were imprinted in him by the power of the One who, through a seraphic work [*operatione seraphica*], purifies, illuminates, and inflames [*purgat, illuminat, et inflammat*]."[35] These three hierarchical activities—the work of sanctifying grace—flow forth from the Crucified Christ in Bonaventure's theology.[36] Here in Chapter 13 of the *Legenda maior*, he likewise affirms that the wounds of the stigmata are a holy sign that Francis's devotion to the Crucified has caused him to be fully conformed to his Beloved.

For those who are the least bit familiar with the Seraphic Doctor's theology, however, these observations surrounding the significance of the stigmata are not new. What needs to be added to our reading of Chapter 13 involves how we interpret what is understood by the "perfection" signified by these wounds: The stigmata should not be interpreted as a stopping point in some sort of bottom-up mystical journey through which Francis ascends from the world and into God so as to never again descend. Rather, if the stigmata are the outward sign of Francis's inner perfection, they signify that the "hierarchical activities" of purification, illumination, and perfection have all become fully "activated" within him. Tellingly, for example, the Seraphic Doctor begins Chapter 13 of the *Legenda maior* in the following way:

It was custom for the angelic man [*angelico viro*] Francis never to rest from the good, rather, like the heavenly spirits on Jacob's Ladder, he was either ascending into God [*ascendebat in Deum*] or descending to his neighbor [*descendebat ad proximum*]. For he had so prudently learned how to divide the

---

34. *Leg. Maj.* 13.10 (8, 545).
35. *Leg. Maj.* 13.7 (8, 544).
36. See Chapter 7.

time given for merit, that sometimes he devoted himself to working for the benefit of his neighbors and dedicated the remaining time to tranquil contemplation.[37]

The significance of Bonaventure's use of the symbol of Jacob's Ladder in this passage cannot be overstated. We have already seen this symbol used by the Seraphic Doctor repeatedly: He employs it in his discussion of the hierarchical activities of the macrocosm within his sermon *De sancti angelis*;[38] the symbol also reappears frequently in his theology in order to describe the ascending, descending, and returning valences at work within the hierarchical soul;[39] and finally, there are parallels between the Seraphic Doctor's use of this symbol and his claim that Christ is the Ladder upon which grace flows throughout the hierarchies so as to purify, illuminate, and perfect all rational creatures.[40] For Bonaventure, as I have already argued, the symbol "enfleshes his discursive speculations"[41] surrounding grace and hierarchy.[42] In his theology—whether with respect to the macrocosm or the microcosm—to be conformed to God and to receive the divine similitude through sanctifying grace is to be transformed into a Jacob's Ladder. Here, we see how Francis can truly be said to embody Bonaventure's doctrine of grace, in that Bonaventure explicitly calls Francis a "Jacob's Ladder," one who can be called "perfect" only insofar as he prudently learned to divide his time between contemplative "ascent" and a "descent" through meritorious action. Importantly, moreover, it is within the Seraphic Doctor's ensuing account of the stigmata in Chapter 13 of the *Legenda maior* that we can also begin to identify significant differences between his own account of the "hierarchical soul" and the angelic anthropology of the twelfth-century Victorine, Thomas Gallus.

Indeed, in contrast to Bonaventure's portrait of Francis, the Victorine had notably relegated his angelic anthropology entirely to the realm of contemplation, at one point even exclaiming in his commentary on the *Song*, "it is not for the contemplative man to stretch out

<hr>

37. *Leg. Maj.* 13.1 (8, 542).

38. See again my treatment of this sermon in Chapter 3.

39. See Chapter 4–5.

40. See my introduction to Chapter 7.

41. Again, I borrow this phrase from Jay M. Hammond, "Appendix: Order in the *Itinerarium*," 198.

42. See Katherine Wrisley Shelby, "Grace, Hierarchy, and the Symbol of Jacob's Ladder," 207–28.

for the care of others, but only to his own interior orders."[43] Unlike Gallus, Bonaventure was a follower of the little poor man from Assisi, whose way of life and stigmatized body contextualized his entire theological project, including his understanding of grace and its related effects within the human person. As the Seraphic Doctor reports in Chapter 13 of the *Legenda maior*, "the angelic man Francis descended from the mountain, carrying with him the likeness of the Crucified, not on tablets of stone or on panels of wood carved by artisans, but written in the members of his flesh *by the finger of the living God*."[44] Through the stigmata, Francis can truly be called a *vir hierarchicus*, an angelic man whose very flesh has been conformed to the object of his affection, Christ. In the prologue to the *Itinerarium*, Bonaventure had insisted that the only way the mind can be uplifted to an affective union with Christ is "through a most burning love of the Crucified," the sort of love, he wrote, which "so absorbed the mind of Francis … that his mind became apparent in his flesh."[45] No longer relegated only to the realm of the intelligible, as is arguably the case with Gallus's own notion of the hierarchical soul, St. Bonaventure's account of what it means to be "holy" pours forth into the sensible realm through Francis's sacred wounds. He not only has a hierarchical soul, but indeed can be called a hierarchical *man*: one who has been sanctified in both soul and body through the sacred stigmata.

This difference between the angelic anthropologies of the Franciscan and the Victorine further significantly underscores the idea that the "perfective moment" in the *Legenda maior* cannot be confined only to a consideration of Francis's "own interior orders." When the Seraphic Doctor writes in Chapter 13 that "the angelic man Francis descended from the mountain, carrying with him the likeness of the Crucified," this claim indeed foreshadows another rather crucial moment within his account of the hierarchical soul in *Hex.* 22. There, when the Seraphic Doctor transitions from his discussion of the ascending valence within the hierarchical soul to his discussion of the descending valence, following Gallus, he details how the former culminates in the order of the seraph, represented by charity. Once the soul has thus ascended

---

43. Thomas Gallus, *Commentaires du Cantique des cantique*, 84: "… et nota quod non est viri contemplativi intendere cure animarum aliarum, sed tantum suis interioribus ordinibus."

44. *Leg. Maj.* 13.5 (8, 543).

45. *Itin.* prol. 3 (5, 295).

to the seraphic order (again following Gallus), Bonaventure proceeds to describe how the charity of the seraph overflows through the lower eight angelic orders within the soul. This descending valence is organized by the Seraphic Doctor into three categories: First, the seraphim, cherubim, and thrones "receive" divine illuminations in the descending valence; second, the dominions, virtues, and powers next "maintain" these illuminations within the soul; and third, the principalities, archangels, and angels "freely pour out" these illuminations outward to others in the final act of descent.[46] In other words, whereas the ascending movement within the hierarchical soul ends with the level of the seraph in *Hex.* 22, the descending movement begins with the seraph. Of this "beginning," Bonaventure notes:

For the soul to receive these lights, it needs vivacious desire, perspicacious scrutiny, and tranquil judgments. For the contemplative soul is not without vivacious desire. Anyone who does not have this has nothing of contemplation, for the source of lights is from the highest things to the lowest things, and not the other way around. This vivacious desire corresponds to the seraphim, which is ardent like fire; and so fire has the greatest signification in scripture. Moses ascended to the summit of the mountain to this burning fire, and nevertheless he first saw that fire at the foot of the mountain. For Moses could not have descended for the purposes of teaching the people [*ad erudiendum populum*], unless he had first ascended to that fire. Thus, desire disposes the soul for receiving light.[47]

Within Bonaventure's portrait of the hierarchical soul in *Hex.* 22, the contemplative union with God experienced by the soul at the level of the seraph is the "fire" that ignites the soul to descend from charity to "the humility of following [*ad humilitatem obsequii*]." Moses ascends the mountain of contemplation, which then enables his descent "for the purposes of teaching the people." Bonaventure's use of this same Old Testament trope in his discussion of the stigmata in the *Legenda maior* is in no wise accidental. It suggests that Francis's wounded flesh, though a sign that he has indeed ascended to the fiery summit of the seraphic order, also signifies that he comes down from the mountain and goes back out into the world.

---

46. I discussed these different valences at length in Chapter 5. See *Hex.* 22.28 (5, 441): "But this has to happen according to the powers of the soul, which are three according to Dionysius: receiving, maintaining, and distributing, so that we might copiously receive, copiously maintain, and freely pour out, whence, '*freely you have received, so freely give.*'"

47. *Hex.* 22.29 (5, 441–42).

This is corroborated when readers of the *Legenda maior* turn from Chapter 13 to Chapter 14 of the text. As Armstrong and Hammond have both already noted, within the macrostructure of the text, Chapters 14–15 correspond with the hierarchical activity of perfection and treat the subjects of Francis's death and canonization, respectively. Bonaventure begins Chapter 14:

Thus now fixed with Christ to the cross in both flesh and with his spirit, Francis not only burned with a seraphic love in God but also was thirsting with Christ Crucified for the multitude of those to be saved. Since he could not walk because of the nails coming out of his feet, he had his dying body carried around the cities and towns so that others would be animated to carry the cross of Christ. He was also saying to his brothers: "Brothers, let us begin to serve the Lord our God because up until now we have done little." He also burned with a great desire to return to his beginning in humility [*flagrabat etiam desiderio magno ad humilitatis redire primordia*], that he might minister to the lepers as he did at the beginning, and so that he might once again treat his body like a servant as he did formerly, which was already collapsing from work. With Christ leading, he resolved to do mighty deeds, and even with weakening limbs, he was hoping to triumph over his enemies in a new battle with a strong and fervid spirit. For there is no place for apathy or laziness where the goad of love always urges to greater things [*amoris stimulus semper ad maiora perurget*]. But there was in him such a harmony of flesh and spirit and such readiness for obedience, that, when he struggled to attain all holiness [*sanctitatem*], not only did the flesh not resist it, but it even tried to run ahead.[48]

The stigmata were a sign of Francis's sanctity, a sign that he had indeed been transformed into a *vir hierarchicus* "in both flesh and spirit." As one "fixed with Christ to the cross," however, the Poverello is not a *vir hierarchicus* only insofar as he experienced a contemplative union with God through the miracle of the stigmata; rather, he is "hierarchical" insofar as this union causes him to "thirst with Christ crucified for the multitude of those to be saved," to "burn with a great desire to return to the humility he practiced at the beginning; to nurse the lepers as he did at the outset" of his ministry. "With Christ as leader, he resolved to 'do great deeds,'" writes Bonaventure. This passage foreshadows the Seraphic Doctor's remarks concerning holy desire and the seraphic order within the hierarchical soul in *Hex.* 22. There, the soul can only be

---

48. *Leg. Maj.* 14.1 (8, 545).

called "hierarchical" insofar as it descends from the burning charity of the seraph for the purposes of "teaching the people," a desire which will lead finally to the soul's descent to its neighbor in "the humility of following."[49] Here in the *Legenda maior*, the miracle of the stigmata similarly incites Francis with "a great desire to return to the humility he practiced at the beginning." The Poverello does not cease being a Jacob's Ladder after his miraculous experience; rather, his reception of the stigmata signifies that his whole person—both his spirit and his body—has been inflamed by the burning love of the seraphic order for the purposes of descending to his neighbor.

This is further significant inasmuch the Seraphic Doctor defines hierarchical perfection according to the movements of the Hierarch throughout salvation history as the Uncreated, Incarnate, and Crucified Word. We recall that, according to Bonaventure, Christ can be called the Hierarch because he descended from glory in an act of complete, kenotic humility to be united to lowly human flesh,[50] and hierarchy is only fully "upheaved" on the cross, where the Incarnate Word descends to the point of suffering and death as the Crucified Word. Francis, likewise, can be called hierarchical because his own experience of union with God incites him to descend to the leper, the lowest and most despicable sort of flesh in his own day. His stigmatic wounds themselves evoke this imagery of descent, whereby what is most divine—what is most holy—is not a mystical experience that takes place apart from the world; rather, Francis's holiness breaks through his flesh in a way that incites longing within him to embrace what is most lowly, most despicable, and that which suffers most within the world.[51] Unlike in Gallus's angelic anthropology, Bonaventure's inclusion of the flesh within his account of Francis's "hierarchization" necessitates that he not confine his discussion of holiness to an account of Francis's "own interior orders"; rather, if the hierarchical soul functions perfectly, then the charity of the seraph will overflow in the descending valence, not only to enliven the "interior orders" within Francis's soul, but also inundating outwardly through meritorious actions toward the Poverello's leprous neighbor as well. Francis is a saint because he has been made "as like

<hr>

49. See again *Hex.* 22.33 (5, 442).

50. See Chapter 7.

51. See Timothy J. Johnson, "Speak Lord, Your Servant Is Listening: Obedience and Prayer in Franciscan Spirituality," *The Cord* 42, no. 2 (1992): 36–45.

as possible" to the Hierarch, the Incarnate and Crucified Word, whose own descent to lowly human flesh and death on the cross represents the perfection of every hierarchy. Francis himself can be called "perfect," "holy," and "hierarchical" because his spiritual ascent leads him back to "the beginning," to the flesh of the leper in the "humility of following" after the example of Christ.

Lest readers be tempted to read Bonaventure's portrait of Francis in the *Legenda maior* as an anomaly, however, we need only turn from the *Legenda maior* to Bonaventure's sermons on St. Francis to confirm this "shape" of sanctity in his thought.[52] On October 4, 1267, the Seraphic Doctor preached both a "Morning" and "Evening" sermon on St. Francis to his brothers in Paris, both of which expound upon Is 42:1: "Behold my servant whom I uphold, my chosen in whom my soul delights; I have put my spirit upon him, he will bring forth justice to the nations."[53] Bonaventure devotes both sermons to an explanation of Francis's remarkable holiness, and uses this text from Isaiah to define sanctity for his brothers:

For the root of perfect sanctity [*perfectae sanctitatis radix*] rests in deep humility [*humilitate profunda*]; the height of sanctity [*celsitudo sanctitatis*] rests in proven virtue [*virtute probata*]; but the diffusion of perfect sanctity [*diffusio sanctitatis perfectae*] rests in full charity [*caritate plenaria*]. For humanity is received by God through deep humility; we are made acceptable to God in proven virtue; but we are raised up to the Lord and inclined to our neighbor in the fullness of charity. Thus, St. Francis is commended by these words for his deep humility, through which he was received by God, as is noted when the text says: *Behold my servant whom I uphold*. Second, he is commended for his proven virtue, through which he is made pleasing to the Lord, when it says: *my chosen in whom my soul delights*. Third, he is commended for the fullness of his charity, through which he was carried into God and opened himself for the sake of his neighbor, when it says: *I have put my spirit upon him*, etc. Who, then, is the one who is perfectly holy [*perfectus sanctus*]? Hear: it is he who has within himself deep humility, proven virtue, and full charity. The root of sanctity begins in humility [*in humilitate incipit*], it is accomplished in proven virtue [*in virtute probata proficit*], and it is consummated in the fullness of

---

52. For more on the theology of Bonaventure's sermons on Francis, see especially Zachary Hayes, "The Theological Image of St. Francis of Assisi in the Sermons of St. Bonaventure," in *Bonaventuriana: Miscellanea in onore di Jacques Guy Bougerol, OFM*, ed. Chavero Blanco (Roma: Edizioni Antonianum, 1988), 323–45.

53. *Sermo 57*, in *SD* 2, 749: "*Ecce servus meus, suscipiam eum, electus meus, complacuit sibi in illo anima mea, dedi Spiritum meum super illum et iudicium gentibus proferet, Isaiae 42.*"

love [*in caritate plenaria consummatur*]. Humility causes us to be received by God, virtue makes us pleasing to God, but the fullness of charity causes us to be totally carried into God [*in Deum totaliter excedamus*] so that we might communicate what we have to others [*aliis communicemus quod habemus*].[54]

Bonaventure will continue both his "Morning" and "Evening" sermons on St. Francis to expound upon each one of these three characteristics of the Poverello's "perfect sanctity," whereby his Morning Sermon treats Francis's deep humility and perfect virtue, while his Evening Sermon is devoted to a discussion of Francis's perfect charity. The same threefold rhythm that drives the Seraphic Doctor's discussion of the Poverello's sanctity in the *Legenda maior* likewise informs this shorter piece of hagiography, with "humility" corresponding to the purgative moment, "virtue" corresponding to the illuminative moment, and "charity" corresponding to the perfective moment. Once again, all three hierarchical activities are required in order for the saint to achieve "perfect sanctity." The perfective moment, as Bonaventure elaborates it in his Evening Sermon on St. Francis, is, moreover, not confined only to a discussion of Francis's ascent to a contemplative union with God; rather, as indicated in his above remarks, perfect charity causes the saint to "be totally carried into God *so that we might communicate what we have to others* [my emphasis]." The goal of a hierarchy is to conform rational creatures to the Trinity by transforming them into a divine similitude; the rational creature can only become like God through a hierarchy, however, insofar as it possesses what Bonaventure calls in *II Sent.* "the fruitfulness of plenitude [*plenitudinis ubertatem*] … namely, in this, that [the creature's participation in a hierarchy] would not only suffice for themselves, but also, because of the plenitude of charity and grace, that it would enable them to assist others [*alios adjuvare*]."[55] The Poverello's saintly perfection as Bonaventure describes it in his Morning Sermon on St. Francis corresponds with this previous assertion about what hierarchy means: Francis is perfect because he enjoys this "fruitfulness of plenitude" (*plenitudinis ubertatem*)—he has been "totally carried into God" in such a way that he can "communicate to others" the *influentia* of grace that he has so perfectly received.

In his Evening Sermon, then, Bonaventure opens his discussion of this sort of charity by writing:

<hr>

54. *Sermo 57*, in *SD* 2, 751.
55. Again, see *II Sent.* d. 9, prol. (2, 462).

Third, he is commended for the fullness of his love when the text says: *I have put my spirit upon him, he will bring forth justice to the nations.* Paul says in his Epistle to the Romans: *The love of God has been poured into our hearts through the Holy Spirit who has been given to us.* The Holy Spirit is given when charity is given. The Lord placed *His Spirit* in Francis, and afterwards, he gave *justice* [*dedit iudicium*]. Thus we read in the Gospel: *For it is not you who speak, but the Spirit of the Father who is speaking in you.* It says that God gave the *Spirit over him.* Who is this Spirit? It is the Spirit who made it possible for him to teach others [*qui alios posset docere*], that is, he gave Francis a hierarchical spirit [*dedit ei spiritum hierarchicum*]. For it is written: *By his Spirit the heavens were adorned.* And Gregory writes: "The adornments of heaven are the virtues of the preachers." I say that God gave to Francis a purgative [*purgativum*], illuminative [*illuminativum*], and perfective spirit [*perfectivum spiritum*], because the Spirit of the Lord first purified him, secondly illuminated him, and thirdly made him perfect.[56]

A hierarchical spirit, for Bonaventure, is a spirit that descends "to teach others" in charity. God gave Francis this spirit to purify, illuminate, and perfect him for the purposes of "giving justice," so that Francis's seraphic charity would overflow to others through his teaching, preaching, and service to the lepers. This is what "holiness" means according to the Seraphic Doctor.

One technically need not look further than Francis to see how Bonaventure's systematic doctrine of grace walks hand in hand with his hagiographical examinations of sanctity. The Poverello embodies his doctrine of grace: As one in whom "the grace of God our Savior has appeared in these last days," Francis is a *vir hierarchicus,* one who has been made "as like as possible to God" in both soul and body. The three hierarchical activities that characterize the macro-, intermediate-, and microstructures within the *Legenda maior* itself are likewise always at work within Francis. For Bonaventure, the Poverello is a Jacob's Ladder, one who has achieved saintly perfection not in the sense that he has arrived at a contemplative union with God that causes him to leave the world; rather, Francis's hierarchical spirit is so enlivened that he can truly be said to spiral between the heights of a seraphic embrace with God and the despised flesh of the lepers in his midst. In Francis, Bonaventure's doctrine of grace finds flesh.

56. *Sermo 57,* in *SD* 2, 767–68.

The Virgin Mary: The *Mulier hierarchica*

As important as they are, Bonaventure's hagiographical treatments of Francis are certainly not the only texts from which to glean an understanding of his theology of sanctity. His *Sermones de sanctis* remain largely unstudied by Bonaventurean scholars. While English translations of his sermons on St. Francis from this collection have appeared (including the Morning and Evening Sermon on St. Francis cited above),[57] most of these sermons remain un-translated and have garnered relatively little interest among both scholars of the Seraphic Doctor and scholars of medieval sermons. Alongside the *Legenda maior* and *Legenda minor*, however, they provide some of the richest and most extensive material pertaining to Bonaventure's teachings on sanctity. Jacques Guy Bougerol's edition of the *Sermones de sanctis*, culled down to Bonaventure's authentic sermons in contradistinction to the collection that appears in the eighth volume of the *Opera omnia*,[58] includes twenty-nine sermons on various saints. As mentioned before, Johnson has argued that Bonaventure intended through them to present the saints as "incarnate 'forms' of divine grace" to urge his brothers to spiritual reform.[59] Here, I examine a selection of these sermons to confirm their continuity with his systematic doctrine of grace in this respect. These saints are holy, as we shall see, because they, like Francis, have been "hierarchized" into a divine similitude. Since the dates and specific contexts of these sermons all vary (Bougerol orders them according to the liturgical calendar), my analyses of these texts will be thematic, highlighting points of theological continuity between Bonaventure's various presentations of different saints and his systematic doctrine of grace. I begin with the Virgin Mary.

Indeed, with the exception of Bonaventure's hagiographical literature on Francis, nowhere is my claim that the saints embody his theology of grace more apparent than in his sermons on Mary. Bougerol's edition of the *Sermones de sanctis* include ten sermons devoted to her:

---

57. English translations of Bonaventure's sermons on Francis appear in *FAED* 2, 508–24, 718–68; and in Eric Doyle, trans. and ed., *The Disciple and the Master: St. Bonaventure's Sermons on St. Francis of Assisi* (Chicago: Franciscan Herald Press, 1983).

58. See especially Bougerol, introduction to *SD* 1, 3–64, and my note about this regarding the *Sermones de sanctis* edition above.

59. See again Johnson, "Reform, Hagiography, and Sanctity," 189, as well as my longer quotation of this article in my introduction above.

three for the Feast of her Purification;[60] two for the Feast of the Annunciation;[61] four for the Feast of her Assumption;[62] and one for the Feast of her Nativity.[63] There are only twenty-nine authentic sermons included in Bougerol's edition to begin with, so these sermons on Mary comprise roughly a third of the Seraphic Doctor's known or affirmed extant sermons on the saints. Space does not permit my drawing from each of these ten sermons in great detail, but it is nonetheless important to underscore that these collectively remain a rich resource for various avenues of further research for Bonaventurean scholars, including most especially the Seraphic Doctor's Mariology,[64] his Ecclesiology,[65] and his theology of hierarchy.[66] The collection of sermons devoted to Mary in the *Sermones de sanctis* are replete with explanations of the latter and thus provide an excellent resource for further demonstration of my argument in this chapter that the saints in Bonaventure's theology embody his doctrine of grace. My own comments will here focus on *Sermo 39* in Bougerol's edition, which is the first sermon within that collection treating the theme, *"On the Purification of the Blessed Virgin Mary,"* since this especially lends itself to providing evidence for this claim with respect to Mary. If Francis can be called a *vir hierarchicus* in the *Legenda maior*, as this sermon shows, it is only because Mary was first a *mulier hierarchica*.

Bougerol gives a probable date of February 2, 1268, for this text, the

---

60. *Sermo 39*, in *SD* 2, 516–39; *Sermo 40*, in *SD* 2, 539–48; *Sermo 41*, in *SD* 2, 548–54.

61. *Sermo 42*, in *SD* 2, 554–63; *Sermo 43*, in *SD* 2, 563–78.

62. *Sermo 49*, in *SD* 2, 641–53; *Sermo 50*, in *SD* 2, 653–59; *Sermo 51*, in *SD* 2, 660–67; *Sermo 52*, in *SD* 2, 667–78.

63. *Sermo 53*, in *SD* 2, 679–84.

64. For more on Bonaventure's Mariology and accompanying bibliography, especially as it is expounded in Bonaventure's sermons on the saints, see especially J. Isaac Goff, *"Mulier amicta sole:* Bonaventure's Preaching on the Marian Mode of the Incarnation and Marian Mediation in his Sermons on the Annunciation," in *Medieval Franciscan Approaches to the Virgin Mary: Mater sanctissima, misericordia, et dolorosa*, ed. Steven J. McMichael and Katherine Wrisley Shelby (Leiden: Brill, 2019), 53–83. Goff provides a fine and thorough examination of Bonaventure's sermons on the Annunciation while also providing a useful general introduction to the Seraphic Doctor's Mariology. It is my hope that my own examination of one of Bonaventure's sermons on Mary's Purification will serve as a companion to Goff's excellent work in this respect. See also Hellmann, *Divine and Created Order*, 161–63, where he further corroborates my claims with respect to Mary's sanctity as I will expound them, below, summed up in his subheading: "The Mother of God Is the Most Ordered Soul."

65. See also Goff, *"Mulier amicta sole."*

66. I have already examined another sermon from the *Sermones de sanctis*, namely, *Sermo 54, De sanctis angelis* in *SD* 2 to expound upon Bonaventure's theology of hierarchy in Chapter 3.

first and longest of three sermons on Mary's Purification in his collection.[67] Perhaps given at Paris, without a definite date, the context for the sermon is not known for sure.[68] The sermon builds from Bonaventure's interpretation of Mal 3:3b: "He shall purify the sons of Levi, and shall refine them as gold, and as silver, and they shall offer sacrifices to the Lord in justice."[69] After a protheme,[70] the Seraphic Doctor suggests that this verse can be interpreted in a twofold way: The first part of the verse, "He shall purify the sons of Levi . . .," refers to "the purification of the glorious Virgin," which "signifies the purification of the ecclesiastical hierarchy." Accordingly, the second part of the verse, ". . . and they shall offer sacrifices to the Lord in justice," refers to the oblation of the Savior, who brings sacrificial justice in the New Testament by means of Mary's purity.[71] The sermon unfolds these themes by providing an extended meditation on Mary's purity in relation to the purity of the ecclesiastical hierarchy. For all those who have received grace through the oblation of the Savior in the ecclesiastical hierarchy, Mary is the exemplar of purity, one who was perfectly sanctified through grace. "The purification of the glorious Virgin signifies the purification of the ecclesiastical hierarchy in two ways," as Bonaventure writes, "one through baptismal grace, another through penitential grace."

He next explains that there are two general types of sin which separate people in the Church from the Kingdom of God, original and actual sin, while insisting that everyone within the ecclesiastical hierarchy must be purified from both types of sin. Original sin is met by baptismal grace, while actual sin is retracted through penitential grace. It will be Bonaventure's task throughout the sermon, then, to show how Mary was also:

Purified in this twofold way, namely, *interiorly according to truth* [*interius secundum veritatem*] and *exteriorly according to representation* [*exterius*

---

67. See *SD* 2, 517.

68. See Johnson, "Reform, Hagiography, and Sanctity: Bonaventure's Sermons on the Saints," 195. Johnson there discusses the dating for Bonaventure's sermon on St. Agnes, which I will discuss further below, and which is pertinent here with respect to Bougerol's dating for this sermon on Mary's purification: "The audience for Bonaventure's *Sermo 37* is unclear, although the date may be 21 January 1268, according to Bougerol. There is no rubric that clarifies where the sermon took place, but Paris would be the strongest possibility given Bonaventure's tendency to remain in that region during the winter months."

69. *Sermo 39*, in *SD* 2, 517.

70. Based on Prv 15:26: "*Abominationes sunt Domino cogitationes malae et purus sermo et pulcherrimus firmabitur.*"

71. *Sermo 39*, in *SD* 2, 519.

secundum repraesentationem] [my emphasis]; and thus she needed baptismal grace [*gratia baptismali*] or its equivalent, because she was conceived in the common way [*quia secundum communem usum concepta fuit*] and thus contracted original sin [*ideo peccatum originale contraxit*]; but she did not need penitential grace [*gratia paenitentiali*] because she did not commit actual sin [*peccatum actuale*].[72]

Expounding upon both points as Bonaventure discusses Mary's "two-fold purification" throughout the remainder of the sermon will serve the purpose of demonstrating my argument that Mary can be said to embody his doctrine of grace. If Francis is the *vir hierarchicus,* Mary is the *mulier hierarchica,* apart from whom no one in the ecclesiastical hierarchy could be purified.

Mary's "Interior Purification according to Truth"

First, Bonaventure discusses Mary's interior purity. The Seraphic Doctor here must address an obvious problem: If Mary "was conceived in the common way and thus contracted original sin," how was she purified from original sin? How, likewise, can she signify the ecclesiastical hierarchy's purification from original sin? Bonaventure answers these questions by suggesting that Mary, though "conceived in the common way," was nonetheless preserved from the effects of original sin insofar as the inflowing of sanctifying grace was gifted to her while she was still in her mother's womb. Bonaventure is careful to show how the "integrity of [Mary's] human nature [*integritas humanae naturae*]" was preserved through sanctifying grace despite her "common" birth. The Virgin, according to Bonaventure, "was interiorly purified in truth through the reception of sanctifying grace, by which she was purified by that perfect purification which is designated in Prv 25:4: *'Take away the rust from the silver, and there shall come forth a most pure vessel.'"* As he explains, "The integrity of [Mary's] human nature" is designated by the *"silver,"* while the *"rust"* signifies the original sin she contracted in her mother's womb. The removal of rust from the silver signifies the sanctifying grace "by which she was sanctified in the womb so that she might be made into a *most pure vessel*; she was sanctified through an excellent grace through which original sin was deleted from her with respect to its stain, namely, in her mind; with respect to what followed,

---

72. *Sermo 39,* in *SD* 2, 519–20.

namely, in her sensuality; and also with respect to its cause, namely, in its root, from the union of the soul with faulty flesh."[73]

Mary thus stands out amid humanity as one who received the *influentia* of sanctifying grace in the womb (*influxum gratiae sanctificantis in utero*), so that "neither the spot nor subsequent sin nor the cause of sin would remain in her."[74] She was purified in this way, moreover, "so that she might conceive the Son of God," through whom the Church would be fecundated [*fecundatur*] and purified from its own spots through the waters of baptismal grace.[75] After Christ, in other words, Mary is representative of what human nature looks like apart from original sin. In this way, she is the exemplar for the "interior" purification of the ecclesiastical hierarchy; had she not been sanctified in the womb, the waters of grace that wipe away the spot of original sin would not flow into anyone.

Mary's "Exterior Purification according to Representation"

Second, and most importantly for our present purposes, Bonaventure next discusses how the Church nonetheless "frequently suffers defeat in its members."[76] Those within the Church *in via* continuously commit sin even after they have received sanctifying grace, so they continuously need penitential grace as well.[77] Again, Mary serves as an exemplar for this penitential grace for those within the ecclesiastical hierarchy: But how?

Unlike those within the Church, Mary was sanctified while still in the womb and thus never committed any actual sins. According to Bonaventure, those who have committed actual sins and who still belong to the Church *in via*, require penitential purification of three types: (1) Legal penance, represented by Moses, who fasted for forty days so that he might receive the Law; (2) prophetic penance, represented by Elijah, who fasted for forty days so that he might arrive at "the secret colloquy of God [*secretum colloquium Dei*]"; and (3) evangelical penance, represented by Christ, who fasted for forty days "before he began

73. *Sermo 39*, in *SD* 2, 520.
74. *Sermo 39*, in *SD* 2, 520.
75. *Sermo 39*, in *SD* 2, 521.
76. *Sermo 39*, in *SD* 2, 522.
77. For more on actual sin, as well as the concept of sin in general, in Bonaventure's theology, see especially Johnson, "Part III: On the Corruption of Sin," in *Bonaventure Revisited*, 169–94; de Wacther, *Le péché actuel selon Saint Bonaventure*.

to preach [*antequam inciperet praedicare*]."[78] Bonaventure's elaboration of these three types of penitence reinforces what ought by now be familiar themes. First, he explains, fear of judgment through God's Law leads to the penitential purification of those in the Church, since this fear of judgment will lead those within the ecclesiastical hierarchy to repent of their guilt.[79] Second, a "more excellent [*excellentior*]" type of penitence is that which can be associated with Elijah. This "prophetic" type of penitence arises from the "ardor of emulating justice [*ardore emulationis iustitiae*]" and leads to a burning charity. Repenting of their sins, those within the ecclesiastical hierarchy receive the Holy Spirit, which ignites in them a fiery love for God and their neighbor.[80] Finally, Bonaventure's explanation of the third type of "evangelical" penance builds upon Tb 12:9, "For alms delivereth from death, and the same is that which purgeth away sins, and maketh to find mercy and life everlasting," in order to argue that the Church is most perfectly purified when it practices works of mercy.[81] These three penitential remedies correspond with the hierarchical rhythm that structures Bonaventure's portrait of the Poverello in the *Legenda maior* and in his sermons on St. Francis. Because they will continue to commit actual sins even after they have consented to receiving the *influentia* of sanctifying grace, those in the Church *in via* continuously need to keep submitting themselves to grace through legal penance, or their adherence to the Law inspired by fear of punishment (purification); through prophetic penance, or their burning love for God and neighbor inspired by the charity of the Holy Spirit, which leads them, like Elijah, to "the secret colloquy of God" (illumination); and through evangelical penance, which leads them to follow Christ through works of mercy (perfection).

What, though, does any of this have to do with Mary? Since she did not ever commit any actual sins, Mary was perfectly purified in all three of the above-mentioned ways, as Bonaventure writes: "But all these purifications were designated in the Glorious Virgin."[82] It is only

---

78. Before making these associations, Bonaventure provides a rather lengthy description of why the number forty is associated with penitential grace in the first place. See *Sermo 39*, in *SD* 2, 523–24, at 523: "Igitur in numero quadragenario designatur integritas paenitentiae: et est in Maria non propter eam sed propter Ecclesiam.…"

79. For Bonaventure's discussion of "legal" penitence, see *Sermo 39*, in *SD* 2, 524–25.

80. For Bonaventure's discussion of this "prophetic" type of penitence, see *Sermo 39*, in *SD* 2, 525.

81. See especially *Sermo 39*, in *SD* 2, 525.

82. *Sermo 39*, in *SD* 2, 524.

after elaborating on all three types of penance that Bonaventure returns to consider Mary:

[Evangelical purification] presupposes the other two types of purification, namely, the purification of Moses and Elijah…. These three purifications are ordered in this way, because what is from fear is like a foundation; what is from the sweetness of divine mercy is what completes it. And so the first is purgative [*purificativa*]; the second is purgative and illuminative [*purificativa et illuminativa*]; but the third is purgative, illuminative, and perfective [*purificativa, illuminativa, et perfectiva*]. These three existed simultaneously [*haec tria simul fuerunt*] in the glorious Virgin. For she is *totally beautiful* and *no stain is within* her. She had within herself the total adornment of the ecclesiastical hierarchy; and in this way, she is the beauty of the celestial hierarchy. *For she is the Purgatrix, Illuminatrix, and Perfectrix* [my emphasis]. We have been failed unless the name of the Virgin means these three things. For "Mary" is interpreted as the sea of bitterness, as the one who has been illuminated, and as the Mistress; she receives purgative, illuminative, and perfecting graces [*suscepit gratias purgativas, illuminativas et perficientes*]. She had purgative graces inasmuch as she was a sea of bitterness, having the most vehement sorrow, as it is written: *And your soul will be pierced with a sword.* She had illuminating graces because she was totally illuminated, and thus can rightly be called, "Mary." The first illumination came to her from the conception of the Word, about which the celestial hierarchy dares not even say anything. Finally, she had perfecting graces because she was perfect by the highest perfection. And because she had these three graces, thus she was the *Purgatrix*, the *Illuminatrix*, and the *Perfectrix*. The most common interpretation of Mary is as the "Star of the Sea," and in this interpretation, all others can be understood…. The glorious Virgin is the star of the sea, purifying, illuminating, and perfecting those who are in the seas of this world. We are thus following the star of the sea, being purified through the sighs of bitter compunction, being illuminated through the zeal of illuminating truth, and being perfected through the vow of perfection.[83]

The Seraphic Doctor will hereafter devote the remainder of *Sermo 39* to an extended reflection of how those within the ecclesiastical hierarchy may thus look to the "Star of the Sea" to follow her along the path of purgation, illumination, and perfection. I here offer three observations with respect to connecting this portrait of Mary with my previous comments regarding the sanctity of the Poverello.

First and most obviously, Bonaventure here explicitly calls Mary

---

83. *Sermo 39*, in *SD* 2, 526–27.

the Purgatrix, Illuminatrix, and Perfectrix. Free from original sin, as he elaborated in the first part of *Sermo 39,* the "Glorious Virgin" in Bonaventure's theology is representative of what human nature was created by God to be—namely, a similitude of the uncreated hierarchy that has been purified, illuminated, and perfected by the *influentia* of sanctifying grace. Because she receives the *influentia* of sanctifying grace in the womb, she is freed from committing any actual sins insofar as she is always perfectly hierarchical—she *is* the Purgatrix, Illuminatrix, and Perfectrix. St. Francis becomes a *vir hierarchicus* after his conversion, but Mary, by contrast, was perfectly sanctified even in her mother's womb: She is and always has been a *mulier hierarchica.* Like Francis, and indeed even more than Francis, Mary embodies the Seraphic Doctor's doctrine of grace in this way.

Second, Bonaventure's insistence in *Sermo 39* that these three hierarchical activities existed "simultaneously" in Mary walks hand in hand with his doctrine of grace as he treats it in other texts. Her perfection is founded upon her purification and illumination, as the Seraphic Doctor makes quite clear, but once she has reached the level of perfection, the other two activities do not cease to work within her. This idea certainly concurs with Bonaventure's more systematic descriptions of what a "hierarchical soul" looks like in his other works. Mary is hierarchical—she is the Purgatrix, Illuminatrix, and Perfectrix—because these three activities are always at work within her.

Third, and closely related to this second point, is Bonaventure's association of the "perfective moment" here with works of mercy. Like in Part 5 of the *Breviloquium* and in Chapters 13–14 of the *Legenda maior,* "illumination" leads the soul to a charity that inflames the person with love of God and neighbor in *Sermo 39.* "Perfection" is then associated with the descent to one's neighbor through preaching, giving alms, and works of mercy. Like Francis, Mary's saintly perfection does not refer to a bottom-up ascent from which she never again descends to help her neighbor; rather, Mary is called the *Perfectrix* because her splendid holiness leads her to a more holy way of life within the world, rather than apart from it.

Crucially, to expand this third point even further, Bonaventure is careful to underscore the fact that the Virgin's perfection is characterized by such works of mercy even unto glory. For example, in his *Sermo 49* "On the Assumption of the Blessed Virgin Mary" written in an unknown year,[84] Bonaventure asserts that Mary was elevated above all the hierarchies—both the ecclesiastical and celestial hierarchies—through her perfect beatitude. Because she is the Purgatrix, Illuminatrix, and Perfectrix, as Bonaventure writes, "she is therefore elevated above the purifying, illuminating, and perfecting angelic hierarchies, and also above the human hierarchy that needs to be purified, illuminated, and perfected."[85] Through her Assumption, Mary can be called "more perfect" than the angels,[86] but even this perfective moment—whereby Bonaventure assigns to Mary a holy authority that surpasses even the most perfect creatures in the celestial hierarchy—should not be understood as a merely static end. As Bonaventure continues *Sermo 49* to elaborate, from her place above all the heavenly and earthly hierarchies, Mary flows forth "the rewards of overflowing mercies [*praesidia supereffluentium misericordiarum*]" to all people.[87] Quite strikingly, the Seraphic Doctor elaborates this point by claiming in his conclusion to *Sermo 49* that Mary is "a place of fruitfulness [*locum ubertatis*]," whom those within the ecclesiastical hierarchy can call upon for help as they strive for glory amidst their struggles *in via*. This word, "*ubertatem*," is the same word used in Bonaventure's prologue to *II Sent.* d. 9 with respect to his claim that a rational creature's participation in a hierarchy likens it to God by causing it to become "fruitful" with respect to its neighbors.[88] Mary, as it were, has been perfectly hierarchized through grace, not because she has ascended above the angels to an unreachable height, but because at the height of her sanctity, she pours forth mercies upon all those who suffer within the hierarchies *in via*. Full of grace, she inflows graces to others in order that others might likewise become sanctified.

84. Bougerol gives a date of August 15 for this sermon, but does not indicate a year.

85. See *Sermo 49*, in *SD* 2, 648.

86. See *Sermo 49* in *SD* 2, and especially the extended discussion of this on 649–50. Significantly, the reason Bonaventure provides for this is due to the fact that Mary—unlike the angels—has both a beatified soul and a beatified body. See esp. 650: "... et beatitudo non esset consummata nisi personaliter ibi esset, et persona non sit anima sed coniunctum, id est corpus et animam...."

87. *Sermo 49*, in *SD* 2, 652. While those *in via* suffer, are "in lack," and seek defense, they seek the place of "fruitfulness," which they can attain by invoking Mary.

88. See again my comments on this phrase in Chapter 3, as well as my recollection of these comments in my treatment of St. Francis above. Most fundamentally, the word '*ubertatem*' recalls a mother who nurses her child at her breast; "breastfulness" might in this case especially be a more suitable translation than "fruitfulness," but I retain the latter for consistency. Nonetheless, more can certainly be said here with respect to the centrality of this feminine imagery within Bonaventure's doctrine of grace.

All these examples suggest that Mary, like Francis, is indeed an "incarnate 'form' of divine grace" in Bonaventure's theology. She, like the Poverello—and indeed even more than the Poverello—embodies the Seraphic Doctor's doctrine of grace insofar as he names her the Purgatrix, Illuminatrix, and Perfectrix who has been the recipient of sanctifying grace even from the womb. Through her sanctity, moreover, the entire Church will be nourished by the fruit of that womb. While my comments here have focused primarily on *Sermo 39* in demonstration of these themes, it must be noted that these are overwhelmingly corroborated throughout Bonaventure's other sermons on Mary in the *Sermones de sanctis,* as we briefly saw above in *Sermo 49.*[89] In equally as explicit ways, these consistently portray the "Glorious Virgin" as a hierarchical woman whose sanctity provides an exemplar of holiness for every rational creature who participates in the dance of the celestial and ecclesiastical hierarchies.[90]

Other Exemplars of Sanctity in the
Sermones de sanctis

What, though, of the other saints treated by the Seraphic Doctor in the *Sermones de sanctis*? While Francis and Mary provide obvious examples from which to glean an understanding of his theology of sanctity, these themes also appear both explicitly and implicitly in Bonaventure's sermons on the larger cast of saints throughout the liturgical year. Like Francis and Mary, these can be called "saints" because they have been conformed to God through the *influentia* of sanctifying grace, which hierarchizes them in both soul and body. Like Francis and Mary, these saints are "fruitful" exemplars of grace whom those in the ecclesiastical hierarchy can follow if they desire to be conformed to Christ. My comments here will highlight two such exemplars in addition to Francis and Mary, namely, Sts. Andrew and Agnes from *Sermo 35* and *Sermo 37,* respectively, before examining two of Bonaventure's sermons for the Feast of All the Saints, *Sermo 60* and *61,* in continued demonstration of these themes. The latter two sermons are especially useful for situating his theology of sanctity within the context of his ecclesiology. I treat

---

89. See especially Goff, "*Mulier amicta sole,*" 53–83.

90. Goff, "*Mulier amicta sole,*" 53–83; Hellmann, *Divine and Created Order,* 161–63.

each of these sermons in the order in which they appear in Bougerol's edition.

Sermo 35 on St. Andrew the Apostle

Johnson also examines Bonaventure's *Sermo 35* on St. Andrew for evidence of his claim that the saints are indeed "incarnate 'forms' of divine grace" in the Seraphic Doctor's *Sermones de sanctis*, noting how Andrew in particular would have "appealed to Bonaventure, no doubt, due to the apostle's status as the first disciple and later crucifixion."[91] *Sermo 35*, as Johnson has shown, was most likely preached to Bonaventure's brothers in Paris shortly before he was elected Minister General and is based on Jb 23:11, "My foot has followed his steps," a verse which would have held deep significance for Bonaventure and his brothers, "since the *Earlier Rule* of the Minorites urged them to follow the '*vestigia*' or 'footsteps' of Jesus Christ."[92] With respect to Andrew, Bonaventure encourages his brothers to understand this verse figuratively. Johnson summarizes the Seraphic Doctor's line of thought in this respect: "God is eternal, invisible, and without a body; thus God's 'foot' is the Eternal Word, Christ. Appealing to a decidedly metaphorical understanding of the body, he argues that just as feet support the entire person, so too, does Christ sustain all that exists."[93] Bonaventure explains this to his brothers:

That *foot*, Christ the eternal Word, *carrying all things*, imprints a twofold vestige in creatures, whether before the incarnation, or afterwards. Insofar as he is the *Wisdom* of God; he imprints the vestige of truth; but insofar as he is the *Power* of God, he imprints the vestige of virtue and sanctity, because it is said of Christ that he is the *Power of God and the Wisdom of God* in 1 Cor 1: 24; for *Wisdom* is of divine things and by *Power* he is sustaining all things. And according to this twofold vestige, he gives to us a twofold faculty, namely, intellective and affective [*intellectivam et affectivam*], one in truth, another in virtue. And this is the twofold perfection of the rational soul [*duplex perfectio animae rationalis*] according to the twofold life, namely, active [*activam*] and contemplative [*contemplativam*]. The active life is what perfects humanity in virtue; the contemplative is what perfects it in contemplation. And this saint

---

91. Johnson, "Reform, Hagiography, and Sanctity," 192.

92. Johnson, "Reform, Hagiography, and Sanctity," 192.

93. Johnson, "Reform, Hagiography, and Sanctity," 192; *Sermo 35*, in *SD* 2, 461.

had this twofold vestige [*duplex vestigium*]; whence it is said in the above: 'My foot has followed his steps.'[94]

The Seraphic Doctor will devote the remainder of the sermon to an explanation of each of these two "vestiges," first explaining how Andrew was imprinted with the vestige of virtue and concluding with an explanation of how he was likewise imprinted with the vestige of truth.

Readers will note that the hierarchical vocabulary which inundates Bonaventure's discussion of Francis and Mary is here not as explicit with respect to Andrew. Andrew's perfection involves the sanctification of his rational soul, which is twofold—rather than threefold, according to the familiar pattern of purification, illumination, and perfection that has commanded our examination of Bonaventure's treatments of the saints thus far. This is perhaps due in part to Bonaventure's context at the time he preached the sermon. Written "in close proximity" to his composition of his *Sentences* commentary, this is an intellectualized sermon intended to appeal to his learned brothers in Paris.[95] His exhortation concerning the rational soul must be read within this university context. The brothers must, like Andrew, be "imprinted" with Christ's virtue and truth if they are to follow the footsteps of Christ as exhorted by their *Rule*. He is essentially telling his brothers—who spend their days studying Aristotle and the rational soul—that the rational soul must yet be touched by Christ if it is to become perfect.

Despite the fact that Andrew is not called a *vir hierarchicus* in *Sermo 35*, Bonaventure's emphasis on the perfection of the active and contemplative lives is nonetheless congruent with his discussions of Francis's sanctity in the *Legenda maior*: The saint, once again, is one who has been perfected in both ways. The rational soul can only become perfect when both its intellective and affective faculties have been imprinted by Christ's Wisdom and Power. This observation becomes significant when we dwell on the conclusion to *Sermo 35*, where Bonaventure discusses how Christ imprinted the vestige of truth, or the "wisdom of God the Father,"[96] within Andrew. Bonaventure focuses on the practical outcome of this with respect to his brothers' studies in a university context: "Andrew was likened unto Christ in the doctrine of truth," he writes, because he followed Christ's footsteps with a "straight foot [*pede*

94. *Sermo 35*, in *SD* 2, 461–62.
95. Johnson, "Reform, Hagiography, and Sanctity," 192–93.
96. *Sermo 35*, in *SD* 2, 466.

directo], a strengthened foot [*pede munito*], and a hastened foot [*pede accelerato*]." He continues: "He followed with a right foot for the purposes of discerning truth; with a strengthened foot for the purposes of defending the truth; and with a hastened foot for the purposes of divulging truth throughout the world. Thus also let us follow in the footsteps of truth."[97] According to Bonaventure in this sermon, Andrew walked with a "straight foot," first of all, because the illumination of faith led him to right belief. Instructed through unction, he defended faith against its detractors with a "strengthened foot." Finally, with a "hastened foot," he went out among the world for the purposes of preaching Christ's truth. [98]

Though the triad of purification, illumination, and perfection does not explicitly appear in *Sermo 35*, this triad of "straightening," "strengthening," and "hastening" through preaching bears a striking resemblance to it. Andrew is imprinted with the vestige of truth and likened unto Christ not so that he can ascend to a contemplative union with God from which he will never again descend *in via*, but so that he can be "straightened," "strengthened," and "hastened" to preach Christ's truth throughout the world. The concludes with an exhortation for the brothers to carry out their Franciscan ministry within the world. The rational soul is imprinted in both its intellective and affective faculties so that it can follow the footsteps of Christ: As one who has been perfected for both the contemplative and active lives, and as one who has been "straightened" and "strengthened," Andrew hastens forward to do God's work.

Sermo 37 on St. Agnes Virgin and Martyr

Whereas these themes are only implicit in *Sermo 35* on St. Andrew, they emerge explicitly in *Sermo 37* on St. Agnes. The precise context and audience for this sermon is unknown, though Bougerol gives a possible date of 21 January 1268.[99] If this were to be confirmed, the Seraphic Doctor would have preached this sermon roughly a week before giving his sermon for the Feast of the Purification of Mary examined above. Notably, a close reading of the sermon on Agnes might confirm the proximity of their composition. It is not at all inconceivable

97. *Sermo 35,* in *SD* 2, 466.
98. *Sermo 35,* in *SD* 2, 466–68.
99. See *SD* 2, 493; Johnson, "Reform, Hagiography, and Sanctity," 195.

to picture the Seraphic Doctor "working out" his thoughts concerning Mary's purity whilst concentrating on Agnes. Like Mary, Bonaventure attributes Agnes's perfect purity explicitly to the fact that she has been made "hierarchical" through grace.

As a whole, the sermon provides an extended meditation concerning how Agnes has been made an *amica* of God through grace, and is based on Bonaventure's reading of Song of Songs 1:8: "To my company of horsemen, in Pharaoh's chariots, have I likened thee, oh my love [*amica*]."[100] The word *amica* as Bonaventure uses it throughout the sermon could be translated as either "friend" or "lover," since the text is—unsurprisingly given both Agnes's status as a Virgin and the scriptural context of the sermon itself—ripe with Bridal imagery. Agnes can be called an *amica* of God first and foremost because of her chaste purity, through which "the glorious virgin drew her heavenly spouse to herself through the integrity of her virginity, not only spiritually, but also bodily, so that she might defend herself and her soul, which is the temple of the Holy Spirit."[101] Because of her purity, "the whole Trinity descends" into Agnes, "the bride of Christ" and *amica* among the daughters of God.[102] As Bonaventure explains of Agnes's holiness:

Chastity is a great virtue. The eternal spouse only loves a chaste soul. Not without cause do the seraphim cry, *holy, holy, holy* [*sanctus, sanctus, sanctus*]. They do not shout, 'great,' 'wise,' or 'just.' Why do the seraphim cry *holy, holy* more than the other angels? Dionysius said what is holy is the same as what is pure [*sanctus idem est quod purus*]. Whosoever enters into understanding wishes no more to stain the body than she wishes to enter the flame of fire. Nothing which is closest to God can be near to God unless it is pure; and so nothing can be joined to God except the love of purity [*amor puritatis*]; and because the blessed virgin was pure in the highest way, so she was spiritually and singularly loved by God.[103]

Here, holiness and purity walk hand in hand. Bonaventure ascribes to Agnes a Seraphic sanctity because her body is "pure in the highest way" through her choice to remain chaste. The purity of her soul walks hand in hand with the purity of her body, and it is only because both remain pure through grace that the seraphim can cry of her, "holy, holy, holy."

---

100. For Johnson's discussion of St. Agnes, see "Reform, Hagiography, and Sanctity," 195.
101. See *Sermo 37*, in *SD* 2, 498.
102. *Sermo 37*, in *SD* 2, 498.
103. *Sermo 37*, in *SD* 2, 499.

confessors in our obedience to justice; through the imitation of the fear of the virgins in our sanctimonious way of life.[114]

The saints in glory—here, the Patriarchs, Prophets, Apostles, Martyrs, Confessors, and Virgins—exemplify the life of grace for those who yet remain in the ecclesiastical hierarchy. Not everyone within the Church will become a saint on par with Agnes, Andrew, Francis, and Mary while *in via*, but everyone who is "born again through baptism" is "made into [a saint]," and thus has the capacity to become "perfect" if he or she follows the example of these "hierarchical" men and women. I will dwell more on this concept in this chapter's conclusion, but, for now, I highlight this passage only to underscore the communion between the saints in glory and those in the ecclesiastical hierarchy below. The entire community of the former provides an "exemplar" for the latter, who must imitate the former if they are to likewise rest finally in the glory of the Heavenly Jerusalem.

In that vein of thought, the remainder of the sermon unfolds these themes in two parts: First, Bonaventure explains very briefly how each of these six categories of saints demonstrate these six "forms of the Spirit" as summarized in the passage above.[115] Second, to conclude the sermon, he focuses on how those within the Church *in via* might "look for that life" of blessedness by imitating the Patriarchs, Prophets, Apostles, Martyrs, Confessors, and Virgins. The very structure of the sermon evokes hierarchy, insofar as it begins by discussing the "descending" valence of sanctity—on one hand, with respect to the macrocosm itself, through the Trinity, Christ, Mary, the celestial hierarchy, the sacraments of the ecclesiastical hierarchy, and finally, the betrothal of the Church to Christ; and on the other hand, with respect to the macrocosm of the communion of saints—before considering how the microcosm of the human person yet *in via* can "ascend" to sanctity through

114. *Sermo 60*, in *SD* 2, 816–17. Bonaventure's predilection for numeric consistency here catches him in a rather unfortunate trap: Readers will note that he begins this portion of the sermon by mentioning the seven gifts of the Spirit, but then proceeds to describe only six. This is surely because there are only "six" categories of saints listed here, presumably to match the sixfold structure throughout the rest of the sermon. The spiritual gift of "piety" is unfortunately dropped by the Seraphic Doctor in his effort to conform the seven gifts with the six types of saints. I have simply left out "seven" in my translation to avoid confusion. Perhaps Bonaventure's use of the word "form" instead of "gift" in this sermon's introduction to these six spiritual gifts is an indication that he or one of his brothers caught his mistake.

115. *Sermo 60*, in *SD* 2, 817–19. See my comment about Bonaventure's naming of six rather than seven gifts of the Spirit in my note above.

what has descended to him. If the person *in via* is faithful in "guarding sanctity" unto glory, Bonaventure finally concludes, then that "blessed life" will have six characteristics.[116] First, it will be glorious because in the life to come, the blessed will follow the way of justice, humbling themselves to show mercy to their neighbors so that these, too, might find life and glory.[117] Second, it will be victorious because the life of blessedness follows upon suffering, and those within it can partake of the tree of life.[118] Third, it will be peaceful and tranquil because peace follows work.[119] Fourth, it will be opulent because all good works are gathered together there, and all will be voluntarily poor.[120] Fifth, it will be "delicious" (*deliciosa*) because as Bonaventure writes: "*They will be drunk from the fruitfulness of your house* [*inebriabuntur ab ubertate domus tuae*], etc., and this follows from abstinence" in the present life.[121] Sixth and finally, it will be eternal, because this follows upon the life of justice. Here, "*Freed now from sin, we will have fruit in sanctification* [*habemus fructum in sanctificationem*], *truly the end in eternal life.*"[122]

According to Anthony Mirabent, the state of glory and state of grace differ for the Seraphic Doctor only in name.[123] Bonaventure's choice to end this sermon by emphasizing the "*ubertatem*" and "*fruit*" of the blessed life further underscores this idea by connecting this discussion of the saints' perfection in glory to his many descriptions of saintly perfection for those *in via*. Though the saints have achieved the final state of rest and tranquility, their perfection *in Patria* is not a static end, but is fruitful—in much the same way that Francis, Mary, Andrew, and Agnes achieved perfect sanctity in this life by becoming "fruitful" through grace. Those within the ecclesiastical hierarchy look to them as exemplars so that they might also ascend to the state of glory, but once there, the "end" they enjoy will not be a wall beyond which they can traverse no further, but a luscious and abundant garden in which they will continue to sprout holy fruit.

116. *Sermo 60*, in *SD* 2, 819.
117. *Sermo 60*, in *SD* 2, 819.
118. *Sermo 60*, in *SD* 2, 819.
119. *Sermo 60*, in *SD* 2, 819.
120. *Sermo 60*, in *SD* 2, 819–20.
121. *Sermo 60*, in *SD* 2, 820.
122. *Sermo 60*, in *SD* 2, 820.
123. See again Mirabent, *La gloria*.

Sermo 61   These hierarchical themes within the context of Bonaventure's ecclesiology emerge again in an even more explicit way in *Sermo 61*. After a protheme about the edification of wisdom,[124] this sermon is structured according to Rv 21:2: "I saw the holy city, the New Jerusalem, coming down out of heaven from God, made ready as a bride adorned for her husband."[125] "In these words," writes Bonaventure, "the solemnity of all the saints is described, because that communion of saints is explained within a metaphor, descending from God [*a Deo descendentis*] and returning or stretching out into God [*in Deum tendentis sive revertentis*].... For He is *the Alpha and the Omega, the beginning and the end*, as it says in Rv 1." The communion of saints, he continues, descends through the gifts of nature and grace, and returns to God through "the merit of virtue" and the "reward of merit"; even more properly, however, he says that it descends "from God through a great many offices" and then "stretches into [*tendentis*]" God "through the uniformity of love [*per uniformitatem amoris*]."[126]

Here, Bonaventure's preoccupation with the "circle" as a summation of his metaphysics again resurfaces through his neoplatonic *exitus-redditus* rhetoric. All things—including the communion of saints—descend from God as their beginning and are ordered back to God as their end. He concludes this introduction by outlining the remainder of the sermon with this same language: "To the commendation of those saints or of that heavenly city," he tells his brothers, "we ought to note that we can speak about it in a threefold way: namely, first with respect to the edification of heaven; second, with respect to its foundation and construction on the earth; and third, with respect to how it must return or be ordered to God."[127] In other words, the very structure of the sermon follows the *exitus-redditus* pattern, beginning from "above," then considering the earth "below," and finally "returning" in the final valence.

My own comments on *Sermo 61* will follow Bonaventure's intended structure for it as such, since close attention to the Seraphic Doctor's explanation of this "descent" and "ascent" of all the saints from and back to God will once again yield important data for how we should

---

124. *Sermo 61*, in *SD* 2, 821.
125. *Sermo 61*, in *SD* 2, 821.
126. *Sermo 61*, in *SD* 2, 821–22.
127. *Sermo 61*, in *SD* 2, 822.

therein regard the moment of "return." Indeed, as I have already argued of his cyclical metaphysics,[128] these descending and ascending valences in his theology of hierarchy are not perfectly comparable to a neoplatonic intelligible circle inasmuch as the return does not end exactly where it began: Once the rational creature returns to the Trinity, it remains in the Trinity by again descending to other rational creatures in love, and vice versa into eternity. In this way, the rational reateure becomes a similitude of the Trinity. The image of the spiral in this sense might be more appropriate for helping us conceive Bonaventure's hierarchical metaphysics, since in his theology of hierarchy and in his doctrine of grace, the return does not simply bring the rational creature to some "end point" on a circle at which the rational creature then stops moving. The rational creature who participates in a hierarchy becomes more and more like God insofar as the return will always yield to another descent in perpetuity so that the rational creature is made capable of ever more fruitful relationships with both God and other rational creatures. There is no final moment of perfection in Bonaventure's cyclical metaphysics; rather, perfection involves continuously moving into ever deeper relationships with God and the rest of creation. Following the descending and ascending movements in *Sermo 61* will help us see how this concept functions in his theology of sanctity as well.

1. *The Construction of the Communion of Saints in Heaven.*　First, the Seraphic Doctor describes how the communion of saints is "built in heaven." The saints in heaven, he tells his brothers, are "made like to their cause [*similior suae causae*]" insofar as they are as close as possible to God; in this sense, they can also be called "deiform." Their deiformity, he continues, results in what he calls "a fourfold commendable condition," which he will spend the next several pages of his sermon explaining for his brothers.[129] The saints are commendable, first and foremost, because they receive an inflowing of power from the Father (*influxum potentiae Patris*) that makes them more glorious than other creatures.[130] They are secondly commendable because they are made beautiful through an inflowing of wisdom from the Son (*influxum sapientiae Filii*),[131] and are thirdly "delicious due to an inflowing of benev-

---

128. For my introduction to this idea, see Chapter 3.
129. *Sermo 61,* in *SD* 2, 822.
130. *Sermo 61,* in *SD* 2, 823.
131. *Sermo 61,* in *SD* 2, 823.

olence from the Holy Spirit" (*deliciosa propter influxum benevolentia Spiritus sancti*).[132] In the same way that the *influentia* of sanctifying grace causes human persons *in via* to become a similitude of the Triune God, in other words, so too does Bonaventure affirm here in the opening of *Sermo 61* that "deiformity" thus also has a Trinitarian shape in the state of glory.

To these three points, however, Bonaventure adds a fourth in further emphasis of this same idea: In addition to receiving an inflowing of power, wisdom, and goodness from the Father, Son, and Holy Spirit, respectively, he says the saints are also "opulent" (*opulenta*) through an "inflowing of overabundance from the God who is one and three" (*influxum exuberantiae unius Dei et trini*). The Seraphic Doctor expounds upon this fourth type of "commendability":

It says opulence on account of the overflowing of every good [*affluentia omnis boni*] ... because there, the one highest good through equivalence is possessed, and for that reason this blessed people sits there in the beauty of peace in an opulent rest in the tabernacle of faith, as is said in Isaiah. And thus, what is expounded in 3 Kgs 10 can be said about that city: *Solomon was made King,* that is Christ, our peaceful King.... In that city, there is *such a multitude of gold and silver which is stone,* because the sweetness and clarity of wisdom and knowledge, by all means that uncreated knowledge, is inflowing [*infunditur*] into each and every Saint according to his or her capacity; and the highest inflowing [*summa influentia*] and the highest opulence [*summa opulentia*] consists in this, because according to Augustine in his book of *Confessions:* "every bit of wealth which is not God, is impoverished," and because the saints *in patria* are enriched by the eternal light of the God who is three and one, thus they are in the highest opulence, and the highest overflowing abundance [*summa affluentia*].[133]

To fully understand what Bonaventure is saying here in *Sermo 61*, it is necessary to recall again his definition of hierarchy from *II Sent.* d. 9.[134] The Seraphic Doctor defines a "hierarchy" first and foremost as God, who is one and three, a perfect community of three divine persons coexisting as one in love, and a fountainhead of overflowing goodness. The deiformity of the saints in *Sermo 61* is attributed to the fact that they receive "inflowings" from all three persons of the Trinity in an immediate way: Though "impoverished" on their own, the saints receive

132. *Sermo 61*, in *SD* 2, 825.
133. *Sermo 61*, in *SD* 2, 826–27.
134. See Chapter 3.

these inflowings of grace in such a way that they also become opulent, an opulence here explicitly defined by Bonaventure as an "overflowing abundance." The saints in glory can be called "deiform" only insofar as this "fourth" point of commendability is added to the previous three. If the Trinity itself is understood by Bonaventure as a fountain of over-flowing goodness, then the saints will only truly be commendable if—having opened themselves up as much as possible for the purposes of receiving God—they themselves overflow this abundance of goodness as well.

2. *The Foundation and Construction of the Communion of Saints on Earth.* The very structure of *Sermo 61* will lend further credence to this theme, insofar as Bonaventure will next "descend" from heaven to speak about the communion of saints on earth. Here, the Seraphic Doctor suggests that the Uncreated Word "builds" heaven by inflowing these four commendations to all the saints therein; on earth, howev-er, the Incarnate Word descends to edify "this city in a fourfold way through grace." For those still *in via* in the ecclesiastical hierarchy, he continues, the Incarnate Word inflows faith into the rational appetite, hope into the irascible appetite, charity into the concupiscible appetite, and "sanctity totally joining them together [*per sanctitatem totius coni-uncti*]"; or, as he alternatively suggests, "through faith in the cognitive faculty [*fidem in potentiam cognitivam*], hope in the potestative faculty [*spem in potentiam potestativam*], charity in the amative faculty [*car-itatem in potentiam amativam*], and sanctity in the operative faculty [*sanctitatem in potentiam operativam*]."[135] Again, the three theological virtues are brought together by a "fourth" inflowing, sanctity. Those *in via* can be called "holy" only when this sanctity resides in the operative faculty of their rational soul; it matters nothing if their natural faculties have been transformed by the theological virtues unless these are put into practice.

3. *How the Communion of Saints Is Ordered to God in the Return.* Finally, then, the third part of the sermon develops how those within the Church *in via* can return to God through these inflowings, namely, when they exercise the four cardinal virtues—prudence, fortitude, temperance, and justice—"not only insofar as they are habitual [*con-suetudinales*], but also insofar as they are political [*politicae*], purgative

135. *Sermo 61*, in *SD 2, 827.*

[*purgatoriae*], and belong to the soul that has already been purified [*animi iam purgati*]."[136] Bonaventure once again emphasizes what ought by now be a familiar theme. The person in whom these virtues have become habitual does not, through them, merely ascend to God so as never to engage the surrounding world; rather, all four virtues are habitual insofar as they better prepare the person to live a holy life within the world until he arrives *in patria*.

This idea is corroborated in the Seraphic Doctor's treatment of the four cardinal virtues throughout the remainder of the sermon, where he identifies these as the "gates" into heaven mentioned in Rv 21:12–13: "And the city had a great and high wall, having twelve gates ... on the east, three gates; on the north, three gates; on the south, three gates; and on the west, three gates."[137] The eastern gate is prudence, and has three doors: memory of past things, understanding of present things, and providence of future things.[138] God opened the gate of prudence "in his nativity and in his way of life, or in his preaching,"[139] and the Friars Minor can follow the way of prudence best when—just as Christ became a poor man—they overcome the shadows of greed and are sent out into the world as little poor ones.[140] The northern gate is fortitude, which Christ likewise opened through his passion, and has three doors: magnanimity in the attack against evil, virility in the pursuit against evil, and patience in perseverance against evil. Bonaventure employs this militant language to describe how those *in via* must remain strong in their resistance of all evils until they reach the heavenly Jerusalem.[141] The southern gate is temperance, opened by Christ in his ascension, and has a door of sobriety in taste, a door for chastity in touch, and a door for honesty in conviction. Ecclesiastical men must especially pass through this gate, since they must be luminaries in their good works.[142] Finally, the western gate is justice, which will be opened for us by Christ in the final judgment and which also has three doors of its own: obedience with respect to one's superiors, modesty with respect to one's neighbors, and mercy with respect to one's inferiors.[143]

---

136. *Sermo 61*, in *SD* 2, 831.
137. *Sermo 61*, in *SD* 2, 831.
138. *Sermo 61*, in *SD* 2, 831.
139. *Sermo 61*, in *SD* 2, 831.
140. See *Sermo 61*, in *SD* 2, 832.
141. *Sermo 61*, in *SD* 2, 832–33.
142. *Sermo 61*, in *SD* 2, 833.
143. *Sermo 61*, in *SD* 2, 833–34.

The "return" of all things to God—the *redditus* of the saints in the act of ascending from earth back to heaven—here explicitly pertains to the life of virtue. All four cardinal virtues must continuously be exercised within the soul of the person *in via* if he hopes to be counted among the communion of saints in heaven. Bonaventure strikingly concludes *Sermo 61* by bringing his listeners back to where he started, writing: "Behold these doors through which the city of the way passes into the city of the Fatherland, so that all of the saints—descending from God through a multiformity of different functions, and returning to God through the uniformity of love—would be wed to its Spouse in a deiform way like an ornate Bride."[144] This conclusion is more meaningful when we consider that the Seraphic Doctor spent the first portion of the sermon describing what this "deiformity" will look like, namely, conformity to the Trinity through an inflowing of power, wisdom, goodness, and sanctity that causes the Saint to "overflow" in abundance. Those who are *in via* may themselves become saints and embark upon the return, but we do well to note that the point of return is itself not a static end, but a fruitful garden, as Bonaventure also emphasized in *Sermo 60*.

Previously, I argued that the image of the "spiral" is perhaps more conducive than that of a "circle" for explaining the dynamic of *exitus-redditus* in Bonaventure's hierarchical metaphysics. Here in *Sermo 61*, the end of the sermon likewise simply ushers us back to the beginning, where we will be directed again to consider the "descent" to the earth, and back up again. For the Seraphic Doctor, this "spiraling" is the business of sanctity, since it is only by continuously descending that the saints continuously ascend, and vice versa even unto glory.

Conclusion

This chapter has argued that the saints embody Bonaventure's doctrine of grace. Looking especially at his *Legenda maior* and a selection of sermons from his *Sermones de sanctis*, it has shown how sanctity has a "hierarchical" shape in his thought. For the Seraphic Doctor, the saint is one who has been conformed to the Triune God through grace by being inwardly and outwardly purified, illuminated, and perfected.

144. *Sermo 61*, in *SD* 2, 834.

Whether with respect to Sts. Francis, Mary, Andrew, Agnes, or even in Bonaventure's sermons for the Feast of All the Saints, these hierarchical activities are always at work within the saint, as this chapter has shown. St. Francis was a *vir hierarchicus* because, even after the contemplative union with God he experienced in the miracle of the stigmata, his body and soul were inflamed for the purposes of descending to the leper in his midst and for "teaching the people." Mary, similarly, is the "Purgatrix, Illuminatrix, and Perfectrix" because the three hierarchical activities of purification, illumination, and perfection have been at work within her since the womb. Through her own "fruitful" and holy womb, grace descends to nourish the entire Church. In St. Andrew, Bonaventure presents for his brothers an exemplar of one who has been perfectly purified for both the contemplative and active life through grace. Even the "vestige of truth" imprinted within him leads him to further ministry within the world. Having achieved the wisdom of the seraph and having been purified in both body and soul, St. Agnes, like Mary, is a hierarchical woman who has been conformed perfectly to the Heavenly Jerusalem. Truly, as also attested in Bonaventure's general discussions of sanctity found in *Sermo 60* and *61* for the Feast of All the Saints, the saints in Bonaventure's theology are microcosms that reflect his hierarchical portrait of the macrocosm, most especially the uncreated hierarchy itself. They embody grace in such a way that the very Trinity descends through them to the ecclesiastical hierarchy, lifting them up so that all might be united through the deifying *influentiam* of the Father, Son, and Holy Spirit in the lap of eternal glory. For the Seraphic Doctor, the saint is like a Jacob's Ladder, one who through grace becomes an ever greater similitude of the Trinity by circling always between perfect contemplation and meritorious action.

We are thereby left with a rather obvious question: What, then, for the rest of us? I here conclude this chapter by proffering a few reflections in answer to this question.

First, as we saw in *Sermo 61* above, the Seraphic Doctor explicitly claims that everyone who receives baptismal grace—who consents to receive the *influentia* of sanctifying grace that can make them as like as possible to the Triune God—"is made into a saint." This is indeed a striking claim: How can it be squared with the fact that, of course, Bonaventure obviously does not think that every Christian is a saint in the same sense as Francis, Mary, Andrew, and Agnes?

These, as we have seen throughout this chapter, can be called "holy" insofar as they have been made perfectly hierarchical. They are "Jacob's Ladders" *in via* as well as in glory. The typical person who has received the *influentia* of sanctifying grace *in via* is made capable of becoming like Francis, Mary, Andrew, and Agnes insofar as they have received this inflowing. However, they will only arrive at perfect holiness—at the order of the seraph, which will then overflow throughout the lower "orders" in their souls, or, in Francis's case, from the wounds of the stigmata—when they "exercise"[145] grace, as prescribed by Bonaventure, for example, in Part 5 of the *Breviloquium*: By affirming the articles of faith; by loving God, their neighbors, and themselves in an ordered way; by obeying the Law; and through prayer. The saints are those who, after consenting to receive the *influentia* of sanctifying grace in acknowledgment of their ontological and moral poverty, continue to recognize their need for grace as "little poor ones in the desert" and who thus never stop receiving grace in willing humility, moving always between contemplation and action. Phrased differently, the saints are those who remain perfectly receptive to the *influentia* of grace throughout their time *in via*, never failing to let the inflowing of grace work these things within them so that they might become ever more like God unto glory. Everyone who has received the inflowing of sanctifying grace within the ecclesiastical hierarchy can become like Francis, Mary, Andrew, and Agnes—or better yet, like Christ the Hierarch—but only to the extent that they thus likewise continue to let grace work within them in this fashion. Because those within the Church will continue to commit actual sins, as we saw in Bonaventure's *Sermo 37* on the Purification of Mary, they will become perfectly sanctified only to the extent that they continue to consent to the work of grace within them and continue to thus merit the Good.

Second, and closely related to this first point, it is useful to consider the purpose of the hagiographical literature considered in this chapter. As I emphasized in the chapter's introduction, Bonaventure wrote both his *Legenda maior* and his *Sermones de sanctis* to urge his Minorite brothers to spiritual reform. In all the texts highlighted here, the

---

145. The phrase, "excercise grace," is admittedly strange, but I here borrow Bonaventure's own words from Part 5 of the *Breviloquium*; the Latin titles of Part 5, Chapters 7–10, of the *Breviloquium* all include the phrase, "*De exercitio gratiae.*" For my explanation of this concept, see Chapter 4.

Seraphic Doctor presents his brothers with exemplars of grace so that they themselves can imitate them. These texts, in other words, show us how his systematic doctrine of grace was practically implemented for the benefit of his fellow confreres, whom he urged to "nakedly follow the naked Christ" with Francis so that they would achieve an ever greater similitude to the Triune God. As Jacques Guy Bougerol once wrote, "Bonaventure does not seek to develop a theology of pure speculation.... Our salvation is at stake. Bonaventure intends to be a theologian for no other reason than to form saints."[146] His brothers might not yet be perfectly hierarchical like Francis, but through these texts, the Seraphic Doctor nonetheless gives his peers a prescription for following the path of the poor one in the desert. He is, indeed, trying to "form saints" among his brothers. As such, we can draw from these texts some general conclusions concerning how the average person who has consented to receive the *influentia* of grace might, according to Bonaventure, follow the saints both up and down the ladder of their "hierarchization."

In this regard, it is necessary to first and foremost emphasize the fact that for Bonaventure, one cannot become a saint apart from the ecclesiastical hierarchy, the Church. As underscored especially by the Seraphic Doctor's comments concerning the communion of saints in *Sermo 60* and *61* above, to receive the *influentia* of sanctifying grace is to be united to all those who participate within Bonaventure's hierarchical conception of the macrocosm. One cannot pass from the path of sanctity *in via* to the "remaining" of deiformity *in patria* apart from this participation in the Church. Those within the Church militant are nourished by the sacraments, which Bonaventure calls "vases of grace," from which "grace is drawn up by the soul" "from the eternal fountain," God. "Just as one who returns to a vase when he requires liquid," writes the Seraphic Doctor in his *IV Sent.*, "so in searching for the liquor of grace and not having it, one ought to hasten back to these sacraments."[147] Partaking in the sacraments ensures that the person *in via* will continue to be bound to this community, apart from which it will be impossible for her to continuously receive grace. The saint cannot be a saint apart from participating in the ecclesiastical hierarchy, through which she receives the sacraments so that her life will be nourished by grace *in via* in expectation of

---

146. Bougerol, *Introduction to the Works of Bonaventure*, 108.

147. *IV Sent.* d. 1, respondeo. I have used here Hellmann et al., trans., *Commentary on the Sentences: Sacraments*, 58.

arriving finally at the Heavenly Jerusalem. To become a saint, the person who receives the *influentia* of sanctifying grace must continuously return to the fountain of grace within this specific context of the Church, through which she is bound to Christ and all other rational creatures who participate in the hierarchies throughout the macrocosm.

Within this context, then, Bonaventure's "prescription" for how one can become a saint is summed up best by his suggestion that the Poverello received the stigmata because he had become a "Jacob's Ladder," and thus had prudently learned to divide the time given him between contemplation and action. In his own examination of the *Legenda maior*, Jay Hammond notes how Bonaventure presents an image of Francis to his brothers that is meant to be both admired and imitated, "whereby the brothers, through the graced activity of purgation, illumination, and perfection, transform themselves into hierarchic men, thereby conforming themselves, like Francis, to Christ."[148] What we have seen throughout this chapter is how the Poverello as well as the other saints treated by Bonaventure in his *Sermones de sanctis*, are themselves "hierarchic" only insofar as the "perfective" moment is at once an "end" and a "beginning." St. Francis, after his stigmata, was ignited through his contemplative experience to descend once again to the leper "in the humility of following." People "exercise" grace so as to become saints when they, like Francis, are always constantly being purified, illuminated, and perfected by the *influentia* of grace. They must themselves become a "Jacob's Ladder," constantly both ascending to God through meditation, prayer, and contemplation,[149] while not forsaking the descent to their neighbors through virtue. For Bonaventure, to be "purified, illuminated, and perfected"—to be holy—is to never cease circling between both.

I conclude with the Seraphic Doctor's advice to his brothers in one of his spiritual tractates, "On the Way of Life."[150] This treatise begins

---

148. Hammond, "Bonaventure's *Legenda maior*," 507.

149. I borrow this from Bonaventure's prescription for the "ascent" to this perfective moment in the prologue to *The Threefold Way*; see *De triplici via* (5, 3): "Sciendum est igitur, quod triplex est modus exercendi se circa hanc triplicem viam, scilicet legendo et meditando, orando, et contemplando." We should here note that Bonaventure's "prescription" for the spiritual life in this text, with its emphasis on the three hierarchical activities of purification, illumination, and perfection, corresponds with this chapter's conclusions concerning how one might "become" a saint in his theology, as he writes: "*Purgatio* autem ad pacem ducit, *illuminatio* ad veritatem, *perfectio* ad caritatem."

150. "De modo vivendi." The Quaracchi editors include this as a "sermon" within Bonaventure's *Sermones de diversis* (9, 723–25). In his introduction to his edition of the *Sermons de diversis* in *SD* 1, however, Bougerol notes that he does not include this text in his

with an exhortation to holiness: "Whoever you are who wishes to attain salvation through faith, hope, and love, it is necessary for you to surrender yourself to three things: namely, to *devout prayer*, to an *honest way of life*, and to *satisfactory confession*." This prescription for sanctity, he continues, is drawn from Micah: "*I will show you, O human, what good is, and what God requires of you: Namely, to make justice*, by confessing truthfully, *and to love mercy*, by living with others in a holy manner, *and to walk solicitously with your God*, vigilantly persisting in your prayers."[151] Later on in the treatise, after emphasizing the importance of persisting in prayer, Bonaventure writes:

And, since Jacob's Ladder is not a place for standing [*non est locus standi*], but for ascending [*ascendendi*] and descending [*descendendi*], so we should not only empty ourselves for devout prayer, but also for an *honest* and holy *way of life*. For the holiness of the way of life consists in two things, namely, in the straightening of justice and in the strictness of discipline. Truly the straightness of justice consists in this: that the will would be rectified for the purposes of rendering to each one what is his, such as subjection and reverence to one's superiors, conformation and benevolence to one's peers, and condescension and care to one's inferiors. For *each and every one* must *administer grace to one another* inasmuch as he receives it, as *good stewards of the manifold graces of God*, as the Apostle Peter teaches. And this same thing happens when help is shown to the needy, education to the ignorant, correction to the lost, support to the wicked, comfort to the afflicted, lifting up to those who have fallen, and compassion to all others who are miserable, as well as peace and love for all other human persons, because this is the summation of all the law and of all justice, according to the testimony of the Apostle, who says: *He who loves his neighbor has fulfilled the law*. And thus he is particularly exhorting us to repay this debt, saying: *Owe no one anything except to love one another....* And this is a correct description of good will, which consists in the rightness of justice, which cannot exist without the sweetness of mercy. But to acquire, increase, and conserve this good will, the *strictness of discipline* is required, whose role it is to organize the spirit of our mind according to a norm and rule according to our *exterior* and *interior* [states].[152]

What is holiness, for the Seraphic Doctor? It is to be ordered interiorly and exteriorly by grace so that, reaching the height of contemplation in a Seraphic embrace with God, we overflow grace to our neighbors

---

own edition because he does not think that it is actually a sermon; rather, 19 manuscripts call it a "*tractatulus*." See *SD* 1, 50.

151. "De modo vivendi" (9, 723).

152. "De modo vivendi" (9, 724).

in humility. We become capable of holiness when we open ourselves up fully to the inflowing of grace, so that through it we can strive after Christ to become—like Francis, Mary, Andrew, Agnes, and the whole communion of saints in heaven—a hierarchical *person*, a "Jacob's Ladder" who never ceases to spiral between God and others with an endless and ever-fruitful love.

CHAPTER 9

General Conclusion

Further Implications

This book has argued that the Seraphic Doctor's doctrine of sanctifying grace is best interpreted through his theology of hierarchy. It has shown how Bonaventure defines sanctifying grace as a "created" *influentia* that "hierarchizes" the entire human person—both soul and body—into a similitude of the Trinity. *Part I* laid the "foundations" for this definition of grace with respect to three historical-theological sources (i.e., Dionysius, Thomas Gallus, and Alexander of Hales) who influenced both Bonaventure's teachings on grace (Chapter 2) and his definition of hierarchy (Chapter 3). Building up from these "foundations," *Part II* turned to a more focused analysis of Bonaventure's doctrine of grace as a topic in its own right. Following Zachary Hayes's intuition that the "element of hierarchy"[1] was an explicit factor in even the Seraphic Doctor's very earliest accounts of soteriology, I chronologically examined four key texts that showed both the evolution of this element within his definition of sanctifying grace and the continuity with respect to that element of his doctrine of grace across the course of his theological career. This examination began by attending to his definition of sanctifying grace as a created "*influentia*" in his *Commentary on the Sentences*

---

1. See again Hayes, *Hidden Center*, 158.

and the *Breviloquium* (Chapter 4) and concluded by analyzing his notion of the "hierarchical soul" as an effect of grace in the *Itinerarium* and the *Hexaëmeron* (Chapter 5). *Part III*, then, explored the implications of this doctrine across several different topics in the Seraphic Doctor's theology, including his theological anthropology (Chapter 6), his Christology (Chapter 7), and, in the climax of our examination, his theology of sanctity (Chapter 8).

Throughout this study, I have endeavored to demonstrate how this marriage between hierarchy and grace in the Seraphic Doctor's theology helps him paint a picture of the sanctified human person as a similitude of the Trinity. The Trinity itself is understood by Bonaventure as an uncreated hierarchy, an ordered relationship of three persons who are perfectly united to one another in love. This, most fundamentally, is what hierarchy means according to the Seraphic Doctor—namely, it means the perfect communion of love in the uncreated hierarchy, a "plenitude" that is abundantly fruitful in the fullness of its love. To be made hierarchical through grace, in turn, simply means that the human person has been made "as like as possible to God" by similarly being made capable of perfect, ordered relationships with God and other rational creatures in the created order of reality. A person becomes holy when she relates to God and the rest of creation in a communion of love, participating in a *circumincessio* that mirrors that within the intra-Trinitarian life.

Sanctifying grace, according to the Seraphic Doctor, causes a person to become holy in this way because it "purifies, illuminates, and perfects" her from within so that the whole person—both soul and body—can be made "upright" for the purposes of loving God above all things and her neighbor as herself. Frequently, Bonaventure employs the symbol of Jacob's Ladder to describe his image of sanctity as such: Like the angels that perpetually circle between heaven and earth in Jacob's dream as described in Gn 28:12, he holds that sanctifying grace hierarchizes human persons by causing them to "ascend" or "return" to a contemplative union with God, represented for Bonaventure by the order of the seraph in Dionysius's celestial hierarchy. This mystical union then leads them to "descend" to their neighbors through love, which will then lead again to the person's renewed "ascent" into contemplation, and vice versa into eternity. Accordingly, a person does not become a similitude of the Trinity through sanctifying grace by simply arriving at an affective union with God that removes her from the rest of the created order of reality; rather, sanctifying grace causes the person to become a similitude of the Trinity only inasmuch as the person who "returns" to God through this seraphic, affective union is invited into ever more fruitful relationships with her neighbor and creation writ large. St. Francis's own experience of this seraphic embrace, whereby he was crucified with Christ the "Hierarch" atop Mt. Alverna, inflamed both his soul and his body, causing him to become a hierarchical "person" who "descended" from the top of the mountain with an even greater love for the leper in his midst. The sanctified person never "arrives" at some sort of "end point" in a bottom-up mystical journey into God: For Bonaventure, the "point" of mystical union with God—the end of the "ascending" valence in the soul's *redditus* to God—is the point at which the person is prepared to once again "descend" to the created order of reality, so that the sanctified person "remains" in God by constantly both "ascending" to God and "descending" to the created order. As Boyd Taylor Coolman has described this concept in Thomas Gallus's angelic anthropology, this image of the "hierarchized person" is thus notably "not a simple circle, not a mere returning to the original point of departure, in order to merely set out on the same course again"; rather, "this dynamic movement *in Deum* is better characterized as a spiral," whereby "'new things' are continually flowing down into the hierarchized soul from her super-abundant Spouse.... There is here an epecstatic dimension to hierarchic human nature, a sense of continual and eternal progress. There is no *static* resting in God, no absolute cessation of the soul's movements.... Never fulfilled, in the sense of filled full, it is always spiraling."[2]

In an amendment to Gallus, Bonaventure, as we saw especially in Chapters 5 and 8, regards this dynamism of the hierarchized soul as an effect of grace, and moreover extends this "spiraling" movement into the sensible realm so as to include the "leper" within it as well. For Bonaventure, sanctifying grace "sanctifies" precisely because it makes the human person into a similitude of the Trinity by causing this dynamism, by inviting her to ever fuller relationships with God and the entire created order of reality as it "inflows" the person's affections and fills her with the "fruitfulness of plenitude" (*plenitudinis ubertatem*)

---

2. Coolman, *Knowledge, Love, and Ecstasy*, 256.

that will cause her to eternally spiral unto and into glory through the fullness of God's overflowing charity.

I here conclude my examination of these concepts with the simple observation that this present study can only just barely crack open the door for understanding them. While *Part III* has been entirely devoted to an exploration of the theological implications of Bonaventure's definition of sanctifying grace as a hierarchizing *influentia*, Chapters 6–8 narrate only some of the rich and manifold ways in which these concepts might indeed play out within and inform our reading of his broader systematic theology. In acknowledgment of the fact that it would truly be impossible to cover everything pertaining to these concepts in the Bonaventurean corpus within the span of this book, I nonetheless will gesture at a handful of possible avenues for further study based upon them. Continued exploration of these topics will be necessary for expanding our understanding of the Seraphic Doctor's doctrine of grace. My gesture toward further areas of study serves the purpose of underscoring certain ways in which his teachings on grace might be useful for contemporary theological reflection in the twenty-first century. The pages that follow are, therefore, an invitation for further research.

Trinitarian Theology

First and foremost, Bonaventure's claim that sanctifying grace hierarchizes human persons is rooted within his view of the Trinity as an "uncreated hierarchy." Quite justifiably and quite rightly, systematic theologians in the twentieth century argue against a view of the Trinity as a hierarchy for myriad reasons. Seeing the Trinity as a hierarchy is especially dangerous because it implies subordination within the relationships between the three persons of the Trinity, and thus verges upon heresy, even as it also justifies the existence of unjust hierarchical power structures within the Church and society writ large. Even though Bonaventure defines the "uncreated hierarchy" as a hierarchy without subordination in the prologue to *II Sent.* d. 9, his understanding of the Trinity as hierarchical is indubitably too problematic for contemporary theological inquiry.

Though we cannot reclaim this particular aspect of the Seraphic Doctor's theology of hierarchy for ourselves, the fact that he unfolds his entire doctrine of grace from his doctrine of the Trinity is still significant. Sanctifying grace, as we have repeatedly witnessed in Bonaventure's writings, purifies the soul so as to make it a "daughter" or "son" of the Father. It illuminates the soul so as to prepare it for a bridal union with its Spouse, the Son. It finally perfects the soul by causing it to become a temple of the Holy Spirit, the uncreated gift of grace that is gifted *with* and *in* the created gift of sanctifying grace. To be thus graced, for Bonaventure, is to become a similitude of the entire Trinity, whereby the soul relates in an ordered and indeed immediate way to all three persons within the Triune God. Most fundamentally, the "story" of sanctifying grace in Bonaventure's theology is the "story" of the human person's *reductio* into the First Principle. Once she has returned to God through sanctifying grace, she remains in God by continuously relating to all three persons of the Trinity. To be hierarchized through grace, for Bonaventure, is to constantly be "purified, illuminated, and perfected" from within. Once it reaches the pneumatological level of perfection, the soul does not cease being illuminated by the Son or purified by the Father; rather, the work of grace is to cause all three hierarchical activities within the soul so that the human person can always be thus united to the Father, Son, and Holy Spirit through a dynamic *circumincessio* that mirrors that within the intra-divine life.

This "Trinitarian" emphasis within Bonaventure's doctrine of grace might perhaps be a useful point of departure for scholars interested in contemporary systematic questions surrounding Trinitarian theology. Theologians in the present day continue to wrestle with Karl Rahner's famous axiom, "The immanent Trinity is the economic Trinity, and vice versa."[3] The Seraphic Doctor's doctrine of grace and its accompanying "comprehensive Trinitarianism" might be quite useful for theologians seeking ways to more clearly articulate the relationship between the immanent and economic Trinity, even as it might likewise be useful for those who are rather simply looking for ways to explain how the doctrine of the Trinity remains applicable for the lived experience of persons of faith in the modern world.

---

3. For this axiom, see Karl Rahner, *The Trinity*, trans. Joseph Donceel (New York: Herder and Herder, 1970). For a selection of other more recent systematic explanations of the doctrine of the Trinity, see Khaled Anatolios, *Retrieving Nicaea: The Development and Meaning of Trinitarian Doctrine* (Grand Rapids, MI: Baker Academic, 2011); Leonardo Boff, *Trinity and Society*; Walter Kasper, "Part III: The Trinitarian Mystery of God," in *The God of Jesus Christ: The New Edition* (New York: T&T Clark International, 2012), 233–316; Catherine Mowry LaCugna, *God for Us: The Trinity and Christian Life* (San Francisco: Harper Collins, 1991); and Moltmann, *The Trinity and the Kingdom*.

Pneumatology

Relatedly, while I explored the relationship between Bonaventure's teachings on hierarchy, grace, and Christology extensively in Chapter 7, much more remains to be said about how those teachings relate to his pneumatology. As we first saw in his treatment of the "hierarchical" effects of grace in Part 5 of the *Breviloquium*, Christ's role in the Seraphic Doctor's account of grace is repeatedly associated explicitly with his various descriptions of the illuminative way. After the soul has been freed from its "mercenary," sinful ways and thus purified for a relationship with the Father, Bonaventure holds that grace works *in* and *with* the free will so that it then "branches out" into the virtues, spiritual gifts, and beatitudes; in this way, the soul is illuminated by grace for a contemplative union with Christ, the Bridegroom. These first two hierarchical activities in Bonaventure's theology of grace always yield to the third, the moment of perfection whereby the soul is transformed into a Jacob's Ladder through grace and becomes capable of meritorious actions and works of mercy toward her neighbor. This moment of perfection is always pneumatological: As Bonaventure writes in the *Breviloquium,* it is here that the soul becomes a temple of the Holy Spirit.

Though much scholarly attention has been given to both his broader Trinitarian theology and his teachings on Christology, his pneumatology and treatment of the Holy Spirit in these respects remain largely neglected topics in Bonaventurean studies. Especially given the prevalence of Joachimism among the Franciscans in his own day, how might attentiveness to his pneumatology within this account of the effects of grace in the soul—both on its own, but also with respect to its intertwinement with his Trinitarian theology and Christology—tell us something about the perceived role of Joachim in Bonaventure's theology? Moreover, inasmuch as pneumatology, even as a topic outside of Bonaventurean studies, tends to be neglected in comparison to the Trinity or Christology, perhaps attention to this particular facet of the Seraphic Doctor's theology might also play a role in helping contemporary theologians iterate more precise teachings on the role of the Holy Spirit in the Christian life. Inasmuch as the moment of operative "perfection" in Bonaventure's notion of the hierarchical soul is always connected with the Spirit, how might Christians perceive the work of

the Spirit in the present-day Church through this insight? Reflecting
on the ways in which Christians are related to one another through the
Spirit and are only "perfected" insofar as grace leads them to others
within the Church could have broad implications for ecclesiology, perhaps even in an ecumenical context.

Ecclesiology

Relatedly, in addition to my neglect of the Holy Spirit, my treatment
of grace has for the most part concentrated on its role in purifying,
illuminating, and perfecting the individual. There nevertheless—and
very regrettably—has not been ample room here to expound at length
upon what this means within the context of Bonaventure's ecclesiology.
I attended briefly to the grace of the sacraments as they "flow forth"
from the wounds of the Crucified Christ in Chapter 7, and likewise
gestured there to the "grace of headship" or capital grace that flows
forth from the Incarnate Christ so as to unite the members of his body
in the Church through the *influentia sensus et motus*. Bonaventure's ecclesiology was also pertinent for reading his *Sermones de sanctis* when I
attended to them in Chapters 3 and 8, but much more work remains by
way of expounding the implications of Bonaventure's doctrine of grace
for his ecclesiology in a systematic way.

It would perhaps be useful to envision a project that brings together
the Seraphic Doctor's doctrine of grace with both his pneumatology
and his ecclesiology since, in his account of grace, it is through the
Holy Spirit that the sanctified microcosm of the human person finds
herself in communion with the macrocosm—both the celestial and ecclesiastical hierarchies. According to Bonaventure, the uncreated gift
of grace, the Holy Spirit, dwells within the sanctified soul as charity.[4]
For him, all persons who consent to receive the "created" *influentia* of
sanctifying grace are bound together by this uncreated gift of charity,
so that they all might become members of Christ's body, the Church.
As he writes in Part 4 of the *Breviloquium:* "And since the Holy Spirit, who is charity and is possessed by charity, is the source of all the
spiritual gifts, thus, when the Holy Spirit descended, the fullness of
these gifts was poured out in order to bring the mystical body of Christ

---

4. See esp. *I Sent.* d. 17, p. 1, a. 1, q. 1, resp. (1, 294–96).

to perfection."[5] As Peter Damian Fehlner has commented regarding this relationship between pneumatology, grace, and the Church in Bonaventure's ecclesiology:

Sanctity is not simply an affair of the individual and his God. It is something to be realized in and through a community. Nor can it be realized in simply any community, but only in that community which is supernatural by nature, which is the community united by the Spirit of the Father and Son…. It is the unity of the Church in charity which is the perfection of those persons who share in the divine nature…. In the last analysis the whole complex of relations that comprise the mystery of the Church is the manner in which the rational creature comes to participate in the life of God as God lives it…. [The rational creature's] entire *raison d'etre* in the supernatural order is to partake of a community life that alone gives meaning to the existence of the individual. Supernaturally, human life has no meaning apart from the Church, the body of Christ, animated by the Holy Spirit. The resultant communion of the multitude of believers is a communion of charity, modeled after that of the Trinity. Or, that which proceeds from God by way of liberality (grace) in a special way returns to him through an ever more perfect conformity to the most blessed Trinity.[6]

Fehlner's comments concerning the role of grace in Bonaventure's ecclesiology coincide quite well with everything this book has argued regarding the sanctity of the individual. The perfection of the hierarchical person cannot take place, for the Seraphic Doctor, apart from the communion of the Church, to which the sanctified individual is bound through the charity of the uncreated gift, the Holy Spirit. How Bonaventure's hierarchical anthropology in particular might be useful for further expounding his ecclesiology with respect to being united by charity, and how his doctrine of grace might thus also speak to theologians working in the field of ecclesiology in the present day, remains to be unpacked.

Social and Environmental Justice

In Chapter 7, I explored the role of sanctifying grace in Bonaventure's theological anthropology to argue, largely against a recent critique against it, that human persons are indeed ordered to beatitude in his theology. According to him, the need for the "special *influentia*" of sanctifying

---

5. *Brev.* 4.10 (5, 252).
6. See Fehlner, *The Role of Charity in Bonaventure's Ecclesiology*, 95.

grace is built into the very fabric of creation, insofar as human persons need sanctifying grace to become a similitude of the Trinity. There, we also saw that, since Bonaventure's theology is unabashedly anthropocentric, the entire created order of reality, which includes sensible as well as intelligible creation, is ordered to God by being ordered to the similitude as well. True to his Franciscan identity, Bonaventure's doctrine of grace has profound cosmic implications. As he writes in his *Commentary on the Sentences*, the human person can only pass from "being" to "well-being," from the image to the similitude, by ordering sensible and irrational creatures to their end in God as well.

Simply put, the story of grace in Bonaventure's theology is in no wise simply a story about "the forgiveness of *my* sins." To be forgiven is to be made capable of holy, ordered relationships, not only between the individual and God, but between the individual and the entire created order of reality. Through the *influentia* of sanctifying grace, the individual becomes capable of relating to all of creation through the charity of the Spirit. This includes, of course, the flesh of the leper, as in Bonaventure's hagiographical portrayals of Francis's sanctity, but it also includes every piece of irrational creation, which can only enjoy its own *reductio* into the Trinity through the similitude received by the human person through sanctifying grace. Sin, for Bonaventure, leaves us "mercenaries," inwardly focused on our own good to the detriment of all persons and all created things around us; grace, in contrast, opens us up so that we can become "extroverts" who relate to the created order of reality through the charity of the Holy Spirit. Human persons are only "perfected" through grace when they come down from the mountain of contemplation and attend to creation through works of mercy once again.

This intuition, though simplistic, could be quite useful for systematic theologians concerned with issues surrounding social and environmental justice in the present day. The graced person in Bonaventure's theology cannot, by definition, turn a blind eye to the alien, the orphan, and the widow in her midst. Likewise, the graced person cannot, by definition, turn a blind eye to the sensible and irrational creation whose own "well-being" is ordered to the contemplative vocation that characterizes Bonaventure's theological anthropology.

Especially in the Western world, the narrative of grace heard from the popular pulpit is often a narrative that merely attends to the ascending valence of the hierarchical soul: The person of faith needs grace so that her sins can be forgiven and so that she can find eternal happiness with God. Bonaventure's "graced" angelic anthropology alternatively serves as a poignant reminder for persons of faith in the modern world that this ascent is only the beginning; that the descent to one's neighbor and the world must always follow; and that only through perpetual "ascents" and "descents" does the person of faith remain in God. Grace is not a zap of lightening that "forgives my sins" and ushers me immediately to heaven; rather, it is a continuous inflowing between the person of faith and God that only remains continuous when the person remains receptive to it in a posture of humility. The human person's receptivity to grace, then, ensures her continued "circling" or "spiraling" between contemplation and action, between God and the world. The Seraphic Doctor's doctrine of grace in this respect especially might be useful for theologians eager to direct persons of faith in the modern world from the story of "me" to the story of "us," which—in the spirit of Pope Francis's encyclical, *Laudato si'*—includes the entire created order of reality.

Grace in Bonaventure's Wisdom Theology

Following from this point, we can finally turn to the question with which this book began.[7] Most commonly, the Seraphic Doctor's doctrine of grace has been treated within the context of his "wisdom theology." Ephrem Longpré, Christopher Carpenter, Zachary Hayes, and Gregory LaNave, while perhaps disagreeing about some of the finer points concerning how these two concepts relate,[8] have nonetheless all shown the inseparability of Bonaventure's notions of theological *sapientia* (wisdom) and *sanctitas* (sanctity). As these scholars have all variously argued, for the Seraphic Doctor, sanctity is required of the theologian: In order to do theology well, the theologian must possess the

---

7. This portion of the chapter has been revised and published as, Shelby, "*Vir Hierarchicus* and the Goal of Theology," 159–71. It is reused with permission here.

8. See especially LaNave, introduction to *Through Holiness to Wisdom*, 14–26, for a discussion and overview of several different approaches to this subject. For a select bibliography on the subject, see also Bougerol, *Introduction to the Works of Bonaventure*; Carpenter, *Theology as the Road to Holiness in St. Bonaventure*; and Zachary Hayes, "Franciscan Tradition as a Wisdom Tradition," *Spirit and Life: A Journal of Contemporary Franciscanism* 7 (1997): 27–40. See also my introduction to this bibliography, as well as my introduction to Bonaventure's "wisdom theology" and the Bonaventurean Question, in Chapter 1.

gift of grace which unites her to the "First Principle," the Trinity, and which also thus distinguishes her from those who merely philosophize. His doctrine of grace is thus most often treated within this particular context in order to discuss how, through grace, the theologian can attain "wisdom." As I nonetheless intimated in Chapter 1, these accounts of Bonaventure's wisdom theology have tended to treat his doctrine of grace as one "step" within a larger argument. It is only now—after encountering that doctrine as a topic *in se*—that we are prepared to approach the role of sanctity in Bonaventure's wisdom theology for ourselves.

In the prologue to his *Commentary on the Sentences,* the Seraphic Doctor defines the goal of theology as follows:

> For if we consider the intellect *in itself,* thus it is properly called speculative and is perfected by a habit which is the grace of contemplation [*contemplationis gratia*], and is called *speculative science.* But if we consider it as having originated to be extended *to work,* thus it is perfected by a habit that exists so that we might become good [*ut boni fiamus*], and this is *practical* or moral *science.* But if we consider it from a middle point of view, as having originated to be extended *to the affect* [*extendi ad affectum*], so it is perfected by a middle habit between the purely speculative and the purely practical [*habitu medio inter pure speculativum et practicum*], and which is encircled by both [*complectitur utrumque*]. And this habit is called *wisdom* [*sapientia*], which simultaneously designates the cognition and affection…. Whence, it is for the sake of contemplation, and so that we might become good; but principally, it is so that we might become good [*ut boni fiamus*].[9]

I contend that Bonaventure's articulation regarding the goal of theology here only makes sense after one has attended to his doctrine of grace and accompanying notion of the "*vir hierarchicus*" as I have thus expounded it throughout this book. Whereas previous scholarship on Bonaventure's wisdom theology tends to emphasize the speculative goal of the above definition, oftentimes to the detriment of the practical, the Seraphic Doctor's angelic anthropology—especially as he readapts and revises it from Thomas Gallus within his doctrine of grace—provides the vocabulary with which to understand exactly what this definition means.

Indeed, as we have seen over and over again throughout the Seraphic Doctor's various discussions of the effects of grace within the human

9. *I Sent.* prooem. q. 3, conc. (1, 13).

soul, he claims that the soul can be made "hierarchical" through grace only inasmuch as the contemplative, affective union with God experienced at the level of the seraph then yields to a descent back into the world, as is clearly indicated in the *Breviloquium*, the *Hexaëmeron*, and in his presentation of St. Francis as the *"vir hierarchicus"* in the *Legenda maior* and in his sermons on St. Francis. Sanctity, in Bonaventure's doctrine of grace, has a definite shape: It is hierarchical. Symbolized by the scriptural image of Jacob's Ladder, the sanctified soul is characterized by endless "ascents" and "descents" through which it remains in God as a similitude of the Trinity. The seraphic order within his angelic anthropology, or namely, the point at which the soul is united to the Bridegroom through an affective union that fecundates the descending valence "back down to the humility of following," as he writes in the *Hexaëmeron*, is the fulcrum around which this circular way of remaining in God revolves. For Bonaventure, contemplative union with God is not the top of a bottom-up mystical ladder that, once reached, represents the "end" of the rational creature's spiritual journey; it is, rather, a beginning, an affective union that fecundates all the rational creature's interior powers so that it bleeds out into the world through "works of mercy," as demonstrated especially in St. Francis's experience of the stigmata, which renewed his desire to minister to the lepers as he had at the beginning of his ministry.

This hierarchical shape of sanctity, as it were, pertains to the Seraphic Doctor's words concerning the goal of theology in his prologue to the *Commentary to the Sentences* because it helps us to understand how contemplation and praxis relate within his definition of theology as *sapientia*, as an affective habit that we do "primarily so that we might become good." By attending to his naming of Francis as a *"vir hierarchicus,"* we can begin to understand these theologian-saints. For Bonaventure, the theologian ought to aim at nothing less than becoming "hierarchical," than ascending to the contemplative union with God that will nonetheless irrevocably set him or her ablaze with a desire to irradiate the influence of grace to others. In the same way that Bonaventure regards St. Francis as a "Jacob's Ladder," so, too, should the theologian ascend through her speculative pursuits to taste the charity of the seraph and—like Francis—be conformed to Christ the Hierarch. She will only be conformed, however, when she also descends from contemplation to praxis, to teach her neighbors in humility. The Seraphic Doctor's claim in his *Commentary on the Sentences* that the end of theology is both speculative and practical but primarily practical is nothing but an early articulation of this same idea. To strive for contemplation through the work of theology is to strive, through grace, to become holy in this way, to learn how to love God so that we might be molded to love the leper as well.

These insights can perhaps be of service to those theologians who continue to wrestle with Bonaventure's doctrine of grace within the context of his wisdom theology. Rather than treating the former in light of the latter, however, this study has hopefully shown how speculation regarding the goal of the Seraphic Doctor's wisdom theology is more fruitfully approached by first attending to grace.

To Dance in the Light of Grace

My own work in expounding the Seraphic Doctor's theology through-out this book has, admittedly, relied heavily upon grace. Following the spirit of Bonaventure's claims concerning the relationship between contemplation and praxis, it is perhaps here fitting to close by moving from a consideration of these theological concepts and into a more concrete realm.

A few blocks away from the Notre Dame Cathedral in Paris, pil-grims can round the corner to find themselves confronted with the Pal-ais de la Cité on the Île de la Cité. If they stand in a short line and pass through the security gates of the Palais, they can then enter a courtyard where, in front of them and hidden by the walls of the Palais from the outside, the Sainte-Chapelle will loom silently before them. This crown of High Gothic architecture, though much smaller than Notre Dame, is nonetheless its equal in grandeur, famed especially for its stained-glass windows that stretch a few yards from the floor of the chapel and all the way up to the vaulted ceilings. The windows essentially serve as the chapel's walls. Walking up the rounded staircase that leads from the ground floor and into the chapel itself, the space inevitably invites pilgrims to turn their gaze upwards and about them. Each pane of mul-ticolored glass in every window works together to weave a tapestry of light: If one enters the chapel on a cloudy day, and the clouds move and sway to conceal and then re-reveal the sunlight, the sunbeams dance among the panes of glass, illuminating reds and greens and blues and yellows at different angles that paint the chapel with holy light.

Turning around toward the entrance of the chapel, the pilgrim will see a rose window that, like the windows throughout the rest of the space, occupies most of the wall above the doorway. A giant sphere of light, colored panes of glass revolve in concentric circles within it around the central image of Christ. Though the space itself symbolizes God's transcendence as the dance of light in the stained glass pulls the pilgrim's gaze heavenward, one is nonetheless struck by the fact that—in looking upward—each pane of glass, from the lowest to the highest, is an indispensable player in this show of light. In the same way that the concentric circles of the rose window above the chapel's exit pull the eye to Christ the Center, so also every pane of glass—and indeed, every element within the chapel—directs the eye to what is "around" as well as to what is "above." The pilgrim is only uplifted to consider God's transcendence by being pulled into a relationship with everything that surrounds her.

Since Sainte-Chapelle was consecrated in 1248, perhaps Bonaventure himself would have been one such pilgrim as a young student reading Lombard's *Sentences* under his teacher, Alexander of Hales, at the University of Paris. Where my own explanations of the theological concepts within his exquisite doctrine of grace—including even my feeble attempts to utilize his own symbols to help us envision these concepts—have surely fallen short, perhaps this final image might illuminate the beauty of that doctrine for his readers. Every person who receives the gift of sanctifying grace is like one pane of glass in Sainte-Chapelle: On our own, we are certainly still beautiful and capable of being illuminated by the light of God, but it is only when we are placed alongside every other piece of glass—when we begin to relate to everything that surrounds us above and below—that divine light will truly begin to dance amid us all. To receive the light of grace, for St. Bonaventure, is to be invited into this dance, this panoply of holy light through which all human beings are uplifted into God by being drawn into relationships with one another.

BIBLIOGRAPHY

Primary Sources

Primary sources will be alphabetized according to the first name of the author of the work cited. English translations of Bonaventure's works are referenced below according to the order in which they were printed in *The Works of St. Bonaventure* series rather than alphabetically (St. Bonaventure, NY: Franciscan Institute, 1996–2016), vols. 1–17; alternative translations of those works are listed in the chronological order they appeared alongside the corresponding work in that series where appropriate.

Alexander of Hales. "I prologhi delle 'Postilla' ai vangeli synottici di Alessandro di Hales." Edited by Alexander Horowski. *Collecteana Franciscana 77* (2007): 27–62.

———. *Quaestiones disputatae de gratia: editio critica.* Edited by Jacek Mateusz Wierzbicki. Studia Antoniana 50. Rome: Antonianum, 2008.

———. *Quaestiones disputatae secundum Alexandrum de Iudicio.* Edited by Alexander Horowski. *Collecteana Franciscana 75* (2005): 27–101.

———. *Summa theologica Doctoris Irrefragabilis Alexandri de Hales Ordinis Minorum.* Quaracchi: Ex Typographia Collegii S. Bonaventurae, 1924.

———. *Tractatus Magistri Alexandri de significationibus et expositione sacrarum Scripturarum.* Edited by Alexander Horowski. "Tractatus Magistri Alexandri de significationibus et expositione sacram Scripturam: Introduzione ed Edizione Critica." *Collecteana Franciscana 79* (2009): 5–44.

Anselm. *Cur Deus homo* (PL 158: 359).

Augustine. *Serm. 169,* 11.13 (PL 38: 923). Translated by Edmund Hill in *Sermons (148–183) on the New Testament,* 231. Works of St. Augustine 3/5. New Rochelle, NY: New City Press, 1992.

Bonaventure. *Doctoris Seraphici S. Bonaventurae Opera omnia,* vols. 1–10. Quaracchi: Ex Typographia Collegii s. Bonaventurae, 1882–1902.

———. *Opere di San Bonaventura.* Edited by Jacques Guy Bougerol, Cornelio del Zotto and Leonardo Sileo. Vols. 1–4, 10–12. Roma: Città Nuova Editrice, 1992–2005.

———. *Sermons de diversis*. Edited by Jacques Guy Bougerol. 2 vols. Paris: Les éditions Franciscaines, 1993.

Hugh of St. Victor. *De sacramentis* (*PL* 176: 173–618A).

John Scotus Eriugena. "De caelesti hierarchia." *Dionysius Areopagita secundum translationem quam fecit Iohannes Scotus seu Eriugena*. Iohannes Scottus seu Eriugena, LLA 696. Turnhout: Brepols, 2015.

Peter Lombard. *Petri Lombardi: Sententiarum libri IV.* Edited by Joannes Aleaume, Francisco Garcia, Jacques-Paul Migne, et al. Paris: Migne, 1841.

Selected Works in Translation

Bonaventure. *On the Reduction of the Arts to Theology*. Translated by Zachary Hayes. The Works of St. Bonaventure 1. St. Bonaventure, NY: Franciscan Institute, 1996.

———. *Itinerarium mentis in Deum*. Translated by Philotheus Boehner and Zachary Hayes. The Works of St. Bonaventure 2. St. Bonaventure, NY: Franciscan Institute, 2002.

———. *The Journey of the Mind to God*. Translated by Philotheus Boehner and edited by Stephen F. Brown. Hackett: Indianapolis/Cambridge, 1993.

———. *Into God: Itinerarium mentis in Deum of Saint Bonaventure; An Annotated Translation*. Translated by Regis J. Armstrong, OFM, Cap. Washington, DC: The Catholic University of America Press, 2020.

———. *Disputed Questions on the Mystery of the Trinity*. Translated by Zachary Hayes. The Works of St. Bonaventure 3. St. Bonaventure, NY: Franciscan Institute, 2002.

———. *Disputed Questions on the Knowledge of Christ*. Translated by Zachary Hayes. The Works of St. Bonaventure 4. St. Bonaventure, NY: Franciscan Institute, 2006.

———. *Writings Concerning the Franciscan Order*. Translated by Dominic Monti. The Works of St. Bonaventure 5. St. Bonaventure, NY: Franciscan Institute, 1994.

———. *Collations on the Ten Commandments*. Translated by Paul Spaeth. The Works of St. Bonaventure 6. St. Bonaventure, NY: Franciscan Institute, 1996.

———. *Commentary on Ecclesiastes*. Translated by Campion Murray and Robert J. Karris. The Works of St. Bonaventure 7. St. Bonaventure, NY: Franciscan Institute, 2004.

———. *Commentary on the Gospel of Luke, Chapters 1–8*. Translated by Robert J. Karris. The Works of St. Bonaventure 8:1. St. Bonaventure, NY: Franciscan Institute, 2001.

———. *Commentary on the Gospel of Luke, Chapters 9–16*. Translated by Robert J. Karris. The Works of St. Bonaventure 8:2. St. Bonaventure, NY: Franciscan Institute, 2003.

———. *Commentary on the Gospel of Luke, Chapters 17–24*. Translated by Robert J. Karris. The Works of St. Bonaventure 8:3. St. Bonaventure, NY: Franciscan Institute, 2004.

———. *Breviloquium*. Translated by Dominic Monti. The Works of St. Bonaventure 9. St. Bonaventure, NY: Franciscan Institute, 2005.

———. *Writings on the Spiritual Life*. Translated by Edward F. Coughlin. The Works of St. Bonaventure 10. St. Bonaventure, NY: Franciscan Institute, 2006.

———. *Commentary on the Gospel of John*. Translated by Robert J. Karris. The Works of St. Bonaventure 11. St. Bonaventure, NY: Franciscan Institute, 2007.

———. *The Sunday Sermons of St. Bonaventure*. Translated by Timothy J. Johnson. The Works of St. Bonaventure 12. St. Bonaventure, NY: Franciscan Institute, 2008.

———. *Disputed Questions on Evangelical Perfection*. Translated by Thomas Reist and Robert J. Karris. The Works of St. Bonaventure 13. Emendatio. St. Bonaventure, NY: Franciscan Institute, 2008.

———. *Collations on the Seven Gifts of the Holy Spirit*. Translated by Zachary Hayes. The Works of St. Bonaventure 14. St. Bonaventure, NY: Franciscan Institute, 2010.

———. *Defense of the Mendicants*. Translated by Jose de Vinck and Robert J. Karris. The Works of St. Bonaventure 15. St. Bonaventure, NY: Franciscan Institute, 2008.

———. *Commentary on the Sentences: Philosophy of God*. Translated by R. E. Houser and Timothy Noone. The Works of St. Bonaventure 16. St. Bonaventure, NY: Franciscan Institute, 2016.

———. *Commentary on the Sentences: Sacraments*. Translated by J. A. Wayne Hellmann, Timothy LeCroy, and Luke Davis Townsend. The Works of St. Bonaventure 17. St. Bonaventure, NY: Franciscan Institute, 2016.

———. *Bonaventure on the Eucharist: Commentary on the Sentences, Book IV, dist. 8–13*. Translated by Junius Johnson. Dallas Medieval Texts and Translations. Louvain: Peeters, 2017.

———. *Collations on the Hexaemeron. Conferences on the Six Days of Creation: The Illumination of the Church*. Translated by Jay M. Hammond. The Works of St. Bonaventure 18. St. Bonaventure, NY: Franciscan Institute, 2018.

———. *Collations on the Six Days*. Translated by José de Vinck. The Works of Bonaventure 5. Paterson, NJ: St. Anthony Guild Press, 1970.

Francis of Assisi: Early Documents. Edited by Regis J. Armstrong, J. A. Wayne Hellmann, and William J. Short. Vols. 1–3. New York: New City Press, 1999–2002.

Peter Lombard. *The Sentences: Book 1*. Translated by Giulio Silano. Toronto: Pontifical Institute of Mediaeval Studies, 2007.

———. *The Sentences: Book 2*. Translated by Giulio Silano. Toronto: Pontifical Institute of Mediaeval Studies, 2008.

———. *In hierarchiam caelestem S. Dionysii (PL 175:923A–1154C)*.

Pseudo-Dionysius the Areopagite. *Corpus Dionysiacum* (PG 3:119–1122).

———. *Pseudo-Dionysius: The Complete Works.* Translated by Colm Luibheid. Edited by Paul Rorem. New York: Paulist Press, 1987.

Thomas Gallus. *Commentaires du Cantique des cantiques.* Edited by Jeanne Barbet. Textes philosophiques du Moyen Âge 14. Paris: Béatrice-Nauwelaerts, 1967.

———. "Commentaire sur Isaïe de Thomas de Saint-Victor." Edited by G. Théry. *La vie spirituelle* 47 (1936): 146–62.

———. *Explanatio in libros Dionysii.* Edited by Declan Anthony Lawell. *CC CM* 223. Turnhout: Brepols, 2011.

———. *Glose super angelica ierarchia: Accedunt indices ad Thomae Galli opera.* Edited by Declan Anthony Lawell. *CC CM* 223A. Turnhout: Brepols, 2011.

Secondary Sources

Modern authors are arranged alphabetically. Multiple titles by the same modern author are arranged in ascending chronological order; if two works by the same author are from the same year, these are arranged alphabetically.

Anatolios, Khaled. *Retrieving Nicaea: The Development and Meaning of Trinitarian Doctrine.* Grand Rapids, MI: Baker Academic, 2011.

Armstrong, Regis J. *The Spiritual Theology of the "Legenda major" of Saint Bonaventure.* PhD diss., Fordham University, 1974.

———. J. A. Wayne Hellmann, and William J. Short, eds. *Francis of Assisi: Early Documents.* Vols. 1–3. New York: New City Press, 1999–2002.

Barnes, Corey. "Part IV: On the Incarnation of the Word." In Monti and Shelby, *Bonaventure Revisited,* 195–214.

Benson, Joshua. "Structure and Meaning in St. Bonaventure's *Quaestiones Disputatae de Scientia Christi." Franciscan Studies* 62 (2004): 67–90.

———. "The Christology of the *Breviloquium.*" In Hammond et al., *A Companion to Bonaventure,* 247–87.

Blanco, Chavero. *Francisco de Assis, Imago Dei: Aproximación a la antropologia teológica de san Buenaventura.* Murcia: Espigas y Azucenas, 1993.

Blastic, Michael W. "Prayer in the Writings of Francis of Assisi and the Early Brothers." In *Franciscans at Prayer,* edited by Timothy J. Johnson, 3–29. Leiden: Brill, 2007.

Boehner, Philotheus. *The History of the Franciscan School.* Vol. 1, *Alexander of Hales.* St. Bonaventure, NY: Franciscan Institute, 1943.

———. Introduction to *Itinerarium mentis in Deum.* Translated by Zachary Hayes, 9–32. Works of St. Bonaventure 2. St. Bonaventure, NY: Franciscan Institute, 2002.

Boff, Leonardo. *Trinity and Society.* Translated by Paul Burns. Maryknoll, NY: Orbis Books, 1988.

Bougerol, Jacques Guy. *Introduction to the Works of Bonaventure.* Translated by José de Vinck. Paterson, NJ: St. Anthony Guild Press, 1964.

———. "Saint Bonaventure et le Pseudo-Denys l'Areopagite." *Études Franciscaines* 18 (Supplément Annuel 1968): 33–123.

———. "Le rôle de l'*influentia* dans la théologie de la grâce chez Bonaventure." *Revue Théologique de Louvain* 5 (1974): 274–300.

———. *Saint Bonaventure: Études sur les sources de sa pensée.* Northampton: Variorum Reprints, 1989.

———. Introduction to *Sermons de diversis* 1, edited by Jacques Guy Bougerol, 3–64. Paris: Les éditions Franciscaines, 1993.

Brown, Stephen F. Introduction to *The Journey of the Mind to God.* Translated by Philotheus Boehner. Indianapolis: Hackett, 1993.

———. "Declarative and Deductive Theology in the Early Fourteenth Century." In *Was ist Philosophie im Mittelalter?* Edited by J. A. Aertsen and A. Speer, 648–65. Berlin: W. de Gruyter, 1998.

———. "The Intellectual Context of Later Medieval Philosophy: Universities, Aristotle, Arts, Theology." In *Medieval Philosophy*, edited by John Marenbon, 188–201. Routledge History of Philosophy 3. London: Routledge, 1998.

———. "Walter Burley, Peter Aureoli and Gregory of Rimini." In *Medieval Philosophy*, edited by John Marenbon, 368–85. Routledge History of Philosophy 3. London: Routledge, 1998.

———. "Late Thirteenth Century Theology: '*Scientia*' Pushed to Its Limits.'" In '*Scientia*' und '*Disciplina*'. *Wissenstheorie und Wissenschaftspraxis im 12. Und 13. Jahrhundert*, edited by Rainer Berndt, Matthias Lutz-Bachmann, and Ralf M. W. Stammberger et al., 249–60. Erudiri Sapientia. Studien zum Mittelalter und zu seiner Rezeptionsgeschichte 3. Berlin: Akademie Verlag, 2002.

———. "Declarative Theology after Durandus: Its Presentation and Defense by Peter Aureol." In *Philosophical Debates at Paris in the Early Fourteenth Century*, edited by Stephen F. Brown, Thomas Dewender and Theo Kobusch, 401–21. Studien und Texte zur Geistesgeschichte des Mittelalters 102. Leiden-Boston: Brill, 2009.

Brunette, Pierre, and Paul Lachance, eds. *The Earliest Franciscans: The Legacy of Giles of Assisi, Roger of Provence, and James of Milan.* New York: Paulist Press, 2015.

Burns, J. Patout. "Grace." In *Augustine through the Ages: an Encyclopedia*, edited by Allan D. Fitzgerald, OSA, 391–98. Grand Rapids: William B. Eerdmans, 1999.

Carpenter, Christopher. *Theology as the Road to Holiness in St. Bonaventure.* New York: Paulist Press, 1999.

Coakley, Sarah. "Re-Thinking Dionysius the Areopagite." *Modern Theology* 24, no. 4 (2008): 531–40.

———. *God, Sexuality, and the Self: An Essay on The Trinity.* Cambridge: Cambridge University Press, 2013.

Colberg, Shawn M. *The Wayfarer's End: Bonaventure and Aquinas on Divine*

Rewards in Scripture and Sacred Doctrine. Washington, DC: The Catholic University of America Press, 2020.

Coolman, Boyd Taylor. "The Medieval Affective Dionysian Tradition." *Modern Theology* 24, no. 4 (2008): 615–32.

———. "Hugh of St. Victor's Influence on the Halensian Definition of Theology." *Franciscan Studies* 70 (2012): 367–84.

———. "Thomas Gallus." In *The Spiritual Senses: Perceiving God in Western Christianity,* edited by Paul L. Gavrilyuk and Sarah Coakley, 140–58. Cambridge: Cambridge University Press, 2012.

———. "'In whom I am well pleased': Hugh of St. Victor's Trinitarian Aesthetics." *Pro Ecclesia* 23, no. 3 (2014): 331–54.

———. *Knowledge, Love, and Ecstasy in the Theology of Thomas Gallus.* Oxford: Oxford University Press, 2017.

———. "Part II: On the Creation of the World." In Monti and Shelby, *Bonaventure Revisited,* 141–67.

Cousins, Ewert H. *Bonaventure and the Coincidence of Opposites.* Chicago: Franciscan Herald Press, 1978.

Coyle, Justin Shaun. "An Essay on Theological Aesthetics in the *Summa halensis.*" PhD diss., Boston College, 2018.

Cullen, Christopher. *Bonaventure.* New York: Oxford University Press, 2006.

———. "Bonaventure on Nature before Grace: A Historical Moment Reconsidered." *American Catholic Philosophical Quarterly* 85, no. 1 (2011): 161–76.

Cusato, Michael F. "Francis and the Franciscan Movement (1181/2–1226)." In *The Cambridge Companion to Francis of Assisi,* edited by Michael J. P. Robson, 17–33. Cambridge: Cambridge University Press, 2012.

———, Timothy J. Johnson, and Steven J. McMichael, eds. *Ordo et sanctitas: The Franciscan Spiritual Journey in Theology and Hagiography. Essays in Honor of J. A. Wayne Hellmann, OFM Conv.* Leiden: Brill, 2017

Davies, Rachel. *Bonaventure, the Body, and the Aesthetics of Salvation.* Cambridge: Cambridge University Press, 2020.

Davis, Robert Glenn. *The Weight of Love: Affect, Ecstasy, and Union in the Theology of Bonaventure.* New York: Fordham University Press, 2017.

Delcorno, Carlo. *Exemplum e letterature: tra Medievo e Rinascimento.* Bologna: Mulino, 1989.

Delio, Ilia. *Crucified Love: Bonaventure's Mysticism of the Crucified Christ.* Quincy, IL: Franciscan Press, 1998.

Dettloff, Werner. "'*Christus tenens medium in omnibus*': Sinn und Funktion der Theologie bei Bonaventura." *Wissenschaft und Weisheit* 20 (1957): 28–42, 120–40.

De Wachter, Maurits. *Le peche actuel selon Saint Bonaventure.* Paris: Éditions Franciscaines, 1967.

Doyle, Eric, trans. and ed. *The Disciple and the Master: St. Bonaventure's Sermons on St. Francis of Assisi.* Chicago: Franciscan Herald Press, 1983.

Dumont, Louis. *Homo hierarchicus: The Caste System and Its Implications.* London: Paladin, 1972.

Falque, Emmanuel, and Laure Solignac. "Penser en franciscain." *Études Franciscaines* 7, no. 2 (2014): 297–325.

———. *God, Flesh, and the Other.* Translated by William Christian Hackett. Evanston, IL: Northwestern University Press, 2015.

Fehlner, Peter D. *The Role of Charity in the Ecclesiology of St. Bonaventure.* Rome: Editrice Miscellanea Francescana, 1965.

Ferzoco, George. "The Context of Medieval Sermon Collections on Saints." In *Preacher, Sermon, and Audience in the Middle Ages*, edited by Carolyn Muessig, 279–92. Leiden: Brill, 2002.

Gaillardetz, Richard. "The Ecclesiological Foundations of Ministry within an Ordered Communion." In *Ordering of the Baptismal Priesthood*, edited by Susan Wood, 26–51. Collegeville: Liturgical Press, 2003.

Gerken, Alexander. *Theologie des Wortes: Das Verhältnis von Schöpfung und Inkarnation bei Bonaventura.* Düsseldorf: Patmos-Verlag, 1963.

Gilson, Etienne. *The Philosophy of St. Bonaventure.* Translated by Dom Illtyd Trethowan and F. J. Sheed. New York: Sheed and Ward, 1938.

Giltner, J. Alexander, and J. A. Wayne Hellmann. "Part VI: On the Sacramental Remedy." In Monti and Shelby, *Bonaventure Revisited*, 273–95.

Goff, Jared. "Part I: On the Trinity of God." In Monti and Shelby, *Bonaventure Revisited*, 97–139.

———. "*Mulier amicta sole*: Bonaventure's Preaching on the Marian Mode of the Incarnation and Marian Mediation in his Sermons on the Annunciation." In *Medieval Franciscan Approaches to the Virgin Mary: Mater sanctissima, misericordia, et dolorosa*, edited by Steven J. McMichael and Katherine Wrisley Shelby, 53–83. Leiden: Brill, 2019.

Golitzin, Alexander. "Dionysius Areopagita: A Christian Mysticism?" *Pro Ecclesia* 12, no. 2 (2003): 161–212.

———. *Mystagogy: A Monastic Reading of Dionysius Areopagita.* Collegeville: Cistercian Publications, 2013.

Gonzales, San Martin, and José Miguel. "Gratia." In *Dizionario Bonaventuriano*, edited by Ernesto Caroli, 438–49. Milano: Editrice Francescane, 2008.

Guardini, Romano. *Die Lehre des Heil: Bonaventura von der Erlösung: ein Beitrag zur Geschichte und zum System der Erlösungslehre.* Düsseldorf: L. Schwann, 1921.

———. *Systembildende Elemente in der Theologie Bonaventuras: Die Lehren vom lumen mentis, von der gradatio entium und der influentia sensus et motus*, edited by Werner Dettloff. Leiden: Brill, 1964.

Hammond, Jay. "Appendix: Order in the *Itinerarium mentis in Deum*." In J. A. Wayne Hellmann, *Divine and Created Order in Bonaventure's Theology*.

———. "Bonaventure's *Itinerarium*: A Respondeo." *Franciscan Studies* 67 (2009): 301–21.

———. "Bonaventure's *Legenda maior*." In Hammond et al., *A Companion to Bonaventure*, 453–508.

———, J. A. Wayne Hellmann, and Jared Goff, eds. *A Companion to Bonaventure.* Brill's Companions to the Christian Tradition 48. Leiden: Brill, 2014.

———. "The Textual Context." In Monti and Shelby, *Bonaventure Revisited*, 9–72.

Hayes, Zachary. *The Hidden Center: Spirituality and Speculative Christology in St. Bonaventure.* New York: Paulist Press, 1981.

———. "The Theological Image of St. Francis of Assisi in the Sermons of St. Bonaventure." In *Bonaventuriana: Miscellanea in onore di Jacques Guy Bougerol, OFM,* edited by Chavero Blanco, 323–45. Roma: Edizioni Antonianum, 1988.

———. "Franciscan Tradition as a Wisdom Tradition." *Spirit and Life: A Journal of Contemporary Franciscanism* 7 (1997): 27–40.

———. Introduction to *Collations on the Seven Gifts of the Holy Spirit.* Translated by Zachary Hayes, 7–25. Works of St. Bonaventure 14. St. Bonaventure, NY: 2008.

———. "Bonaventure's Trinitarian Theology." In Hammond et al., *A Companion to Bonaventure,* 189–214.

Hellmann, J. A. Wayne. *Divine and Created Order in Bonaventure's Theology.* Translated by Jay M. Hammond. St. Bonaventure, NY: Franciscan Institute, 2001.

———. and Timothy LeCroy, Luke Davis Townsend. "Historical Introduction." In *Commentary on the Sentences: Sacraments,* edited by J. A. Wayne Hellmann, Timothy LeCroy, and Luke Davis Townsend, 7–26. Works of St. Bonaventure 17. St. Bonaventure, NY: Franciscan Institute, 2016.

Horowski, Alexander. "Doni dello Spirito Santo nella theologia di Alessandro di Hales." *Naturaleza y Gracia* 55, no. 2 (2008): 477–517.

Hughes, Kevin L. "Bonaventure *Contra mundum*? The Catholic Theological Tradition Revisited." *Theological Studies* 74, no. 2 (2013): 372–98.

Hülsbusch, Werner. *Elemente einer Kreuzestheologie in den Spätschriften Bonaventuras.* Düsseldorf: Patmos-Verlag, 1968.

Ivanovic, Filip, ed. *Dionysius the Areopagite between Orthodoxy and Heresy.* Newcastle, UK: Cambridge Scholars, 2011.

Johnson, Elizabeth. *She Who Is: The Mystery of God in Feminist Theological Discourse.* New York: Crossroad Publishing, 2014.

Johnson, Timothy J. "Speak Lord, Your Servant Is Listening: Obedience and Prayer in Franciscan Spirituality." *The Cord* 42, no. 2 (1992): 36–45.

———. "Reading between the Lines: Apophatic Knowledge and Naming the Divine in Bonaventure's Book of Creation." *Franciscan Studies* 60 (2002): 139–58.

———. "Dream Bodies and Peripatetic Prayer: Reading Bonaventure's *Itinerarium* with Certeau." *Modern Theology* 21, no. 3 (2005): 413–27.

———. "Prologue as Pilgrimage: Bonaventure as Spiritual Cartographer." *Miscellanea Francescana* 106–7 (2006–2007): 445–64.

———. Introduction to *The Sunday Sermons of Saint Bonaventure.* Translated by Timothy J. Johnson, 11–58. Works of St. Bonaventure 12. St. Bonaventure, NY: Franciscan Institute, 2008.

———. "Dieter Hattrup and Bonaventure's Authorship of the '*De reductione*.'" *Franciscan Studies* 67 (2009): 139–58.

———. "*Item ordinetur de Legenda Beati Francisci*: A Prolegomena to the Study of Bonaventure's *Legenda minor.*" *Frate Francisco* 76, no. 1 (2010): 225–39.

———. *The Soul in Ascent: Bonaventure on Poverty, Prayer, and Union with God.* 2nd ed. St. Bonaventure, NY: Franciscan Institute, 2012.

———. "Bonaventure as Preacher." In Hammond et al., *A Companion to Bonaventure*, 403–34.

———. "Place, Analogy, and Transcendence: Bonaventure and Bacon on the Franciscan Relationship to the World." In *Innovationen durch Deuten und Gestalten: Klöster im Mittelalter zwischen Jenseits und Welt*, edited by Gert Melville, Bernd Schneidmüller, and Stefan Weinfurter, 83–96. Regensburg: Verlag Schnell and Steiner, 2014.

———. "Part III: On the Corruption of Sin." In Monti and Shelby, *Bonaventure Revisited*, 169–93.

———. "Reform, Hagiography, and Sanctity: Bonaventure's Sermons on the Saints." In Cusato et al., *Ordo et sanctitas*, 186–206.

———. "*Wisdom Has Built Her House; She Has Set Up Her Seven Pillars*: Roger Bacon, Franciscan Wisdom, and Conversion to the Sciences." In *The English Province of the Franciscans (1224–c.1350)*, edited by Michael J. P. Robson, 294–315. Leiden: Brill, 2017.

———, Marie Kolbe Zamora, and Katherine Wrisley Shelby, eds. *Bonaventure: Friar, Teacher, Minister, Bishop; A Celebration of the Eighth Centenary of His Birth. Conference Proceedings from "Frater, magister, minister, et episcopus: The Works and Worlds of St. Bonaventure," at St. Bonaventure University, July 12–15, 2017.* St. Bonaventure, NY: Franciscan Institute, 2020.

———. "Place, Person, and Prayer in the *Summa Halensis.*" In Schumacher, *The Summa Halensis: Doctrines and Debates*, 325–42.

Karris, Robert J. Introduction to *Commentary on the Gospel of John.* Translated by Robert J. Karris, 1–32. Works of St. Bonaventure, 11. St. Bonaventure, NY: Franciscan Institute, 2007.

———. Introduction to *The Disputed Questions on Evangelical Perfection.* Trans. Robert J. Karris and Thomas Reist, 7–28. Works of St. Bonaventure, 13. St. Bonaventure, NY: Franciscan Institute, 2008.

Kasper, Walter. *The God of Jesus Christ: The New Edition.* New York: T&T Clark International, 2012.

Kaup, Julian. "Christus und die Kirche nach der Lehre des hl. Bonaventura." *Franziskanische Studien* 26 (1939): 333–44.

Kienzle, Beverly Mayne, ed. *Models of Holiness in Medieval Sermons: Proceedings of the International Symposium (Kalamazoo, 4–7 May 1995).* Textes et études du Moyen Âge 5. Louvain-La-Neuve: Fédération Internationale de Instituts d'Études Medievales, 1996.

Kuntz, Paul. "The Hierarchical Vision of St. Bonaventure." In *Atti del Congresso Internazionale per il VII Centenario di San Bonaventura da Bagnoregio: San Bonaventura, Maestro di vita Francescana e di sapienza Christiana; Roma, 19–26 settembre 1974*, edited by A. Pompei, 233–48. Rome: Pontificia Facoltà Teologica San Bonaventura, 1976.

LaCugna, Catherine Mowry. *God for Us: The Trinity and Christian Life.* San Francisco: Harper Collins, 1991.

LaNave, Gregory. *Through Holiness to Wisdom: The Nature of Theology according to St. Bonaventure.* Rome: Instituto Storico dei Cappuccini, 2005.

———. "Knowing God through and in All Things: A Proposal for Reading Bonaventure's '*Itinerarium mentis in Deum.*'" *Franciscan Studies* 67 (2009): 267–99.

———. "Bonaventure." In *The Spiritual Senses: Perceiving God in Western Christianity*, edited by Paul L. Gavrilyuk and Sarah Coakley, 159–73. Cambridge: Cambridge University Press, 2011.

Lawell, Declan Anthony. "*Ne de ineffabili penitus taceamus:* Aspects of the Specialized Vocabulary of the Writings of Thomas Gallus." *Viator* 40, no. 1 (2009): 151–84.

———. "*Spectacula contemplationis* (1244–46): A Treatise by Thomas Gallus." *Recherches de théologie et philosophie médiévales* 76, no. 2 (2009): 249–85.

———. Introduction to *Thomae Galli: Explanatio in libros Dionysii*, edited by Declan Anthony Lawell, vii–ix, xxiii–xxxii. CC CM 223. Turnhout, Brepols, 2011.

Longpré, Ephrem. "Bonaventure." In *Dictionnaire de spiritualité.* Vol. 1. Col. 1768–1843. Paris: G. Beauchesne et ses fils, 1937.

Louth, Andrew. *Denys the Areopagite.* Wilton, CT: Morehouse, Barlow, 1989.

Luyckx, Bonifaz Anton. *Der Erkenntnislehre Bonaventuras.* Munich: Baeumker-Beiträge, 1923.

Maranesi, Pietro. *Verbum inspiratum: Chiave ermeneutica dell'Hexaëmeron di San Bonaventura.* Rome: Instituto Storico dei Cappuccini, 1996.

Marthaler, Berard. *Original Justice and Sanctifying Grace in the Writings of Saint Bonaventure.* Rome: Editrice Miscellanea Francescana, 1965.

McElrath, Damian, ed. *Franciscan Christology.* St. Bonaventure, New York: Franciscan Institute, 1980.

McGinn, Bernard. *The Foundations of Mysticism: Origins to the Fifth Century.* The Presence of God: A History of Western Christian Mysticism 1. New York: Crossroad, 1991.

———. *The Growth of Mysticism: Gregory the Great through the Twelfth Century.* The Presence of God: A History of Western Christian Mysticism 2. New York: Crossroad, 1994.

———. "Thomas Gallus and Dionysian Mysticism." *Studies in Spirituality* 8 (1998): 81–96.

McGrath, Alister E. *Iustitia Dei: A History of the Christian Doctrine of Justification.* 2nd ed. Cambridge: Cambridge University Press, 1998.

Milbank, John. *The Suspended Middle: Henri de Lubac and the Debate Surrounding the Supernatural.* Grand Rapids, MI: William B. Eerdmans, 2005.

Mirabent, Antonio Briva. *La gloria y su relación con la gracia según las obras de San Buenaventura.* Barcelona: Editorial Casulleras, 1957.

Mitzka, Franz. "Die Lehre des hl. Bonaventura von der Vorbereitung auf die heiligmachende Gnade." *Zeitschrift für katholische Theologie*. 50, no. 1 (1926): 27–72; 50, no. 2 (1926): 220–52.

Moltmann, Jürgen. *The Trinity and the Kingdom: The Doctrine of God.* San Francisco: Harper and Row, 1981.

Monsour, H. Daniel. *The Relation between Uncreated and Created Grace in the Halesian* Summa: *A Lonerganian Reading.* PhD diss., Toronto School of Theology, 2000.

Monti, Dominic, and Katherine Wrisley Shelby, eds. *Bonaventure Revisited: Companion to the Breviloquium.* St. Bonaventure, NY: Franciscan Institute, 2017.

———. Introduction to *Bonaventure Revisited*, edited by Monti and Shelby, 7–16.

Nguyen van Si, Ambroise. *La théologie de l'imitation du Christ d'aprés Saint Bonaventure.* Roma: Editizione Antonianum, 1991.

O'Meara, Thomas F. "Beyond 'Hierarchology': Johann Adam Möhler and Yves Congar." In *The Legacy of the Tübingen School: The Relevance of Nineteenth-Century Theology for the Twenty-First Century*, edited by Donald J. Dietrich and Michael J. Himes, 173–91. New York: Crossroad, 1997.

Osborne, Kenan B., OFM. *The Franciscan Intellectual Tradition: Tracing its Origins and Identifying its Central Components.* The Franciscan Heritage Series 1. St. Bonaventure, NY: Franciscan Institute, 2003.

Osborne, Thomas M. "*Unibilitas*: The Key to Bonaventure's Understanding of Human Nature." *Journal of the History of Philosophy* 37, no. 2 (1999): 227–50.

Perl, Eric D. *Theophany: The Neoplatonic Philosophy of Dionysius the Areopagite.* Albany, NY: State University of New York Press, 2007.

Principe, Walter H. *Alexander of Hales' Theology of the Hypostatic Union.* Vol. 2. *The Theology of the Hypostatic Union in the Early Thirteenth Century.* Studies and Texts 12. Toronto: Pontifical Institute of Mediaeval Studies, 1967.

Quaracchi editors. "Prologue generalis." In *Summa theologica Doctoris Irrefragabilis Alexandri de Hales Ordinis Minorum.* Tome 1, Book 1. Quaracchi: Ex Typographia Collegii S. Bonaventurae, 1924.

Quinn, J. F. *The Historical Constitution of St. Bonaventure's Philosophy.* Toronto: Pontifical Institute of Mediaeval Studies, 1973.

Raby, Elyse. *Toward an Intercorporeal Body of Christ: A Study in Ecclesial Body Images.* PhD diss., Boston College, 2021.

Rahner, Karl. "La doctrine des sens spirituels au Moyen Âge, en particular chez saint Bonaventure." *Revue d'ascetique et de mystique* 14 (1933): 263–99.

———. "The Doctrine of the 'Spiritual Senses' in the Middle Ages." In *Theological Investigations.* Vol. 18. Translated by Edward Quinn. New York: Crossroads, 1983.

———. *The Trinity.* Translated by Joseph Donceel. New York: Herder and Herder, 1970.

Ratzinger, Joseph. *The Theology of History in St. Bonaventure.* Translated by Zachary Hayes. Chicago: Franciscan Herald Press, 1971.

Rézette, Jean Pierre. "Grace and similitude de Dieu chez saint Bonaventure." *Ephemerides theologicae Lovanienses* 32 (1956): 46–64.

Rist, John. "Love, Knowing, and Incarnation in Pseudo-Dionysius." In *Traditions of Platonism: Essays in Honour of John Dillon*, edited by John J. Cleary, 375–88. Brookfield, VT: Ashgate, 1999.

Rocco, Giuseppe. *L'antropologia in San Bonaventura*. Vicenza: Editrice Veneta, 2009.

Roques, René. *L'universe Dionysien: Structure hiérarchique du monde selon le Pseudo-Denys*. Aubier: Éditions Montaigne, 1954.

Rorem, Paul. *Biblical and Liturgical Symbols within the Pseudo-Dionysian Synthesis*. Studies and Texts 71. Toronto: Pontifical Institute of Mediaeval Studies, 1984.

———. *Pseudo-Dionysius: A Commentary on the Texts and an Introduction to Their Influence*. New York: Oxford University Press, 1993.

———. "Dionysian Uplifting (Anagogy) in Bonaventure's *Reductio*." *Franciscan Studies* 70 (2012): 183–88.

Ruello, Francis. Introduction to *Un commentaire vercellien du* Cantique des cantiques: *'Deiformis anime gemitus,'* 7–93, edited by Jeanne Barbet. Translated by Francis Ruello. Turnhout: Brepols, 2005.

Ruh, Kurt. "Thomas Gallus Vercellensis." In *Geschichte der abendländischen Mystik*, 59–81. Die Mystik des deutschen Predigerordens und ihre Grundlegung durch die Hochscholastik 3. Munich: Verlag, 1996.

Rydstrøm-Poulsen, Aage. *The Gracious God: Gratia in Augustine and the Twelfth Century*. Copenhagen: Akademisk Forlag, 2002.

Schmutz, Jacob. "The Medieval Doctrine of Causality and the Theology of Pure Nature (13th to 17th Centuries)." In *Surnaturel: A Controversy as the Heart of Twentieth-Century Thomistic Thought*, edited by Serge-Thomas Bonino and translated by Matthew Levering, 203–50. Ave Maria, FL: Sapientia Press, 2009.

Schumacher, Lydia, ed. *The Summa Halensis: Sources and Context*. Veröffentlichungen des Grabmann-Institutes zur Erforschung der mittelalterlichen Theologie und Philosophie 65. Berlin: De Gruyter, 2020.

———. *The Summa Halensis: Doctrines and Debates*. Veröffentlichungen des Grabmann-Institutes zur Erforschung der mittelalterlichen Theologie und Philosophie 66. Berlin: De Gruyter, 2020.

———. *The Summa Halensis: The Legacy of Early Franciscan Thought*. Veröffentlichungen des Grabmann-Institutes zur Erforschung der mittelalterlichen Theologie und Philosophie 67. Berlin: De Gruyter, 2021.

Shelby, Katherine Wrisley. "Bonaventure on Grace, Hierarchy, and the Symbol of Jacob's Ladder." In Cusato et al., *Ordo et sanctitas*, 207–28.

———. "Part V: On the Grace of the Holy Spirit." In Monti and Shelby, *Bonaventure Revisited*, 215–43.

———. "Sanctifying Grace and the Threefold Way in the *Summa Halensis*." *Franciscan Connections: The Cord—A Spiritual Review* 68, no. 3 (2018): 10–16.

———. "The *Vir hierarchicus* and the Goal of Theology according to St. Bonaventure." In *Bonaventure: Friar, Teacher, Minister, Bishop. A Celebration of the*

Eighth Centenary of his Birth. Conference Proceedings from "Frater, Magister, Minister, et Episcopus: The Works and Worlds of St. Bonaventure," at St. Bonaventure University, July 12–15, 2017, edited by Timothy J. Johnson, Marie Kolbe Zamora, and Katherine Wrisley Shelby, 159–71. St. Bonaventure, NY: Franciscan Institute, 2021.

———. "Thomas Gallus' *Explanatio* and Dionysian Thought." In *Victorine Restoration: Essays on Hugh of St. Victor, Richard of St. Victor, and Thomas Gallus,* edited by David Orsbon and Robert J. Porwoll, 297–327. Turnhout: Brepols, 2021.

Silic, Rufin. *Christus und die Kirche, ihr verhältnis nach der lehre des heiligen Bonaventura.* Breslau: Müller and Seiffert, 1938.

Solignac, Laure. *La voie de la ressemblance: Itinéraire dans la pensée de saint Bonaventure.* Paris: Hermann, 2014.

Stang, Charles M. "Dionysius, Paul, and the Significance of the Pseudonym." *Modern Theology* 24, no. 4 (2008): 541–55.

Tavard, George H. *Transiency and Permanence: The Nature of Theology according to St. Bonaventure.* St. Bonaventure, NY: Franciscan Institute, 1954.

Tedoldi, Fabio Massimo. *La dottrina dei cinque sensi spirituali in San Bonaventura.* Rome: Pontificium Athenaeum Antonianum, 1999.

Théry, Gabriel. "Thomas Gallus et Egide d'Assise: le traite *De septem gradibus contemplationis.*" *Revue néoscolastique de philosophie* 36 (1934): 180–90.

Veuthey, Leon. *La filosofia Christiana di San Bonaventura.* Rome: Miscellanea Francescana, 1996.

Volf, Miraslov. "'The Trinity Is Our Social Program': The Doctrine of the Trinity and the Shape of Social Engagement." *Modern Theology* 14, no. 3 (1998): 403–23.

von Balthasar, Hans Urs. *The Glory of the Lord: A Theological Aesthetics.* Translated by Erasmo Levis-Merikakis, Andrew Louth, Brian McNeil et al. San Francisco: St. Ignatius Press, 1982–1989.

Walsh, James A. "Thomas Gallus et l'effort contemplatif." *Revue d'histoire de la spiritualité* 51 (1975): 17–42.

———. *The Pursuit of Wisdom and Other Works by the Author of the Cloud of Unknowing.* New York: Paulist Press, 1988.

Wawrykow, Joseph Peter. *God's Grace and Human Action: 'Merit' in the Theology of Thomas Aquinas.* Notre Dame: University of Notre Dame Press, 1995.

Weber, Hubert Philipp. *Sünde und Gnade bei Alexander von Hales.* Innsbruck: Tyrolia, 2003.

———. "Alexander of Hales's Theology in His Authentic Texts (Commentary on the *Sentences* of Peter Lombard, Various Disputed Questions)." In *The English Province of the Franciscans (1224–c.1350),* edited by Michael J. P. Robson, 273–93. Leiden: Brill, 2017.

Abelard, Peter, 63–64
activity, 1, 10, 32–34, 36–40, 73–74, 77, 88–90, 92, 97, 101, 105–6, 135–36, 141, 202, 259, 312, 346
Acts of the Apostles, 26, 83
Adam, 91, 172, 236–39
affective 4, 21, 43–44, 47–48, 50–56, 176–77, 183–84, 187, 189–90, 239, 277–78, 310, 327–29, 351, 360. *See also* union, affective
Agnes of Rome, 300, 329–33, 343–44, 348
Alan of Lille, 291n121
Albert the Great, 120n12
Alexander IV, Pope, 59
Alexander of Hales, 8, 23–25, 56–76, 99, 122, 124, 127, 130, 132–33, 349, 363
Andrew the Apostle, 327–29, 344, 348
angel, 14, 32, 38, 47, 82, 96, 98, 101n54, 103, 105, 109, 111–12, 141, 160, 174, 179, 181, 229–30, 245, 254n24, 293, 296, 300, 306–7, 325, 330, 350. *See also* archangels; seraph
angelic anthropology, 47–56, 73–76, 166, 166n3, 175–76, 176*t*, 177, 180–82, 184, 187, 191, 194, 239, 251, 278, 290, 298, 309–10, 313, 331, 351, 358–59. *See also* hierarchical soul
Anselm, 45, 248, 251–53, 253n22, 265, 265n53

Anthony of Padua, 46, 57–58
anthropocentrism, 216, 221, 357
anthropology, 358; angelic, 47–56, 73–75, 166, 166n3, 176, 176*t*, 177, 180–82, 184, 187, 191, 194, 239, 251, 278, 290, 298, 309–10, 313, 331, 351, 358–59; in *Collationes in Hexaëmeron*, 192; descent and, 360; in Gallus, 47–56, 73–74, 166, 166n3, 176, 176*t*, 177, 180–82, 184, 187, 191, 194, 239; hierarchy and, 356; human nature and, 221, 241; inflowing and, 203; *influentia* and, 206; personhood and, 216; saints and, 298; salvific history and, 290; theological, 192, 194, 200–43, 266, 350, 357
apophatic turn, 27–29
appetite, 49, 176*t*, 217, 220, 239, 340
Aquinas. *See* Thomas Aquinas
archangels, 32, 49, 103, 105, 176*t*, 181–82, 182*t*, 185*t*, 186, 189*t*, 311
Aristotle, 4, 8, 24, 58, 217, 266n55, 328
Armstrong, Regis J., 301–3
ascension, 79–80, 106, 181–84, 182*t*, 193, 245, 272n67, 280, 287, 310–11, 335–37, 360
assimilation, 70, 73, 89, 97, 134, 136–38, 141, 143–44, 147, 149–50, 151*t*, 153, 159n89, 161–63, 194, 226, 277; First Principle and, 135, 148